Daoist Identity

DAOIST
IDENTITY

History, Lineage, and Ritual

EDITED BY LIVIA KOHN AND HAROLD D. ROTH

University of Hawai'i Press
Honolulu

02 03 04 05 06 07   6 5 4 3 2 1

Library of Congress Cataloging-in-Publication Data

Daoist identity : history, lineage, and ritual / edited by
Livia Kohn and Harold D. Roth.
    p.   cm.
Includes bibliographical references and index.
ISBN 0–8248–2429–6 (cloth : alk. paper)—
ISBN 0–8248–2504–7 (pbk : alk. paper)
    1. Tao.   I. Kohn, Livia   II. Roth, Harold David.
B127.T3 D36   2002
181'.114—dc21   2001053064
Designed by Kenneth Miyamoto

Printed by The Maple-Vail Book Manufacturing Group

Dedicated to
Michel Strickmann

Contents

Acknowledgments   ix

LIVIA KOHN AND HAROLD D. ROTH
      Introduction   1

Part I Early Formations

1. TERRY F. KLEEMAN   Ethnic Identity and Daoist
      Identity in Traditional China   23

2. TSUCHIYA MASAAKI   Confession of Sins and Awareness
      of Self in the *Taiping jing*   39

3. PETER NICKERSON   "Opening the Way": Exorcism,
      Travel, and Soteriology in Early
      Daoist Mortuary Practice and Its
      Antecedents   58

Part II Texts and Symbols

4. MARK CSIKSZENTMIHÀLYI
      Traditional Taxonomies
      and Revealed Texts in the Han   81

5. SUZANNE CAHILL   Material Culture and the Dao:
      Textiles, Boats, and Zithers in the
      Poetry of Yu Xuanji (844–868)   102

6. MABUCHI MASAYA   A Mid-Ming Reappraisal of the
      Laozi: The Case of Wang Dao   127

Part III Lineages and Local Culture

7. EDWARD L. DAVIS   Arms and the Dao, 2: The Xu
                            Brothers in Tea Country   149

8. MORI YURIA   Identity and Lineage: The *Taiyi*
                            jinhua zongzhi and the Spirit-Writing
                            Cult to Patriarch Lü in Qing China   165

9. SHIGA ICHIKO   Manifestations of Lüzu in Modern
                            Guangdong and Hong Kong: The
                            Rise and Growth of Spirit-Writing
                            Cults   185

Part IV Ritual Boundaries

10. CHARLES D. ORZECH   *Fang Yankou* and *Pudu:* Translation,
                            Metaphor, and Religious Identity   213

11. MITAMURA KEIKO   Daoist Hand Signs and Buddhist
                            Mudras   235

12. MARUYAMA HIROSHI   Documents Used in Rituals of Merit
                            in Taiwanese Daoism   256

13. ASANO HARUJI   Offerings in Daoist Ritual   274

Glossary   295
Names of Authors Cited   309
List of Contributors   311
Index   315

Acknowledgments

This volume is the result of a three-day conference, held at the Breck-inridge Conference Center of Bowdoin College in York, Maine, May 29–June 1, 1998. Twenty scholars from Japan and the United States— all specialists of various aspects of Daoism— met to discuss the difficult and heretofore unexplored question of Daoist identity. The Japanese scholars who attended the conference were part of a study group from the Tokyo area known as the Dōkyō bunka kenkyū kai, or Society for the Study of Daoist Culture. The group had also sponsored a first international meeting in 1995, which resulted in the publication of the conference volume, *Dōkyō no rekishi to bunka* (The History and Culture of Religious Taoism), edited by Yamada Toshiaki and Tanaka Fumio (Tokyo: Hirakawa, 1998). While the first meeting discussed various issues in the history and worldview of Daoism, the Breckinridge meeting looked specifically at the question of Daoist identity from a number of perspectives.

Both the book and the conference would not have been possible without the active and cheerful cooperation of many people. First, there are the participants, both paper presenters and discussants, whose research, engagement, and efforts are at the very root of the work. We would like to extend our hearfelt gratitude to them all, and especially to our Japanese organizers, Yamada Toshiaki and Tanaka Fumio, as well as our American discussants, Stephen R. Bokenkamp, Russell Kirkland, and Benjamin Penny, for being such wonderful colleagues and creating such an engaging discussion.

As for organizing the meeting, we owe a great debt of gratitude to American Council of Learned Societies, whose generous financial support made this most memorable experience possible. The unbureaucratic and friendly cooperation of Jason Parker was, especially, a pleasure to experience, and we are most happy to thank him. Also of great help was the Office of Sponsored Programs at Boston University, especially David Berndt and Phyllis Cohen. Their work made administering the grant easy and allowed timely payments to all concerned parties. Moreover, Gail Berneike made our stay at the Breckinridge Center comfortable and delightful, going to no end of trouble to keep us all pleasantly housed, fed, and entertained. Our only problem was the shortness of the stay, but we all have taken wonderful memories home with us.

During the conference, we greatly relied on the help of two graduate students, James Miller (Boston University) and Zhonghu Yan (Brown University), who set up the conference room, ran the tape recorders, and kept us all well watered during the discussions. They also contributed valiantly to the publication effort, Zhonghu by translating the chapter by Asano, and James by creating a set of typed transcripts of the discussions—more intelligent and, certainly, more intelligible than they seemed at the time. Another graduate student, Louis Komjathy (Boston University), moreover, helped greatly with the editing process, converting files, entering changes and characters into the computer, and pointing out errors and technical problems. The efforts of these three on our behalf were invaluable, and we are most pleased to thank them now.

Introduction

Livia Kohn and Harold D. Roth

Identity

The concept of identity is vague and diffuse. The word, originally related to the Latin *idem,* indicates sameness and lack of change or deviation and is, indeed, still used in this sense, most commonly in its adjectival form, "identical." The Latin word *identitas,* on the other hand, comes closer to our general sense of the term, indicating "the way in which the *substantia* of an entity remains the same despite all the changes undergone by its *accidentes*" (Van der Ven 1994, 28). In other words, at the most elementary level, identity is the continuity of an inherent substance or solidity, however perceived, that lasts through all the various transformations its carrier might undergo.

In Western thought, the concept of identity has developed through three major phases of definition and usage. It was first used by rational thinkers from the Enlightenment to the nineteenth century, then developed in great intricacy by psychologists in the twentieth century. In the last few decades, it has become the focus of scholars of theology and religion. Rational thinkers such as Locke, Leibniz, Kant, and Kierkegaard saw identity as mainly a function of consciousness, a personal sense of reflection and self-awareness created actively by the thinking, rational ego. "Only that of which we were conscious belonged to our identical self" (Mol 1976, 56); the term referred to a taken-for-granted continuity in the way people think of and evaluate themselves.

Psychologists such as William James, Sigmund Freud, and Erik Erikson took on the concept next and expanded its application to the emotional dimension of humanity, defining identity as a personal sense of sameness that "arises from the resemblance and continuity of our feel-

1

ings" (James 1890, 1:459) and that is intricately tied up with our internal drives and sexuality. Erikson, in particular, made identity the cornerstone of his psychological theory, defining it as "a persistent sameness within oneself" while also sharing one's "essential character" with others (Mol 1976, 57). This represents a first foray into defining identity not merely on the basis of the individual but also as a function of social groups and larger communities. Erikson enhanced this view in studies of the Sioux, through which he found that identity among what he termed primitive societies was less the "unconscious striving for continuity of personal character" (Erikson 1960, 51) than a reservoir of collective integrity that placed and protected the individual. He then came to distinguish true identity from synthetic identity—a pervasive sense of wholeness based on a sound mutuality between individual and group versus an overwhelming feeling of totality created by an arbitrary delineation of self and others (Erikson 1964, 92; Mol 1976, 57). He focused strongly on the concept of boundaries in identity formation, insisting that every sense of identity is closely tied up with both its inner delimitations and its surrounding structures, and pointing out that despite the desired sense of sameness and continuity, boundaries of identity must remain flexible and open to change. Whereas true identity has this flexibility, synthetic identity is rigid and unmovable, leading to tensions and personality disorders. While one major danger to identity, then, is this inner rigidity, which he calls "identity-foreclosure," the opposite is also problematic: identity diffusion, where boundaries are kept too open and fluid and the sense of sameness is lost (Mol 1976, 58). One can also describe the two problem areas as an overemphasis on the ego, on the one hand, and an excessive other-directedness, on the other. Identity, as it evolves from the work of Erikson, is, therefore, seen as the continuous balancing of a sense of self between the demands of the individual versus those of society, between an attitude of inner openness and self-centered rigidity.

Developing the work of Erikson, the theologian and anthropologist Hans Mol has created an even more complex understanding of identity, relating it actively to systems of belief and religious practice. He begins by defining identity generally as a "stable niche in the whole complex of physiology, psychology, and social patterns of interaction" that is characterized by a continuous regularity of worldview, emotional reactions, and patterns of behavior (Mol 1976, 8). It evolved historically even among early humanity as a means of survival, of "man's evolutionary necessity to cope successfully with his environment" (Mol

1976, 31), and can be described as a balancing of two opposite forces or tendencies: *differentiation* and *integration*. Differentiation means the development of new, increasingly complex, and forever changing conditions; left unchecked or not properly adapted to, it leads to heterogeneity, incoherence, and an overall sense of meaninglessness in the person or group (Mol 1976, 28). Integration means the establishment of a stable, strong, organized system with clear boundaries and a firm set of responses; it leads to a sense of belonging and wholeness (Mol 1976, 32, 35); but if left without challenge, integration can result in personal or social rigidity and become an obstacle to successful adaptation.

The key point of identity for Mol, therefore, is the creation of a stable system both within the self, as a sense of wholeness, and in society, as a mode of fruitful interaction. Identity is not so much a given, whether rational or emotional, but a process—it has moved far away from its original Latin definition as *substantia* and grown into an ongoing activity that we all engage in all the time. Outlining this identity as process in more detail, Mol describes it with the term *sacralization*. Sacralization is "a process by means of which on the level of symbol-systems certain patterns acquire the same taken-for-granted, stable, eternal quality which on the level of instinctive behavior was acquired by the consolidation and stabilization of new genetic materials" (1976, 5). In other words, to create a sense of identity, people make the choice to elevate certain patterns to sacred status, that is, place them in the position of being unchanging and eternally valid. Developing thereby "a system of meaning, or a definition of reality that modifies, obstructs or (if necessary) legitimates change" (1976, 6), they find feelings of belonging, of rightness, and of wholeness in their world.

The patterns, moreover, that are being selected to serve as the mainstays of the identity process tend to involve rational, emotional, and behavioral components and can be divided into several distinct groups. Mol distinguishes four: a conscious creation of order in a set of beliefs, which he describes as "objectivation"; an emotional attachment to ideas, people, or groups that creates a sense of belonging, which he calls "commitment"; a concrete and practical choice of certain key sets of formal behavior, described as "ritual"; and the reinforcement of the overall worldview and people's actions through tales and stories, which he calls "myths."[1]

Objectivation, to begin, is the "tendency to sum up the variegated elements of mundane experience in a transcendent frame of reference where they can appear in a more orderly, more consistent, and more timeless way" (1976, 206). It is the creation of meaning and order through a set of beliefs and in a specific interpretation of reality. Meaning, in this context, indicates a set of taken-for-granted interpretations and a choice of ultimate reference points that answer the "why" of existence and drive out feelings of meaninglessness and loss (1976, 69). To create meaning, symbol systems are developed that help people manipulate their environment and find a sense of security and competence in it. The systems involve values, criteria of validity, patterns of logic, and a distinct perspective on the world in addition to a set of substantive beliefs, rules, and prohibitions and a specific understanding of technology (Hardin and Kehrer 1978, 84–85). The notion of objectivation, moreover, follows Berger and Luckmann and their understanding of the sociology of knowledge (1967), which postulates that human beings, in order to survive, need to create meaning in themselves and their environment and that "there is no such thing as uninterpreted reality" (Mol 1976, 68). Choosing specific concepts and beliefs to create meaning and wholeness, people also develop a predisposition toward new social forms. For example, by placing themselves in a religious community that focuses predominantly on a transcendent world or deity, they see themselves as outside the established society and become able to overcome this society's restrictions and limitations. The creation of new social forms, in which women are equal or people from different ethnic backgrounds are actively integrated, can often be related to the choice of certain new and transcendent beliefs over traditional patterns (Mol 1983, 29).

Commitment, next, is defined as the "focused emotion or emotional attachment to a specific focus of identity. It is an anchoring of the emotions in a salient system of meaning—social, group, or personal, whether abstract or concrete" (Mol 1976, 216). By channeling major feelings, even passions, toward a specific idea, deity, or person, commitment affords the individual a higher level of integration and creates a sense of emotional consistency and predictability. It enhances the definiteness of who one is and dictates one's choices of behavior and role in the world, and these, in turn, provide a yet greater sense of continuity and stability. Commitment becomes most obvious in cases of conversion, when people leave one set of emotional support behind and turn to something new. Moving from meaninglessness to meaning, from alienation to integration, from anomie to order (Mol 1976, 67), they become devout and dedicated followers of their new focus—

often a charismatic leader—and change their identity in the process. Commitment is often characterized by feelings of awe and reverence, commonly called "faith," and is very evident in the willingness to sacrifice objects of value or even oneself for the cause, group, or belief (Mol 1976, 227). Commitment, while necessary to create a sense of personal stability, can also become extreme and lead to the complete surrender of the person and to the establishment of cults. The example Mol cites is the People's Temple in Jonestown (1983, 32). Here, as in other cases of intense commitment, the focus was a person who represented an ideal rather than an abstract sense of belief or value; intentional segregation of members was used to enhance and empower group identity.[2]

Ritual, the sacralization of behavior, is the third method by which identity is created. It is described as repetitive, emotion-evoking action, a systematic and patterned focus of behavior that reinforces social cohesion and personal integration (Mol 1976, 13). Rites, more specifically, are a "means of articulating and reiterating a system of meaning. They act out and sacralize sameness. They restore, reinforce, or redirect identity. They maximize order by strengthening the place of the individual in the group or society, and vice versa by strengthening the bond of a society vis-à-vis the individual. They unify, integrate, and sacralize" (Mol 1976, 233). The repetitive action of the rites reinforce and validate both personal identity and the social structure, also affording a "recommitment to memory of a system of meaning" and thus strengthening commitment and belief (Sinha 1978, 141). Anxieties on various levels are mitigated, whether created by social restraints, collective guilt, or personal conscience. The sameness and predictability of the rites, then, serve to integrate the identity of the participants and support the customs and habits of the group. Yet rites also allow the articulation of aggressive and destructive actions, thereby controlling and curbing them; they reinforce the boundaries of group and personal identity. Special rites, moreover, enhance the community while providing different focal points of identity, so that rites of passage bridge major changes in the status of community members (e.g., initiations, weddings) and restore community and personal identity after a major disruption (e.g., funerals) (Mol 1976, 238).

Myths, finally, and their correlates, theological stories and symbolic tales, provide a "shorthand for basic personal and social experiences" and thereby sacralize experience, "holding arbitrariness at bay and reinforcing identity" (Mol 1976, 246). They interpret reality, often depicting it in terms of dramatic conflict, showing the interlocking and continuously interacting pattern of contrasting elements and opposites. They do not present just one mode of action or attitude but point out the mutual interaction and simultaneous presence in the world of diversity and integration, conflict and union (Mol 1983, 65). Often using sexual imagery, they show how opposites attract, interact, create harmony, and divide again—coming together yet remaining always inherently apart. Myths represent an "emotion-laden assertion of man's place in the world" (Mol 1976, 14), which they sacralize through recurrent narration. Telling stories and providing relevant symbols, they reinforce the reality created through other forms of sacralization and help people find their way in day-to-day living.

Mol makes it clear that while his analysis of the four major patterns of the creation and maintenance of identity is based on and can best be seen in a religious context, it is by no means limited to it. Rather, sacralization is an ongoing process that places concepts, attachments, and behavior patterns in a position of taken-for-granted–ness—and by no means do they have to be religiously sponsored or transcendent to fulfill their function as mainstays of identity. Focusing more on the specific problem of religious identity, on the other hand, some recent studies have concentrated on the comparative roles of *ethnicity* and *culture*. The consensus is that religious identity is, by necessity, shaped through culture and ethnic background, shown in the facts that different groups following the same religion perform rites and interpret beliefs differently depending on their cultural and ethnic background (e.g., Roman Catholics in different countries; see Lewins 1978) and that as cultures change so do the ideals and practices of their relevant religions (e.g., Roman Catholicism in modern societies; see Greinacher 1994; King 1994). Roman Catholic leaders afford a yet completely different perspective on religious identity, first defining an abstract sense of the Church (as the only and unfailing means to salvation), then shaping believers' personal and social identities in accordance with it, and, finally, dealing with the inevitable conflicts either by ignoring them or by judging and punishing them in a strict scheme of hierarchy and authority (see Borras 1994). The problem that is raised in this context, however, which is of wider interest, is the notion of a *plurality* of identities within the same overall organization, which necessitates the ranking of beliefs, convictions, commitments, and formal sets of behavior. It illustrates the dynamics of a living religious community and the ongoing process of identity formation in the shaping of both ideals and realities (see Van der Ven 1994, 30–32).

Daoism

This plurality of identity is a point most obviously valid in Daoism, which during the more than two thousand years of its existence has evolved in close interaction with the other major traditions of China, notably Confucianism, Buddhism, ethnic creeds, and popular religion. To the present day, the religion thus consists of a multiplicity of beliefs and practices, a fact that has presented a major challenge to scholars attempting to grapple with what exactly Daoism is. This challenge, as well as the development of the religion itself, can well be understood as the continuous interaction of the two forces of differentiation and integration, the move to change in accordance with political and economic developments and to adopt ever new forms and patterns from a variety of different souces versus the urge to create stability and continuity through the establishment of belief systems, lineage lines, rituals, and valid myths.

Over the centuries, different aspects and schools of Daoism have favored different modes of sacralization and identity formation, each placing its key emphasis on one pattern and paying less attention to the others. Thinkers or literati Daoists, often working in the wake of Laozi and Zhuangzi, thus have opted to formulate belief systems, yet they were also committed to their inspiring models and their myths and followed regimens of ritually formalized self-cultivation to enhance the philosophers' concepts in their lives. The members of the early movements, Great Peace and Celestial Masters, focused on ritual patterns and behavioral models, but they also had a clear belief system—including a new level of transcendence that allowed them to experiment with new social forms and ethnic integration—and required a strong commitment of members to the group, as expressed in sexual rites and the use of confession rather than medicine to heal diseases.

The major medieval schools of Shangqing and Lingbao, as well as the integrated organization of Daoism in the Tang dynasty, developed most strongly through the adaptation of Buddhist elements: beliefs, lineage structures, organizations, rituals, and symbols. These schools contributed to the development of several completely different forms of Daoism. The same pattern holds true again for the many schools and trends of modern Daoism since the Song dynasty, in which the area of adaptation and merging has been popular religion and regional cults (and, most recently, health practices) rather than Buddhism. Through it all, Daoism has grown and flourished and changed—every time a new level of differentiation has occurred, new forms of integration have emerged (and are still emerging), leaving both believers and scholars at a loss when trying to pinpoint a continuous line, the one firm inner *soliditas* of Daoism.

Any fruitful discussion of Daoist identity, in light of these observations, must first of all do away with the futile endeavor to find permanence and solidity in the tradition and begin by looking at identity as process. Rather than focusing on one, single static item, it must study the dynamics of identity in various areas of sacralization and specific situations—historical periods, schools, and local communities. Approaching the problem from this perspective, the conference on Daoist identity came to concentrate on four distinct areas of Daoist identity formation, three of which match the sacralization patterns described by Mol. We found that identity developed through the creation of belief systems focusing on the Dao, commonly expressed in and transmitted through texts (= objectivation). Daoist identity also grew from the establishment of lineages that often combined local and popular or ethnic bonds with certain religious ideas and practices (= commitment). Then again, the religion shaped its self-understanding through ritual practices, and here especially through the establishment of firm boundaries vis-à-vis Buddhism in the middle ages and popular religion in modern Daoism (= ritual). In addition, the early movements (Great Peace and Celestial Masters) were found to represent thoroughly fascinating case studies of Daoist identity, since they were such close-knit communities that set themselves up to be intentionally different through beliefs, group cohesion, and rituals yet could not help absorbing and using common cultural and ethnic patterns and the practices of popular religion. A case study of the early movements is presented first in this volume, followed by more topic-centered presentations that span various periods of history.

To summarize the volume's conclusions: there are certain general or typical patterns in Daoist identity formation. To begin, objectivation occurs in a Daoist context through specific key ideas or concepts that tend to lie at the root of sustaining belief systems. These concepts are the Dao as the underlying force of the world, the pure world of the spirits and gods, and the notion of a self harbored and supported by the all-pervasive Dao that is also present in every individual's body, mind, and spirit. These beliefs tend to be expressed and transmitted in writing, so that the written word, and by extension the sacred text, emerges as the major concrete focus of this form of identity. Whether the texts are the works of Laozi and Zhuangzi that have continued to inspire literati Daoists, religious texts that were handed down in strict lines of masters and disciples (thus creating commitment), or poetic stanzas and metaphors that expressed the writer's innermost feelings, objectivation in Daoism appears as a predominantly literati enterprise, in which words and concepts take precedence over personal or group cohesion and the practice and cultivation of rituals.

This impression, of course, may well reflect the lopsided view of the modern scholar who only has access to the texts that formulate the concepts and cannot see the accompanying interpersonal relationships, annual rites, and daily regimens. Still, one may suspect that every formulation of a Daoist belief system carried a certain degree of commitment and social interaction and came with sets of formalized behaviors, if only the repeated recitation and honoring of the sacred text.[3] These literati Daoists, therefore, even though they do not belong to organized groups or engage in obvious rituals, must not be ignored. After all, they call themselves Daoist and create their identity with the help of Daoist concepts while also helping to form an identity for the religion. For scholars, the most important lesson to be learned from these cases is to treat all representatives of a tradition with respect and not bring in their own prejudices. As emerged clearly from the discussions at the conference, one should not, as one participant offered, "hesitate to see Yu Xuanji as a Daoist poetess, because she is too violent," nor should one categorically claim that all "Daoism is about gods and sin." The religion has many facets, and we need to listen closely and carefully to all those who claim affiliation with it to see just how they shape it and are shaped by it.

Commitment in Daoism, next, was found most clearly expressed in a sense of lineage, the major means by which the religious content (ideas and rites) were transmitted from master to disciples, continuing an original revelation from the deity, or immortal, to the founder, or patriarch, of the school. Identity through lineage is thus of both this world, through the link with the living master, and the otherworld, through the active connection with the deity. Then again, identity through commitment can be created ex post facto through the active and conscious establishment of a lineage consisting largely of historical, legendary, and divine personages. Inspiring saints, former seekers, and immortals who went their own way and were often eccentric wanderers with a distinct dislike for all forms of organization and structure would then be turned into masters of the ideas and practices of specific schools and venerated as patriarchs.[4] The construction of lineages in this way shows most clearly the patterns of differentiation and integration at work in the religion. That lineage is central in Daoism is no accident, since lineages form the backbone of Chinese social organization in general. The primary among them is, of course, the family, honored and worshiped in the ancestral cult. But there are also local elites that organize themselves in lineages; the political aristocracy has a clear sense of ranks and hierarchy; and the intellectual aristocracy tends to organize itself in schools of thinkers, poets, and painters. Religious lineages share the characteristics of all these lines, following similar structures and imitating the family model.

Identity created through lineage, next, carries over into the ritual sector when specific groups set up rules for moral purity, rites for initiation and ordination, and other unique ways of life (through special clothing, facial marks, diets, and so forth). Specifically religious rituals among Daoist groups, however, had to contend most vigorously with the fact that many of their forms were adapted from either Buddhism or popular religion. Clear boundaries had to be established to keep Daoist rites functional for Daoist identity. Throughout history, Daoist communities have been open to others and have welcomed outsiders and non-Daoist ways. Daoist temples, therefore, often were and are community temples; Daoist offerings have included blood sacrifices in adaptation of popular practices; Daoist hand gestures and incantations have integrated Buddhist mudras and mantras; Daoist rituals of salvation of the dead have been similar to Buddhist and popular practices; and even the uniquely Daoist practice of sending announcements, petitions, and memorials to the celestial administration has involved addressing popular and foreign gods.

To delineate a Daoist identity through ritual, scholars must examine the rites for their uniquely Daoist aspects. Thus, for example, Daoist ritual gestures can be described as unique in that the different parts of the hand are correlated with different aspects of the cosmos, and even though the gesture may have an Indian name and imitate Buddhism, its cosmic meaning and impact on the universe are strictly Daoist. Similarly, there may be offerings of pigs and other animals during a Daoist *jiao,* but they are placed far away from the most holy activity. The ritual banquet, moreover, in Buddhism enacts the welcome that a host extends to his or her guest; in Daoism it is an audience with the celestials. And, most importantly, the Daoist priest becomes, for the duration of the ritual, a celestial officer, his or her task the conveyance of formal orders to the heavenly administration. He or she is not a supplicant, a mediator, or a meditator but an officer with rank and regalia. His or her interaction with the divine is almost exclusively through written documents that are often lengthy, convoluted, and penned in formal classical Chinese. Although specific acts, symbolic objects, or chanted formulas may have been adopted from other traditions, they were yet translated succesfully into a Daoist context and have come to serve the world of the Dao, reinforcing both the identity of the individual and the group as Daoist.

In all these ways of forming Daoist identity, specific concepts, images, metaphors, and symbols play a pervasive role, constructing a valid network of ideas and a flow of narrative to show how to be Daoist in this world. Although myths per se were not singled out as a category in the contributions or discussions at the conference, their presence through images and symbols is ubiquitous, appearing in all the various venues of Daoist identity.

The Contributions

The first part of this volume discusses the specific ways of forming identity in the early Daoist movements, the Way of Great Peace and Celestial Masters. In chapter 1, "Ethnic Identity and Daoist Identity in Traditional China," Terry Kleeman raises a number of questions from both early and modern sources pertaining to the issue of how Daoist religious movements dealt with peoples of different ethnic backgrounds. He argues that from its very inception as an institutionalized religion, Daoism has been significantly shaped by non-Chinese ethnic groups, and he demonstrates that even today, archaic forms of Daoism survive among non-Chinese peoples long after they have died out among the Chinese.

Taking the case of the Ba minority in second-century C.E., Sichuan, Kleeman explores the reasons for their initial attraction to the religions of the Celestial Masters, how the early Daoist movement assimilated elements of Ba popular religious beliefs, and how the Ba were able to retain various aspects of these beliefs as well as their unique ethnic identity while still embracing and being embraced by this new religious and political movement. Kleeman concludes that the earliest Celestial Masters community in Sichuan was multiethnic, and he further traces a liberal Daoist approach to ethnic minorities into later centuries, touching upon an ethos that emerged from the Daoist self-conception as a universal religion, which finally changed with the intense nationalism of the Song period. He also touches upon the fascinating case of the modern Yao peoples of Southeast Asia who maintain a Daoist priesthood and religious institutions long since abandoned among ethnic Chinese. In the end, Kleeman raises a number of issues about the interpenetration of Daoist identity and ethnic identity that can serve as the basis for future research.

Tsuchiya Masaaki, in his chapter, "Confessions of Sins and Awareness of Self in the *Taiping jing*," presents a careful analysis of the rituals of confession undertaken by members of the Way of Great Peace in order to cure ailments and diseases, adumbrating how they were conducted and why they were believed to be efficacious. The penitent frequently entered into a private chamber in order to ritually purify herself or himself through physical and mental fasting, concentrating on various gods that resided in the inner organs of the body, and self-reflecting to determine which of her or his deeds were evil. This was followed by a public confession of sins, possibly self-punishment, and the eventual curing of the affliction.

A singularly fascinating aspect of Tsuchiya's presentation is his explanation of the underlying mechanism of this expiation of guilt. While it may have been the case that in earlier times, sin was forgiven or punished directly by an anthropomorphic god, the explanation provided in the *Taiping jing* details how this takes place. According to the text, Heaven, Earth, and Humanity form an intricately related triad, interacting through the medium of *qi* (vital energy). Evil deeds alter the *qi* and the entire being of the sinner, creating a disharmony with Heaven, causing the spirit to flee the body, and bringing on disease. Ritual purification in the meditation chamber and public confession cause certain significant alterations in the mind and *qi* of the supplicant, which are then communicated directly to Heaven through *qi*. Heaven recognizes the renewal of a sincere will and the restoring of harmony by mercifully removing the ailment.

While presenting the confession ritual as a unique contribution of Daoism to Chinese culture, Tsuchiya shows that the penitents' identities as persons are transformed into ones as Daoists as they come to see themselves first as sinners, then as entities inhabited by gods and demons. By gaining Daoist identities, their very bodies are transformed from physical mechanisms and networks of vital energy into powerhouses of the Dao. They are healed because they become more one with the Dao, believing the Dao to pervade them and reside in them in the form of body divinities. The key to identity is their individual acceptance of a distinctive set of beliefs about the divine order of the Dao, activated further through commitment and ritual.

Also focusing on the early movements, and specifically on their mortuary rituals, is Peter Nickerson's chapter, "Opening the Way: Exorcism, Travel, and Soteriology in Early Daoist Mortuary Practice and

Its Antecedents." The rites were established at the end of the Han dynasty on the basis of an already existing mortuary practice used in folk religious culture, while adding a Daoist soteriological dimension. Later-Han tomb contracts and "grave-securing writs" served to secure the release of the dead from the underworld ruled by the Yellow Monarch to eternal repose in the tomb. Nickerson demonstrates that Daoists grafted their own soteriology onto this burial practice and adapted the writs to a new use: aiding the spirits of the deceased on a journey (with origins in early Chinese shamanism) from the tomb into a better life in Heaven. As Mark Csikszentmihàlyi also argues in the following chapter, this provides clear evidence that the organized Daoist movements of the late Han dynasty did not emerge ex nihilo but had their origins in pre-existing social institutions and practices. Also, the belief in a heavenly source of retribution for sin evident in the *daotan* communities studied by Shiga and in the *Taiping jing*, as analyzed by Tsuchiya, can be seen again in the form of a heavenly judgment of the spirit of the deceased. Activating the belief in an all-powerful cosmic rule of the Dao, mortuary practices in the early movements reconfirmed the Daoists' sense of order and belonging and reinforced their commitment to the religion.

Moving away from the early movements and to the discussion of specific modes of identity formation, three contributors discuss the process of objectivation or the establishment of identity through belief systems, cosmology, and sacred texts. Csikszentmihàlyi's chapter, "Traditional Taxonomies and Revealed Texts in the Han," addresses the issue of Han antecedents of Daoism and its various religious institutions. Arguing that it is not reasonable to assume, as many scholars have, that Daoist institutions arose ex nihilo, he demonstrates the existence of earlier Han-dynasty social institutions that showed close parallels with those of the early Daoist communities.

Of particular interest to him is the transmission of esoteric texts—associated with mantic practices, medicine, and self-cultivation, reasonably labeled as "Huang-Lao"—and their associated techniques in lines of masters and disciples that were outside officially sanctioned circles. Such committed master–disciple communities often centered on specific locations, "salons," and there is considerable evidence that their social forms and the texts they transmitted played important roles in the origins of later Han Daoism. That these may have been overlooked, he argues, is due to a lack of clarity about earlier forms of textual taxonomies, such as the classifications of philosophers in several pre-Han sources and those provided by the Han historians in the *Shiji* and *Hanshu*. Csikszentmihàlyi shows how each had a specific ideological purpose that often obscured the sociological bases of these thinkers and caused scholars to assume there were none. This, in turn, has prevented scholars from seeing the sociological and ideological background of the late-Han Daoist movements that he points out here.

Next, Suzanne Cahill's chapter, "Material Culture and the Dao," describes a similar search for personal yet Daoist identity in the case of the Tang poetess Yu Xuanji (844–868), intellectual, courtesan, and Daoist nun. For her, the religion offered a haven of security after she suffered in the world of marriage and politics. She was ordained and formally established in the organization, yet her self-understanding came from her embracing of a key set of Daoist beliefs and a sense of divine order rather than from her official status or performance of rituals. Once removed from the society that had wounded her, she could vent her anger against it in an aggressive poetry, finding herself and her own true voice, while at the same time emphasizing the value of Daoist ideas as a venue for self-expression. This self-expression appeared in many symbolic images that revolved around three areas: textiles, which often symbolized her limitations as a woman; the boat, which often symbolized her freedom in wandering with the Dao; and the zither, which often symbolized her longing to find a true friend who could really understand her, "one who recognizes my sound."

Cahill finds in Yu Xuanji an extremely intelligent, well-read, and passionate woman who was unable to realize her deepest nature in conventional society because of the limiting roles it inflicted on women. Only through Daoist literature and practice was she able to put aside her bitter feelings over her lot and discover her freedom, expressed through imaginative wanderings and passionate poetry and in the tranquility of remote mountain hermitages.

A different case of Daoist identity created through the objectivation of cosmological beliefs is that of the philosopher Wang Dao (1487–1547), a student of both Wang Yangming and Zhan Ruoshui, who forged his own unique synthesis of the harmony of the three teachings. As presented by Mabuchi Masaya in his chapter, "A Mid-Ming Reappraisal of the *Laozi*," Wang Dao took from the *Laozi* the message that to be truly moral beings, humans must look to the ultimate source of benevolence and rightness. It was not to be found in Wang Yangming's "innate knowledge of the good," which he felt was contaminated by selfish thought, but rather in the pure and tranquil substance of the mind, the Dao. Mabuchi finds that Wang Dao was more a literati, or intellectual, than a practicing, or ordained, Daoist, who was not committed to a specific group following a set of ritual practices. Still, he found a Daoist identity for himself as a Ming-dynasty thinker, mediated entirely through the written word of the *Laozi*. The text provided him with a truth and a sense of order, more so than the more commonly preferred Confucian classics. The key to his thinking was the concept of the Dao and its expression in the ancient scripture, the way it was activated in the context of his particular lifetime and personal experience. Was he a Daoist? By his own definition, most certainly. And he did, in his own way, contribute to the later development and expansion of the Daoist tradition.

Moving away from the more intellectual pursuit of divine order and toward emotional commitment in the formation of Daoist identity, three studies look at modern Daoist lineages in relation to local and popular cults. First, Edward Davis, in his "Arms and the Dao, 2: The Xu Brothers in Tea Country," deals with the local temple cult of the Xu brothers that began in south China in the tenth century and later grew into a widely popular sect, investigating its historical origins, sociological role, and religious activities. The Xu brothers were worshiped in life as local heroes and in death as Daoist transcendents, and their ancestral cult was given imperial recognition by the Ming Yongle emperor, resulting in the inclusion of its text in the Daoist canon of 1445.

Despite these obvious links with Daoism, Davis demonstrates that very few of the cult's religious beliefs and cultural activities, centered in its main temple, Lingji gong, can be labeled "Daoist." While cultic practices included spirit-writing and mediumism, they also involved a variety of local seasonal ceremonies, Buddhist-inspired rituals, and the promotion of a major local teaching academy. Taken together, these seem as much expressions of the social and political aims of local literati families as forms of religious aspirations. Commitment to locality and lineage, as it were, was expressed through objectified beliefs and formal rituals, showing the close interconnection between religion and local culture.

Mori Yuria, in his chapter on the *Jinhua zongzhi* (known in the West as *The Secret of the Golden Flower*), discusses problems of identity and lineage, showing how different redactions of the text were used for lineage construction and membership identification in the early and middle Qing dynasty. Identifying six distinct redactions of the text printed between 1775 and 1921, he concentrates his analysis on three of them, those by Shao Zhilin (1775), Jiang Yupu (1803), and Min Yide (1835).

He shows how each redactor, by textual editing and through the addition or deletion of prefaces, claims the text as an authentication of his or her lineage and his or her own membership in it.

The principal reason for this lies in the putative origins of the text at a Daoist altar in Jiangsu province, where it was produced through spirit-writing that communicated the ideas of "Patriarch Lü." It was originally produced in the Jingming (Pure Brightness) lineage of the Quanzhen (Complete Perfection) school, and its later redactors were able to remove it from its lineal origins and claim it as proof of their own by reworking the connection from Patriarch Lü directly to themselves and their lineage. Thus, though a Jingming text for Shao, the *Jinhua zongzhi* was used as a Tianxian (Heavenly Immortal) lineage text by Jiang and a Longmen (Dragon Gate) lineage text by Min. The case presents an illuminating example of commitment to a deity linked creatively with commitment to specific masters and lineages and the continuous overlap between the two.

Shiga Ichiko, next, in her "Manifestations of Lüzu in Modern Guangdong and Hong Kong," takes up the same issue in the context of the origins and development of *daotan,* or Daoist temple societies, in nineteenth- and twentieth-century south China. She shows that contrary to accepted scholarly opinion, *daotan* are genuinely lay movements that originated with the gentry but over the course of time spread to include people from all walks of life. Many maintain close ties with the official Quanzhen school, but they are not sanctioned or sponsored by it. They have been involved in a wide variety of social activities, from providing retreat facilities through charitable relief to the promulgation of morality books. Their focus of commitment is based on locality and the social and cultural ties already present, yet reinforced through the manifestation and communication of the deity. Yet again, Daoist identity appears in close interaction with cultural, local, and ethnic patterns.

The last part of this volume concentrates on identity formation and reinforcement through ritual, focusing on the delimitation of boundaries vis-à-vis Buddhist and popular practices. First, Charles Orzech compares two similar rituals in his chapter, "*Fang Yankou* and *Pudu.*" The esoteric Buddhist *fang yankou,* or "release of the flaming souls," is a form of saving the dead from the punishments of hell. It has, at first glance, many striking parallels with the Daoist *pudu,* or "rite of universal salvation," in terms of material details, technical terminology, the use of "Brahma-language," mantras, and mudras, and also in terms of the overall ritual structure and conception.

However, questioning the very notion of "syncretism," and replacing it with the analytical tools of translation theory, Orzech demonstrates not that the two rituals are a combination of elements that should be separated as parts of two distinct systems, but rather that the Daoist rite can properly be understood as a "translation," in which the multilayered South Asian metaphoric complex of the *fang yankou* is mapped onto a different multilayered East Asian metaphoric complex. As such, it represents, in Tony K. Stewart's terms, an example of "metaphorical equivalence" rather than one of "syncretism." In other words, the *pudu* does not represent an appropriation of the *fang yankou* but rather a translation of its ritual program into a distinctly Daoist performance based on its own cosmology and metaphors. Though boundaries are clearly established, the ritual, however Buddhist in appearance, emerges as ultimately Daoist.

Mitamura Keiko reaches similar conclusions in her chapter, "Daoist Hand Signs and Buddhist Mudras," in which she provides an inventory of Daoist hand signs and shows how they developed between the Tang and Ming dynasties. She then compares them to esoteric Buddhist mudras and examines their indigenous origins. She argues that there are two general types of signs, those developed in apparent imitation of Buddhist mudras and those that are uniquely Daoist, both used in rituals for protection from disasters, exorcising demons, and healing diseases.

Mitamura traces the origins of Daoist hand signs to early shamanistic rituals continued in the practices of the *fangshi* and transmitted through them into Daoism. She shows evidence of their use in conjunction with incantations and talismans to ward off evil influences (recorded by Ge Hong) and shows possible evidence of their use in Lingbao texts and Tang works. Under the influence of esoteric Zhenyan Buddhism in the eighth century, Daoists combined the symbols and styles of Buddhist mudras with their own finger techniques. At first thoroughly imitating Buddhist terminology, they gradually translated it into their own distinctive cosmology and metaphors, yielding a more dynamic system of hand signs. Again, the ritual reinforces the specific Daoist sense of order and commitment, however apparently Buddhist it may appear.

Another dimension of Daoist ritual uniqueness is the extensive use of written documents, discussed by Maruyama Hiroshi in his "Documents Used in Rituals of Merit in Taiwanese Daoism." Concentrating on the "ritual of merit" of a modern successor of the *pudu,* as practiced in southern Taiwan, he analyzes three complementary sets of

texts collected locally. They present five sets of ritual documents, including, among others, the Announcement, the Writ of Pardon, and
the Precious Litany to the Rulers of Darkness. Comparing these contemporary ritual presentations with Song-dynasty sources, Maruyama
demonstrates a lineage continuity among some of them and points
out certain patterns of historical development. He documents the remarkable continuity of rituals while also showing the impact of cultural and historical changes on their expression.

The last chapter, Asano Haruji's "Offerings in Daoist Ritual," presents a comprehensive list of offerings used in both *zhai* (purification
ceremonies) and *jiao* (sacrificial offerings). They include incense,
flowers, candles, tea, wine, fruit, grain products, baked goods, writing
utensils, and meat. Most are common to all Chinese traditions. The
notable exception is writing utensils, which are not offered elsewhere
but in Daoism symbolize the strong emphasis placed on written communication with the otherworld. The other unusual feature is the presence of meat offerings at Daoist rituals, which were proscribed in the
early Daoist religion, partly because the pure Dao does not feed on
blood, partly to distinguish Daoist rites from those of popular religion.
Today, to accommodate folk religious beliefs and maintain a clientele
among popular practitioners, meat is offered in rites directed to the
Jade Emperor, to appease recently deceased souls and hungry ghosts,
and at the specific request of the family that sponsors the ritual.
Nonetheless, it is never placed in a central position in the ritual space
but always set up on a side table. Although compromising with current popular culture and the practical demands of the people, Taiwanese Daoists yet maintain their boundaries and conserve the integrity and unique identity of their rituals.

Notes

1. Mol describes these elements variously in his writings. For objectivation,
see Mol 1976, 202–215, and Mol 1983, 18–31; for commitment, see Mol 1976,
216–232, and Mol 1983, 32–47; for ritual, see Mol 1976, 233–245, and Mol
1983, 48–60; for myths, see Mol 1976, 246–261, and Mol 1983, 61–73. The elements also appear in case studies and theoretical evaluations by various scholars convened at a conference on the subject and published in Mol 1978.

2. For a study of another segregated group in this context, see Shaffir 1978.

3. For a documentation of the formalized cultivation practices of the early
Daoists that are most commonly regarded as mere "thinkers," see Roth 1999.

4. A study of these patterns in the case of specific Daoists and lineages of
the Yuan and Ming dynasties is found in Reiter 1988.

Bibliography

Berger, Peter L., and Thomas Luckmann. 1967. *The Social Construction of Reality*. London: Penguin Press.

Borras, Alphonse. 1994. "The Canonical Limits of Catholic Identity: Some Problematical Situations." In *Catholic Identity*, ed. by James Provost and Knut Walf, 47–59. London: SMC Press.

Erikson, Erik. 1960. "The Problem of Ego Identity." In *Identity and Anxiety*, ed. by Maurice R. Stein, Arthur J. Vidich, and David M. White, 37–87. Glencoe, Ill.: Free Press.

————. 1964. *Insight and Responsibility*. New York: Norton.

Greinacher, Norbert. 1994. "Catholic Identity in the Third Epoch of Church History." In *Catholic Identity*, ed. by James Provost and Knut Walf, 3–14. London: SMC Press.

Hardin, Bert L., and Guenter Kehrer. 1978. "Identity and Commitment." In *Identity and Religion*, ed. by Hans Mol, 83–96. Beverly Hills, Calif.: Sage Publications.

James, William, 1890. *Principles of Psychology*. New York: Holt.

King, Geoffrey. 1994. "Identity, Law, and Culture." In *Catholic Identity*, ed. by James Provost and Knut Walf, 38–46. London: SMC Press.

Lewins, Frank W. 1978. "Religion and Ethnic Identity." In *Identity and Religion*, ed. by Hans Mol, 19–38. Beverly Hills, Calif.: Sage Publications.

Mol, Hans. 1976. *Identity and the Sacred*. New York: The Free Press.

————, ed. 1978. *Identity and Religion*. Beverly Hills, Calif.: Sage Publications.

————. 1983. *Meaning and Place: An Introduction to the Social Scientific Study of Religion*. New York: Pilgrim Press.

Reiter, Florian C. 1988. *Grundelemente des religiösen Taoismus: Das Spannungsverhältnis von Integration und Individualität in seiner Geschichte zur Chin-, Yüan- und frühen Ming-Zeit*. Stuttgart: Franz Steiner Verlag.

Roth, Harold D. 1999. *Original Tao: Inward Training and the Foundations of Taoist Mysticism*. New York: Columbia University Press.

Shaffir, William. 1978. "Witnessing As Identity Consolidation: The Case of the Lubavitcher Chassidim." In *Identity and Religion*, ed. by Hans Mol, 39–58. Beverly Hills, Calif.: Sage Publications.

Sinha, Manju, and Braj Sinha. 1978. "Ways of Yoga and the Mechanisms of Sacralization." In *Identity and Religion*, ed. by Hans Mol, 133–150. Beverly Hills, Calif.: Sage Publications.

Van der Ven, Johannes A. 1994. "The Communicative Identity of the Local Church." In *Catholic Identity*, ed. by James Provost and Knut Walf, 26–37. London: SMC Press.

Part I
Early Formations

1

Ethnic Identity and Daoist Identity in Traditional China

Terry F. Kleeman

The ancient Chinese portrayed themselves as an island of civilization in an ocean of barbarism, as a beacon of light surrounded by insignificant others who, if intelligent, were fascinated by Chinese culture and actively sought to assimilate into it and, if not, were recalcitrant recidivists who deserved to be subjugated militarily or driven from the region by force. The reality was much more complex. Recent archaeological discoveries make evident that the Neolithic period saw a variety of advanced regional cultures stretching from Hangzhou Bay to Liaoning, and that the culture of the traditional heartland was by no means the most advanced among them. During the Shang and Western Zhou dynasties, non-Chinese intermarried with Chinese kings and joined them in military expeditions. In the Eastern Zhou, "barbarians" attended interstate conferences and, judging from the resplendent remains of the Zhongshan state, enjoyed a lifestyle comparable in most respects to that of the Chinese. The barbarians are usually thought of as geographically beyond the borders of Chinese civilization, but in fact, there were non-Chinese tribes in the hills and wilds across China (Prusek 1971). As late as the fifth and sixth centuries C.E., peoples identified as Man-barbarians were a constant threat to public safety in Central China.[1] Today, China shares its territory with fifty-five officially recognized non-Chinese peoples speaking over 150 distinct languages and worshiping a wide variety of gods and ghosts.

Daoism is properly dubbed China's indigenous higher religion. It is the culmination of an array of distinctively Chinese beliefs, practices, and movements, including popular deity worship and ancestor veneration, traditional ritual practices of the state and home, self-cultivation practices and medicine, cosmological speculation, the political philosophy of the Huang-Lao school, the cult of immortality, Han Confucianism, and the apocryphal writings (*chenwei*). Daoism is not the national religion of China in the way that Shintō serves that function in Japan by encompassing all indigenous cults and beliefs. On the contrary, Daoism is a militantly reforming faith that consciously rejects significant parts of traditional practice as heretical, even evil. Still, it has come over time to enjoy pride of place in the Chinese religious world. Moreover, it has eventually incorporated into its pantheon a select group of the most influential popular gods, and Daoist priests regularly officiate at ceremonies honoring gods of the larger popular pantheon. In this sense, Daoism is quintessentially Chinese, an expression of the Chinese spirit and the Chinese historical experience.

It is surprising, therefore, that a cursory examination of the history of Daoism shows that non-Chinese ethnic groups have played a significant role in Daoism from the beginning, that Daoism remains an influential religion among ethnic minorities within and outside China even today, and that archaic forms of Daoism survive among non-Chinese peoples that are no longer to be found among the Chinese. The topic of this chapter is the role of non-Chinese peoples and their beliefs in Daoism, the influence Daoism has exerted and continues to exert on these peoples, and the significance of a multiethnic Daoism for our study of the religion. Since this is a vast topic, I will focus on some of the more significant evidence and point out where I believe further research would prove fruitful.

Early Sichuan and the Foundation of Daoism

The earliest and most prominent encounter with non-Chinese ethnic groups occurred at the time of Daoism's founding. The story of Zhang Ling's immigration from Jiangsu to Sichuan and his subsequent revelation from the divinized Laozi in 142 C.E. is well known and generally accepted, despite the lack of corroborating evidence in contemporary documents. Less attention has been paid to what he found upon his arrival in western China. The Sichuan region possesses a long history of settlement, and the recent discoveries at Sanxingdui, dating to the Shang and Western Zhou periods, have confirmed the sophistication of its indigenous culture. The Qin conquest in the late fourth century B.C.E. initiated a period of intensive colonization, including forced resettlement on a large scale that permanently changed the face of the region (Sage 1992, 107–142). Thanks, in part, to the efforts of the legendary educator Wen Weng, Sichuan soon became a center of learning. By the Western Han period, the area was already contributing officials of the rank of the Three Dukes and Nine Ministers (*sangong jiuqing;* Chen 1980, 176–177) as well as the period's most prominent poet, Sima Xiangru. During the Wang Mang interregnum, Sichuan was an important center for the development of the apocryphal literature.

One might expect that by the end of the Han dynasty, the area would have been thoroughly sinicized and integrated into Chinese culture. Such was not the case. Instead, we find in Sichuan a congeries of ethnic groups living intermixed with the ethnic Chinese (*zaju*) and in segregated communities, reflecting a range of assimilation from near merger in the large urban centers to preservation of the original tribal society in the mountains and remote areas. This was particularly true in the areas of eastern Sichuan that had once been part of the Zhou-period kingdom of Ba. The Ba were an ancient people, first entering Chinese history around 700 B.C.E. They were warriors who gloried in their military prowess, celebrating it in martial songs and dances so full of vibrant energy that they enthralled the first emperor of the Han dynasty and were adopted into the repertoire of court performances. They also maintained an unusually high standard of living for a group comprised essentially of hunter-gatherers with limited agriculture, though not so high as the settled agriculturalists of the Chengdu plain. The secret to this high culture was, no doubt, their service as mercenaries to their neighbors to the east (Chu) and west (Shu) but may also have been founded in their role as salt producers and traders. In any case, the Ba were unique among China's neighbors in developing a distinctive script of their own (actually two scripts, though one may have been of limited function). This limited literacy may have been one factor in their ability to resist assimilation, as may have their different lifestyle.

For whatever reason, there were large numbers of identifiably Ba peoples living in Sichuan during the second century C.E., when Daoism was taking form.[2] They were locked in an adversarial relationship with local representatives of the Chinese state, who sought to integrate the wealth and power of unassimilated Ba tribes into the Chinese administrative framework and thereby provoked repeated rebellions. When the Daoist message of deliverance spread through the region, the Ba flocked to its banner, with Ba kings, marquises, and other local elites leading groups numbering in the thousands to adopt the new faith and join the apocalyptic kingdom in Hanzhong.[3] We do not of-

ten think about the early Celestial Masters as a multiethnic community, but non-Chinese peoples must have comprised a significant portion of their population.

This situation raises a number of questions concerning how Daoism related to the native beliefs of the Ba. First, what can we say about
Ba religion? Since the lifestyle of the Ba seems to have focused on hunting, fishing, and warfare, we might expect religious beliefs related to
these activities to loom large. Representations of hunting and warfare, no doubt understood to include potent magic that would lead
to success at these endeavors, seem to have made up the famous Ba
Yu dances.[4] Stories of tigers being hunted by Ba tribesmen, of people
turning into tigers, and of tiger worship predominate in the historical record for this region. Material objects confirm this emphasis, with
numerous representations of tigers on weapons, musical instruments,
and the like. Snakes and birds, especially the cormorant, are important secondary motifs. Finally, we find among people of Ba descent
names referring to tigers, such as Li Hu who led his followers to join
the Celestial Masters at the time of the Hanzhong community
(*Huayangguo zhi* 9.119, 5). Clearly, a tiger spirit and other zoomorphic
spirits played a role in Ba religion. The were-tiger theme may reflect
the presence of shamans who were thought to transform themselves
into tigers or to use these mighty beasts as their familiars. In other respects, we can probably assume that Ba religion resembled that of the
indigenous peoples of southwest China today, that is, the worship of
nature, hero, and ancestral spirits by tribal shamans who play a
significant role in the direction of the group. Given the long history
of Han domination by the second century C.E., it is likely that there
was some intermixture of Chinese popular beliefs and deities; the degree of this influence, no doubt, varied with the degree of contact with
and assimilation into Chinese culture. In fact, although indigenous
beliefs would have included distinctive autochthonous spirits, the overall tenor of Ba religion, with its presumed emphasis on the shamanic
control of demonic spirits, does not seem all that different from the
contemporary popular Chinese religion, as revealed in recent years
by scholars such as Harada Masami (1963; 1967), Donald Harper
(1985), and the late Anna Seidel (1987).

One is struck by accounts of mass conversions among the Ba to
Celestial Masters Daoism. Local leaders converted with their entire
communities; Li Hu's group alone comprised more than 500 families, perhaps some 2,500 individuals. Some migrated to Hanzhong to
participate directly in Zhang Lu's millennial kingdom, but others

maintained a base of support in northeastern Sichuan to which he could retreat when Cao Cao pressed him.

The most detailed comment in historical sources concerning why the Ba were attracted to the new religion is the following:

> Their race (*zhongdang*) was strong and brave; by custom they were fond of necromancer shamans (*guiwu*). At the end of the Han, Zhang Lu occupied Hanzhong, teaching the common people the way of the ghosts (*guidao*). The Zong people revered and believed in him. (*Huayangguo zhi* 9.119, 4–5)

The exact sense of this "way of the ghosts" is uncertain. One source tells us that initiates to the movement were referred to as "ghost troopers" (*guizu*), and an inscription from 173 records a Daoist initiating god with the title "ghost soldier" (*guibing*).[5] We also know that members of the church possessed certificates of ordination called registers, which specified the number of spirit generals they had at their command; these generals and their troops, once freed from the civilizing control of the Dao, would revert to demonic status, as detailed in one of the early scriptures of the movement, the *Nüqing guilü* (Ghostly Ordinances of Nüqing, HY 563). But the Celestial Masters also condemned popular cults in no uncertain terms and rejected the blood sacrifice that was at their root. It is also interesting to note that among the modern Gelao, descendents of the Lao who invaded Sichuan in the fourth century, the primary religious officiant is sometimes referred to as *daoshi,* or Daoist priest, but the most common title is *guishi,* or "master of the ghosts."[6] Another intriguing parallel is the Lord of Ghosts, the priest of the Black Man-barbarians, a figure directly ancestral to the Zimo of the Yi peoples (Nuosu) of southwestern Sichuan and Yunnan province today.[7] The words of the *Xin Tangshu* (New Book of the Tang) in describing this figure recall earlier descriptions of the Ba:

> The tribesmen have great reverence for ghosts. The officiant at sacrifices is called the Lord of Ghosts. Each year every household must contribute an ox or sheep, which is brought to the home of the Lord of Ghosts and sacrificed. In sending off or welcoming demons there is always a great flourish of weapons, inevitably resulting in conflict and blood feuds. (222c.6315)[8]

Thus we may conclude that the control of demonic forces was an important aspect of the Daoist priest or libationer's social role and that this mastery was influential in gaining adherents for the new faith.

What else in the Celestial Masters' message would have appealed to the Ba? We know that a central element of the new faith was a focus on sin, on the supernatural bureaucracy that observed, recorded, and punished sin, and on a method to erase sin through the submission of documents to the Three Offices (*sanguan*) confessing to the sin, through repentance, and through works of penance. Judging from modern, anthropological parallels, it is unlikely that the Ba shared this concern, but it is possible that the doctrine was effective in proselytization, much as Christian tales of hellfire and brimstone have scared countless indigenous peoples across the world into converting.[9]

More likely, it was the social content of the new faith that drew the Ba. We know that they had repeatedly rebelled in protest against exorbitant taxes and other unfair treatment. The Celestial Masters replaced the local representatives of the central government with libationers (*jijiu*) who demanded only a modest, fixed contribution of rice from each family. The onerous demands of corvée labor were replaced with more modest requirements for participation in communal projects like repairing roads, which also served as penance for sins and as a merit-making activity. We do not know exactly how the famous "lodges of righteousness" (*yishe*) functioned, but there was at least some provision for the indigent and starving. All of these features were part of a larger message of social justice that was founded in the ideal of Great Peace, or Great Equity (Taiping). One can well imagine the appeal egalitarianism would have had for an oppressed minority like the Ba. The millenarian ideal that was the culmination of this doctrine would have held a similar attraction. Instead of facing the unsavory choice of abandoning their culture in order to assimilate or maintaining their culture at the cost of continued oppression, the world to come held out a new possibility, a new and perfect world where Chinese and Ba would share a common identity as "seed people."[10]

We must conclude, I believe, that the earliest Celestial Masters community was truly multiethnic, accepting people from a variety of ethnic backgrounds as equal members of the new faith. This was an unprecedented event in Chinese history and deserves far more recognition than it has received. It had always been the case that barbarians were free to absorb the transforming influence of Chinese civilization and merge into the Chinese populace. Here we find culturally and ethnically distinct peoples forming a new union with the Chinese while maintaining their own identity as Ba.

The Ba Create a Daoist Kingdom

When Cao Cao conquered the Hanzhong state, huge numbers of Daoists were forcibly transferred to other parts of the country, primarily to the area around the capital of Ye and to the northwest (modern Shaanxi and Gansu). It would seem that most of the Ba were moved to the northwest. Reliable records for the third century are rare, but the Celestial Masters faith maintained some semblance of organization at the same time that the movement was spreading across North China. We cannot know to what degree the Daoists of Shaanxi and Gansu remained under the administrative control of some central successor to Zhang Lu, but they did retain their Daoist identity and practices.

At the end of the third century, a large body of refugees, predominately non-Chinese and Daoist, were driven south by civil unrest, natural disasters, and famine.[11] Members of the Li family, descendents of Li Hu who originally hailed from Dangqu in eastern Sichuan, but more recently from Tianshui in Gansu, were pushed forward as leaders of this stream of immigrants, hundreds of thousands strong. They moved south into Hanzhong, then through the passes into Sichuan, returning after a century to the land of their origin. There the immigrants took up the menial jobs normally open to refugees, but when local officials sought to drive them back north, they arose in rebellion, with Li Te and then his son Li Xiong at their head, and established a state called Great Perfection (Dacheng). The name, taken from a prophetic passage in the *Shujing* (Book of Documents), denoted a land of Great Peace, and the state was built in part upon the expectations of a savior figure surnamed Li who would appear as an avatar of the divine Laozi and establish a utopian kingdom in this world. When Li Xiong assumed the imperial throne, he was installed in his office by Long-lived Fan, a Daoist sage, possibly of Ba ethnicity himself, who confirmed that Xiong was indeed the one destined to rule. Fan was made Chancellor and State Preceptor (*guoshi*), and his son succeeded him in that position. Although they do not seem to have been especially active politically, the Fans continued to guide the state and its rulers, and when the state was finally conquered by the Jin, it was the son, Fan Ben, to whom surviving officials turned in one last, desperate attempt to restore Great Perfection.

For the brief half century of its existence, Great Perfection was in some sense a realization of the Daoist utopian ideal. Here, as in the lost Hanzhong community, Chinese and non-Chinese lived in harmony

and equality, enjoying the limited government and lenient punishments associated with Daoist rule.[12] But it is important to note that
the Ba did not lose their own ethnic identity in the process of adopting their new Daoist one. Instead, Daoism seems to have functioned
effectively to create a new community, establishing interpersonal ties
and patterns of cooperation that spanned the divide of ethnicity.

Daoist Views of Non-Chinese Ethnic Groups

Looking outside that original community at the way non-Chinese were
portrayed in Daoist scriptures and essays, we find a certain ambiva-
lence. From the *Dadao jia lingjie* (Family Commands and Precepts of
the Great Dao),[13] we know that Zhang Lu continued to keep watch
over his flock from the other world and communicated through spirit
possession, as did the Dao (i.e., the Supreme Lord Lao himself). The
official in charge of these divine communications was the Determiner
of Pneumas (Jueqi) or Controller of Determinations (Lingjue). A
Tang encyclopedia of Daoism, the *Sandong zhunang* (Bag of Pearls of
the Three Caverns, HY 788) records this official's duties as follows:

> He is in charge of ghostly pneumas. When a man or woman is possessed
> by this pneuma and transmits words, the Controller of Determinations
> is instructed to distinguish whether [the revealing spirit] is Chinese,
> Yi, Hu, Rong, Di, Di[a], or Qiang, and whether the message is authentic
> or not. (7.19a)[14]

Here we see that communications from non-Chinese peoples were
not rare. Moreover, while the source of such communications had to
be determined, there is no blanket statement that messages from non-
Chinese were to be excluded from consideration. This reflects a continuing openness toward non-Chinese peoples during the mid-third
century.

There is also evidence that the Daoists did not believe their message was disseminated only to the Chinese. The great cultural hero
Shun is said in a Daoist scripture to have received an esoteric work on
alchemy from an enigmatic western barbarian (*ronghu*).[15] Further, in
describing the entire corpus of sacred scriptures revealed from the
beginning of time up until its end, the *Zhengyi fawen jingtu kejie pin*
(Chapter on Codes and Precepts of Scriptures and Diagrams from the
Zhengyi Canon), quoted in the *Daojiao yishu* (Nexus of Meaning for
the Teachings of the Dao, HY 1121; ca. 700 C.E.), lists 123,000 chap-

ters of scriptures revealed to the Chinese and 84,000 chapters revealed to the barbarians of each of the four directions (2.11b). These scriptures entrusted to the non-Chinese are described as being composed of "overlapping principles, the same words expressed differently." This same viewpoint is expressed in the early literature on the conversion of the barbarians (*huahu*) and in the polemical debates of the fifth and sixth centuries. There Buddhism is often viewed as a deviant and inferior form of Daoism. Laozi, having proceeded into the Western Regions, found it necessary to modify his teachings in view of the lustful, avaricious character of the native peoples, resulting in the strict discipline of the Buddhist path, with its stress on celibacy, vegetarianism, and asceticism. While this position is a rejection of certain aspects of the foreign faith, it affirms the basic value of Buddhism much as Zhiyi's "discrimination of the teaching" (*banjiao*) affirmed while simultaneously denigrating all the other types of Buddhism abroad in his day. The passage from the *Zhengyi fawen* would seem to take a further step, arguing that all barbarians in every direction have been vouchsafed holy scriptures with the same basic message as the sacred tomes of the Daoist canon.

Whatever the utopian dreams of Great Peace, we should not imagine that the early Daoist church itself was a wonderland where traditional views of class and race were wholly forgotten. A good corrective is to be found in the instructions for ordaining menials and non-Chinese in the *Zhengyi fawen taishang wailu yi* (Ceremony for External Registers of the Most High, from the Zhengyi Canon, HY1233), in which Daoist openness is tempered by traditional Chinese ideas of the relationship of barbarians to non-Chinese culture (4a–5a).[16] In addition to expressly linking non-Chinese with slaves, maidservants, and retainers, this document advises the supplicant to admit plainly his or her origin among the Man, Mo, Di, or Lao and to proclaim that although sins in previous lives led to this mean birth, he or she bears no resentment. Note the explicit acknowledgment that the non-Chinese involved may be from outside the borders of the state or from the wild, uncivilized regions within a Chinese county. It was the individual's ugly, evil nature that caused him or her to be born in the border wastes, where the rites and morality are unknown, yet even in this muck and mire their "good roots,"[17] sown through meritorious actions in a previous life, still survive and have led them to live among the Chinese, where they will be nurtured by the Daoist codes (*daoke*). Beyond adopting a Chinese surname and personal name, the aspiring Daoist had to learn to write proper ritual petitions.[18] Thus although membership was open to all, there were yet some elements of Chinese culture that non-Chinese had to be prepared to master in order to join the Daoist community.

Is there a pattern in these early relations with non-Chinese peoples? One might expect that attitudes and policies that were appropriate in second-century Sichuan, where there was comparative peace between settled indigenous ethnic groups and Chinese inhabitants of long standing, would be abandoned or transformed in the volatile atmosphere of post-317 China, when the northern half of China had been lost to a variety of non-Chinese forces that periodically menaced the remnant southern territories. Kristofer Schipper discerns a pattern of interaction whereby Daoism initially conceived of itself as a universal religion that saw Buddhism as a sibling faith but gradually moved to a position that saw all foreign religions as antithetical to its message while fostering a rapprochement with Confucianism (Schipper 1994, 63). He sees the culmination of this trend in the mid-Tang dynasty, at the time of the composition of the *Yuqing jing* (Scripture of Jade Purity, HY 1300)[19] during the reign of Emperor Xuanzong (r. 712–755), and notes that by late imperial times, relations between Daoism and Confucianism had again worsened to the point that arguments originally directed toward Buddhism were then targeted at the Daoists. This at least provides a working hypothesis to test and refine. Future research should focus on confirming and specifying more accurately these transition points, then delving more deeply into the reasons behind this transformation.

There are, of course, many more points worthy of study with regard to the ethnographic history of Daoism. The period of the Song, when Neo-Confucianism assimilated elements of Buddhist and Daoist doctrine to produce an intensely nationalistic, antiforeign philosophy, and the Yuan, when the Complete Perfection Daoists were actively courting the Mongols while many officials retired rather than serve a foreign conqueror, would be particularly interesting objects of study in this regard.

Daoism and Modern East Asian Ethnicities

The final topic I would like to broach involves the role Daoism plays among the non-Chinese peoples of modern China. The most dramatic example is the Yao people, who once lived in south China but now are also found in the hilly regions of Southeast Asian countries like Thailand, Laos, and Vietnam.[20] The Yao people maintain a universal Daoist priesthood; every member of the community passes through successive ordinations confirmed by an ever more exalted register, just as the Celestial Masters Daoists once did. Social position within Yao society is based on one's position within the church. Although there is not a complete identity of secular and ecclesiastical authority, the highest-ranking secular and religious figures within a village are pretty much on a par in terms of power and influence. The Yao incorporate certain indigenous gods, notably the founder Panhu, within their pantheon, so there has been a certain amount of adaptation over the centuries to specifically Yao cultural patterns. However, it is still remarkable that they have maintained a non-Chinese society over an extended period based upon the strictures and beliefs of a distinctively Chinese religion.

The Yao case raises an important question for the history of Daoism as a whole: when did the uniquely Daoist type of social organization, typical of the earliest Daoists and now found among the Yao, disappear among the Chinese? Today, Daoist priests in Chinese communities are priests without a congregation, hired on an ad hoc basis by members of the community to perform periodic and occasional rites. The Yao must have learned their Daoism when the old system was still intact. The scriptures and god images used by the Yao point to a date no earlier than the Song; rituals of the *Tianxin zhengfa* (Correct Rites of the Heavenly Heart) heritage seem to loom large among their practice. The Song and Yuan periods also saw the establishment of numerous large Daoist abbeys (*daoguan*) in Sichuan, Yunnan, and Guizhou (Duan 1992, 71). If this dating is correct, we can assume that the original Daoist social order must have survived in recognizable form until the eleventh or twelfth century in parts of South China. Because of the paucity of records concerning Daoism in standard sources, we have heretofore largely relied on the dating of scriptures and other religious documents to trace the development of Daoism through the ages. If our tentative conclusions concerning the Yao are correct, this suggests that we may be able to date developments in Daoist practice by looking at Daoism's diffusion into new regions and its acceptance by non-Chinese peoples.[21] A similar study might be conducted by looking at elements of Daoist culture that were transmitted to neighboring cultures like those of Korea and Japan.

Although the details are not nearly so well known as in the case of the Yao, Daoism is found among many of the ethnic minorities who currently live or once lived within the borders of modern China. One of the more prominent examples is the group meetings in Yunnan centering on the recitation of Daoist scriptures, sometimes referred to in the literature as Grotto Scripture Congregations (Dongjing hui) or August Scripture Congregations (Huangjing hui), depending on whether their primary scripture is the *Dadong zhenjing* (Perfected Scripture of the Great Grotto) or the *Yuhuang benxing jing* (Scripture of the Original Actions of the Jade August One; see Song 1985; Yang 1990). At present there are no Daoist priests associated with these groups, but their history remains unclear, and it seems unlikely that they chose such key Daoist scriptures by chance.

The status of Daoism, including the presence of ordained Daoist priests and Daoist scriptures, among the ethnic minorities of China and mainland Southeast Asia is perhaps the most exciting aspect of this problem. We are still at the beginning stages of this study, and so far most of our information comes from anthropologists with limited expertise in Daoism. Hence, what information we have is not always reliable. Still, surveys of the religions of ethnic minorities seem to find some Daoist influence among most of the peoples of Southwest China. There are major surveys of the region under way that bring together ethnographers and experts in Chinese religion, including one led by John McRae at Indiana University and another based in Japan in which Maruyama Hiroshi is participating. We can look forward to better, more sophisticated data in the near future. We should start honing our questions. We would profit by knowing in each case: How long have the members of the ethnic group been in contact with Daoism? What elements of Daoist belief and practice have they adopted? What accommodation has been made to indigenous gods and beliefs? Is knowledge of spoken or written Chinese necessary to participate in Daoist-derived activities? How do living practitioners understand their role as non-Chinese vis-à-vis this originally Chinese religion? Is Daoist influence among their people growing or waning? Have Daoist beliefs and practices in any sense facilitated their interactions with the Chinese?

Conclusion

For most of human history, the nature of ethnic identity has gone unexamined. Born into a given milieu, one adopted the prevailing definitions of one's region, one's social class, and one's family in sorting out the complex questions of who belonged with whom. In recent years, we have come to question most of these assumptions. We now assume that ethnic identity is culturally constructed, that it bears only a tenuous relationship to genetics, language, and history. Still, China challenges the limits of our understanding of ethnic identity. The development of a Chinese identity based primarily on cultural assumptions, the variety and diversity of non-Chinese peoples who came into contact with the Chinese over time, the complex interaction of cultural borrowing in both directions that took place among these peoples, all give pause to even the most limited definitions of ethnic identity. And yet, to understand the Chinese cultural experience, we must try to make some sense out of the rich record of interaction among the peoples of East Asia.

Religion is no less problematic a term when applied to this region. Although as an analytic category, its existence cannot be denied, there is no single emic category that is coterminous with what we mean by "religion" in the Western academy. Even foreign religions such as Buddhism transformed in a variety of ways when they entered China, and we are coming to talk about Chinese Buddhisms that vary internally to a surprising degree over time and space. Daoism is no simpler a concept, even in the narrow definition advocated in this chapter. The early Daoists drew upon a number of diverse intellectual traditions and incorporated elements from the religious practices of a number of disparate groups.

In this chapter, I have focused on how Daoism as a Chinese religious tradition interacted with the indigenous beliefs of the non-Chinese ethnic groups who have since its inception constituted a significant portion of its followers. I believe that further progress in this respect will require careful attention to all of these questions: What did it mean to be Chinese, and how was this cultural identity defined against that of non-Chinese peoples? What elements of individual and communal worldview, moral values, and practice were religious in nature, and did they, in fact, as a whole, constitute a religion or religions? Finally, what did it mean to be Daoist? What portions of the totality of religious experience were subsumed under this rubric, what beliefs or practices observed by those who were at least nominally Daoist should be excluded from their Daoist identity, and what beliefs or practices followed by other members of the community were eschewed by those claiming to be Daoists? I have offered here, and in my other published work, some suggestions concerning each of these questions. I hope that this will provide a starting point for further discussion of this important topic.

Notes

1. This was one of the themes of the presentation by Andrew Chittick, "Xiangyang Local Society under the Liu-Song Regime," at the Association for Asian Studies Annual Meeting, Washington, D.C., March 1998.

2. The two ethnonyms most closely associated with them at this time were Banshun Man or Board-shield Man-barbarians, referring to a distinctive feature of their traditional armament, and Zong, referring to their special tax status.

3. Stein points out the military significance of these people to the fledgling state (1963, 21–23). He also provides an able refutation of claims that these people were in any sense Tibetans, though I think he still gives too much credence to the consistency in usage of some more general ethnonyms.

4. On the Ba Yu dances, see *Jinshu* 12.693–694; Dong 1987, 167–177.

5. The original text of this inscription can be found in *Lixu* 3.8a–b. See the discussion of its interpretation in Kleeman 1998, 69n28.

6. *Zhongguo ge minzu zongjiao yu shenhua dacidian* "Gelaozu bufen." Schafer notes that during the Tang, the leaders of the Cuan people of Yunnan were "Great Ghost Masters" (1967, 49). On the Gelao and their relationship to the Lao, see Rueh 1957; Pulleyblank 1983.

7. The Yi are a particularly apt comparison because they, like the Ba, were famed primarily as warriors and practiced only limited agriculture, yet maintained a relatively robust culture, which included their own written language, and a distinct ethnic identity that resisted assimilation for many centuries. The Ba did not, so far as we know, become wealthy by subjugating another ethnic group and using them as agricultural slaves or serfs, as the Black Tribes Yi did with the White Bones, a group composed primarily of Lao and other conquered Yi tribes. See Von Glahn 1987, 24–26, 33–38.

8. This translation is adapted from Von Glahn 1987, 26. If the Ba followed a similar system, the annual tithe of five bushels of rice must have seemed a good equivalent to the contribution of meat to the sacrifice. There was also a distinction among the Black Man between the Great Lord of Ghosts who ministers to a large settlement and the normal Lord of Ghosts for smaller groups; this parallels the Celestial Masters hierarchy of Great Libationers and Libationers.

9. A good example of the difficulties in transmitting this sort of message is found in the documentary *Between Two Worlds: The Hmong Shaman in America* (Taggart Siegel and Dwight Conquergood, producers 1986). When a Christian missionary lectures a Hmong shaman on humankind's sinful nature and the need for Christ's redemption, the shaman turns to one of his family members and says in Hmong, "I have committed no sin." That the message eventually penetrates is shown by the high rate of conversion to Christianity by the Hmong in America.

10. On the seed people (*zhongmin*), see the classic article by Yoshioka Yoshitoyo (1976).

11. The following account is based primarily upon Kleeman 1998.

12. On this topic of early Daoist utopias, see Stein 1963.

13. Contained in *Zhengyi fawen Tianshi jiaojie kejing* (HY 788); see Bokenkamp 1997, 149–185. This text dates to 255 or shortly thereafter.

14. This passage, though from a Tang compilation, seems early, particu-

larly in its use of "Qin" to stand for Chinese. This usage is found in the *Dadao jia lingjie* and would seem to tie both sources to the early church when it was still centered in the northwest.

15. See *Yunji qiqian* (HY 1026), 85.1b–2b, quoting the *Taiji zhenren feixian baojian shangjing xu.*

16. *Zhengyi fawen taishang wailu yi* 4a–5a. Schipper tentatively dates this scripture to the fifth or sixth century (see Schipper 1994, 74). The translated passages, later, were made with reference to Schipper's translation of this section.

17. This term *"shan'gen,"* representing the originally Buddhist term *"kusalamūla,"* refers to merit won through virtuous action that results in an auspicious encounter with the true teaching or a worthy teacher in a later lifetime.

18. This is made clear in the following section of the *Wailu yi* (HY 1233), which details the petition of thanksgiving to be submitted three days after ordination (5ab). There, we are told, if the new Daoist is as yet unable to complete the petition, someone can "lend a hand" (*jiashou*), presumably meaning that they would take hold of and direct the writer's hand, and if even that proved impossible, a teacher or friend could write the petition on behalf of the newly ordained priest.

19. The full title is *Taishang dadao yuqing jing*, which Schipper translates as "Book of the Precious Purity of the Exalted Great Dao."

20. On the Yao and Daoism, see Shiratori 1975, 1981; Strickmann 1982; Skar 1992. In an article studying the Yao charter myths, ter Haar (1998) points out that the physical membership of the Yao community has been rather fluid, with Chinese and members of other ethnic groups redefining themselves as Yao, and Yao becoming Chinese. This has interesting implications for the process by which the Yao adopted Daoism.

21. Admittedly, such an approach would face many obstacles. One would first, for example, have to determine what premodern ethnic group can be reliably identified with the modern one and when and where they lived, then look for proof that they were converted to Daoism directly by the Chinese rather than hearing of it from some other minority group. On his website (http://www.let.leidenuniv.nl/bth/yao.htm), ter Haar has argued that the Yaos' adoption of Daoism is later than the Song. If true, this would push the survival of true Daoist communities in China even later.

Bibliography

Bokenkamp, Stephen R. 1997. *Early Daoist Scriptures.* Berkeley: University of California Press.

Chen Cheng-siang. 1980. *A Geographical Atlas of China.* Hong Kong: Cosmos Books.

Dong Qixiang. 1987. "Ba Yu wu yuanliu kao." In *Ba Shu kaogu lunwen ji*, ed. by Xu Zhongshu, 167–177. Beijing: Wenwu.

Duan Yuming. 1992. *Xi'nan simiao wenhua.* Kunming: Yunnan jiaoyu.

Harada Masami. 1963. "Minzoku shiryō to shite noboken." *Philosophia* 45:1–26.

———. 1967. "Bokenbun ni mirareru meikai no kami to sono saishi." *Tōhō shūkyō* 29:17–35.

Harper, Donald. 1985. "A Chinese Demonography of the Third Century B.C." *Harvard Journal of Asiatic Studies* 45:459–498.

Kleeman, Terry F. 1998. *Great Perfection: Religion and Ethnicity in a Chinese Millennial Kingdom.* Honolulu: University of Hawai'i Press.

Prusek, Jaroslav. 1971. *Chinese Statelets and the Northern Barbarians, 1400–300 B.C.* Dordrecht, Netherlands: Riedel.

Pulleyblank, E. G. 1983. "The Chinese and Their Neighbors in Prehistoric and Early Historic Times." In *The Origins of Chinese Civilization*, ed. by David N. Keightley, 411–466. Berkeley: University of California Press.

Rueh Yih-fu. 1957. "Laoren kao." *Bulletin of the Institute of History and Philology*, Academia Sinica 28:727–771.

Sage, Stephen. 1992. *Ancient Sichuan and the Unification of China.* Albany: State University of New York Press.

Schafer, Edward H. 1967. *The Vermilion Bird: T'ang Images of the South.* Berkeley: University of California Press.

Schipper, Kristofer M. 1994. "Purity and Strangers: Shifting Boundaries in Medieval Taoism." *T'oung Pao* 80:61–81.

Seidel, Anna. 1987. "Traces of Han Religion in Funeral Texts Found in Tombs." In *Dōkyō to shūkyō bunka*, ed. by Akizuki Kan'ei , 714–733. Tokyo: Hirakawa.

Shiratori Yoshirō. 1975. *Yōjin monjo.* Tokyo: Kōdansha.

————. 1981. "The Yao Documents and Their Religious Ceremonies." In *Proceedings of the International Conference on Sinology: Section on Folklore and Culture*, Academia Sinica 311–318.

Skar, Lowell. 1992. "Preliminary Remarks on Yao Religion and Society." Unpublished typescript.

Song Enchang. 1985. "Dali he Lijiang daojiao gaikuang" In *Yunnan minzu minsu he zongjiao diaocha*, ed. by Yunnan sheng bianjizu, 119–124. Kunming: Yunnan minzu.

Stein, R. A. 1963. "Remarques sur les mouvements du taoïsme politico-religieux au IIe siècle ap. J.-C." *T'oung Pao* 50:1–73.

Strickmann, Michel. 1982. "The Tao among the Yao." In *Rekishi ni okeru minshū to bunka*, ed. by Sakai Tadao sensei koki shukuga kinen no kai, 23–30. Tokyo: Kokusho kankōkai.

Ter Haar, Barend. 1998. "A New Interpretation of the Yao Charters." In *New Developments in Asian Studies*, ed. by Paul van der Velde and Alex McKay, 3–19. London: Kegan Paul International.

Von Glahn, Richard. 1987. *The Country of Streams and Grottoes: Expansion, Settlement, and the Civilizing of the Sichuan Frontier in Song Times.* Cambridge, Mass.: Council on East Asian Studies, Harvard University Press.

Xueyuan, ed. 1990. *Zhongguo ge minzu zongjiao yu shenhua dacidian.* Beijing: Xueyuan.

Yang Cenglie. 1990. "Lijiang Dongjing yinyue diaocha." In *Lijiang wenshi ziliao* 9:114–138.

Yoshioka Yoshitoyo. 1976. "Rikuchō Dōkyō no shumin shisō." In *Dōkyō to bukkyō* 3:223–283. Tokyo: Kokusho kankōkai.

2

Confession of Sins and Awareness of Self in the *Taiping jing*

Tsuchiya Masaaki

In the Way of Great Peace (Taiping dao) under the leadership of Zhang Jue in the later Han, the formal confession of sins was practiced. As the *Dianlue* (Scriptural Abstracts) says, as cited by Pei Songzhi in his commentary to Zhang Lu's biography in the *Sanguo zhi* (Record of the Three Kingdoms):

> In the Way of Great Peace, the leader wrote talismans and wove spells, holding on to a bamboo staff of nine sections. He told the sick people to knock their heads to the ground and remember their sins, then gave them a talisman, burned and dissolved in water, to drink. Those who got gradually better and were healed by this treatment were called good believers in the Dao. Those who showed no improvement were considered faithless.
>
> The methods of Zhang Xiu were by and large the same as those of Zhang Jue. In addition, he established a so-called chamber of tranquility or oratory, where the sick would retreat to reflect on their wrong-doings. . . . Also, he appointed so-called demon soldiers who were in charge of the prayers for the sick.
>
> To perform these prayers, they would write down the sick person's name while formally reciting his intention to expiate all sins. This would be done three times: the first version was offered to Heaven by being exposed on a mountain; the second was offered to Earth by being buried in the earth; and the third was offered to Water by being thrown into a stream. Together they were known as "petitions to the Three Bureaus." (*Sanguo zhi* 8.264; Kobayashi 1991, 21)

The text here uses the expression *siguo,* "to remember one's sins" or "to meditate on one's trespasses." This compares to the term used in the contemporaneous *Hou Hanshu* (History of the Later Han), *shouguo,*

"to face one's sins" (71.2299). What both texts refer to by these words
is a formal ceremony of confession, used as a method of inner cleansing and easing sickness. The same notion is also apparent in the biography of Zhang Daoling in Ge Hong's *Shenxian zhuan* (Biographies
of Spirit Immortals):

> Zhang Daoling made it a rule that sick people should write down all
> the sins they had committed since they were born and cast these writ-
> ten confessions into a stream of water, vowing to the gods that they
> would sin no more, on penalty of death. (*Taiping guangji* 8.56; Giles
> 1948, 61)

This matches the description of the rite found in the *Sanguo zhi*, in
each case the emphasis being clearly placed on the remembrance and
written documentation of past sins.[1] The sources thus shed some light
on the practices undertaken in Zhang Jue's Way of Great Peace as well
as in the Celestial Masters led by Zhang Daoling and Zhang Lu.[2]

Similar formalities of confession were also undertaken in medieval
Daoism. As Lu Xiujing's (406–477) *Daomen kelue* (Abridged Codes for
the Daoist Community, HY 1119) says,

> The ill were not to take medicines or use the acupuncture needle or
> moxa. They were only to ingest talismans, drink water [into which the
> ashes of the talisman had been mixed], and confess all their sins from
> their first year of life. Even all those who had committed capital crimes
> were pardoned, and of those whose symptoms had accumulated and
> who were distressed by major illnesses, none were not healed. (Nick-
> erson 1996, 352–353)

Again, we have in the *Santian neijie jing* (Scripture of the Inner
Explanations of the Three Heavens, HY 1196), also of the early fifth
century:

> Those afflicted with illness who are above the age of seven—that is, the
> age of cognition—are to personally seek forgiveness for their trans-
> gressions and to employ all proper offerings, protocols, petitions, and
> talismans. For even long-standing diseases or difficult maladies that
> physicians cannot cure, one need only to take refuge in the divine law
> and confess in order to be immediately cured (1.6b; Bokenkamp 1997,
> 216–217)

These ideas of healing were found not only among the southern Ce-
lestial Masters, for even in the north we find highly similar notions. Kou
Qianzhi's (365–448) so-called "New Code," the *Laojun yinsong jiejing*
(Scripture of Recited Precepts of Lord Lao, HY 783), has a relevant rule:

> If among the people of the Way there is sickness or illness, let it be an-
> nounced to every home. The Master shall first command the people
> to light the incense fire. Then the Master from inside the chamber of
> tranquility, and the people on the outside, facing toward the west with
> their hair unbound, striking their heads to the ground, shall confess
> and unburden their sins and transgressions. (16a; Mather 1979, 117)

After the fifth century, the texts begin to change as they increasingly
reflect the influence of the Buddhist practice of *chanhui,* or "penitence
and regret" (see Kuo 1994), one example being the sixth-century
Zhengyi weiyi jing (Scripture of Dignified Observances of Orthodox
Unity, HY 790), which contains two entries using the term in the description of formal confessions.

Ōfuchi Ninji, in his recent analysis of the early Daoist practice of
confession, has come to characterize it by six points:

(1) Confession was directly related to sickness, which was thought
    to be caused by sins.
(2) This view in turn was based on the notion that human behavior
    was supervised and evaluated according to its good and bad
    qualities by a supernatural administration of gods and spirits;
    this concept was significantly different from that held commonly
    in pre-Qin times and documented in texts like the *Mozi.*
(3) Confessions also contained a traditional Confucian element
    in that penitents had to kowtow to the gods and beg for the
    forgiveness of their sins.
(4) The formalities took place in a separate meditation hut or other
    isolated place, like the chamber of tranquility, or oratory.
(5) Confessing sins in order to heal diseases had the effect of
    lightening the penitents' burdens and making them feel lighter;
    this was completed by the religious purification of "talisman
    water" (*fushui*), which enhanced the psychological effect of
    the confession.
(6) Other religions, especially Christianity and Buddhism, have sim-
    ilar practices of formal confession. Compared with these, the
    Daoist ones appear less based on a deep inner feeling of guilt;
    they are, it seems, a more utilitarian and this-worldly measure
    of concrete, practical relief (Ōfuchi 1991, 87, 92–93, 163).

Unlike Ōfuchi Ninji, who denies any Buddhist influence on the early
Daoist practice, Fukui Kōjun has argued that it reflected a great degree of similarity (1987a, 44; 1987b, 91). Then again, Yamada Toshiaki, in his discussion of Daoist *zhai* rituals, argues that in their development from Han-dynasty purification rites to the full-blown Rites of

Mud and Soot (*tutan zhai*) in the fifth century, formal confessions and the breast-beating of the Way of Great Peace were integrated. As the rite was expanded to include the purification of both body and mind, the possibility to express one's shouldering of sins through self-punishing acts came to be of increasing importance (Yamada 1994). Most recently, Yoshikawa Tadao has studied the oratory, or chamber of tranquility (*jingshi*), as the concrete setting of formal confessions, describing its origins and development under both Daoist and Buddhist aspects in some detail. He has also successfully elucidated the consciousness of sin that prevailed among the medieval Chinese (see Yoshikawa 1998; also 1987; 1992; 1994).

Following in the footsteps of these eminent scholars and their research, in this chapter I would like to discuss the setting and special characteristics of early Daoist confessions, examining them particularly in regard to the fifth and sixth points made by Ōfuchi and focusing on their practice as undertaken in the Way of Great Peace and as documented in the *Taiping jing* (Scripture of Great Peace).

The *Taiping jing* has come down to us in only one edition, that contained in the Ming-dynasty Daoist canon, which consists of fifty-seven scrolls. As mentioned in the Buddhist text *Mouzi lihuolun* (Mouzi's Examination of Doubts) of the second or third centuries C.E., the original *Taiping jing* of the Way of Great Peace had 170 scrolls, which means that a good two-thirds of the text is lost. As a result, there are many doubts regarding the integrity of the transmitted text, which scholars have tried to resolve in various ways.

Among Japanese scholars, the first to take up the issue was Fukui Kōjun. He suggests that the transmitted *Taiping jing* was first compiled in the Yuan dynasty on the basis of a text called *Taiping dongji jing* (Scripture the Pervasive Ultimate of Great Peace) in 170 scrolls, which in turn was put together in the Six Dynasties and survived throughout the Tang and Song (see Fukui 1936; 1937). In contrast, Yoshioka Yoshitoyo, who focused his examination on the Dunhuang fragments of the text (found in S. 4226), concludes that our *Taiping jing* is the remnant of a version created under the Chen emperor Xuandi (r. 658–682), which conflated the *Taiping dongji jing* and the surviving fragments of the ancient text (1970, 150). Yamada Toshiaki, next, follows Yoshioka and elucidates the different versions more clearly in a study of the meditation technique of "guarding the One" (1999, 27–48). In addition, Ōfuchi Ninji has shown convincingly that our *Taiping jing* contains some content that could not have been written by men of the late Six Dynasties (1957); the same point is also made by the Chinese scholar

Wang Ming, who furthermore provides evidence that the text's language in many instances reflects Han-dynasty rather than later usage (1984, 183–200).[3] To conclude, we may say that the transmitted *Taiping jing*, which forms the basis of my study, contains information and material that go back to the ancient movement and show the early Daoists' ideas of self and world.

The following study, then, is based on an interest not only in the early history of Daoism, but more generally in the phenomenon of traditional Chinese autobiography. The latter was characterized by Kawai Kozō as follows:

> Autobiography in traditional Europe developed from the regret of personal misdeeds and the confession of sins, from formulating the wrongs one had done and thus from the reflection of the difference between one's former (good) self and one's recent (sinful) self. This kind of elementary examination of the self lies at the root first of "spiritual self-advancement," then of European autobiography. In China, in contrast, there was in general no comparable regret of one's deeds and confession of sins, nor was there the formal pronouncement of one's wrongs. (Kawai 1996, 5)

In a highly similar argument explaining the absence of self-searching autobiography in China, Wu Peiyi says:

> The two major groups of Chinese self-literature we have dwelt upon, spiritual and fictional autobiographies, have one thing in common: an affirmation of the self. The tortuous quest in the first and the exuberant display in the second were both predicated on a fundamental optimism. If the autobiographer finds fault with his life at this or that point, he is usually sustained by hope. There may be occasions for despair, but never harsh self-stricture. (Wu 1990, 207)[4]

Not entirely convinced by these arguments, I would like to suggest that there exists a deeper dimension of Chinese autobiography that goes back to in-depth self-examinations first practiced among the Daoists of the Way of Great Peace. To appreciate this deeper dimension more fully, it is necessary to understand the ancient texts and their views on their own terms rather than through modern concepts. The following is an attempt in this direction.

Confessions in the Way of Great Peace

In early Daoism, confessions were practiced with the aim of healing illness and disease. How were these two thought to be connected? Why should enumerating one's sins have an impact on one's physical well-being?

Ōfuchi explains the connection in his fifth point by suggesting that confessions served to alleviate feelings of sinfulness and badness, thus relieving the psychological stress that may have caused somatic symptoms and therefore aiding in the healing of illness. I would agree that certainly a psychosomatic element plays a role in the procedure; however, in the ancient sources the understanding of the effect of confessions has nothing to do with stress relief. Rather, they insist that the sins of the past are the immediate cause of illness and disease. How, then, do the sins come to cause illness? What are the ways in which moral behavior affects physical health in traditional Daoist thought?

The *Taiping jing* explains the interaction of sins and diseases by first pointing out that there are three key factors in the universe: Heaven, Earth, and humanity. They are the three forms into which primordial energy (*yuanqi*) divided at the time of creation (66.236). This primordial energy is the root of all, the spirit root (*shen'gen*) of all existence. The spirit root divides into the three factors, then also manifests in three psychosomatic factors: spirit (*shen*) associated with Heaven; essence (*jing*) associated with Earth; and the vital energy (*qi*) of harmony associated with humanity (154.728).

Within this cosmic system, human beings contain the powers of Heaven and Earth and represent a microcosm of the larger universe. The roundness of the human head resembles Heaven; the square shape of the feet imitates Earth; the four limbs match the four seasons; and so on (35.36).[5] According to the *Taiping jing*, Heaven, Earth, and humanity are, therefore, equally made from primordial energy; they are not only connected intimately but also stand in direct analogy to one another. The intimate connection between Heaven, Earth, and humanity, then, leads to the phenomenon that when the ruler follows the Dao, the proper way of the cosmos, Heaven and Earth rejoice; when he or she loses the Dao, disasters and strange occurrences appear (18.17). In an analogous way, when the ruler in the human body—the microcosmic replica of Heaven and Earth—loses the Dao and commits evil, the body suffers disasters, that is, it falls ill.

Just as disasters visit the planet as direct effects from Heaven, so the human body is subject to immediate reverberations of its evil deeds. Just as Heaven loves good and loathes evil, so whenever a human being commits a bad deed, Heaven manifests its displeasure by visiting sickness upon his or her body. According to the *Taiping jing*, sickness is, therefore, the expression of displeasure at human misdeeds on the side of the spirit(s) of Heaven (*tianshen*) and not the automatic effect of an imbalance or disharmony of energy. Whenever someone commits an evil act, the flow of the energy of Heaven and Earth is cut off, and the person can no longer recognize his or her destiny (*ming*), that is, the moral duty in life, and will accordingly lead a life akin to that of beasts. Heaven and Earth hate this state of affairs and, as a result, cause the person to fall ill (96.425). Also, when the energy in the body is no longer in harmony, its spirit and essence will take off. The reason for this is that spirit and essence love to be in a pure place, and when the body becomes defiled, they dislike it so much that they leave (18.27). The reason, in turn, why the body is defiled is that the person has committed a sin. This shows clearly that in this early thinking the concepts of sin and defilement were intimately connected.

To make the spirit return to the body, which will also effect a cure for the illness, the defiled body must be purified. To this end, Daoist followers practiced *zhaijie* as well as sitting in an "incense chamber" and meditating on the images of the gods who resided in the body's inner organs. *Zhaijie* at this time indicated formal measures of purification that involved fasting and living only on pure energy, keeping one's eyes averted from all evil and nastiness, practicing bodily refinements, and abstaining from sexual activities and passions (42.90). Meditation (*jingsi*) was especially emphasized as a remedial method in the *Taiping jing* and had to do with the belief that the good spirits would come into the body if and when they were visualized within—as would the bad. The "incense chamber" (*xiangshi*) indicates the oratory, or *jingshi* (73.306, 110.534, 35.46; see Yoshikawa 1998). Prepared by *zhaijie* and meditation and placing themselves in the incense chamber, Daoists would then undergo formal confessions. The act of confession, then, was a key measure in the purification process, as it was thought to aid the expulsion of the defilement of sin that had infiltrated the body.

The actual confession ritual, moreover, consisted of the verbal formulation of one's sins and offered an opportunity to identify the ones responsible. A pertinent example is not found in the *Taiping jing* itself but in the *Jinshu* (History of the Jin Dynasty):

> Wang Xianzhi once fell ill, and his family decided to have a ritual of petitioning on his behalf. The invited Daoist master had him confess his sins and to this end asked him a number of relevant questions. He answered: "There is nothing sinful I can think of in particular, except

maybe the fact that I divorced my wife, Chi Daomao." This lady was the
daughter of Chi Tan. Wang Xianzhi died soon thereafter. (80.2106; see
also Bokenkamp 1997, 253n20)

So Wang's illness and death in this account were related to his sin
of divorcing his wife, Chi Tan's daughter. Since he was a member of
the southern aristocracy several hundred years after the Way of Great
Peace, it is hard to tell whether his experience reflects earlier practices. On the other hand, it is one of the few incidents described in
the texts. Let us, therefore, take a closer look. The Daoist master begins to prepare the ceremony by asking the sick person to examine
his or her behavior from the early stages of life to the time of the illness. Once a foundation is established in the form of a list of the patient's good and bad deeds, it is possible to judge which one or ones
might have been the immediate cause for the illness at hand. To do a
proper evaluation, this implies, the sick person should be conscious
of a number of rules and precepts, the breaking of which might constitute a sin; he or she would need a measurement against which to assess the deeds.

Should the sick person be unable to think of any sins or bad deeds,
the master might prompt him or her by listing the rules and precepts.
The imagination-based reflection of one's former deeds to find out
one's sins and the pointing-out of possible misdeeds by others in this
system aid the patient in the recognition of certain sins as the possible cause of the condition. This, in turn, serves to develop a certain
level of interior moral self-awareness, which finds different forms of
expression. As the *Taiping jing* says:

> People today behave in a stupid and superficial way, then get sick and
> die, never once taking proper refuge in Heaven. If only they confessed
> their sins before their entire family, beat their breasts, and kowtowed
> deeply to Heaven, seeking help and begging for mercy, Heaven would
> certainly—at least after a few days—grant them forgiveness. (114.621)

The activity of confession and breast-beating, it seems, went on for
several days, allowing the expression of the patient's self. Not taking
refuge in Heaven alone, according to this, however, did not make a
person a sinner. Rather, the formal status of sinner came only with the
act of confession and the official begging of Heaven's mercy. As penitents formally confessed their sins (*shouguo*) and beat their breasts
(*zibo*), they would repeatedly throw themselves to the ground and
knock their heads (*koutou*), repenting their sins and accusing themselves of various misdeeds (114.591). The *Taiping jing* also uses the ex-

pression *zize*, or "self-blame," indicating that people would "meditate on their sins and think of the burden thus accumulated" (107.555). The formal confession of sins, therefore, also included the opportunity for self-blame, which in turn was a way of developing shame within the person for the sins committed. The ceremony then offered a chance to show this inner shame to the entire community and thus be exonerated (154.719).[6] The effect was the same as that described in Zhang Daoling's biography cited earlier, that is, penitents would recognize their sins, feel ashamed of them, and then vow "to the gods that they would sin no more, on penalty of death."

In addition, it seems that, at least in the middle ages, penitents would also undergo harsh self-punishments, or aggressions against themselves (*zinue*). Why would they do that? The *Taiping jing* does not give a coherent answer to this question, but it does speak about aggression and hurt exerted toward others and visited upon sinners by Heaven:

> Even if Heaven has indicated that it will kill the sinners, they yet pray for long life and put their faith in Heaven, as if nothing was wrong. Even if Heaven has begun to punish them, they yet cry out to Heaven and Earth and loudly wish for forgiveness. This is because they do not understand the importance of their own sins.
>
> Then Heaven tests them, leads them off, and even throws them into a far-off, deserted wilderness, so that they may come to know themselves. If you want to know what this kind of judgment feels like, just think of the examination of a criminal by an enlightened ruler. If he confesses his crimes and accepts the blame for them, the ruler will not have him killed. It is just the same with Heaven.
>
> Depending on the greatness of the misdeeds, the culprit will be given a prison sentence—a harsh one for major sins, a light one for lesser ones. This way he can expiate his crime. And if he has come to know himself properly, then even should he have to die, he will not feel hatred and not cry out against the judgment. (117.663)

According to this, the suffering inflicted upon sinners matches the weight and seriousness of their sins. Accordingly, if sinners understand the causes and reasons for their sufferings and recognize the impact of their own behavior, then they achieve a certain level of self-awareness and self-consciousness. When undergoing a formal rite of penitence, it is, therefore, adequate that the sinners subject themselves to punishments matching their trespasses. The self-punishing acts during such a rite are, therefore, undertaken in anticipation of the punishments Heaven would eventually mete out, sinners putting them on themselves to avoid later inflictions. The formal rite of confession, in turn, becomes part of the self-punishment undergone in fear of Heaven.

Self-Blame and Confession

If formal confession is part of self-punishment, how then are the sins formulated, and what exactly is the effect of this action? There are no pertinent examples in the *Taiping jing*, but the expression "self-blame" occurs variously in sources of the Later Han period. One case is the exposure of King Tang of the Shang in a rainmaking ceremony after the country had suffered from a prolonged drought. The story first appears in pre-Han literature (see Zheng 1957), where it is mentioned twice, in the *Lüshi chunqiu* (Spring and Autumn Annals of Mr. Lü) and in the *Xunzi* (Works of Master Xun). The first version runs:

> Tang himself entered the mulberry forest to pray. He said: "If I, the ruler, have sinned, then let the people not be blamed; but if the people have sinned, then let me, the ruler, take the blame! Let not the highest god and otherworldly spirits harm the destiny of the people for the personal incompetence of my single person!"
>
> Having said this, he cut off his hair and had his hands tied, making himself into a sacrificial victim. Thus he prayed to the highest god. The people greatly rejoiced at his actions, and a great rain fell. (*Lüshi chunqiu* CH.479; see Wilhelm 1971, 106–107; Schafer 1951)

Then again, the *Xunzi* has:

> On the occasion of the drought, Tang prayed: "Is my government not properly regulated? Does it cause the people grief? Why has the rain not come for so long a time? Are the palaces and chambers too glorious? Are the women of the harem too numerous? Why has the rain not come for so long a time? Are reed mats and sackcloth being offered in bribe? Do slanderers flourish? Why has the rain not come for so long a time? (*Xunzi* 24.504; Knoblock 1994, 323–324)

The king's prayer in the first version begins with the assumption that the continued drought is to be blamed on a specific sin. If the sin is the emperor's, then he is a major sinner who deserves to die. If it is the people's, then the emperor will take it upon himself. In either case, he shoulders the responsibility for the well-being of the realm and is considered a sinner. As he recognizes himself as such, he undergoes the appropriate punishment of exposure and offers himself as a sacrifice. Heaven accepts this and promptly sends down rain. The second version, too, begins with the assumption that sin causes the drought. It acknowledges the possibility that the sin is the emperor's by mentioning his self-examination, but ultimately in this reading he does not commit any wrong. As a result, the emperor is not a sinner, and the drought is an unwarranted oppression on the side of Heaven. As the emperor exposes himself, Heaven recognizes its wrong and sends down rain.

Looked at from the perspective of self-blame, the two versions are significantly different. In the first, the emperor sees himself as a sinner and becomes an appropriate sacrificial victim, thus accepting blame upon himself. In the second, he is free from sin and, therefore, does not take any blame.

The story developed further under the Han and appears in Wang Chong's *Lunheng* (Balanced Discussions):

> According to legend, after seven years of drought King Tang exposed himself in prayer in the mulberry forest, blaming himself for six faults. Then Heaven sent down rain. The king said: . . . [as in *Lüshi chunqiu*].
>
> [This is like] one person sitting on a dais and another kowtowing to him below, begging him for something. As the one on top hears the lower person's words, he feels compassion and concedes to the request. However, if the top man could not hear the lesser one's words, then even if the latter implored him most movingly, he would not get anything. Now, the distance between Heaven and humanity is not only that between above and below a dais. How then could Heaven, however much King Tang blames himself, hear his pleas and send rain in response? (*Lunheng* 16.245; see Forke 1972)

Wang Chong, although overall critical of the basic idea that Heaven can hear anything, in his retelling of the story mixes the perspective of the two pre-Han versions and interprets the king's list of sins as an indication of self-blame. He does so because he places the incident in the wider cultural context of self-examinations and formal confessions, already practiced in his time.

As his words also confirm, confession begins by examining the sins committed, then moves on to an organized list of them. As the sins are made public, shame is felt and blame is formally accepted by the self—marking self-blame as an essential part of confession and, therefore, also of the development of a critical, moral self-awareness.[7]

Heaven and Human Consciousness

Confessions and acts of self-blame are, therefore, self-inflicted punishments that anticipate the suffering Heaven is expected to mete out in recompense for the sins committed. Their purpose is to get Heaven to grant forgiveness for those sins—an idea common to both the Daoist text and the King Tang story.

To be more specific, a *Taiping jing* passage cited earlier states that confession, beating the breasts, kowtowing, and begging for mercy certainly would cause Heaven to forgive the penitent's sins (114.621). This mercy is the compassion and pity felt by Heaven on behalf of the sinner. Similarly, in the story of King Tang, Heaven is moved by the suffering to which the ruler subjects himself, communicating his sincere intention to the powers above. Both the *Taiping jing* and the story of King Tang, therefore, hold that if one acknowledges oneself as a sinful person and communicates one's sincere intention to Heaven, the latter will certainly grant forgiveness. However, how is Heaven thought to recognize and understand this human effort at sincerity and self-blame?

Heaven and humanity might, as in the illustration used by Wang Chong, be seen as two interacting agents, of equal sensory power but different position in the scale of things, so that the human being needs only to voice his or her faults loudly in order to be understood and recognized. In this model, Heaven is a personified celestial power, which has an auditory sense to hear human pleas and recognize human sincerity. Equally anthropomorphic is Heaven's reaction of pity and compassion, the basis for the forgiveness offered to the sinner.

While this model may be at the root of the King Tang story, it is not dominant in the *Taiping jing*. Here, Heaven and Earth, on the one hand, and humanity, on the other, are linked primarily through their common bond of *qi*-energy. As consciousness arises in the human being, so his or her *qi* is activated; this, in turn, has the ability to move and respond to Heaven and Earth. Utmost sincerity (*zhicheng*), then, is the state within human beings that most closely matches the virtue of Heaven and Earth as they create and nurture the myriad beings. Human beings receive life from their father and mother only because Heaven and Earth, in their sincere virtue, cause this to happen. As a result, Heaven and Earth expect human beings to turn toward the good and develop a similar sincerity in their actions. Ideally, therefore, a human being should always first reflect on the will and tendencies of Heaven and Earth before doing anything.

Within human beings, moreover, the heart/mind is the highest among the five inner organs, the seat of spirit and sagacity, and the residence of pure yang *qi* within the body. In the system of the five phases, it is associated with fire, a fire that burns within people to match the glory and brightness of Heaven. Similarly, the sun, the concentrated yang energy of the sky, is the ruler of fire and the most honored among all celestial entities. It, too, is a source of great light and bright radiance. In people, similarly, a mind of utmost sincerity burns with warm fire and shines forth with great brightness, matching the power of the sun. The spirit of the heart/mind, moreover, rises up to communicate the mind's sagacity to the sun, which, in turn, transmits this pure intention to Heaven. This is the pathway by which utmost sincerity in humans can move the spirit powers of the universe and spread purity all around, including also throughout the body (*Taiping jing* 96.426).

The way human consciousness impacts Earth is understood along similar lines. Most purely, when people are in a state of utmost sincerity, they are free from thoughts and radiate pure yang energy. Now, if they have thoughts while in deep sincerity, the heart/mind feels burdened and in pain, both heart and stomach are upset, and the person cannot eat or drink. The force that causes the mind to be filled with thoughts and enter this painful state is the intention (*yi*). The nature of the intention is benevolence, and among inner organs it is associated with the liver. The liver being further connected with the eyes, when humans are in a state of sincerity with thoughts, they often shed tears.

In addition, thinking (*si*) is associated with the spleen. Just as the heart is the seat of pure yang, so the spleen is associated with pure yin. It is thus related to Earth. As thoughts arise in a state of sincerity of pure yang, the heart is pained, tears come to the eyes, and the spleen is activated. As this sincerity is further spread into the four directions, the intention is carried far off and communicates with outside forces. Its nature being yin, it expresses itself in melancholy and sadness, which, in turn, carried by the yang force of the mind, comes to communicate with Earth. Earth, in turn, reports the person's mental state to the spirits of Heaven. This is the way in which human consciousness moves Heaven and Earth (*Taiping jing* 96.426).

The interaction of humanity with Heaven and Earth in this model is, therefore, explained through the actions of *qi* in its various forms and associations with the five inner organs and the five phases. This, however, does not yet explain how Heaven can have the human characteristics of hearing, feeling compassion, and granting forgiveness. Even in the *Taiping jing*, it appears, Heaven is personified enough to allow for certain human characteristics and for mercy felt in response to human sincerity. Sins, then, are dissolved through the feeling of merciful compassion on the side of Heaven. And the undergoing of formal confessions, especially in their extreme form, including self-blame and punishment, is the key means of gaining a reaction of compassion from Heaven. It is analogous to the feelings evoked in a human judge when confronted with a penitent criminal. This analogy can be substantiated in three different points.

First, according to the *Taiping jing*, Heaven and humanity are not only related through their mutual correspondence but also through the fact that the human body is a microcosmic replica of the greater universe and thus parallel to Heaven in structure. Similarly, human society and celestial society are structured alike. In both, there is a hierarchical administration, and Heaven in this is personified as the Lord of Heaven (*tianjun*), the senior executive officer who evaluates and judges human behavior. As the *Taiping jing* says:

> If one dares to come forward and beg life from the Lord of Heaven, one must not have any egotistic desires. . . . One should rather speak in plain and straightforward words and clearly state one's rights and wrongs to the various department heads. On this basis, the Lord of Heaven will judge the merits of one's case. . . . Even if one has committed a major evil and is facing death, one should desire to straighten out and repent one's wrongdoing, resolve to do only good and abstain from all evil, reflect on one's deeds day and night. Then one's sin can be forgiven. . . .
>
> Common people don't usually realize it, but Heaven sends out its emissaries to observe and record their sins, and whether big or small, Heaven knows them all. Heaven keeps detailed ledgers of good and evil, recording all deeds by month and day, and using them to decide the length of people's lives. If they don't abstain from committing evil, upon death they will enter the realm of demons, where they will be examined by the spirits of Earth and their answers measured against the recorded behavior. Then they are made to reflect on their sins and have to undergo punishment, finally learning to be submissive and obedient. (110.524–526)

According to this, the Lord of Heaven has the assembled underlings and lesser spirits keep detailed records of people's good and bad deeds, which the Lord of Heaven then uses as the basis for moral judgments. The world of the spirits is organized hierarchically, like a human government, with the Lord of Heaven at the top. Confession is important even after death, when the spirits of Earth examine the sinner and make the accuracy of the report the basis for the punishment to follow. The deeds recorded in the ledgers have to match those enumerated during confession; if they don't, the spirits will interrogate for as long as it takes the sinner to recognize his or her own evil.

Second, according to the legal thinking of the time, if a criminal would acknowledge guilt and confess, he or she would be pardoned. The *Hou Hanshu* has the story of Wu You, a famous judge who was confronted with the case of Sun Xing, a tax collector who had taken some of the state's money to buy his father new clothes. The father, however, was not pleased to receive illicit presents, and as a result, Sun Xing felt deeply ashamed. He entered the private chamber of the judge, taking the offending garment along, and confessed his deed. Wu You, acknowledging the sincere intention of both father and son and accepting the latter's confession, granted him forgiveness (64.2101). This story documents that criminals who would voluntarily confess their deeds could expect to be pardoned in the ancient legal system. Analogous to this, Heaven as the supreme judge of all humanity would tend to grant forgiveness to all those repenting and confessing their sins.

Third, as did Sun Xing in the above case, many protagonists of popular court cases enter the judge's private chamber and engage in self-blame. The term used for this chamber is *he,* which literally indicates a small side door, and by extension refers to the doorway that separates the official from the private quarters of an imperial administrator (see Sahara 1989; Yoshikawa 1998, 74). The *Hanshu* presents the case of Tian Yannian who let himself be bribed by an enemy agent, then closed the private side door behind him and entered into a *zhaishe,* or purification room, to reflect in loneliness (90.3666). The private quarters of senior officials were, therefore, often also purification places, or rooms for solitary reflection and study.

In addition, rooms used for confession in the *Taiping jing* are also called *zhaishi,* or purification chambers. It says: "If you want to escape from danger, follow instructions carefully, enter a purification chamber and make sure the door is closed firmly behind you, lest others enter by mistake" (154.723). As both types of rooms have the word *zhai* in their names, it is likely that they were facilities for the practice of *zhaijie,* or purification and abstention. The same kind of room was also called a *jingshi,* or chamber of tranquility, as described earlier. In addition, according to Yoshikawa's recent studies, the chamber of tranquility had a close connection with the Han official *qingshi,* or chamber of interrogation, and the term *jingshi* as likely as not derived from *qingshi* (1998, 66). In other words, the religious practice of confession

in the Way of Great Peace closely imitated the legal practice of inter-
rogating criminal suspects.

Conclusion

Several notions have become clear in the above discussion. To begin,
the confession of sins in the Way of Great Peace is based on an understanding of *qi* as the key connecting factor between the universe
and humanity. Heaven, Earth, and humanity are connected and in harmony through the continuous flow of *qi*, and just as Heaven sends
down disasters if the king lacks virtue, so it visits disease upon the body
if the human being commits evil. Sickness is a state in which the harmony of the body's *qi* with the forces of the universe is interrupted.
In such a state, the spirit inherent in the person feels defiled and flees
to avoid contamination. It can be brought back into the mind and body
only through proper purification and self-reflection. The confession
of sins, then, fulfills the function of providing a means of purification
of body and mind. As the sick person undergoes confession, he or
she inevitably reflects upon the self and reaches a state of increased
self-awareness.

While this self-awareness finds expression in the punishments sinners inflict upon themselves, it is also responsible for the sense of personal guilt and shame that is experienced during confession and self-
punishment. The latter is especially designed to anticipate any further
sufferings Heaven might inflict, and confession in this respect serves
to convey the sinner's sincere consciousness of fault to Heaven with
the aim of engaging the latter's compassion and finding forgiveness.
The way sins are exonerated in the religion, moreover, closely reflects
the way in which official judges have dealt with criminals, punishing
them if unrepenting or leaning toward pardon if they confess. Heaven
and humanity are one system, organized in a parallel fashion, from
their overall structure to the specific actions undertaken.

Confession and self-blame on occasion are formal ways of enacting
even the death penalty for a given sin. In this case, they serve to avoid
death, and the sinner, fully penitent, vows never to commit the same
act again. In some ways, the formal confession can thus be described
as a performance, during which the old self—the sinner—is left behind and a new self—the penitent—is found. The performance,
moreover, involves close reflection on the existence and nature of one's
self, from its beginnings through its development to its present state
and possible renewal. The *Taiping jing* says accordingly:

Your destiny rests mainly with yourself—why would you kowtow and invoke Heaven? Your own self is what has to be purified—who else could you possibly cleanse? Your own self is what should be loved—who else could you possibly love? Your own self is what should be perfected—who else could you possibly perfect? Your own self is what has to be reflected on—who else could you possibly have memories of? Your own self is what has to be blamed—who else could you possibly find guilt in? . . .

   If you continue to commit evil without stopping, negative reports to Heaven will also never cease and you will bring death upon yourself. You must know the rules and precepts! If you commit evil, it is you alone who will shoulder the burden—nobody else will take it for you! (110.527)

This establishes a close and severe connection between the individual's sins and punishments. Despite the fact that overall the Later Han dynasty saw individuals as parts of larger community organizations and tended toward communal responsibility and punishment, the Way of Great Peace, operating at the same time, strongly proposed an individualistic vision of guilt and sin, emphasizing personal responsibility. Although a comparison with Western religions might seem simplistic, the early Daoist understanding of sin and blame is highly similar in its complexity and cannot be put aside merely as a utilitarian measure used for the curing of diseases. The intensity and depth of self-awareness exhibited in the ancient writings on confession clearly show that Chinese culture did not lack in self-reflection and critical self-evaluation, but document that it had its own highly developed visions of the functioning and structure of human self and consciousness.

Translated by Livia Kohn

Notes

   1. As the *Shenxian zhuan* says, "If they would unexpectedly fall sick, they would forthwith proclaim their misdeeds; thus on the one hand they obtained healing, and on the other were moved to shame and remorse which deterred them from sinning again" (Ōfuchi 1991, 152).
   2. The latter is described in the *Hou Hanshu:*

   Zhang Lu, *zi* Gongqi, . . . organized his followers into several groups. Initial practitioners were "demon soldiers" (*guizu*), later they would advance to "libationers" (*jijiu*). Each libationer was in charge of a group of followers, and those who ruled a particularly

large group were known as "village heads" (*litou*). They demanded
highest sincerity and faith and would not tolerate any falseness or
cheating. When someone fell sick, they would make him or her
confess all sins. (72.2435)

3. Further arguments for the early date of certain ideas and terms of the
Taiping jing, including a detailed examination of relevant sources, are found
in Fukunaga 1987; Maeda 1994.

4. He documents this point by examining not only early confessions among
Daoist movements but also Shen Yue's *Chanhui wen* (On Confession); Wang
Ji's (1498–1583) *Zisong* (Self-Criticism); Zhu Hong's (1535–1615) *Zize* (Self-
Accusation); Liu Zongzhou's (1578–1645) *Renpu* (Life Chronology); and
other works, especially of the Ming and Qing dynasties. See Wu 1996. Other
studies of the subject include Tsuchiya 1994; and on the Western aspects, especially Foucault 1997.

5. This reflects mainstream Chinese cosmology. See *Huainanzi* 7; *Chunqiu
fanlu* 13.

6. The text has, "If a person has a sin within his belly, why would his face
be red?" For more on shame in the *Taiping jing*, see Miyakawa 1983, 489.

7. A similar argument can be made from Shen Yue's *Chanhui wen;* see Wu
1990, 209.

Bibliography

Bokenkamp, Stephen R. 1997. *Early Daoist Scriptures.* With a contribution by
Peter Nickerson. Berkeley: University of California Press.

Forke, Alfred. 1972. *Lun-Heng: Wang Ch'ung's Essays.* 2 vols. New York: Paragon.
Originally published 1907.

Foucault, Michel. 1997. "Technologies of the Self." In *Michel Foucault's Ethics:
Subjectivity and Truth,* ed. by Paul Rabinow, 223–252. New York: The New
Press.

Fukui Kōjun. 1936–1937. "Taiheikyō no ichikōsatsu." *Waseda daigaku Tōyōshi
kai kiyō* vols. 1 and 2.

———. 1987a. "Dōkyō no kisoteki kenkyū." Tokyo: Risōsha. Also reprinted
in *Fukui Kōjun chōsaku shū* vol. 2. Kyoto: Hōzōkan.

———. 1987b. "Tenshidō to bukkyō no kōshō." In *Fukui Kōjun chōsaku shū*
vol. 1. Kyoto: Hōzōkan.

Fukunaga Mitsuji. 1987. *Dōkyō shisōshi kenkyū.* Tokyo: Iwanami.

Giles, Lionel. 1948. *A Gallery of Chinese Immortals.* London: John Murray.

Kawai Kozō. 1996. *Chūgoku no jiden bungaku.* Tokyo: Sōbunsha.

Knobloch, John. 1994. *Xunzi: A Translation and Study of the Complete Works.*
Books 17–32 vol. 3. Stanford: Stanford University Press.

Kobayashi Masayoshi. 1991. "The Celestial Masters Under the Eastern Jin and
Liu-Song Dynasties." *Taoist Resources* 3.2:17–45.

Kuo, Li-ying. 1994. *Confession et contrition dans le bouddhisme chinois du Ve au Xe
siècle.* Paris: Ecole Française d'Extrême-Orient.

Maeda Shigeki. 1994. "Zaishutsuhon 'Taiheikyō' ni tsuite." In *Dōkyō bunka e
no tenbō,* ed. by Dōkyō bunka kenkyū kai,153–179. Tokyo: Hirakawa.

Mather, Richard B. 1979. "K'ou Ch'ien-chih and the Taoist Theocracy at the Northern Wei Court, 425–451." In *Facets of Taoism,* ed. by Holmes Welch and Anna Seidel, 103–122. New Haven: Yale University Press.

Miyakawa Hisayuki. 1983. *Chūgoku shūkyōshi kenkyū.* Kyoto: Dōhōsha.

Nickerson, Peter. 1996a. *"Abridged Codes of Master Lu for the Daoist Community."* In *Religions of China in Practice,* ed. by Donald S. Lopez Jr., 347–359. Princeton: Princeton University Press.

Ōfuchi Ninji. 1957. "Taiheikyō no raireki ni tsuite." *Tōyōgaku* 27.2: 252–276.

———. 1991. *Shoki no dōkyō.* Tokyo: Sōbunsha.

———. 1997. *Dōkyō to sono kyōten.* Tokyo: Sōbunsha.

Pei, Yiwu. 1990. *The Confucian's Progress: Autobiographical Writings in Traditional China.* Princeton: Princeton University Press.

Sahara Yasuo. 1989. "Kandai no kangi to zokuri ni tsuite." *Tōhō gakuhō* 61:95–163.

Schafer, Edward H. 1951. "Ritual Exposure in Ancient China." *Harvard Journal of Asiatic Studies* 14:130–184.

Tsuchiya Masaaki. 1994. "Gokan ni okeru shika to shuka ni tsuite." In *Dōkyō bunka e no tenbō,* ed. by Dōkyō bunka kenkyūkai, 271–293. Tokyo: Hirakawa.

Wang Ming. 1960. *Taiping jing hejiao.* Beijing: Zhonghua.

———. 1984. *Daojia he daojiao sixiang yanjiu.* Beijing: Zhongguo shehui kexue chubanshe.

Wilhelm, Hellmut. 1971. *Frühling und Herbst des Lü Bu-wei.* Düsseldorf: Diederichs.

Yamada Toshiaki. 1994. "Dōkyō ni okeru saihō no seiritsu." In *Ajia ni okeru shūkyō to bunka,* ed. by Tōyō daigaku kenkyūhan, 309–338. Tokyo: Tōyō University.

———. 1999. *Rikuchō dōkyō girei no kenkyū.* Tokyo: Tōhō shoten.

Yoshikawa Tadao. 1987. "Seishitsu kō." *Tōhō gakuhō* 59:125–162.

———. 1992. "Rikuchō Zui-Tō jidai ni okeru shukyō no fūkei." *Chugoku shigaku* 2:151–174.

———. 1994. "Chūgoku rikuchō jidai ni okeru shukyō no mondai." *Shisō* 1994/4:99–118.

———. 1998. *Chūgokujin no shūkyō ishiki.* Tokyo: Sōbunsha.

Yoshioka Yoshitoyo. 1970. *Dōkyō to bukkyō* vol. 2. Tokyo: Kokusho kankōkai.

———. 1976. *Dōkyō to bukkyō* vol. 3. Tokyo: Kokusho kankōkai.

Zheng Zhenduo. 1957. *Tangdao pian.* Beijing: Gudian.

3

"Opening the Way"
Exorcism, Travel, and Soteriology in Early Daoist Mortuary Practice and Its Antecedents

PETER NICKERSON

The Celestial Masters in Chinese Religious History

Zhang Daoling and his followers clearly effected a religious revolution. They inaugurated a new dispensation that defined itself, then as now, not in relation to Buddhism or "Confucianism," but rather in antithesis to the false gods whom the benighted populace worshipped with blood offerings. Though the early Daoists spoke of high antiquity, of the Yellow Emperor, Yu the Great and the famous immortals of the Zhou dynasty, . . . the social history of Daoism begins with the founding of the Way of the Celestial Master in the second century A.D.

Thus, I am proposing to use the word *Daoist* only in referring to those who recognize the historical position of Zhang Daoling, who worship the pure emanations of the Dao rather than the vulgar gods of the people at large, and—I may add—who safeguard and perpetuate their own lore and practices through esoteric rites of transmission (Strickmann 1979, 165–166).

A working definition of Daoism more elegant and practical than Michel Strickmann's has yet to be proposed. In one stroke—by highlighting the essential distinction between Daoism and the popular religion of sacrificial god-cults and related practices—it freed Daoist studies from that tired sinological notion according to which "all that which is neither Buddhism nor Confucianism is Daoism." In another respect, however, the view that Daoism appeared as an entirely unprecedented ("revolutionary") alternative to a debased popular religion of blood sacrifice has been shown to be in need of revision. Largely owing to a great expansion in the excavated archaeological record and resultant work on Han and pre-Han magico-religious traditions (see, e.g.,

Harper 1978; 1982; 1985; 1987; 1998), a new appreciation of the pre-history of Daoism has emerged.

Of special significance for our purposes is Anna Seidel's work on the "tomb ordinances" or "tomb contracts" (*muquan* and related arti-facts) of the Han, especially the genre of "grave-securing writs" (*zhenmu wen*): texts from the Latter Han (first–second centuries C.E.) written on earthenware jars and buried together with the dead (see Seidel 1982; 1987a; 1987b). Written as edicts emanating from a Celestial Monarch (Tiandi) and delivered by his Envoy (Tiandi shizhe), the grave-securing ordinances command a minor spirit-bureaucracy of the tomb to conduct the deceased to the underworld (which also has its own magistrates, prisons, and systems of taxation and corvée) and place him or her securely in the charge of the underworld adminis-tration. According to Seidel, the people of the Han who used the writs expected that the dead would be treated like criminals: because of mis-deeds committed when alive, they would be imprisoned by the au-thorities. The grave-securing writs, therefore, also sought the "libera-tion" (*jie*) of the dead—that is, their release from the prisons of the earth to the secure dwellings of their tombs (Seidel 1987a; 1987b).[1] The religion of the grave-securing writs was both bureaucratic and eth-ical, in Seidel's analysis. The motif of judicial trial for past sins, fol-lowed by imprisonment and release, has remained central to Chinese death ritual until today.

Though it does not possess all the features Seidel identified with the "religion of the Celestial Monarch," a rather typical grave-securing writ, from the late second century, reads, in part, as follows:

> In the second year of Xiping, in the twelfth month [early 174], whose first day is *yisi*, on the sixteenth day which is *gengshen*, the Envoy of the Celestial Monarch declares to—the rulers of the left, the right, and the center of the Zhang family's three mounds and five tombs, the Assis-tant of the Sepulcher, the Director of the Sepulcher, . . . the Hostel Chief of the Gate of the *hun*-soul, . . . and the others, [and also] dares to announce to the Assistant of the Mound, the Sire of the Tomb, the Subterrestrial Two Thousand Bushel Officials, . . . the Squad Chiefs of Haoli, and the others:
>
> Today is auspicious and good, and for no other reason [is this an-nouncement being made], but only because the deceased, Zhang Shu-jing, had a barren fate, died young, and is due to return below and [en-ter] the mound and tomb.
>
> The Yellow Monarch [Huangdi] gave birth to the Five March-

mounts, and he rules over the registers of the living. He summons the
hun- and *po*-souls, and rules over the records of the dead. . . .[2]

For this reason are offered: medicine for exemption from forced labor, with the desire that there will be no dead among those of later generations; nine roots of ginseng from Shangdang, with the desire that
they be taken in replacement of the living; lead men, to be taken in replacement of the dead; and yellow beans and melon seeds, for the dead
to take to pay the subterrestrial levies. . . . Let the odium of the soil be
driven off, with the desire that evil be kept from propagating.

Once these orders have been transmitted, the civil servants of the
earth shall be bound, and are not to trouble the Zhang household
again. Quickly, quickly, in accordance with the statutes and ordinances.
(Ikeda 1981, 273, no. 6)

Seidel correctly categorizes the "religion of the Celestial Monarch"
(*tiandi jiao*) that underlay the grave-securing writs as a type of "proto-
Daoism." While it is not clear in the above document whether the
"odium of the soil" is the result of the deceased's misdeeds or simply
the irritation of the earth spirits as a result of the introduction of the
polluting corpse into their realm—the line between pollution and
moral malfeasance in early Chinese religion is often a fine one—the
notion of a bureaucratic administration of the underworld (the "civil
servants of the earth") overseen by a celestial deity and his underlings
clearly anticipates Daoist cosmology. In a later description, Seidel even
more boldly ascribes "many beliefs and practices of the early Daoist
church (e.g., the bureaucratized heavenly and netherworldly hier-
archies)" to "the religion of a literate class outside of officialdom—
village elders, exorcists and specialists in funerary rites—since at least
the first century C.E." (Seidel 1990, 237). The Daoist religion was less
of a novelty than accounts that contrast it only with spirit-mediumism
and sacrificial cults would imply.

Nonetheless, Seidel concludes that Daoism involved an entirely "new
soteriological paradigm." Daoism introduced into the bureaucratic
framework of the proto-Daoist religion of the Han grave-securing writs
the goals and lore of the elite immortality cult, with its graceful transcendents and fantastically adorned celestial landscapes. Ordinary
people could aspire to more than a dreary existence under the earth
as resentful subjects of the administration of the shades. The Daoist
religion promised, instead, "liberation" from death and promotion to
celestial transcendence (Seidel 1987a, 47–48).

Angelika Cedzich has further expanded this line of thought through
her ground-breaking analysis of the early Celestial Masters' ritual of

petitioning the celestial authorities (*shangzhang*) and the use of the petitioning ritual in handling the spirits of the unquiet dead (1987). In her analysis, the paradigmatic break between the beliefs about the afterlife implied by the grave-securing writs and Daoist ideas of salvation was even sharper than Seidel's work might imply. The purpose of the grave-securing writs was at its root exorcistic: their chief goal was to get the potentially malevolent spirits of the dead away from the living and keep them away. Only with the advent of the Way of the Celestial Master was an attempt made instead to save the dead, to *integrate* them into a greater "social" body together with the living—the bureaucracy of the Daoist church and the Daoist cosmos. In Daoism the use of ritual to install the deceased in a secure and pleasant post in the afterworld ensured the salvation of the dead. But the Daoists thus did not simply propose a new kind of soteriology: by insisting on salvation rather than mere exorcism, Daoists *created* the first indigenous soteriology (see Cedzich 1987, 42–60; 1993; Seidel 1988).

Implicit in the views of Strickmann, Seidel, and Cedzich is the idea that the advent of Daoism, as represented by the Way of the Celestial Master, involved a significant rupture in Chinese religious history. The early Daoists' treatment of the dead, in which a soteriological ritual and ideological paradigm was adopted in place of an exorcistic one, meant a complete reconfiguration of the Chinese religious universe. Daoism promised salvation in heaven for the worthy—in contrast with the pre-Daoist and proto-Daoist notion of an afterlife for all in the Yellow Springs and/or the tomb. It thereby advocated, in Joseph Needham's terms, a conception of the afterlife that was otherworldly and ethically polarized—rather than this-worldly and nonethical (Needham 1974, 77–113). Hence, one infers from these scholars' analyses, although the proto-Daoist religion of the grave-securing writs might, like Daoism proper, have involved the idea of an afterworld bureaucracy that could hold the dead accountable for their misdeeds, the Celestial Masters and their heirs placed those beliefs within cosmological and moral contexts that differed radically from what had gone before.

The vocabulary with which the "Daoist revolution" is described— New Dispensation, New Testament, reformation, revolution—testifies amply to the roots of such periodizing schemes. Behind this periodization is an evolutionary typology of religions that opposes "higher" religion—which is otherworldly in its cosmology and has an afterlife that is ethically polarized, and an approach to the dead that is soteriological—to a more primitive antecedent that is this-worldly, does not apply ethical criteria to the determination of afterlife destinations, and is sacrificial or exorcistic in its dealings with the spirits of the dead. Thus the issue of the place of Daoism in the history of Chinese religion has come to be discussed in terms of questions about death: the cosmology of the afterlife, the means of determining who goes where, and the rites conducted in the attempt to secure good destinations for the departed. This chapter supports a claim that differs significantly from the views of the scholars discussed above: Daoist soteriology involved no revolution, no fundamental paradigmatic shift, from the religious treatments of death that had preceded it.

Precursors of Daoism: Archaic Death Ritual

In ancient times, the hazards posed by death often were handled by figures who might, with varying degrees of specificity, be termed shamans. One of the earliest literary traces of archaic, nonclassical mortuary rites centers on the description of the *fangxiang shi* or "exorcist." According to the *Zhouli* (Rites of Zhou) of the Warring States Period,

> The duty of the *fangxiang shi* is to cover himself with a bearskin, [a mask having] four eyes of gold, a black upper garment, and a vermilion lower garment. Grasping his halberd and brandishing his shield, he leads the hundred functionaries in the seasonal No [the "Great Exorcism" held on the eve of the La, or New Year] in order to search through the rooms and drive out pestilences. (3.475; see Granet 1926, 1:298; Kobayashi 1946; Bodde 1975, ch. 4; Boltz 1979)

In the Great Exorcism the *fangxiang* was assisted by 120 (or 240, 60, or 24) youths and twelve dancers in animal masks and costumes, and he invoked in an incantation twelve demon-animal servants to devour the specters due to be exorcised. But what is of greatest importance here is that the *fangxiang* was also said to have had duties during royal funerals. The *Zhouli* continues,

> In great funerals he goes before the coffin. When the grave has been reached he enters the pit and with his halberd strikes the four sides in order to drive out the *fangliang* [demon]. (31.12a–b [3:475])

Other early shamanic figures involved with the dead included the court shamans who exorcised corpses before rulers might approach them—and, of course, Shaman Yang (Wu Yang), who summoned the soul in the *Chuci* (Songs of the South). It might further be claimed that, whether one terms all of them shamans or not, at the least these figures represented a common type of archaic religious practitioner, one whose activities involved exorcism, soul-summoning, and masked dancing.[3] Ying Shao (c. 140–206) comments concerning the function of masks in popular death ritual in a way that establishes a very close link between masked performances and the summoning of the soul:

> The *hun*-soul vapor of the deceased floats about. Therefore one makes a griffon head [mask] (*qitou*) to preserve (*cun*) it. [The term *qitou*] indicates that the head is monstrously huge. Sometimes the griffon head is called striking-the-pit (*chukuang*). This is a special local term. (*Fengsu tongyi* 1.88; *Taiping yulan* 552.10a [3.2501])

Ying Shao's remark echoes the statement in the *Liji* (Book of Rites) that after death the *hun*-soul vapor has "nowhere it does not go, nowhere it does not go" (10.19b [5.194A]). However, for those who practiced the rites described by Ying Shao, this clearly was not regarded as a good thing. Instead, *qitou*, "griffon heads" (Schafer 1987, 78) or spirit masks, were employed to keep the soul from wandering away (see Lewis 1990, 312*n*106).

Given its role in the protection of the deceased—here the soul rather than the body—together with what might be an allusion to the exorcist's striking of the sides of the grave-pit, the griffon head mask would appear to be linked, at least functionally, to the *fangxiang*. This identification is made explicitly in Duan Chengshi's *Youyang zazu* (Miscellanea from Youyang), where the nature of the performances involving the masks is also clarified:

> When a person dies nowadays, there is someone who acts and plays music that is called "funeral music." The griffon head is that by which the *hun*-soul vapor of the deceased is secured. One name for [the performer] is Fright, because his clothing and coverings are frightening. Others call him Crazed Suspicion (*kuangzu*). If he has four eyes he is called a *fangxiang;* if he has two eyes he is called a dervish. (13.69–70; see Kiang 1937, 92–93)

The griffon head thus refers both to the mask and to the ritualist who wore it. As shown by the numerous regional names provided by Ying Shao and Duan Chengshi, there must have been many local varieties of such funeral performances, involving masked players who danced, perhaps in a state of ecstatic trance—the monster masks and frenzied dancing certainly suggest shamanism.[4] Their work was probably intended to drive away the demons that would eat the corpse (a goal attributed to the work of the *fangxiang*) and (at least by the time of the Latter Han, when Ying Shao wrote) also to prevent the soul from wandering or dispersing. The soul so protected was in all likelihood then provided with permanent lodgings in the tomb.

These funeral rites must have been much like the Nuo, or Great Exorcism, itself. While the Nuo was a seasonal rite aimed at specters of age, dirt, and decay, the death rite sought to neutralize all the hazards death created: for the deceased, attacks by demons of putrefaction or by the fierce demonic creatures the soul would encounter were it to wander too far; for the survivors, the pollution of the corpse and the potential hostility on the part of the spirit of the deceased. The central feature in both cases was the exorcistic masked dance by the *fangxiang* (or the related *qitou*) accompanied, Marcel Granet suggests, by drumming and "cris provoquaient des états d'extase et de possession" (Granet 1926, 333). Analysis has revealed a continuous tradition of exorcism and shamanism that during funeral rites employed masked dancing, music, and chanting.

The Post-Mortem Journey in Daoist Mortuary Ritual

Many parallels in medieval Daoist texts can be found for the archaic and proto-Daoist rites. Here I will examine just one, from the *Yaoxiu keyi jielü chao* (Breviary of Rules, Rituals, Precepts, and Statutes Essential to Practice; HY 463; see Cedzich 1987, 14–15). The last two *juan* of this work (15 and 16) contain precise instructions for the funerals of Daoist priests, based on a tradition the ritual master Zhu Faman traces to "the greater Master Meng," Meng Jingyi (fl. 480), as well as to three other individuals: "the Lesser Master Meng," identified by Isabelle Robinet as Meng Zhizhou of the Liang (502–550; Robinet, 1977, 99); and Shijing gong (Sir Stonewell) and Zhang Xu, whom I have not been able to locate in other sources. Zhu presents his version as a "synthesis" (*huihe*) of the work of his four predecessors, and he is so scrupulous in his attribution of various sections of the ritual or different variations to his four sources that there is little reason to distrust his claim that he represents a tradition whose development over two centuries or more was well documented.

The text is quite detailed and represents, to my knowledge, a relatively untapped source for the study of medieval funerals. Particularly noteworthy is the way in which the classical form is retained—the rite is divided into the standard categories found in the *Yili* (Protocols and Rites) and other early ritual texts, such as the "lesser dressing" (*xiaolian*) of the corpse, the "greater dressing" (*dalian*), or coffining, and so forth, and the same general sequence is followed. At the same time, new Daoist procedures are interwoven into that structure. This suggests that there was little inherent conflict between Daoist (and quite likely Buddhist) mortuary ritual and "Confucian" ritual forms until that conflict was created by the Neo-Confucians of the Song (see Davis 2001).

The *Yaoxiu keyi*'s funeral for priests shows how the Daoist synthesis of the late Six Dynasties and the Tang incorporated both of the key tributaries of the larger stream of the Daoist ritual tradition, not only the Lingbao scriptures, but also the Way of the Celestial Master. This is also borne out by the *Zhengyi lun* (Discourse on Upright Unity) attributed to Meng Jingyi.[5] It argues precisely for the unity of the Way of the Celestial Master and the revelations of Lingbao: "The teachings of Zhang [Daoling] and Ge [Xuan, fl. 200; traditionally the first recipient of the Lingbao scriptures] are entirely the same and share a single function" (HY 1218, 3b2).

Continuities among archaic, proto-Daoist, and medieval Daoist mortuary rites are evinced by two ritual documents whose use is prescribed by the *Yaoxiu keyi*. The first of these, called an "Announcement" (*yiwen*), is, like the proto-Daoist grave-securing writs of the Han, in fact a form of tomb ordinance. (One difference between this document and other tomb ordinances is the identity of the issuer of the Announcement, the Celestial Elder [Tianlao], but this difference may not be so great as initially appears.)[6] It is to be written either on plain silk or paper, recited during the ceremony, and then placed in the coffin for burial together with the corpse.

The "Announcement" in the *Yaoxiu keyi* first provides a form for listing the scriptures, registers, and talismans received by the departed during his lifetime (which may or may not be placed together with the corpse in the tomb), together with the other grave goods: clothing and the articles appropriate to the priestly profession, such as ink stone, paper, brushes, petition-table, and incense burner. The text continues:

> The Celestial Elder announces to—the Heavenly One and the Earthly Two; . . . the Elders of Haoli; the Two Thousand Bushel Officials beneath the soil; . . . the Inspector of the Gate of the *Hun*-soul; . . . and the Envoys in Charge of Talismans:[7]
>   Now (so-and-so), a disciple of the Three Caverns, from (such and such a) village, township, district, commandery, and region, a male born in (such and such a) year, who lived (so many) years, died this month on (such and such a) day at (such and such a) time. Having declared his lifespan exhausted, suddenly he gave up [his life] in order to be

transformed anew. His *hun*-soul will ascend to heaven, and his form will enter the earth to dwell. Now he is going to return to a brick tomb established on a mountain in (such and such a) township and village.

(So-and-so) when he was alive abandoned the profane and followed a Master, requesting that the Way allow him to leave the world to seek learning and to wear at the waist the great scriptures, talismans, charts, and declarations of the Three Caverns of Shangqing. He is carrying all of these back to the Grand Yin (Taiyin), along with winter and summer clothes, ornaments, and implements, altogether including (such and such) varieties, his pine coffin and the gear used for the funeral and the burial and the preparations therefor.

When this talisman arrives, attentively lay to rest and conceal his form and bones; vigilantly guard the scriptures and treasures; guide, cap, and gird him. Order your subordinates to greet and escort him, and not to impede him. Let him go directly and without obstruction to his place of concealment. Do not allow the demons of other surnames dwelling [in graves] nearby, to left or right, or to east, west, south, or north, to appropriate his name or assume his surname, thus falsely giving rise to theft. Clearly receive these talismanic orders; do not disobey them. Let all be in accordance with the statutes and ordinances of the Nüqing Edicts of the Demon Laws of the Grand Mysterious Capital. (*Yaoxiu keyi* 15.14ab; see Nickerson 1996)

The text attributes this form of Announcement to (the greater) Master Meng (16.4b); it should, therefore, date from about the year 480. Despite the passage of time and the emergence of the mature Daoist tradition, the "Announcement" here still resembles very closely the Han grave-securing writs: besides the overall similarity of form—the identical roles of the Celestial Elder and the Celestial Monarch's Envoy, the members in common of the underworld pantheon, and the "talismanic orders" that must be obeyed "in accordance with the statutes and ordinances"—the "Announcement," like the writs, seems primarily to be concerned with securely placing the deceased, together with his grave goods, in the tomb, the "place of concealment" (*zangsuo*). The post-mortem journey's final destination seems less than inviting.

Soteriology in the Medieval Daoist Synthesis

But as the second key ritual document in the funeral directions of the *Yaoxiu keyi* shows, the overall intent of the mortuary rite remains soteriological, in a manner that is highly consistent with the journey paradigm, which I will try to show is characteristic of the Daoist tradition as a whole. The text prescribes the sending up of a petition (*zhang*) in conjunction with the burial of the document in the tomb—as does the early Lingbao work *Miedu wulian shengshi miaojing* (Miraculous Scripture of Salvation through Extinction by Revivification of Corpses through Fivefold Refinement, HY 369; see Bokenkamp 1989). The form of petition set out in the *Yaoxiu keyi* reads, in part, as follows:

> [Since the deceased had become] bound by his sins and his [allotment] of trespasses had been filled, his body became exhausted and his spirit departed. In this month on (such and such a) day at (such and such a) time he took his leave of heaven and earth and sank forever down to [the realm of] the officials of the soil. Having [prepared] the precious scriptures, talismans, charts, ritual implements, clothing, and other articles he possessed in life, we then today at (such and such a) time sealed [them together with] his enshrouded and encoffined corpse in the mound and sepulcher.
>
> We fear that in life [the departed] may have committed a capital crime, or that the demons of stale vapors [that enforce] prohibitions and taboos or the wicked and false sprites of mountains and rivers will block the deceased and not open the way. Also we fear that the subterrestrial rulers of the four seasons, the Elders of Haoli, the Assistant of the Mound and the Sire of the Tomb, and the Subterrestrial Two Thousand Bushel Officials will not lay him to rest and conceal him.
>
> Respectfully we list the scriptures and funerary objects and transfer each item as per the document. And respectfully we prostrate ourselves on the earth and offer up a petition, inviting our superiors—the Envoy who Descends to the Corpse, and the Lord and Clerks in Charge of Funerals—to descend together and supervise the funeral and lay to rest [the deceased's] skeleton and spirit, giving him everlasting peace in Haoli and reincarnation in accordance with his karma. (16.3b–4a)

Here, very similar to the late-Han grave-securing writs, the principal fear surrounding death and burial is that the deceased will be held responsible for sins, the "capital crimes" he committed during his life, or for the breaking of the rules governing burial—the "prohibitions and taboos"—and that this will cause the chthonian spirits to harass him.

The body/spirit dualism that differentiates the Daoist from the proto-Daoist handling of death is expressed strongly, if not without some ambiguity. The death is first described in terms of the exhaustion of the body and the departure of the spirit (*shenjin shenshi*). However, the deceased is treated as a unitary being: we are told simply that "he"—the text fails to introduce a new subject, which therefore remains the "disciple of the Three Caverns, (so-and-so)" of the very first line— "sank forever down to [the realm of] the officials of the soil." The petition next addresses only the burial of the grave goods and the corpse.

The initial body/spirit (*shen/shen*) bifurcation resurfaces, however— and even more explicitly—as the petition goes on to detail the fears felt by the survivors on behalf of the deceased. The spirit, for which the way to the beyond must be opened, is treated separately from the body, which must be laid to rest in the tomb. Regarding the spirit, the text worries that the demons of "stale vapors [that enforce] prohibitions and taboos" might hold the deceased accountable for his sins and thus "block [him] and not open the way." But while the spirit is to be sent on its way to heaven, the body is to be "laid to rest and concealed" (*an yin*), provided that the cooperation of those ubiquitous spirits of the tomb—the Elders of Haoli, the Assistant of the Mound, the Sire of the Tomb, and so on—can be secured. Corpse and spirit must be brought to their appropriate, and separate, resting places so that eventually the deceased may be "reincarnated in accordance with his karma." Or as the "Announcement" had stated: "His *hun*-soul will ascend to heaven, and his form will enter the earth to dwell."

The *Yaoxiu keyi*'s funeral rite, in fact, demonstrates how Daoism's soteriological concerns—and the related separation of spirit and body—were handled within the pre-existing framework of mortuary thought, according to which death was a journey requiring exorcistic protection. The apparent ambiguities just pointed to—where the deceased is alternately treated as a single entity and as a compound of body and spirit—point to a kind of historical accretion. As in the Han grave-securing writs, the whole person of the deceased, including both the material and the more ethereal components, is first installed in the tomb: he is to "go directly and without obstruction to his place of concealment," "forever down to [the realm of] the officials of the soil." At that point, however, the destinies of body and spirit diverge. Though both might initially enter the tomb, it is the body alone that will remain in its dwelling place in the earth, while the spirit will continue on and ascend to heaven (or be reincarnated—this, of course, is another ambiguity that pervades Chinese notions of post-mortem fates). Hence the *Yaoxiu keyi*'s funerary petition addresses two distinct groups of spirits: one to settle the body in the tomb, and one to open the deceased's way to heaven.

The process of historical accretion that resulted in the construction of Daoist soteriology on the foundation of pre- and proto-Daoist traditions of mortuary exorcism was expressed in Daoist ritual through a homologous temporal dualism. The first journey of the deceased was to the tomb and the underworld; the soul alone subsequently undertook the second journey—to the heavens or other pleasant afterworld realms. This appears to have been a common notion concerning death during the Six Dynasties. An example is Huangfu Mi, whose religious world seems primarily to have been molded by New Text Confucianism. In his writings, he expresses a similar view: while the corpse will remain in the grave, the *hun*-soul will ascend after burial from the grave to the heavens (see Knapp 1998).

The journey paradigm remained as the model used to represent the transformations of death: the visible journey of the deceased to the tomb was simply duplicated on the invisible plane as the ascent of the spirit. Like the corpse, it too had to be bathed, clothed, and girded (cf. *Miedu wulian jing* 7b–8a). Just as the *fangxiang* led the funeral procession, "opened the way" to the tomb, and then entered the grave and drove off the demons that might devour the deceased, and just as proto-Daoist ritualists placed grave-securing writs in the tomb to finalize the transfer of the deceased to the underworld regime and protect deceased and survivors from the "civil servants of the earth," so medieval Daoists used their apotropaic documents to control the spirits of the earth and the tomb in order to secure both legs of the journey of death. In fact, not only the funeral ritual of the *Yaoxiu keyi*, whose beginnings go back to the late fifth century, but also the c. 400 Lingbao scriptures and certain excavated Celestial Master tomb ordinances, which span the period from 433 to 520, testify to the existence of a common medieval Daoist conception of death and its dangers, and of the ritual means to be employed in order to combat those dangers (see Nickerson 1996, ch. 3).

Passage and Paradigm in Daoist Mortuary Rites

In her essay on the Han grave-securing writs, Anna Seidel has stated that, by grafting notions of celestial transcendence that had developed as part of the immortality cult of the Han elite onto the popular religion of the grave-securing writs, Daoism created a "new soteriological paradigm" that "infused beauty, mystery and hope into the gray and legalistic spirit hierarchy of the Celestial [Mon]arch" (Seidel 1987a, 47–48). Whether one finds this to have been the case depends largely on how one defines the term "paradigm." Certainly, the notion that there was somewhere beyond the grave for ordinary souls to go (other than unhappily wandering the earth) was new, and Seidel's work shows brilliantly how Daoists were able to incorporate the goal of celestial transcendence into their bureaucratized (if not "gray and legalistic") rites for the dead.[8] However, if one understands "paradigm" in accordance with its basic meaning of "an accepted model or pattern"— as Thomas Kuhn has defined it in his application of the term to the history of science (1970, 23)—what is interesting is that Daoism was able to incorporate these new ideas *without developing a new pattern* for representing the process of death and afterlife. From the standpoint of the Kuhnian understanding of scientific revolutions, the duplication of the journey to the grave on a spiritual level would seem to have been precisely the application of an old pattern—the exorcistically protected journey—to new "data": the peregrinations of the soul of the deceased in an expanded invisible world. Thus, to that extent, there was no paradigmatic break, no revolution in soteriology.

More detailed morphological analysis of Daoist death ritual and its predecessors will help substantiate this view. Here I employ the (by now well-worn) framework for the study of the structure of mortuary rites proposed by Arnold van Gennep in his seminal *Rites of Passage* (1960, ch. 8, esp.163–164). As a rite of passage, a funeral can be considered in terms of three stages: (1) separation—whereby the ties between the deceased and the survivors are severed; (2) an intermediate, liminal phase of transition; and (3) incorporation, which effects the entry of the deceased into the land of the dead or other new place or state. These divisions are by no means clear-cut: burial, for instance, may be considered as separation, the removal of the dead from the presence of the living, but also as a rite of incorporation, as in the case of societies in which the dead are considered to dwell in the grave.

In early China, the most visible and tangible funerary rite of passage was the funeral procession itself, whereby the departed was removed from the dwellings of the living (separation), conveyed to the burial site (transition), and lodged in the tomb, which at least from Warring States times onward was conceived as a home for the dead (incorporation).[9] The centrality of the journey as a metaphor for the transition from life, through death, to afterlife is thus perfectly understandable: the most important rite of passage was, in fact, a plainly visible journey. Moreover, while van Gennep has noted that "the journey to the other world and the entrance to it comprise a series of rites of passage whose details depend on the distance and topography of that world" (1960, 153), the reverse is also true: when death is conceived as a journey, a culture's notion of travel molds the conception of death.

The mortuary passage was not the only kind of journey in early China that necessitated exorcistic rites. Kiang Shao yuan, in his classic study of ancient Chinese beliefs associated with travel, and particularly their relationship to demonology, reached the following conclusion:

> The ancients, when they left their homes or their native states, believed themselves to be continually exposed to the attacks of supernatural beings. . . . It was because of these immaterial beings that travelers needed to fear so many difficulties, privations, and perils. In order to prevent them, cope with them, or remedy them, the ancients made use of a great number of recipes. (Kiang 1937, 127, 129)

Later Daoists and magico-religious practitioners of similar ilk continued such traditions. Best known is Ge Hong's discussion in his *Baopuzi* ([Book of] The Master Who Embraces Simplicity) of "ascending mountains" (*dengshan;* ch. 17), a dangerous undertaking that required the prior knowledge of all manner of esoteric techniques.

Closer to our immediate topic, when the *fangxiang shi* opened the way for the funeral procession and drove the demons of putrefaction from the grave—and the *fangliang* and its ilk were also among the most common nemeses of travelers (Kiang 1937, 169–216)—this constituted in an important sense simply another type of travel exorcism: the provision of apotropaic protection for a procession. In that role, the *fangxiang* followed in the footsteps of his patron deity, Chiyou, also a guardian of processions.[10]

A similar convergence of travel and mortuary ritual is evident in the case of the ancient travel sacrifices, the *zu* and the *ba*. The *zu* could serve as a farewell ceremony for a living wayfarer but could also be performed before the setting out of the funeral cortège, or as a seasonal ritual to send off (and hence exorcise) wandering souls. Chiyou was also a tutelary god of the *zu*. The *ba* was structurally homologous with the pattern of sacrifice and exorcism outlined by Wang Chong (27–91) with reference to the appeasement of earth spirits offended by the construction of houses (or graves) and was carried out (in conjunction with the *zu*) to drive off the malevolent spirits of the mountain paths and make the traveler's way secure. Rituals for travel, death, and exorcism were thus inextricably linked (Nickerson 1996, 208–220).

Nor was this ritual interrelationship disturbed by the incorporation within the Daoist religion of new concepts centered around judgment in the afterlife and the possibility that souls could enjoy either transcendent bliss in the heavens or imprisonment and torture in the "earth prisons." No radically new model for the post-mortem journey had to be developed. Instead, the pre-existing pattern was replicated on an additional level: the endpoint of the initial journey—the tomb—simply became the starting point for a new peregrination. Burial placed the deceased in the charge of the spirits of earth and tomb, after which the second journey commenced. It was the function of the death ritual to ensure that those spirits acted as dutiful escorts for the soul's trip to the beyond, rather than as malevolent demons that could detain the soul or attack it on the road.[11] The parallelism between the physical journey of the funeral procession and the invisible journey of the soul should not be surprising: that the treatment of the corpse tends to be structurally parallel to beliefs about the fate of the soul was the essential principle established in Robert Hertz's pathbreaking study of mortuary rites (see Hertz 1960).

"Among the reasons for [the Daoists'] success," Seidel writes, "was no doubt the fact that they proposed a way out of the dilemma of physical death . . . [and] eventually came to devise means to save even those who had already become wretched demonic shades" (1982, 225, 230). The appeal of early Daoist soteriology must have been that much stronger because of what it could provide, not only for those among the living who were concerned about their own fates, but especially for all (nearly everyone, if one follows Seidel's reading) who were anxious about their ancestors. Daoism allowed a means of redressing the balance between unfilial, self-interested terror of the dead and filial fear on their behalf.

Early Daoist mortuary ritual gained the salvation of the dead by means of the transformation of the initially unfilial rites of exorcism themselves. Ancient travel sacrifices and funeral rituals exorcised the enemies of the traveler/deceased and, simultaneously, sent off—and thus, in effect, exorcised—the traveler/deceased him- or herself. Daoist rites of salvation, by consigning the well-fed and properly clothed soul securely to some pleasant region of the afterlife, similarly made certain that the dead would not come back and harm the living. On the other hand, the successful transfer of the dead to higher realms, while satisfying the ubiquitous imperative of the Han grave-securing writs—"let living and dead take separate paths"—also satisfied moral and emotional demands that one's forebears be well treated. Filial concerns for the welfare of an ancestor were addressed through precisely the same means as were necessary to exorcise the enemies of the deceased—and the deceased her- or himself.

Indeed, one way in which Kuhn's work may be more relevant to the history of Daoism concerns his idea that "paradigms gain their status because they are more successful than their competitors in solving a few problems that the group of practitioners has come to recognize as acute," and, therefore, "those unwilling or unable to accommodate their work to [a prevailing paradigm] must proceed in isolation or attach themselves to some other group" (1970, 19, 23). The early Daoists, by proposing a bureaucratized version of the exorcistic ritual model that could be embraced as a means of providing for the welfare of one's ancestors, might be understood as having developed such a new, more successful paradigm of practice. Daoists designed their rituals in part, perhaps, with a view toward supplanting those who were the Daoists' ritual competitors on the local scene, in particular spirit-mediums and diviners, who were apt to have provided the primary ritual recourse for common people troubled by the consequences of death. The chief factor affected by the Daoist bureaucratization of popular ritual may have been not ritual structure, in the broadest sense, but ritual personnel: bureaucratized religion is best handled by priestly bureaucrats, not by illiterate shamans or spirit-mediums.

Early Daoist ritualists appropriated the paradigm of the journey—as guided by apotropaic escorts like the *fangxiang*, the mythic Chiyou, or the Celestial Monarch's Envoy—and adapted it to the framework of the Daoist religion. That journey was then extended by replication: the old model of the funeral procession (and the preparations for it, like the bathing and clothing of the corpse) was duplicated in the form of the soul's invisible journey from the tomb to transcendence. In insisting upon bureaucratic means to handle the problem of salvation, which previously had been dealt with (if at all) through sacrifice, as in the classical ancestral cult (in theory denied to commoners), Daoism simply emphasized the most bureaucratic aspects of an already bureaucratized mortuary tradition (one that had begun during the mid-Eastern Zhou[12] and culminated with the grave-securing writs). The paradigm was old, but exorcism and bureaucracy had been made newly soteriological.

Notes

1. Concerning my use of "tomb ordinance" and related terminology for these artifacts, see Nickerson 1996, 134–141. As to the philological determinations that motivated text-critical and translation choices for the texts ad-

duced in this study, the interested reader is again referred to Nickerson 1996, especially chs. 2–3.

2. The Yellow Monarch (Huangdi), according to Sarah Allan's speculation, was the ruler of the Yellow Springs (Huangquan), the earliest recorded underworld destination for the dead in Shang mythology. See Allan 1991.

3. The notion of shamanism has inspired much debate in comparative religious and anthropological literature and in the study of early Chinese history. The present study largely circumvents this debate, resolution of which is not essential to its purposes. Considering the centrality—in depictions of Siberian shamans, in discussions of shamanism worldwide, and in portrayals of the ancient Chinese *fangxiang, qitou,* and their ilk—of animal masks and animal familiars, music, chanting, and dancing, and the recovery of wandering souls, it seems appropriate to term those Chinese figures shamans as well.

4. The *Shuowen jiezi* (9A.446B–47A) and its commentary by Duan Yucai (1735–1815) also confirm the identification of the griffon head and the *fangxiang.*

5. The attribution of the *Zhengyi lun* to Meng Jingyi is made in the *Nanshi* (6.75.1879). However, the content of the essay as represented by the *Nanshi* does not correspond with the text as preserved in the Daoist canon. It seems possible that the text as it appears in the *Daozang* was put together by a redactor with a particular object in mind, namely the demonstration of the consistency of the Celestial Master practice and the rituals of Lingbao.

6. The Celestial Elder is mentioned in several early sources of indeterminate date, and in the *Shuoyuan* of Liu Xiang (c. 79–6 B.C.E.), as a subordinate of and adviser to the Yellow Monarch (18.11a). The Celestial Elder was also reputed to have been particularly well versed in military affairs. Thus, as a subordinate of the Yellow Monarch, he fits the same pattern as the Envoy vis-à-vis the Celestial Monarch of the grave-securing texts and, therefore, would seem quite an appropriate figure to proclaim tomb ordinances. Moreover, since he is the instructor of the Yellow Monarch, he bears an additional resemblance to Laozi, who was the Monarch's preceptor according to the Huang-Lao school (see Seidel 1969)—and Laozi also issued commands to the earth spirits in excavated Daoist tomb ordinances (see Nickerson 1996, ch. 3).

7. In Daoism, these spirits become messengers "attached to talismans": *zhifu.* They play this role repeatedly in the modern Zhengyi rituals described by John Lagerwey (1987, 88, 127, 131, 226–227). However, these same *zhifu* also appear much earlier in the context of demonology and divination. See, for example, *Qianfu lun* 6.25.348, 358; *Lunheng* 3.24.1014–1015.

8. The origin of these novel soteriological concepts is a distinct and difficult question. The belief in "otherworldly immortality," that is, "transcendence" or *xian*-hood—as opposed to a state of "no death" (*busi*) that was merely the prolongation of worldly longevity—may have first appeared in the late fourth century B.C.E. (see Yü 1965, 91). The notion of a celestial transcendence—of *tianxian,* such as those who "ascended to heaven in broad daylight," versus *dixian,* immortals who remained on earth—also emerged early, perhaps in the second century B.C.E. It was, however, only explicitly enunciated later, in the Eastern Han or early in the Six Dynasties period (Needham 1974, 104–111). Whether it was under the influence of Buddhism or simply

as a result of internal development that the concept of "otherworldly immortality," which had become increasingly seen as dependent on moral behavior, fused with the juridical morality of the grave-securing writs is a question that cannot be fully resolved here, although a further possible motivation will be suggested later.

9. The tomb may always have been the only dwelling place for the dead in the case of commoners, to whom ancestral worship and its temples and shrines were in theory denied. Moreover, the same may have been the case for members of the educated Han elite, even those who embraced dualistic notions of the *hun* and *po* souls. See Seidel 1982, 107; Wu 1988, 96–100. This interpretation is, of course, consistent as well with my reading (following Bokenkamp 1989) of the "Summons of the Soul" and other sources concerning the rite of soul recalling, which views that ritual largely as a post-mortem procedure intended to guide the soul into the tomb.

10. Chiyou is best known as the enemy of the Yellow Monarch who met the monarch's accession with armed opposition. However, the relationship between the two is more complex than simply that of vanquished and victor: Chiyou is elsewhere named as a servant or escort of the Yellow Monarch (*Hanfeizi* 3.44.). More significantly, Chiyou was associated closely with the *fangxiang* (*Wenxuan* 2.19a [46A]; see Knechtges 1982, 217). Finally, Anna Seidel has linked Chiyou to the Envoy of the Celestial Monarch (Seidel 1987a, 34–37).

11. The links with travel ritual are also strengthened by the fact that certain of the spirits addressed in Daoist tomb ordinances were as much spirits of roads as of tombs. For example, one passage in the *Wushang biyao* of 574 (25.6a8–10), quoting a Sanhuang text, mentions "Hostel Chiefs and Boundary Patrollers of the Crisscrossing Paths." Hostel Chiefs appear numerous times in tomb ordinance texts, and Boundary Patrollers on the Paths are invoked in a Han grave-securing writ (Ikeda 1981, 271, no. 3).

12. For traditions of mortuary bureaucratization prior to the grave-securing writs, see Falkenhausen 1994; Harper 1994; and Nickerson 1996, ch. 2.

Bibliography

Allan, Sarah. 1991. *The Shape of the Turtle: Myth, Art, and Cosmos in Early China.* Albany: State University of New York Press.

Bodde, Derk. 1975. *Festivals in Classical China.* Princeton: Princeton University Press.

Bokenkamp, Stephen R. 1989. "Death and Ascent in Ling-pao Taoism." *Taoist Resources* 1.2:1–20.

Boltz, William G. 1979. "Philological Footnotes to the Han New Year Rites." *Journal of the American Oriental Society* 99:423–439.

Cedzich, Ursula-Angelika. 1987. "Das Ritual der Himmelsmeister im Spiegel früher Quellen: Übersetzung und Untersuchung des liturgischen Materials im dritten chüan des *Teng-chen yin-chüeh.*" Ph.D. diss., Julius-Maximilians-Universität, Würzburg, Germany.

———. 1993. "Ghosts and Demons, Law and Order: Grave Quelling Texts and Early Daoist Liturgy." *Taoist Resources* 4.2:23–35.

Davis, Edward. 2001. *Society and the Supernatural in Song China.* Honolulu: University of Hawai'i Press.

Falkenhausen, Lothar von. 1994. "Sources of Taoism: Reflections on Archaeological Indicators of Religious Change in Eastern Zhou China." *Taoist Resources* 5.2:1–12.

Granet, Marcel. 1926. *Danses et légendes de la Chine ancienne* 2 vols. Paris: F. Alcan.

Harper, Donald. 1978. "The Han Cosmic Board (*Shih*)." *Early China* 4:1–10.

———. 1982. "The *Wu Shih Erh Ping Fang:* Translation and Prolegomena." Ph.D. diss., University of California, Berkeley.

———. 1985. "A Chinese Demonography of the Third Century B.C." *Harvard Journal of Asiatic Studies* 45:459–498.

———. 1987. "Wang Yen-shou's Nightmare Poem." *Harvard Journal of Asiatic Studies* 47:239–283.

———. 1994. "Resurrection in Warring States Popular Religion." *Taoist Resources* 5.2:13–28.

———. 1998. *Early Chinese Medical Literature: The Mawangdui Medical Manuscripts.* London: Kegan Paul.

Hertz, Robert. 1960. "A Contribution to the Study of the Collective Representation of Death." In *Death and the Right Hand.* Trans. by Rodney and Claudia Needham. Glencoe, Ill.: Free Press.

Ikeda On. 1981. "Chūgoku rekidai boken ryakkō." *Tōyōbunka kenkyūjo kiyō* 86:193–278.

Kiang Chao-yuan. 1937. *Le voyage dans la Chine ancienne, considéré principalement sous son aspect magique et religieux.* Trans. by Fan Jen. Shanghai: Kelly & Walsh.

Knapp, Keith. 1998. "The Religious Vision of the Third Century Writer and Recluse Huangfu Mi." Paper presented at the conference "Society, Culture, and Religion in Medieval and Early Modern China: In Celebration of David Johnson's Sixtieth Birthday." University of California, Berkeley.

Knechtges, David R., trans. 1982. *Wenxuan or Selections of Refined Literature* vol. 1. Princeton: Princeton University Press.

Kobayashi Taichirō. 1946. "Hosō kueki kō." *Shinagaku* 11:401–447.

Kuhn, Thomas. 1970. *The Structure of Scientific Revolutions.* Chicago: University of Chicago Press.

Lagerwey, John. 1987. *Taoist Ritual in Chinese Society and History.* New York: Macmillan.

Lewis, Mark. 1990. *Sanctioned Violence in Early China.* Albany: State University of New York Press.

Needham, Joseph. 1974. *Science and Civilisation in China* vol 5.2. Cambridge: Cambridge University Press.

Nickerson, Peter. 1996. "Taoism, Death, and Bureaucracy in Early Medieval China." Ph.D. diss., University of California, Berkeley.

Robinet, Isabelle. *Les commentaires du Tao tö king jusqu'au VIIe siècle.* Paris: Mémoires de l'Institut des Hautes Etudes Chinoises.

Schafer, Edward. 1987. "Consolidated Supplements to *Matthews.*" Berkeley: private distribution.

Seidel, Anna. 1969. *La divinisation de Lao tseu dans le taoïsme des Han.* Paris: Publications de l'Ecole Francaise d' Extrême Orient.

————. 1982. "Tokens of Immortality in Han Graves." *Numen* 29:79–114.

————. 1987a. "Traces of Han Religion." In *Dōkyō to shūkyō bunka,* 21–57. Festschrift for Akizuki Kan'ei. Tokyo: Hirakawa.

————. 1987b. "Post-Mortem Immortality, or: The Taoist Resurrection of the Body." In *Gilgul: Essays on Transformation, Revolution and Permanence in the History of Religions,* ed. by S. Shaked, D. Shulman, G. G. Stroumsa, 223–237. Leiden: E. J. Brill.

————. 1988. "Early Taoist Ritual." *Cahiers d'Extrême-Asie* 4:199–204.

————. 1990. "Chronicle of Taoist Studies in the West, 1950–1990." *Cahiers d'Extrême-Asie* 5:223–347.

Strickmann, Michel. 1979. "On the Alchemy of T'ao Hung-ching." In *Facets of Taoism: Essays in Chinese Religion,* ed. by Holmes Welch and Anna Seidel, 123–192. New Haven: Yale University Press.

Van Gennep, Arnold. 1960. *The Rites of Passage.* Trans. by Monika B. Vizedom and Garbrielle L. Caffee. Chicago: University of Chicago Press.

Wu Hung. 1988. "From Temple to Tomb: Ancient Chinese Art and Religion in Transition." *Early China* 13:78–115.

Yü, Ying-shih. 1965. "Life and Immortality in the Mind of Han China." *Harvard Journal of Asiatic Studies* 25:91.

Part II
Texts and Symbols

4

Traditional Taxonomies and Revealed Texts in the Han

MARK CSIKSZENTMIHÀLYI

The subject of this chapter is the limitation imposed by the use of traditional taxonomies on the writing of the early history of Daoism. As a preface to this discussion, it is worth briefly exploring another area in which the restrictiveness of these taxonomies has clearly been demonstrated. Recent archaeological discoveries in China, in particular the finds at Mawangdui and Guodian, have catalyzed the reevaluation of traditional categories used to describe late Warring States and Qin-Han thought. The discovery of the texts originally identified as the *Huangdi sijing* (Four Classics of the Yellow Emperor) has led to widespread speculation about the nature of the category Huang-Lao, a term usually rendered in English as the "Yellow Emperor and Laozi," first used around 100 B.C.E. by Sima Qian in the *Shiji* (Historical Records; see Kondō 1997). The discovery of versions of the *Wuxing pian* (Essay on the Five Kinds of Action) at both sites provides an opportunity to refine our understanding of the Zi Si and Mengzi strain of the early Ru tradition, first mentioned as a distinct category in the third century B.C.E. text *Xunzi* (Writings of Master Xun; see Pang 1980). These are only two of the many texts that have given intellectual historians an opportunity to put old wine back into old bottles— that is, to pour textual content that had long been missing into containers bearing labels that have been preserved. At times, these labels have been applied without analyzing how such newly excavated texts are related to received categories. Specifically, the practice of reading a text labeled "Huang-Lao" as the product of a tradition that is different from the Ru tradition assumes these labels had distinct sociological meanings when the texts were composed and that these meanings were mutually exclusive.[1]

I will question this assumption in the first part of this chapter by adopting a skeptical approach to the received taxonomies and by attempting to draw a set of analytical distinctions that the use of these taxonomies obscures. Based on these distinctions, I will propose a new map of Warring States and Qin-Han textual production, one that is based on differing sociological conditions of production rather than on received taxonomies. Finally, I will use this map to locate continuities between self-cultivation practices used by divination and medical specialists in the Han and some of the practices of early Daoist communities.

One of the criteria that will be central to this examination is the means by which authority is ascribed to a text. In particular, attention will focus on a category of text characterized not by its link to a worthy minister or famous sage of the past, but by its revealed nature or its quality of incipience in natural patterns. There has been a long-standing controversy over the degree to which Warring States texts like the *Laozi* are connected with the foundational Daoist movements of the late Han, what is still sometimes misleadingly referred to as the relation between "philosophical" and "religious" Daoism. This chapter argues that the latter movements must not be studied in isolation from their antecedents but suggests that the *Laozi* is not the right place to start. By attempting to establish a continuity between second-century Daoist communities and their precursors in the semi-official and private academies of the Han, I will outline a genealogy connecting late Warring States self-cultivation practices, Han medical and divination traditions, and early Daoist communities.

The Sociology of Early Chinese Traditions

Any sociological approach to religious traditions must begin by acknowledging the important pioneering effort of Max Weber to develop a typology of such traditions in general and to describe Chinese traditions in particular. Weber's treatment of Confucianism and Daoism in *The Religions of China* (1951) has been justly criticized for its ahistorical approach to China. Authors such as Bryan S. Turner have rightly pointed out the problems inherent in Weber's assumption of the timeless and continuous qualities of the "East" (1981, 277–278).[2] Weber's sociology posits the existence of several types of religious founder, but these ideal types are for the most part based on Indo-European models. The application of this typology, in *The Sociology of Religion* (1963), was the occasion for Weber's pronouncement that Confucius was an "academic teaching philosopher" and not a "prophet" (1963, 53).[3] Since Weber saw early Confucianism not as the routinization of the charisma of a sage leader but, instead, as a diffusion of other aspects of Chinese society, he did not see it as the same kind of phenomenon as some Western religious movements. An example of a very different picture is Asano Yūichi's recent portrait of Confucius as a charismatic founder figure in the Weberian sense, one who had the implicit goal of setting up a new social order to succeed the Zhou (1997, 17).

As this example demonstrates, the fact that the same labels are applied over time to very different social entities complicates the task of historicizing early Chinese religious traditions. Therefore, the first step in refining the sociological understanding of religious traditions in early China must be to examine historical descriptions of these traditions and the circumstances of the composition of these descriptions.

What were the traditions in early China? The simplicity of this question is deceptive, because descriptions of the early Chinese intellectual landscape do not employ uniform terms and criteria. As mentioned above, many taxonomies of these traditions imposed labels on earlier periods in a post-facto manner. Some writers divided the landscape based on the content of a set of texts (e.g., *zongheng*), others on a "motto" or basic philosophical position (e.g., *ming*), and others on the putative authorship of, or central figure in, a set of texts (e.g., Mo). Texts themselves may be grouped by their primary referents (i.e., what other text is quoted as canonical, e.g., the category of the "six attainments" [*liuyi*], generic [e.g., "military," *bing*] or formal qualities [e.g., "poetry," *shi*]), the basic questions posed or the answers supplied to these questions (e.g., "law," *fa*), or even the primary metaphors used to illustrate these questions and answers (e.g., *dao*). Finally, as in the case of the "classicists" (Ru), a social or official group might also be the basis of a category. In other words, there is nothing approaching a standard rationale for grouping individuals or texts. In the absence of such a rationale, scholars resort to the use of the widely varied types of category mentioned above for the simple reason that such categories hold historical precedence.

As a result, these varied categories are used as units of a common currency, and the differences between their particular natures are diminished or ignored. For example, when the suffix *jia* is affixed—as it routinely is to all but a couple of the cited examples—these groups are often used as if they were of the same sociological type. The use of such traditional categories has the potential to obscure the socio-

logical differences among early traditions because the categories
themselves are treated as similar in kind. Indeed, the early Chinese
conception of what constituted a "tradition" was, to a large extent, con-
tingent on when the judgment was being made.

This chapter will distinguish three stages in the construction of
taxonomies that led to the orthodox bibliographical categories incorporated into the standard histories during the Han dynasty. The
first was the existence of socially distinct institutions predicated on
the transmission of practice during the Spring and Autumn period.
The second was the isolation of master–disciple transmission from its
broader social context as part of a late Warring States effort to make
an ideological point about inconsistencies inherent in that type of
transmission. The third was the emergence of conventional identifications of social categories, in which projections of divisions that existed in government and society defined taxonomies.

These three progressive stages may be distinguished based on the
nature of the criteria singled out to divide the intellectual landscape:
institutional, interpretive, and generic. The sense in which these
terms are used will become clear as each stage is treated specifically;
they are never completely descriptive of each individual stage of taxonomy. However, they do reflect the reality that taxonomies were
compiled for radically different reasons in different periods and also
emphasize the need to examine the motives for their compilation critically. At the same time, it is important to acknowledge that new categories are suited to the nature of this particular inquiry in the same
way that the labels currently used for early Chinese traditions were
suited to the interests of those who developed them.

The Communities of Confucius and Mozi

The prototypes for Warring States models of transmission were the
master–disciple groupings of the Spring and Autumn period, specifically those of Confucius and Mozi. While there is considerable evidence that the groups around these two figures functioned as autonomous communities that distanced themselves from society, this
seems not to have been the case for later social groups asociated with
them. While the evidence indicates that one facet of the communities
surrounding Confucius and Mozi was the master–disciple transmission
of teachings, it was only one facet of what appear to have been complex and independent social organizations.

According to the information about Confucius in the *Lunyu* (Analects) and later sources that describe the composition of the *Mozi* (Writings of Master Mo) or the dynamics of the "Mohist" community, both Confucius and Mozi constructed institutions that operated independently of the social structure. Confucius established a number of measures designed to separate his community of disciples from the customs and values of the broader society. One type of regulation that Confucius instructed his disciples to observe was economic. Just as Weber's "prophet" eschews a regular salary, since "charismatic domination is the very opposite of bureaucratic domination," and "rejects as undignified any pecuniary gain that is methodical and rational" (Weber 1946, 247), so too Confucius taught his disciples that value derived from ritual context. Thus Confucius accepted meat from the nobility that he served (*Lunyu* 7.7) and cherished those who sought his counsel. "Even if it was a carriage and horses, if it was not sacrificial meat, he did not make a ritual bow" (10.23). In this way, the earliest Confucians sought to set themselves apart from ordinary society by suspending accepted economic criteria of value and replacing them with criteria derived from a ritual system of exchange (see also Csikszentmihàlyi 2001, 265–273).

The followers of Mozi formed what was possibly an even more distinct community. While his first- and second-generation followers were not so geographically centralized as those of Confucius in Lu, there are indications that the different groupings were strictly hierarchical. A later chapter of the *Zhuangzi* (Writings of Master Zhuang) says that the different divisions of the Mo lineage "took the 'Great Master' [*juzi*] as their sage" (ch. 33, 10b.1079); it then describes several different groups of followers. The Great Master was able, in the words of Jiang Boqian, to inspire other Mohists to "go through fire and water" and even sacrifice their lives.[4] One anecdote from the *Lüshi chunqiu* (Spring and Autumn Annals of Mr. Lü) reveals that these communities maintained a separate legal code from the state within which they dwelt, executing a patricide despite the contrary ruling of the leader of the state of Qin (55–56).[5] According to the *Zhuangzi*, among the other singular customs observed by the Mohists was the lack of ceremonies at birth and death (10b.1079). These different laws and practices certainly functioned to separate the followers of Mozi from their contemporaries.

These two models indicate that the early followers of Confucius and Mozi lived in communities founded on the maintenance of values different from those of the society at large, values that qualified them to fill a particular social role. Members of the Confucian community were

often asked to serve as stewards (*zai*) of the estates of wealthy landowners (e.g., *Lunyu* 6.5, 6.9, 6.14), but they were expected to continue to
adhere to the alternative system of value, and in some instances this
meant not following their employer's wishes. So, for example, when
a disciple serving as a steward helped the clan that employed him to
collect taxes and added to their already exceptional wealth, Confucius
expelled him from the Ru community (*Lunyu* 11.17). Similarly, the
values of Mohist communities were ideally suited to their particular
role, that of military defensive specialists, in that absolute allegiance
to a leader and a commitment to the equal distribution of resources
were important in a city under siege. The emphasis on praxis was so
strong in these communities that both groups in some way substituted
a different set of relationships for the biological ties of family.

Warring States Taxonomies

Late Warring States writers looked back to the Spring and Autumn
Period as foundational, yet their accounts make it clear that social conditions had changed radically since then. While these later writers discussed the latter-day followers of Confucius and Mozi, they reduced
the social equation to one variable: the transmission of teachings from
one individual to another. This aspect was isolated and made the model
for complex lines of crossgenerational transmissions of teachings as
part of an attempt to diminish the authority of master–disciple transmission itself. Taxonomies of the intellectual landscape in three important late Warring States texts all use the names of individuals and
differentiate these individuals by their teachings or their interpretation of earlier teachings. This may be seen from an examination
of three taxonomies in late Warring States texts. The *"Xianxue"*
(Renowned Learning) chapter of the *Hanfeizi* (Writings of Master Han
Fei) divides Ru and Mo learning into eight and three groups of descent, respectively, each associated with a particular Warring States
figure.[6] The *"Tianxia"* (The World) chapter of the *Zhuangzi* constructs
five (or six) rather different divisions of non-Ru thinkers, each represented by one to three figures, based on criteria that vary from internal practices to philosophical positions.[7] The *"Fei shier zi"* (Against
the Twelve Masters) chapter of the *Xunzi* condemns six pairs of
figures, which are differentiated according to their behavior, the content of their teachings, and their methods of misleading others.[8] In
each of these cases, little mention is made of the Spring and Autumn
period communities surrounding Confucius and Mozi or of latter-day

survivals of their customs or structures. Instead, the emphasis is on the names of individuals and on the fragmentation of the transmission over generations.

The reason for their emphasis on fragmentation has to do with the explicit rhetorical function that these three taxonomies perform. The *Hanfeizi* taxonomy is the first part of a rhetorical strategy to undermine truth claims based on appeals to the authority of the ancient sage kings. After outlining the descent groups from Confucius and Mozi, the writer continues by observing that "what each (group) adopted and ignored (from their founder) was different and contradictory." Thus the *Hanfeizi* taxonomy is in itself a stage in an argument about the inapplicability of past models to the present.

A similar assumption about the fragmentation of knowledge is basic to the *Zhuangzi* and is also the basis of the taxonomy in the *"Tianxia"* chapter. There, the first five descriptions begin with a summary of a particular subgroup of the "ancient methods and techniques" (Guo 10b.1069). Yet the understanding of moderns, as contrasted with the complete understanding of the ancients, is at best partial:

> The people of the world each act on their preferences, and on this basis form their own method (*fang*). It pains me that the hundred schools move along without looking back, and in this manner will certainly never unite. (Guo 10b.1069)

Because humanity has turned a collective back on the unity of knowledge, the best that may be hoped for is the use of a method that preserves one particular aspect of the methods of the ancients.[9] The perspective of the *Zhuangzi,* like that of the *Hanfeizi,* is that fragmentation is an irreversible historical process that is linked to the inability of contemporary humans to nullify their desires. In turn, these desires lead individuals to focus on one particular aspect of the teachings of previous generations.

The taxonomy of the *Xunzi* is exceptional in that while it also emphasized the inevitability of interpretive variation, it alone posited the possibility of the correct transmission surviving across generations. *Xunzi* believed that the "footprints of the ancient sages" could be discovered by attending to the governance of the sage-emperors Yao and Shun and to the righteous acts of Confucius and his disciple Zi Gong. Nevertheless, *Xunzi* did accept the basic thesis of the degradation of information that is the basis of the critique of *Hanfeizi* and *Zhuangzi.*

Each of the three examples of late Warring States taxonomy is presented as proof of the inevitability of the misinterpretation of classical teachings and, as such, is an argument for either the superiority of a novel system of government (*Han Fei*), a natural innateness (*Zhuangzi*), or a particular strain of Confucian fundamentalism (*Xunzi*). As a result, their "interpretation" of a particular ancient teaching essentially differentiates the groupings that are central to these taxonomies.

Taxonomies in the Han Dynasty

During the Han, the criteria according to which previous writers were categorized shifted once more, and again the reason for the shift had to do with changes in the social situation. During the Spring and Autumn period, the terms Ru and Mo referred to communities bound by distinct social relations; during the Warring States period, different taxonomies were largely organized to illustrate differences in interpretation of teachings. For the Han, neither of these two explanations suffices to describe the complex situation. This is partly the result of centralization and the capacity for distribution of texts that the new empire created and partly the result of increased bureaucratization of earlier modes of transmission. The resulting taxonomies were primarily based on conventions surrounding both official and private learning and may be described as "generic," even though they carried over elements of the earlier institutional and interpretive modes.

The most influential taxonomies of the Han period appeared in this atmosphere, as part of the standard histories *Shiji* and *Hanshu* (History of the Han Dynasty). Sima Qian's record of his father Tan's discussion of the "Essentials of the Six Schools" (*liujia zhi yaozhi*) divides those who "work on behalf of government" into the following six groups: yin-yang, Ru, Mo, *ming, fa,* and *daode* (130.3288). Each of these groups is later discussed as a *jia* (with the *daode* group becoming the *daojia*) and are differentiated from each primarily by the methods (*shu*) that might be used to govern, a use to which Sima Qian laments that his father was never able to put them (130.3293).[10]

The Sima taxonomy is similar to those of the Warring States period in that the groups are arranged primarily by maxims and methods. In no case is a group identified by its isolation from the social structure. There are important differences, however, that mark this taxonomy as being substantially different from both types of predecessors. First, with the exception of the surname Mo, proper names are not used to describe the groupings, but instead, key methods are employed. That is, instead of referring to a founder figure, even when such a figure existed, the groups are described according to methods tied to ruler-ship. A second difference is that group membership is not constituted by master–disciple transmission, but in the case of the Ru, at least, by allegiance to a common project: "Now, the Ru take the 'six attainments' as their models (*fa*)" (*Shiji* 130.3290). The Sima taxonomy is, there-fore, tied to the bureaucracy, inasmuch as each group supplies a method for a specific aspect of governing.[11]

This relationship is also characteristic of the thirtieth chapter of Ban Gu's (32–92 c.e.) *Hanshu,* the culmination of an earlier cataloging ef-fort that began in 26 b.c.e. There, Ban divides the written materials that were the product of a survey into six categories, the texts of the "six attainments," the "various masters" (*zhuzi*), "poetry and rhyme prose" (*shifu*), "military texts" (*bingshu*), "algorithms and techniques" (*shushu*), and "recipes and arts" (*fangji*). These categories confirm the trends present in Sima Qian's taxonomy. Most evidently, the treatise is devoted not to a typology of names, or even methods of rulership, but to written materials. Officials collected these materials according to the nature of their position. The classics and "various masters" texts were collected and catalogued by the officials who would use these texts: for example, the "recipes and arts" texts were the responsibility of the physician Li Zhuguo (*Hanshu* 30.1701). In this way, Ban's bib-liography was tied even more closely to the workings of the govern-ment than the Sima taxonomy.

The dominant rationale for taxonomies in the Western Han was the product of a different project than that of the late Warring States writers. As several recent examinations of the Han have emphasized, the three-way homology between the body, the state, and the cosmos was a dominant feature of Western Han intellectual life (see Sivin 1995). The taxonomies of Sima Qian and Ban Gu seek to organize the existing types of expertise in the image of the government itself. Like their Warring States predecessors, the Han writers assumed that orig-inal knowledge degraded but still held out the possibility that the parts could be reassembled to reach that original knowledge again. This stance may be seen from their use of the terms *dao* and *shu* "methods." For Sima Tan, the *daojia* was best able to select methods from each of the other groups and "cause human essence and spirit to be unified" (*Shiji* 130.3289).[12] As such, the Sima taxonomy may be seen as serving the same function as that of the *Xunzi,* to privilege one group as "com-plete" among a number of groups that are partially correct. Ban uses the same metaphor in his discussion of the "various masters":

> The nine lineages [of the various masters] all arose when the kingly
> *dao* had already diminished, the feudal lords use strength to conquer.
> The rulers of this period each ruled for a generation, their likes and
> dislikes leading them each in different directions. This is the reason
> the *shu* of the nine lineages swarmed forth and were created at the same
> time. Each [lineage] drew on a different basis, promoting what they
> were good at and taking it on the road. With these they united the feu-
> dal lords. (*Hanshu* 30.1746)[13]

Ban Gu's understanding is that the Warring States period was a time
when "methods" arose as expedient because the more complete *dao*
had disappeared. Ban Gu uses the same metaphor of "methods" as the
constituent parts of the *dao*—just as the variegated parts of the bureaucracy fit together to create a functioning state, so too were the different genres of writing seen to cumulatively amount to the *dao* of the
ancients. This underlying metaphor provides insight into the reason
why the specialized bureaucracy of the new empire developed the type
of taxonomy that is seen in the writings of Sima Qian and Ban Gu.

The consecutive types of taxonomy outlined above are, of course,
painted with a broad brush and, therefore, contain many generaliza-
tions. However, they do demonstrate real differences in the motives
behind the composition of the taxonomies used to talk about early
China and suggest that, as a result, some of the categories used in different taxonomies may also be different in kind. If this is the case, then
it is quite possible that categories of different taxonomies might overlap or that a particular taxonomy might not be comprehensive. This
preliminary conclusion lays the groundwork for the consideration of
a special subclass of sacred texts that emerge unnoticed among the
categories of traditional taxonomies.

The Emergence of the Category of Revealed Text

Because the categories of the Han dynasty reflect various earlier institutional and interpretive categories filtered through a generic
framework determined by Han organizational forms, they are clearly
not a reliable guide to the sociology of Han thought. While the official
Han taxonomies reflected the organization of the state, a telling alternative is reflected in the second-century B.C.E. *Huainanzi* (Writings
of the Prince of Huainan):

> The average modern person holds the ancient in high esteem, but looks
> askance at the new. Those who work out ways must attribute them to

Shennong [Divine Farmer] and Huangdi [Yellow Emperor], and only then will they be admitted into the debate. . . . Today, if the writings of new sages were to be taken and labelled "Kongzi" [Confucius] or "Mozi," then there would certainly be many disciples who would motion with their fingers and accept them. (ch. 19; 242, 244)

The two tiers of attribution the author complains about are worth noting. The first claims the pedigree of the ancient sage-emperors, while the second claims the pedigree of more recent sages. The types of writings that constituted the Warring States taxonomies, metonymically represented by Confucius and Mozi, are contrasted to writings on methods that are attributed to figures further in the past, like Shennong and Huangdi.

The affiliation of texts with mythical sage-rulers of antiquity such as Shennong and Huangdi became increasingly common during the Han. This practice may be seen as a version of the strategy of "inventing traditions" via the construction of fictive lineages designed to privilege a particular individual or text by providing it with a historical pedigree.[14] As Eric Hobsbawm has shown for Britain, the creation of a venerable past that grounds present institutions in a false cloak of timelessness is something done by many social groups, past and present (Hobsbawm and Ranger 1983, 101–164). Similarly, as the *Huainanzi* points out, in the case of the Han, a particular type of text was valorized by association with extraordinary beings.

Texts related to Shennong and Huangdi or their disciples constitute a significant percentage of some categories of Ban Gu's bibliographic treatise. In particular, these texts constitute 14 percent of the "military," 6 percent of the "algorithms and techniques," and 28 percent of the "recipes and arts" sections of the text (see Csikszentmihàlyi 1994, 145–155, 216–226, 256–266). As such, had Sima Qian decided to group methods by their putative originators, Huangdi and Shennong might have constituted a category unto themselves. But Sima Qian did not see the attribution of the text to an author as the germane criterion for describing it in a taxonomy. So instead of incorporating Huangdi into his generic taxonomy, Sima Qian grouped Huangdi with Laozi and labeled particular individuals as followers of Huang-Lao methods. This may have happened because Sima Qian was attempting to confer authority by implicitly comparing the methods associated with Huangdi and Laozi to texts associated with the Spring and Autumn figures Confucius and Mozi, traditionally grouped as Kong-Mo.

This comparison provides insight into Sima Qian's conceptualization of the Huang-Lao tradition. Huang-Lao was a category created by Sima Qian and retrospectively imposed on a handful of his contemporaries and figures in previous generations. Under this interpretation, attempts at defining Huang-Lao must begin by examining Sima Qian's characterization of Huang-Lao and the realities of his time, and not necessarily the realities of those upon whom he imposed the label Huang-Lao. This explains the lack of a "motto," or general principle, of the type used in Warring States taxonomies that may be used to summarize Huang-Lao thought. Instead of a coherent "philosophy," Huang-Lao is most closely associated with a set of methods deriving from a particular cosmological view during a particular historical moment. This historical conclusion is consonant with Yates's recent observation that texts associated with Huang-Lao are generally based on the knowledge of natural categories and the manipulation of yin-yang correlations (1997, 10–16). This type of category arose only in the Han, and for this reason comparison with categories of earlier pedigree is inherently problematic.

The methods associated with mythical sage-emperors like Huangdi did not claim them as authors but often as recipients of revelation. Han texts portray Huangdi receiving advice on sexual hygiene from Sunü (Pure Woman) and ascending to immortality on the back of a wattle-bearded dragon.[15] Narratives concerning the apotheosis of Huangdi found in the *Zhuangzi* and the *Shiji* share the motif that Huangdi's achievements were predicated on his ability to understand Heaven and the spirit world.[16] Huangdi both symbolized and gave historical grounding to a relationship between Heaven and humankind that was the basis of many self-cultivation methods.

As Anna Seidel has pointed out, the apocryphal *chenwei* tradition draws on a second type of revelation, texts not based on the testimony of deities per se but rather incipient in the patterns of the natural world (1983, 336–342). The representative work in this second category of revelation is the *Yijing* (Book of Changes), a set of patterns that might be accessed by divination because they are incipient in the natural world. This is the message of the *"Xici"* appendix to the *Yijing*:

> Heaven suspends images that manifest good and bad fortune. The sage images himself on them. The [Yellow] River produces its Chart and the Luo [River] produces its Writing. The sage takes them as his standard.[17]

The idea of texts that were in some sense incipient in the natural world was the naturalistic counterpart to the revelation of texts by anthropomorphic deities. Since the simultaneous existence of both views of the cosmos characterized the Han dynasty, the coexistence of these two categories of revelation should not be surprising. Huangdi's use of "spirit stalks" (*shence*) associates him with this kind of natural revelation, too. According to a story recounted in the *Shiji*, Huangdi found a precious tripod (*ding*) containing "spirit stalks" that he used to calculate the calendar, and only then did he ascend to Heaven (12.467). The association of Fu Xi with the revelation of the *Yijing* and of Huangdi with that of methods of transcendence are just two of many instances of revelation texts that became popular in the Han.

As products of revelation, these books were incapable of becoming obsolete in the same way that the Warring States authors felt was inevitable over time. A prose poem written circa 50 C.E. by Feng Yan demonstrates the linkage between natural sources of knowledge and the writings of the ancient sages. Feng links the observation of the natural world, the empirical knowledge of the effects of plants and herbs, and the work already done by Huangdi and Shennong:

> To accord with the alternations of the four seasons and distinguish
>   the benificence of the five types of terrain,
> To judge what is produced on the forested plains and hillsides and
>   discriminate what grows in the rivers and springs,
> To cultivate the essential tasks of Shennong and select the extraordi-
>   nary memorials of [Huangdi],
> To pursue the transmitted teachings of Zhou Qi and surpass the lost
>   traces of Fan Li. (*Hou Hanshu* 28b.90)

The idea of revelation is thereby grounded in precedent, and the successes of the sage-kings demonstrate the authority of methods based on the reciprocity between Heaven and human beings.

Revealed texts may be distinguished from the majority of texts in circulation in the Han not only by their nonhuman origins but also by the fact that they were transmitted in distinct ways. Li Ling notes that texts associated with mantic practices circulated differently from "official" texts, and their divine or semidivine origins imbued them with a value not necessarily associated with other works (1993, 9–10). Michel Strickmann, in his discussion of the revealed nature of the Shangqing corpus, says that one of the more important characteristics of the revealed text is the value associated with the natural limitation on its production (1979, 27). This limitation is consistent with an esoteric mode of transmission. In the second century B.C.E., "secret" recipes were passed down in the salon of Chunyu Yi, who studied yin-yang medical theory and from 181 to 179 B.C.E. apprenticed with Yang Qing. According to the *Shiji:*

> [Yang Qing] had [Chunyu Yi] discard his old recipes and replaced them with his secret recipes. [Yang] passed on the books on [reading] pulse of Huangdi and Bian Que; the method of diagnosing illnesses by the five colors in order to understand whether a person will live or die; and the method of choosing among various differential diagnoses in order to decide whether an illness was terminal. (105.2794–2795)

This master–disciple transmission of texts depends on the limitation of supply to assure its value.

The authority of such texts derives from such a transmission, a value reflected in the example of the *Zhenzhong hongbao yuan bishu* (Pillow Book of Secret Writings from the Garden of Vast Treasures). This text contained a recipe for turning metal into gold that Liu Xiang (d. 6 B.C.E.) claimed to have memorized when his father, a Huang-Lao devotee, attained the book while overseeing the prison in Huainan (*Hanshu* 36.1928–1929). Another tale associated with "pillow books" is the story of Meng Xi, a student of Tian Wangsun:

> Because Meng Xi wanted to be famous he took the *Yijing* as well as other texts on omen-lore and yin-yang based interpretations of disasters and events, and falsely claimed his teacher Tian had been lying on his deathbed with his head pillowed on his roll of inked slips, and that he passed them on to Meng alone. (*Hanshu* 88.3599)

As Seidel has observed, there is a connection between such texts and later Daoist texts whose value is expressed by their nature as "pillow books" (1983, 301).[18]

A more direct link to the tradition of revealed texts in the Han is the account of the *Baoyuan taiping jing* (Scripture of Great Peace and Embracing the Prime) in the *Hanshu*. There, that text is the subject of the same style of claim to revelation by the perfected emissary of Heaven, Chijingzi, or the "Master of Red Essence" (75.3192). This text, the first of several bearing the title *Taiping jing*, bridges the gap between revealed texts that treat mantic practices and revealed texts associated with early Daoist movements.

Modes of Transmission of Revealed Texts

While not much is known about the sociological dimension of the circulation of texts in the later Han, there is evidence of a revival of the type of master–disciple transmission that was earlier identified with the institutional typologies of the Spring and Autumn period. The false claim of direct transmission from an *Yijing* master to the student Meng Xi notwithstanding, the increasingly popular private salons of the Han were a place where revealed esoteric texts were passed on from master to student. Two examples of salons (*suo*) will provide evidence of this emphasis on direct master–disciple transmission: an early-Han example from the *Shiji* and a later one from the *Hou Hanshu*.

A key to understanding the *Shiji* description of Huang-Lao is the account of Yue Chengong who, Sima Qian notes, "excelled at cultivating the doctrines of Huangdi and Laozi, became famous in Qi, and was named 'Worthy Teacher' [*xianshi*]" (80.2436). Yue is identified in the *Shiji* as the teacher of Tian Shu and Gai Gong, who later went on to teach Chancellor Cao—all figures elsewhere identified with Huang-Lao (54.2025, 104.2725). At his salon, located in the state most closely identified with Huangdi, Yue may have been identified as "Jugong,"[19] a title with Mohist overtones (Takigawa 1986, 104). Sima Qian likens the early-Han institution run by Yue to the master–disciple transmissions of the earlier Spring and Autumn period.

In the Eastern Han, transmission of methods in salons grew even more popular, as shown by the example of Yang Hou (fl. 109–149 C.E.), a native of southwestern China. Yang Hou's techniques include *tuchen*, referring to the charts and apocryphal texts that served as the basis of correspondence theory used to interpret portents. After retiring from his official position (a common pattern among such teachers), Yang presided over the largest institution of Huang-Lao learning. Between 141 and 146 C.E.

> [Yang Hou] specialized in Huang-Lao and [organized] the teaching of students. Over 3,000 students had their names written into the register. . . . [When Yang died] his disciples set up a shrine where the Commandery's literary officials and scribes performed a yearly feasting and archery ceremonial, as well as regular sacrifice. (*Hou Hanshu* 30a.1050)

One of the students at Yang's academy was Ren An (124–202 C.E.), who learned Yang Hou's methods so well that his contemporaries said of him: "If you want to understand [Yang Hou], just ask Ren An" (79a.2551). After studying with Yang, Ren An founded his own teaching institution.

The continuities between these institutions and later ones associated with organized forms of Daoism are suggestive but await further study. Another similarity between early Han institutions and early Daoist communities is the title taken by the leaders of these groups.[20]

Such conclusions about the social continuities among modes of transmission of learning in the Han and in Daoist communities are in one sense consistent with the general approach of some scholars who have argued that the term *Daoism* had too often been applied on the basis of ideology rather than social structure and had, therefore, been applied inappropriately. Strickmann influentially summarized this position:

> Whatever its ideological prehistory, this religion came into social being with the Way of the Celestial Master [Tianshi dao] in the second half of the second century C.E., and continues under the aegis of its successors and derivatives at the present day. (1978, 2)

Strickmann's formulation suggests that although previous pseudo-Daoist movements shared ideological elements, the second century C.E. was the first time that Daoism became rooted in the social background that informs it today. Taking Strickmann's dictum seriously requires that we subject the categories we use to critical scrutiny and pay attention to the sociological context of the use and production of texts. As this chapter has shown, the rise of the category of revealed texts and the resulting social dynamics in the Han are sociological continuities between early-Han social groups and early Daoist communities. Given the historical evolution of Han-dynasty taxonomies in early China, it should not be surprising that these taxonomies do not reflect such social dynamics. This indicates that whatever the "ideological prehistory" asserted by traditional taxonomies, the "sociological prehistory" of early Daoist communities may be meaningfully traced prior to the second century C.E. Whether this particular continuity may be pushed further back is unclear, but recent work holds out this possibility.[21] Though consonant with Strickmann's methodology, the above conclusions disagree with his specific result in regard to the origin of the social forms of Daoism.

While certain Warring States texts are cited as the "ideological" precursors of Daoism, it is often assumed that there were no significant forerunners to the social forms that characterized the Celestial Masters and later traditions. In terms of the history of religions, the notion that novel social and religious structures can spring up in this way has a clear and influential predecessor, and that is the idea that divine revelation set Christianity apart from earlier religions. The influence of this idea is such that very few histories of Christianity bother to relate it to other apocalyptic movements seeking independence from the Roman Empire in the second and first centuries B.C.E. (see Daniélou

1964). The idea that Daoist social relations arose ex nihilo similarly gives Daoism a uniqueness and importance that may have been necessary at a time when it was not taken seriously in Western religious studies. The assumption that the social aspects of the Celestial Masters movement was created ex nihilo implies the same underlying valuation of that tradition and privileges the study of those social features in a way that is typical of insider accounts of early Christianity.[22] These preliminary conclusions about continuities between certain Han traditions and early Daoism, then, might indicate a way to extend Strickmann's concerns with social relations in a direction he might not have anticipated.

Notes

The author would finally like to acknowledge the support of the Jesse Ball duPont Religious, Charitable, and Educational Fund during the writing of this chapter at the National Humanities Center, and the helpful comments of Stephen R. Bokenkamp.

1. Recent writings by Qiu Xigui in China (1993, 249–255) and Ikeda Tomohisa in Japan (1993, 36–47) have argued that in the cases of the two texts introduced earlier, the labels being applied to them do not quite match the texts. For some primary sources, the following conventions are used: (1) references to the Standard Histories are to the Zhonghua punctuated edition published in Beijing, e.g., *Shiji* (1959) or *Hanshu* (1962); (2) references to the Thirteen Classics refer to the Zhonghua reprint (1979) of the Qing dynasty blockprint edition of Ruan Yuan's (1764–1849) *Shisanjing zhushu;* (3) other collections cited frequently are the 1983 Beijing Zhonghua edition of *Zhuzi jicheng.* The exceptions are *Zhuangzi* and *Lüshi chunqiu,* which are referenced using Guo Qingfan's *Zhuangzi jijie* and Chen Qiyou's *Lüshi chunqiu jiaoshi* (see below). The numbering of the passages in the *Analects* follows D. C. Lau (1979).

2. What some have objected to as cultural essentialism was also, in terms of its assumption that structural differences between cultures may be expressed in religious forms, a valuable counterweight to the universalist approaches to religions inherited from evolutionary models popular in the late nineteenth century. For example, it was Weber, along with C. K. Yang, who first emphasized the diffuse nature of indigenous East Asian religions and contrasted them with the dominant European traditions possessing an organization separate from the social structure. See Weber 1951, 143.

3. This problem illustrates a limitation of the application of the Weberian conception of religion to early China. Because Weber's discussions are for the most part restricted to independent and self-conscious movements, his perception of the "diffused" nature of early Confucianism leads him to view Confucius as primarily a "philosopher." For a more detailed critique of Weber's reading, see Csikszentmihàlyi 2001.

4. Jiang summarizes the Mohist hierarchy: "Mozi certainly was the ultimate leader in his lifetime, but after his death the *juzi* became the leaders. Those who subsequently became *juzi* derived their authority from the previous ones" (1985, 224). Jiang probably bases this statement about self-sacrifice on the story of Great Master Meng Sheng, who inspired his disciples to face death (Chen, *Lüshi chunqiu*, 1257–1258).

5. Note that the Mohists would be particularly deaf to giving a murderer special consideration based on a family relationship because of their doctrine of caring for all people equally regardless of kinship.

6. The Ru groups are named after masters Zi Zhang, Zi Si, Yanshi, Meng-shi, Qidiao shi, Zhongliang shi, Sunshi, and Yueshi. The Mo groups are called Xiangli shi, Xiangfu shi, and Dengling shi. See *Hanfeizi jijie* 49, in *Zhuzi jicheng* 19.351.

7. Two groups are distinguished by practical as well as philosophical descriptions: (1) Mozi and his disciple Qin Guli; (2) Song Bing and Yin Wen. Three groups are differentiated by doctrinal considerations: (3) Peng Meng and his student Tian Pian, and Shen Dao; (4) Guan Yin and Lao Dan; (5) Zhuang Zhou. A sixth figure is Hui Shi, but since the style of his description differs greatly from that of the others, it is not clear that he is really part of the taxonomy (*Zhuangzi* 10b. 1065–1115).

8. These six groups are: (1) Tuo Xiao and Wei Mou; (2) Chen Zhong and Shi Qiu; (3) Mozi and Song Bing; (4) Shen Dao and Tian Pian; (5) Hui Shi and Deng Xi; (6) Zi Si and Meng Ke. Lu Wenchao notes that the last pair does not appear in the parallel text of the *Hanshi waizhuan* (Han's Separate Transmission of the *Poetry*) and concludes that the passage condemning them was added by Hanfeizi and Li Si (*Xunzi jijie* 6, in *Zhuzi jicheng* 3.57).

9. This view is similar to the one expressed in the *"Jiebi"* (Explaining Unworthiness) chapter of the *Xunzi:* "Those of partial learning observe a corner of the Dao, but cannot understand its totality" (*Xunzi jijie* 21, in *Zhuzi jicheng* 15.262). According to the *Xunzi,* Confucius was the only one who was not partial in this sense.

10. The implication is that to the degree Sima's father Tan had a grasp of the whole spectrum of methods that conferred authority, he was qualified to do so.

11. That his disapproval over the bureaucratization of the Ru was one of the primary reasons that Sima Qian invented the category Huang-Lao and tried to lend prestige to its members is the contention of Mark Csikszentmihàlyi and Michael Nylan, "Constructing Lineages and Inventing Traditions in the *Shiji*" (unpublished manuscript).

12. The relationship between *dao* and *shu* is similar to the way in which, in Jia Yi's (200–168 B.C.E.) *Xinshu* (New Writings), the *dao* is made up of a variety of specific *shu*. See Csikszentmihàlyi 1997.

13. Ban Gu also highlights the calculation involved in these techniques: "Demolishing the great to make it into the small, paring down the distant to make it into the near, this is how techniques of the *dao* do their breaking and splitting, and are difficult to see" (*Hanshu* 30.1767).

14. During the Han, perceived age increased the authority and value of a

text. The fact is lamented by Liu Jia (fl. 157 B.C.E.) in the second chapter of the *Xinyu* (New Sayings). Lu argues that there is something that the present and the past have in common: "[The common people] mistakenly value those things that have been transmitted from ancient times and take lightly those made in the present" (*Xinyu jiaozhu* in *Zhuzi jicheng*, 39).

15. Texts include *Lunheng* (6.12) and *Shiji* (12.468). See Yü 1964; Seidel 1969.

16. *Zhuangzi* 6.467; *Shiji* 12.467–468. See Csikszentmihàlyi 1994, 87–94.

17. *Zhouyi zhengyi* (Proper Interpretation of the Book of Changes), ed. *Shisan jing zhushu*, 7.70. This text is probably a product of the third through first centuries B.C.E. See Petersen 1982.

18. Examples of such works in the bibliographic catalog of the *Jiu Tangshu* (Old History of the Tang Dynasty) are the *Zhenzhong sushu* (Pure Pillowbook) and the *Bian Que zhenzhong bijue* (Secret Pillowbook Formula of Bian Que). See *Jiu Tangshu* 205.5198, 207.5306.

19. The earliest link with the state of Qi is the reference to Huangdi inscribed in the mid-fourth century bronze vessel called the *Chenhou Yinzi dui*. For a discussion, see Csikszentmihàlyi 1994, 70–74. The *Jijie* commentary to the *Shiji* (80.2436) notes that some editions also read Yue Jugong for Yue Chengong, and *Hanshu* 37.1981 has Jugong for the same individual.

20. In 145 C.E. a person taking the title "Yellow Emperor" (Huangdi) led an insurrection in east-central China. It was suppressed, but three years later the "Son of the Yellow Emperor" and the "Perfected" led two nearby insurrections. The more-involved but not completely successful Yellow Turbans movement was an academy before it turned into a rebellion in 184. Its leader, Zhang Jue, according to the *Hou Hanshu*, "took the title 'Great Worthy and Exellent Teacher' and attended to matters with the Dao of Huang-Lao." Even the term "Celestial Masters" is seen in the context of the Mawangdui materials from the late fourth or third century B.C.E., when a figure named such answers one of Huangdi's questions. See *Mawangdui Hanmu boshu* 3.145.

21. Harold Roth has convincingly demonstrated, through a comparison of passages using meditative vocabulary in a variety of early texts, that common forms of meditation existed in the Warring States period (1991). These indigenous meditation practices were in some ways forerunners to later Daoist practice.

22. This episode in the history of Daoism also diverges in some important ways from the implicit precedent in the history of Christianity. First, Christianity is rarely conceived as being defined by its continuous form of social organization; rather, it is seen in terms of the recognition of the authority of a founder figure. This is not the case for later *daojiao*, especially in the light of Kobayashi's point that the term *jiao* was used only in the late Six Dynasties and then in the context of the comparison with Buddhism (1990, 512–521). Second, Strickmann's claim that Daoism "continues under the aegis of its successors and derivatives to the present day" begs the question of what degree of variation in social organization is permissible in such a comparison. Not only was the transmission of Huang-Lao during the Han accomplished through passing on revealed texts, but it fit the pattern of "nuclear, not hierarchical" dissemination that Strickmann proposes. The early Celes-

tial Masters tradition that grew out of the Five Pecks of Rice movement, then, should not necessarily be looked upon as an original social form that appeared out of the blue as "Daoism" in the second century c.e. Rather, it could just as well be examined as the most successful variation on a theme that started at least three centuries earlier.

Specifically, the deep reflection demanded of the sage resembles the type of meditation that scholars since Marcel Granet have theorized was the experiential base of texts like the *Laozi*, *Zhuangzi*, and *Liezi*. While the connotations of the expression "to attend to one's solitude" are not well established, Shimamori Tetsuo's examination of six texts that use the phrase highlights the solitary nature of this approach to self-cultivation in the *Wuxing pian* (1979). On the surface at least, this is not incompatible with the practice of "concealing oneself in a remote place to model the form within oneself [*neixing*]," as recommended to the Yellow Emperor. According to the Mawangdui narrative, prior to his decisive military victory, Huangdi withdrew for three years to a scenic mountaintop to carry out the practice (*Mawangdui hanmu boshu* 1.65). These methods are at least partially echoed in the *Wuxing pian*.

Bibliography

Asano Yūichi. 1997. *Kōshi shinwa*. Tokyo: Iwanami.

Chen Qiyou. 1984. *Lüshi chunqiu jiaoshi*. Shanghai: Xinhua.

Csikszentmihàlyi, Mark. 1994. "Emulating the Yellow Emperor: The Theory and Practice of Huang-Lao, 180–141 b.c.e." Ph.D. diss., Stanford University.

———. 1997. "Jia Yi's 'Techniques of the *Dao*' and the Han Confucian Appropriation of Technical Discourse." *Asia Major* 10.1–2:49–67.

———. 2001. "Confucius." In *The Rivers of Paradise*, ed. by D. N. Freedman and M. McClymond. Grand Rapids, Mich.: William B. Eerdmans Publishing Co.

Daniélou, Jean. 1964. *The Theology of Jewish Christianity*. Chicago: H. Regnery, 233–308.

Elman, Benjamin. 1984. *From Philosophy to Philology: Intellectual and Social Aspects of Change in Late Imperial China*. Cambridge, Mass.: Harvard University Press.

Guo Qingfan. 1961. *Zhuangzi jijie*. Beijing: Zhonghua.

Hobsbawm, Eric, and Terence Ranger, eds. 1983. *The Invention of Tradition*. Cambridge: Cambridge University Press.

Ikeda Tomohisa. 1993. *Baōtai kanbo hakusho gogyōhen kenkyū*. Tokyo: Kūkō shoin.

Jiang Boqian. 1985. *Zhuzi tongkao*. Zhejiang: Guji.

Kobayashi Masayoshi. 1990. *Rikuchō dokyōshi kenkyū*. Tokyo: Sōbunsha.

Kondō Hiroyuki. 1997. "Maōtai kanbo kankei ronsha mokuroku." *Chūgoku shutsodo shiryō kenkyū* 1:251–258.

Li Ling. 1993. *Zhongguo fangshu kao*. Beijing: Renmin zhongguo.

Pang Pu. 1980. *Boshu wuxing pian yanjiu*. Shandong: Zilu shushe.

Peterson, Willard J. 1982. "Making Connections: 'Commentary on the Attached Verbalizations' of the Book of Change." *Harvard Journal of Asiatic Studies* 42:67–116.

Roth, Harold D. 1991. "Psychology and Self-Cultivation in Early Taoistic Thought." *Harvard Journal of Asiatic Studies* 51:599–650.

Seidel, Anna K. 1969. *La divinisation de Lao Tseu dans le taoïsme des Han.* Paris: Ecole Française d'Extrême-Orient.

———. 1983. "Imperial Treasures and Taoist Sacraments: Taoist Roots in the Apocrypha." In *Tantric and Taoist Studies,* ed. by Michel Strickmann, 2: 291–371. Brussels: Institut Belge des Hautes Etudes Chinoises.

Shimamori Tetsuo. 1979. "Shindoku no shisō." *Bunka* 42.3–4:1–14.

Sivin, Nathan. 1995. "State, Cosmos, and Body in the Last Three Centuries B.C." *Harvard Journal of Asiatic Studies* 55:5–37.

Strickmann, Michel. 1978. "The Mao Shan Revelations: Taoism and the Aristocracy." *T'oung Pao* 63:1–64.

Turner, Bryan S. 1981. *For Weber: Essays on the Sociology of Fate.* Boston: Routledge and Kegan Paul.

Weber, Max. 1946. *From Max Weber: Essays in Sociology.* Trans. by H. H. Gerth and C. Wright Mills. New York: Oxford University Press.

———. 1951. *The Religion of China.* Trans. by H. H. Gerth. Glencoe, Ill.: Free Press.

———. 1963. *The Sociology of Religion.* Trans. by E. Fischoff. Boston: Beacon Press.

Yates, Robin. 1997. *Five Lost Classics.* New York: Ballantine Books.

Yü, Ying-shih. 1964. "Life and Immortality in the Mind of Han-China." *Harvard Journal of Asiatic Studies* 25:80–112.

5

Material Culture and the Dao
Textiles, Boats, and Zithers
in the Poetry of Yu Xuanji (844–868)

SUZANNE CAHILL

Yu Xuanji, a poet, courtesan, and Daoist nun, lived a short and violent life near the end of the Tang dynasty (618–907 C.E.). Executed in 868 for murdering her maid, she gained a reputation in later history and literature as a disruptive woman who defied social convention, sexual and intellectual norms, and, ultimately, the law. Fifty of her poems, probably less than a quarter of her total output, survive today in the *Quan Tangshi* (Complete Tang Poetry), abbreviated *QTS*. Biographical accounts of her life first appeared within a few decades of her death. The sources agree on the bare outlines of her life.[1]

Born to common people in the capital city of Chang'an, she was married as a secondary wife to a student named Li Yi (*zi:* Zi'an). He passed the imperial examination after about two years' residence in the capital. Yu Xuanji accompanied him when he returned home to take up an official position. Li's primary wife, waiting at home all this time, was unable to tolerate Yu Xuanji, so Yu moved out. Eventually, she returned to the capital, where she lived in reduced circumstances, working as a courtesan. Soon she took holy orders as a Daoist nun and moved to a convent known as the Belvedere of Universal Propriety (Xianyi guan). Her convent was located close to the courtesans' quarter in town, southwest of the imperial palace. All her adult life she wrote poetry and corresponded with other authors. In 868, accused of strangling her maid, Luqiao, in a jealous rage, Yu was jailed, tried, and executed by decapitation.[2]

Yu Xuanji has always been a controversial figure: admired for her talents and damned for her choices. Her story, linking sex, violence, religion, and talent, has fascinated writers and readers from the late Tang to the present. She appears in literature as the model of evil womanhood that proper young ladies must avoid and reject. Tradition teaches us that because she chose what to do with her own intellect and sexuality, Yu Xuanji came to a terrible end. The 1984 movie *Tang-chao haofang nü* (A Wild Woman of the Tang Dynasty), made by the Shaw Brothers' Studio in Hong Kong, agrees with her major ninth-century biographer Huangfu Mei in taking this message from her life. Critics have assumed that her Daoist vocation was insincere, disguising at best a broken heart and at worst a promiscuous life. Even Robert van Gulik, who portrays the poet sympathetically in his 1968 Judge Dee mystery, *Poets and Murder,* does not take her career as a Daoist nun seriously. Most editors of her works arranged the poems to tell the story of a poor but gifted young girl, hurt by her lover's rejection, who turns for escape first to religion and then to debauchery. Her notorious reputation as an executed criminal makes it difficult to assess her contributions to literature, Daoism, or women's history in China.

If we want to know something about Yu Xuanji, her thought, and her accomplishments, we cannot do better than to study her actual writings in the context of her time. Many people consider the Tang dynasty to be the golden age of Chinese poetry because of the quality and ubiquity of poetic expression during that era. Tang people from all walks of life expressed themselves in verse on any occasion, private or public. The many surviving Tang poems provide a wonderful resource for exploring medieval Chinese life, but they also have limitations as primary sources. Sometimes the exact circumstances that prompted a poem can no longer be discovered; in such cases, our interpretations rely partly on inference. Conventions of language and topic further restricted poems. Finally, they alluded to a long tradition of past literature, not all of which is recoverable today. Yu Xuanji's poems in particular have often been preserved with no information or with misleading information about the events that elicited them. She adheres, although often ironically, to Tang codes of subject and style. She also draws, in a sophisticated and purposeful manner, upon the writings of the past. Despite limitations that force us to speculate about specific facts and situations, and despite constraints created by convention and allusion, her poems disclose a wealth of information about the world of her thought. Her works reveal a startling intellect, an original voice, and a heart longing for the Dao. She expresses her intellect, voice, and feelings within the conventions of Tang poetry.[3]

This chapter investigates three images from Tang material culture that recur in Yu Xuanji's poetry: textiles, boats, and zithers. I link her use of these images with ideas about herself, female roles, the Dao, communication, and companionship. In exploring her use of images from material culture, I hope to bypass Yu Xuanji's seductive notoriety and move right to the heart of her world of thought.

It is a commonplace of Tang poetry that the description of a woman's clothing reveals the state of the woman; that a small boat represents the wandering soul; and that the zither refers to attempts to express oneself. However, Yu Xuanji uses these conventions in many unconventional ways. In her poetry, images of textiles, boats, and zithers express new and personal meanings, connected to her experiences as a poet and as a Daoist nun. This paper examines her images to open a window into her world. When her poems are arranged according to her use of these images, they tell a new tale: the story of a poor but gifted young woman, disappointed in marriage, who turns to the consolations of poetry, Daoist contemplation, same-sex eroticism, and friendship. The multiple meanings of clothes, boats, and music in the poetry of Yu Xuanji can also illuminate medieval Chinese Daoism, material culture, and women's culture. Let us turn now to the poems, looking first at textile images.

Images of Material Culture in the Poems of Yu Xuanji: Images of Textiles

I begin with a short poem on a conventional subject that is startling in its power and rage. The congratulatory title is "Wandering to the South Tower of the Belvedere for Venerating the Perfected (Chongsheng guan), Then Viewing the Place Where Names of New Exam Graduates Are Inscribed." Here Yu Xuanji commemorates an occasion upon which she accompanies a group of new graduates of the imperial examination, an exam in which she could never participate, leading to jobs she could never obtain. On their outing, the group, like countless fortunate graduates before them, climbs the tower at a Daoist temple in Chang'an. Later on, in celebration of their accomplishment, the members inscribe their names in order on a plaque at the Ci'en si (Temple of Mercy and Compassion), a Buddhist temple not far away. The poem conflates the two events. Yu Xuanji begins, conventionally enough, with the distant view, then moves to the closer scene.

> Cloudy peaks fill the eye, releasing spring's brightness;
> One after another, silver hooks arise beneath their fingers.
> Involuntarily I resent the silk netted-gauze robes that hide my lines
>   of poetry;
> Lifting my head, I vainly envy the names on the plank. (*QTS* 9050)[4]

"Silver hooks" refer to her companions' calligraphy. The final couplet expresses the speaker's thoughts. Her silk netted-gauze robes become the target for anger at being excluded from the man's world of writing, examination, and public office. Yu Xuanji equates having to perform the role of woman, by dressing the part, with having to choke back her talents and ambitions. She feels equal to any of her companions. As a poetic conceit, she blames her clothes for the limitations imposed upon her as a woman in Tang China. This attitude is going to get her killed.

Next I turn to her most famous poem, featured in most accounts of her life, including the Shaw Brothers' movie. Traditionally set on the morning of her execution (perhaps a later embellishment of romantic literati), she calls it "Given to a Neighbor Girl." It may be addressed to a former neighbor in the convent or the streets of Chang'an, or to a nearby inmate:

> Shamed before the sun, I shade myself with my netted-gauze silk
>   sleeve,
> Depressed by the spring, reluctant to rise and put on make-up.
> It's easy to find a priceless treasure,
> Much harder to get a man with a heart!
> On my pillow, secretly flow my tears;
> Amidst the flowers, silently my guts are sliced.
> Since I will soon personally be able to peek at Song Yu,
> Why regret Wang Chang? (*QTS* 9047)

(The "man with a heart" [*youxin lang*] is a colloquial term for a compatible lover.) Here the speaker's silken sleeve proves inadequate to hide her when she raises it as a shield against the world. Since it is transparent, it cannot block the sun or the gaze of others. Beautiful garments cannot protect her. Again she berates her clothes, this time for being ineffective. Depressed and ashamed of her situation, cynical about her relationships with men, she laments her broken heart and fractured trust. The last couplet looks ahead to paradise. There she intends to meet Song Yu, a handsome third-century B.C.E. poet, minister of Chu, and disciple of Qu Yuan (340?–278 B.C.E.); both Song Yu and Qu Yuan influenced her writing. Wang Chang appears in Six Dynasties and Tang literature as the fine, marriageable young man next-door. In poetry, he is usually the one who got away. Since the speaker will soon meet her ideal, why mourn her failure to marry a suitable young man such as the fictional Wang Chang?

The next example of Yu Xuanji's poetry, addressed to a Mr. Li, rejects fine textiles as useless luxuries. Several poets sent Yu Xuanji work to read and criticize. Li Ying, who passed the *jinshi* exam in 856 and became Censor in Attendance, was a neighbor, scholar, and former suitor. He wrote Yu Xuanji a now-lost poem "Return from Fishing on a Summer's Day," inviting her comments and also inviting her over for a drink. She replied in a satirical vein, entitling her response "Toasting Li Ying's 'Return from Fishing on a Summer's Day,' Which He Submitted for a Look."

> Although our dwelling places follow along the same lane,
> For years I haven't passed you even once.
> With clear lyrics you urge drinks on the old girl,
> While you break off new branches of fragrant cinnamon.
> Your "Daoist nature" is more ridiculous than my icy, snowy flesh;
> Your "meditating heart" more laughable than my white patterned
>   tabby-weave and netted-gauze silks.
> Although your footsteps may climb to the top of the Empyrean Han
>   (Milky Way),
> You have no road to reach (heaven's) misty waves. (*QTS* 9050)

The title and topic are as polite and conventional as a thank-you note. While Yu at first appears to flatter Li, her tone is sarcastic. She turns down his invitation, complaining he has neglected her, his "old," or former, companion, to pursue new girlfriends ("branches of fragrant cinnamon"). Quoting lines from his poem that include the phrases "Daoist nature" and "meditating (or *chan*) heart," she scoffs at his pretending to be an ascetic while pursuing pleasure and claims that her own white flesh and silken garments are more genuine than his pompous show of austerity. An alternative translation to the third couplet runs:

> My Daoist nature mocks ice and snow;
> My meditating heart laughs at white patterned tabby-weave and
>   netted-gauze silks.

In this case, the author again compares herself favorably to the recipient. As a Daoist nun, she does, in fact, know something about meditating. Here, "white patterned tabby-weave and netted-gauze silks" mean clothes made of expensive and luxurious fabrics. Despite his claims of religious discipline, Li Ying is more caught up in the world than she. Although Li may be successful and famous, climbing to the stars of social acclaim, success in the examinations, and a fine job in the imperial bureaucracy, he still has no way to reach Daoist perfection, including immortality and heaven.

In contrast, Yu Xuanji sends a hymn of praise, opening with a textile image, to a Daoist nun who bears the elevated title of *lianshi,* or "Refined Master" in "I Send the Refined Master a Poem I Wrote About Her."

> Auroral clouds of many colors, cut to make your robes,
> Burgeoning incense emerges from embroidered bed curtains.
> White lotus flowers and leaves (. . .).
> Mountains and waterways spread out (. . .) and disperse.
> Stopping in your steps to listen as bushwarblers talk,
> You open cages and release cranes to fly away.
> In the High Audience Hall, you awaken from a spring sleep,
> In evening rain, just now full and driving. (*QTS* 9047–9048)

(Each set of parentheses represents one missing paragraph.)

"Refined Master" was an honorific title granted to a nun who lived in a convent but had no administrative responsibilities. All she had to do was meditate and practice austerities; her stature as an ascetic brought glory to her establishment. The Refined Master's robes equate her with a Daoist goddess dressed in swatches of the heavens. The clothes are the woman: their qualities stand for her qualities. Her auroral garments provide evidence of her spiritual attainment: her description matches that of Shangqing ("Supreme Clear Realm") divinities found in related scriptures in the Daoist canon. These beautiful goddesses descend from the Daoist heavens, or "clear realms," to instruct mortal men in the arts of eternal life. Yu also compares the Refined Master to the ancient shamanistic goddess who appears in the Han dynasty *Gaotang fu* ("Rhapsody on the High Altar") by Song Yu, preserved in the *Wenxuan.* That elusive deity spent a passionate night with the King of Chu, then abandoned him, to his eternal sorrow. The same language appears in the Shangqing text known as the *Zhen'gao* (Declarations of the Perfected, HY 1011), which describes the meeting of the adept and his seductive goddess-instructress. Yu Xuanji profoundly admires her subject's accomplishments and envies her life of freedom, choice, and ease. The priestess sleeps where she likes and does what she wants with no limitations, restrictions, or penalties. Sexual images of rain and spring sleep suggest her meetings with gods. This poem and the next respond to the Refined Master's accomplishments, sexuality, and charisma. They recommend the author as a companion.

Yu Xuanji addressed another poem to Refined Master Zhao, perhaps the same person. Here Yu takes on the conventional subject of
visiting a recluse without finding him (or, in this case, her) available.
There are poems on this subject by Wang Wei (701– 761), Li Bo (701–
762), and Du Fu (712–770). Even the title follows a Tang formula: "I
Pay a Visit on Refined Master Zhao Without Meeting Her."

> Where are you and your transcendent companions?
> Your green-clothed servant rests alone in the household.
> On the warm stove: remains of your steeped herbs,
> In the adjoining courtyard: boiling tea.
> Painted walls, dim in the lamps' radiance;
> Shadows from banners' poles slant.
> Anxiously I turn my head back again and again,
> At numerous branches of blossoms outside your walls. (*QTS* 9052)

Yu Xuanji takes a conventional subject and gives it her own meaning. Entering a mysterious, deserted household, she discovers that the
Refined Master of the title has just left; her tea and herbs, both still
cooking, reveal her recent presence. Yu Xuanji, searching for a like-
minded friend, longs for Zhao's companionship. She also admires the
nun's lifestyle: the simplicity, security, and aesthetic pleasure appeal
to her. In contrast to the divine clothing worn by the Refined Master
in the previous poem, the servant's clothes here are anonymous and
humble. Her green cotton outfit identifies Master Zhao's servant: she
too is what she wears. "Green-clothed" indicates her class and function but tells us nothing about her as an individual. She is little more
than furniture in the nun's retreat. Finally, the poet departs, with many
a backward glance. Her wishful gaze mistakes climbing flowers on the
wall lit by the setting sun for the rosy garments of the master and her
retinue.

Meanwhile, back in the capital, Yu Xuanji describes her own life at
the end of a neglected alley in the middle of the busy city. Her lover
is long gone, and everyone else seems to have a life. She writes "Late
Spring Sketch":

> In a deep lane, the last gate, few companions or mates,
> Esquire Ruan only here in remnants of my dreams,
> Incense drifting through my netted-gauze silk and white patterned
>   tabby-weave clothing from some other household's dining mats,
> Wind sending the sound of songs from a storied building someplace.
> The street closed, drumbeats rouse me from dawn sleep;
> The courtyard secluded, magpies' chatter mixes with my spring
>   depression.

How could I have kept pursuing affairs among humans?
My ten thousand *li* body is just like an untied boat. (*QTS* 9053)

The first line describes living alone, without friends or resources, in poor quarters (the "last gate") in the capital. This Esquire Ruan is Ruan Zhao, the Eastern Han scholar who met a transcendent one day when he was wandering in the mountains looking for medicinal herbs. After sharing a feast with her for what seemed like a short time, he returned home to discover seven generations had passed. Here the writer equates herself with his transcendent lover, missing her mortal visitor after his departure. The second couplet adds a sad and envious voyeurism: other people have banquets while she sits alone. She feels invaded and excluded as expensive incense from a neighboring household's feast permeates her silken garments and music from a gathering in some fine tall building interrupts her dreams. Clothing here, as always in her poetry, represents the person. She is also acutely sensitive to sound: songs, drums, and magpies depress her.

This poem suggests how the speaker came to be a Daoist nun. After her bitter experiences living alone in the capital, she wonders how she could have been ensnared so long in the world of human affairs and seeks refuge in the convent. The poem closes with a powerful and evocative image of herself. She compares her body, strong enough to go ten thousand *li* without stopping (like a heavenly horse), to an untied boat, cut off from worldly attachments, free at last to follow the Dao. We will consider the image of the boat drifting toward the Dao in detail later. One of Yu Xuanji's central poetic self-representations is the wandering sojourner: an untied boat here, a banished immortal in the next poem.

Alone again in autumn, Yu Xuanji again portrays herself as a wayfaring stranger. Her narrator sings Daoist ritual verses or *qingge* (literally, pure songs), practices Daoist self-cultivation or *yangxing* (literally, nourishing [her] nature), reads Daoist scriptures, and enjoys her melancholy solitude. The title is "Sad Thoughts" (one source has "Autumn Thoughts").

Falling leaves flutter and swirl, joining evening rain;
Alone strumming vermilion strings, I naturally break into pure song.
Releasing my feelings, I stop resenting heartless friends;
Nourishing my nature, I toss off as empty the waves of the bitter sea.
While sounds of leaders' chariots are outside my gate,
Daoist documents and scrolls pile up beside my pillow.
This cotton-clad commoner in the end turns out to be a sojourner
 from the cloudy empyrean,

From time to time passing the green rivers and blue mountains
  (of this world). (*QTS* 9050–9051)

This is a poem of self-consolation. Daoism is a great comfort, allowing her to forget loneliness and betrayal. The narrator portrays herself as a wandering sojourner and banished immortal. Alone on a rainy evening, she plays her zither to express herself. Expressing emotions frees her from their grip. Practicing self-cultivation of the type known as *yangqi*, or "nurturing the breaths," designed to increase health and longevity, brings her peace of mind despite the suffering that is the normal condition of life in this world (the "bitter sea"). Indifferent to the bustle of leaders outside her door, she reads scriptures. The commoner nobody appreciates (herself) turns out to be that well-known figure of legend, the immortal in disguise. In her poetry Yu Xuanji tries on different roles; here, she resembles a banished immortal, temporarily cast down to this world for punishment, soon to return to the glories of the heavens. The simple cotton clothes that give away her class origins are, for the space of a poem, the disguise of a transcendent. As a "cotton-clad commoner," she passes through the moving and transitory beauty of the Chinese landscape, but her true home lies elsewhere. She may be unappreciated, but she knows she is a goddess.

The last poem in this section, "Dwelling in the Mountains on a Summer's Day," depicts the free and easy life of a Daoist recluse in her mountain retreat. But before translating that poem, consider another, a quatrain that probably portrays the same place in spring, called "On a Pavilion Hidden in the Mist":

Its spring flowers and autumn moons enter the verses of my poems;
Its white days and clear nights would suit even far-flung
  transcendents.
Raising my beaded curtains to empty space, I don't lower them
  again;
I've moved a couch so I can sleep facing the mountains. (*QTS* 9051)

Location is important to the poet. In her comfortable and convenient dwelling, suitable for the pickiest transcendent, naturally supplied with flowers, a clothes hanger, and fresh spring water, she drinks wine, reads, chants, and sails. Here is "Dwelling in the Mountains on a Summer's Day," a song celebrating her mountain home:

Moving to obtain a transcendent dwelling, I came to this place;
Its flower thickets are naturally profuse; I haven't pruned.

> In front of the courtyard, a forked tree spreads out as my clothes
>   rack;
> Beneath my seat a new spring floats my wine cup.
> The fence railing obscurely winds away into a deep bamboo path;
> My long cloak of white patterned tabby-weave and netted-gauze
>   silk mixes into my book pile.
> In leisure riding my painted boat, I chant to the bright moon;
> Trusting the light wind to blow me home again. (*QTS* 9053)

This poem has a powerful sense of place. Enjoying seclusion, she contemplates, free from care. She has finally attained the freedom and ease she sought. Not bothering to dress formally, she wears her luxurious cloak of white patterned tabby-weave and netted-gauze silk loosely, so that it tumbles down and plays havoc with her books, knocking the scrolls about. Her clothing expresses an independence, intellectual and financial, she longs for in other poems. Here she acts the part of absent-minded hermit, absorbed in reading and chanting. She imitates her ideals: the Seven Sages of the Bamboo Grove of the past, or Refined Masters like Master Zhao of the present. The author has finally found a "room of her own," a place to write and think.

"Dwelling in the Mountains on a Summer's Day" ends with the image of a little boat. Riding along, she chants to the moon, like Li Bo, another Daoist poet and solitary wine drinker. Engaged in free and easy wandering, allowing her painted boat to follow the wind, she travels like a transcendent.

Images of Boats

Boats small enough to be controlled by one person appear frequently in Yu Xuanji's writing. The boat provides a means of transportation for the fisher person or sojourner. The boat can represent the traveler, the process of moving from one place to another, or a more general transition or transformation. In a mocking poem addressed to Censor-in Attendance Li (*QTS* 9051), his boat refers to the fisherman, home from his wanderings. Usually Yu Xuanji is running the boat. In a traditional genre of poetic travelogue, practiced with originality and passion by the well-known Tang poet Du Fu, Yu Xuanji chronicles her own journeys on the water. One such poem has her "Passing Ezhou" in a decorated boat propelled by both sails and oars:

> Willows brush my orchid oars, flowers fill their branches;
> Beneath the city walls at Stone City (Shicheng), at sunset our sails
>   slow down.

On top of Broken Stele Peak (Zhanbei feng): the tomb of the
    Minister of the Three Lü clans (San Lüshi);
At the Head of Distant Fire Mountain: a five-horse prefect's
    flag.
"White Snow" tunes are lofty, composed about old temples;
"Sunny Spring" songs remain, changed to new lyrics.
Mo Chou's cloud-soul has departed, following the clear Yangzi
    River,
Emptily causing travelers to write a myriad poems. (*QTS* 9053)

Ezhou includes modern Wuchang in Hubei. Stone City is up the
Han River from Ezhou. The "Three Lü clans" are the three royal clans
of the Chu kingdom (Zhao, Chu, and Jing) during the Warring States
period. The minister of the Three Lü clans is Qu Yuan, the great Chu
poet, statesman, and suicide. His poetry had a great influence on Yu
Xuanji, as is evident here with the image of orchid oars. This is one
of several sites associated with his tomb. As in the cases of the Han
lady Wang Zhaojun and Yu the Great, many places claim the honor
of being Qu Yuan's final resting place. (Since Qu Yuan drowned himself, the actual disposition of his body may never be known.) The
mountains named must be visible from the Han River. A prefect who
merits five horses resides at Distant Fire Mountain, his presence indicated by his flags. "White Snow" tunes are traditional old songs,
known for being too high for most people to manage. (An alternative reading of *lou* for *diao* would make this line begin "The White
Snow Storied Building is lofty." The White Snow Storied Building, west
of Stone City, was poised above the Han River.) "Sunny Springs" songs,
in contrast, were modern. Mo Chou was a singer from Stone City, according to the Music Bureau (Yuefu) ballads. Although Mo Chou is
long departed, Yu Xuanji blames her lingering spirit for infecting travelers with the urge to write occasional verse, most of which is drivel.
Now she has added one more herself. The poet uses a conventional
type of writing masterfully and irreverently, poking fun at the genre
while enjoying her ability to perform it. Here the boat seems to be
merely a pleasant vehicle ferrying the traveler from one place to another.

However, her boat signifies more than just a means of transport. It
represents the poet herself. Hers is a "stranger's boat" (*kechuan)* that
belongs nowhere. For example, in "Composition Capturing Willows
by the Riverside," Yu Xuanji inserts the stranger's boat in a riddling
poem on willows. Willows by the riverside are conventional signs of
parting and of fragile female beauty:

Kingfisher blue forms joining on uncultivated riverbanks,
Their misty shapes entering distant buildings,
Reflections spreading out across the autumn river's surface,
Flowers falling on the fisherman's head,
Roots aged, hiding fish caves,
Branches reaching down to fasten the stranger's boat,
Sighing and soughing on a windy, rainy night,
They startle my dreams and increase my depression. (*QTS* 9047)

Here the willows, ghostly in the autumn mist, their almost undifferentiated shapes the iridescent blue-green of kingfisher feathers, catch the stranger's boat and add to her melancholy. This poem on a conventional subject has a personal and poignant meaning at its heart. The wayfaring stranger's boat appears again, in a poem addressed to Li Zi'an entitled simply "Sent to Zi'an":

At our drunken parting feast, a thousand goblets could not dispel
    my sorrow;
Pain at separating: a hundred knots with no place to start untying
    them.
Tender orchids dispersed and done, you return home to your spring
    orchard;
Willows to the east and west moor the stranger's boat.
In our gathering and scattering, I lament that we, like clouds,
    do not settle;
In my compassion and passions, I must imitate the water which
    constantly flows.
At the season of flowers, I know it's hard to meet,
But I cannot bear to get drunk quietly and calmly in my jade storied
    building. (*QTS* 9054)

Yu Xuanji and Zi'an have separated; pain (literally, [pain from severed] intestines caused by separating [*li chang*]) ties her in knots. "Tender Orchid," Huilan, is one of her names; he leaves her to return to his first wife, his home orchard. The speaker is a wayfaring stranger, a wandering boat moored insecurely by willows (signs themselves of parting). If he is inconstant as a cloud, she will study the water that always moves and changes. Water is also a metaphor for the Dao. Although she cannot meet him in the spring, she refuses to follow the passive example of the deserted woman in conventional literature and weep demurely in her secluded women's quarters.

This stranger's boat is often untied. In poems to Li Zi'an, the untied boat seems lost and at loose ends. In poems with Daoist themes, the untied boat is unfettered and free to follow the Dao. Yu Xuanji's "Late Spring Sketch" (see page 108) closes with the line "My ten thousand *li* body is like an untied boat."

Two poems entitled "Going Along the Yangzi River" depict an aimlessly drifting little boat, with implications both erotic and Daoist. The first one runs:

> The great river slants across to embrace Wuchang;
> Before Parrot Island (Yingwu zhou): doors of a myriad households.
> Sleeping in spring in my painted boat; at dawn I haven't had
>   enough,
> Dreaming I was a butterfly seeking flowers. (*QTS* 9051)

Wuchang is a city in Hubei at the meeting of the Han and Yangzi Rivers. Parrot Island is located in the Yangzi River across from Wuchang. Yu Xuanji lived around there for a time. Her "painted boat" could be a courtesan's trysting place, common in Song-dynasty literature, or simply a decorated vehicle. Spring sleep, as in her poem to the Refined Master, has sexual overtones. The last line contains a double meaning. "Dreaming of a butterfly" recalls the famous story of Zhuangzi's dreaming he was a butterfly (chapter 2), which asks us to question the nature of perceived reality. The butterfly seeking flowers, on the other hand, is an erotic image of a man pursuing a woman (see *Chuci* and the works of Song Yu). Here Yu Xuanji uses a man's voice, adopting a conventional expression usually used by males. The object of her desire might be male or female. Several of her poems are ambiguous about the gender of the erotic object. The boat, wending its way between sites along the river, between the Dao and sexual desire, represents the rider, Yu Xuanji.

She again compares herself to a small painted boat in the second poem:

> When misty flowers entered Cormorant Harbor (Luci gang),
> In my painted boat I was still making up poems about Parrot Island.
> I went to bed drunk and woke up chanting poetry, not feeling a
>   thing;
> This morning I am startled to find myself at the head of the Han
>   River. (*QTS* 9051)

Cormorant Harbor is in Hubei near Hanyang, up the Han River from Parrot Island and Wuchang. (The *Quan Tangshi*, for the second line, prefers *yan* to *ti*, producing the alternate reading: "My painted boat was still skirting Parrot Island.") Yu Xuanji presents herself again as a drifting boat. She floats along in a drunken reverie, unaware of her surroundings as she composes poems. Drunkenness in poetry provides a way of talking about altered states of consciousness associated with Daoism and Daoist eccentrics. The speaker wakes up to find herself in an unexpected but familiar place, surprised she has gone so far. In a negative sense, the image of the drunken boat implies she has no control over her life; in a positive sense, it implies she attaches herself to the Dao and goes with the flow.

Another of her poems joins boats and drinking with two of the author's great themes: solitude and communication. Entitled "Handing Over My Feelings," this work idealizes seclusion while it records an attempt to express herself:

> At leisure and retired, with nothing to do,
> I wander alone through the passing scene:
> The moon seen through severed clouds over the Yangzi River,
> A boat with loosened ropes in the middle of the sea.
> My zither I play at Xiaoliang Temple;
> My poems I chant from Yu Liang's tower.
> Thickets of bamboo make do for comrades;
> And pieces of stone are fine for mates.
> Swallows and sparrows I simply treat as nobles;
> Gold and silver I willingly forsake.
> The spring wine filling my cup is green;
> At night the window facing the moon is dark.
> I circle stepping stones around the clean, clear pool,
> Pluck out my hairpin to shine in slender currents.
> I lie in bed, texts and fascicles all around me,
> Then half drunk, get up to comb my hair. (*QTS* 9052)

At ease and unemployed, the speaker compares herself to the moon in a cloudy sky and to a boat drifting freely. She visits sites along the Yangzi River, playing music at an unidentified Buddhist temple. Many temples were named Xiaoliang after the devout Buddhist emperor Liang Wudi (464–549), whose name was Xiao Yan. She chants poems from a tower named after its builder who died around 340 C.E. Her only companions are bamboo and stones; she honors swallows and sparrows as noble guests. Material wealth is not her aim: she finds riches enough in wine, her setting, and her books. Removing her golden hairpin, she sticks it into the stream and combs the current, enjoying the moon's reflection shining off the ornament into the water. The hair in Tang poetry is the woman: letting her hair down, she lets down her own formality and reserve. She does as she pleases, lying in bed surrounded by disorderly books. She romanticizes drunkenness as did Tao Qian (365–427) and Li Bo before her. She is free and easy as a Daoist immortal or "a boat with loosened ropes." This accords with her use of the painted boat in "Dwelling in the Mountains on a Summer's Day" (see pages 110–111), which closes with the speaker riding home on her boat:

> In leisure riding my painted boat, I chant to the bright moon;
> Trusting the light wind to blow me home again. (*QTS* 9053)

She is that unmoored boat drifting along with the Dao, going home to the Dao.

Yu Xuanji's small boats express transition, passage, metamorphoses, and changes of state in the life of an individual. In the poems translated above she gets drunk, sleeps, dreams, and wakes. Boats and water take her from one place to another, one state of consciousness to another, and one condition of existence to another. She moves from city to country, public to private, courtesan to recluse. She floats along through life and change, entrusting herself to the Dao.

Images of Zithers

The table zither (*qin*) is a traditional Chinese stringed instrument favored by Tang literati and courtesans. Many could play it; few could play it well. The zither in Yu Xuanji's poetry represents her attempts to communicate her deepest feelings and find a real companion. She alludes repeatedly to four stories about the zither that stress genuine communication and love. Two concern same-sex friendships; two concern heterosexual love affairs. A poignant tale involves the famous Warring States musician Bo Ya and his friend Zhong Ziqi. Whenever Bo Ya played his zither, his friend instantly knew what Bo Ya was trying to express, whether it was lofty mountains or clear running water. When Zhong Ziqi died, Bo Ya smashed his zither, since there was no longer anyone alive who could really understand him. Then there are the Seven Sages of the Bamboo Grove, eccentric literati of the Three Kingdoms period, intimate friends who drank together and conversed in the languages of music and poetry. Another story concerns the famous Han dynasty poets and lovers Sima Xiangru and Zhuo Wenjun. They were supposed to have met when the recently widowed Zhuo heard Sima playing the zither and singing at a banquet. Yu Xuanji also alludes to the mythical emperor Shun, a paragon of Confucian virtue and the legendary inventor of the zither, and his two loving wives, goddesses of the Xiao and Xiang Rivers. A song addressed to her neighbor mentions Shun's consorts and his zither. Responding to his poem, Yu Xuanji wrote "Following the Rhymes of My Western Neighbor Who Newly Settled In, and Begging for Barley Wine":

> One poem comes and I chant it a hundred times;
> Renewing my passions: Each word resonates like gold.
> Looking west, I already had plans to climb your fence;
> Gazing far off, how can my heart not turn to stone?
> Appointments by the River Han fade into empty space at the end
>   of my view;
> Dreams of Xiao and Xiang Rivers severed, I lay off strumming my
>   zither.
> More intense when we encounter the Cold Food Festival: my home-
>   sick thoughts;
> As for Shuye's good wine: don't ladle it out alone! (*QTS* 9050)

This is a drinking song, of the type made famous by Tao Qian and Li Bo. It also responds to Yu Xuanji's neighbor's poem, using the same rhymes in the same order. Yu Xuanji praises the man, his poem, their old hometown, and his wine. The poem abounds in allusions to lovers. Our speaker casts herself in the role of the eastern neighbor girl, the subject of many earlier male writers (among them Mencius, Song Yu, Sima Xiangru, and Yuan Zhen). While the male writers look east at a beautiful young neighbor girl, Yu Xuanji looks west at a handsome young neighbor man and imagines climbing his fence. Her heart's turning to stone as she gazes into the distance recalls the story of a mountain in Hubei called *Wangfu shi* (Gazing Far-off at Husband Rock); it seems a woman longing for her absent husband climbed a high mountain and looked for him for so long that she turned to stone. Appointments by the Han River refer to the night of Double Seven, the festival of lovers when the Herd Boy and Weaver Girl Stars (Vega and Altair) meet once a year on a bridge of magpies over the Milky Way. The Milky Way, called the Silver, or Starry, Han, is imagined to continue the earthly Han River up into the sky. Such meetings have faded in her memory. Dreams of the Xiao and Xiang Rivers are dreams of water goddesses, patronesses of those southern rivers and subjects of shamanistic hymns attributed to Qu Yuan and collected in the *Chuci*. Consorts of Emperor Shun, inventor of the zither, they wept tears that permanently spotted the bamboo by the riverside when he died. They sometimes appeared to worthy scholars in later periods. The Cold Food

Festival was a late-winter festival of renewal; absent natives of the capital city remembered its celebration in Chang'an with special fondness. (See the exile poetry of Shen Quanqi, ca. 650–713.) Shuye is Xi Kang (223–262), a poet, drinker, zither player, and member of the Seven Sages of the Bamboo Grove. Here she lays off strumming her zither, giving up hope of a spiritual encounter, but not, perhaps, of an evening spent drinking in pleasant company.

In "Early Autumn," the season evokes feelings that translate into pure songs that possess the speaker's zither:

> When tender chrysanthemums hold in their new colors,
> Distant mountains corral evening mist,
> And cool winds startle green trees,
> Then pure rhymes enter my vermilion threads.
> The pensive wife, polychrome tabby-weave silk in her loom,
> Her man on campaign in the heavens outside the passes.
> Wild geese fly, fish stay in the river,
> As if only they would transmit his letters and news! (*QTS* 9052)

Chrysanthemums suggest autumn and the poet Tao Qian, who wrote of seclusion, drinking, and transcendence. As the evenings grow cool, the speaker plays pure songs on her zither. A story enters her instrument and demands expression. She sings about a woman waiting. As Double Seven, the festival celebrating the meeting of the Herd Boy and Weaver Girl, approaches, the weaving wife wishes for news of her wandering man. Textile work is the ultimate woman's work; here is a dutiful and productive wife sticking virtuously to her domestic duties in the absence of her husband. The wife waiting at her loom for an absent husband, an image as old as the *Gushi shijiu shou* (Nineteen Old Songs) of the Han dynasty, is a cliché in the Tang that still has the power to move. He may already be dead—as in a poem by Chen Tao (c. 841) that closes with the poignant image of bones by the riverside that are still living lovers in the dreams of their wives back home. Wild geese and fish, carriers of messages in folk tales, bring her no news. The zither tells a folk tale that harmonizes with the speaker's longing and loneliness.

In "Sad Thoughts" (see page 109), the zither provides a conduit for communication with sources of divine inspiration: "Alone strumming my vermilion strings, I naturally break into pure song." The instrument also allows her to release negative emotions that might otherwise obstruct her spiritual progress:

> Releasing my feelings, I stop resenting heartless friends;

Nourishing my nature, I toss off as empty the waves of the bitter sea.
(*QTS* 9050–9051)

Yu Xuanji sends her sorrows by means of her zither in another
poem, this one addressed to her friend and traveling companion Wen
Tingyun (c. 812–887). He is the only person aside from Li Yi whom
she addresses by his cognomen (*zi*). In "Sent to Wen Feiqing," she berates him for not writing:

Beside the stepping stones of my staircase, disorderly crickets cry out;
On the branches in the courtyard, mist and dew are clear.
In the moonlight, my neighbors' music echoes;
Atop the storied building, distant mountains brighten.
Over my jeweled mat, a cool breeze touches me;
From my turquoise zither, the sorrows I send you arise.
If Lord Xi is too lazy for letters and tablets,
Then what can release my autumn passions? (*QTS* 9053)

This is one of two poems to Wen Tingyun. Here she restlessly describes sensations of the scene all around her on an autumn night. She
hears crickets and her neighbors' music, sees dew on nearby trees and
starlight on distant mountains, and feels a chilly wind. She translates
all these physical sensations into sad music on her zither. The turquoise
zither refers to a famous instrument (Sima Xiangru's?) in a poem by
Li Shangyin (813?–858). Playing the zither is an attempt to reach a
like-minded friend. She then translates the language of music into this
poem. Individual elements of this poem belong to the conventional
lonely, lovelorn autumn poem, but the chaotic pile of images creates
an unbalanced mood that is unconventional. Lord Xi is Xi Kang, the
Six Dynasties Southern poet, eccentric, and member of the Seven Sages
of the Bamboo Grove. He was a handsome fellow, a wild drinker, and
a great companion. In a famous letter to his friend Shan Tao, Xi Kang
claims that he is too lazy and untalented to hold a position at court.
Yu Xuanji flatters Wen Tingyun with the comparison. Her last line goes
beyond the customary request for a reply, sounding desperate for true
communication.

Yu Xuanji describes someone else playing the zither in what is perhaps her clearest expression of lesbian eroticism: a love song addressed
to three orphaned sisters, young courtesans of refined musical and literary ability, who were for a time her neighbors in a guest house. The
title of the poem as it stands is quite long; probably some introductory remarks of the editors are mixed up with a shorter title like "Poem

Composed Following the Rhyme Words of Three Sisters." The title in the *Quan Tangshi* reads: "Guang, Wei, and Pou are three sisters, orphaned when young and accomplished from the beginning. Now they have written these poems, so essential and pure that they are hard to match. How could even the linked verses from the Xie household [i.e., by Xie Daoyun] add to them? There was a stranger coming from the capital city who showed them to me. Consequently, I put these rhymes in order." The poem itself is also rather long:

> Formerly I heard that in the southern nations flowery faces were few,
> But today my eastern neighbors are three sisters.
> In their dressing room, gazing upon one another: the "Rhapsody on the Parrot";
> At their cyan window they must be embroidering phoenix slips.
> Pink fragrant plants fill the courtyard, ragged and jaggedly broken off;
> Green strained wine fills our cups; one after another we put them to our mouths.
> I suspect they once served as girl attendants at the Turquoise Pond (Yaochi);
> Coming in exile to this dusty world, they did not become males.
> I finally venture to compare them to the appearance of Lady Wenji;
> Little Xi (Shi) would be speechless before them; I am still more mortified.
> A single tune of ravishing song—the zither seems far away and indistinct;
> While the four-strings are lightly strummed, they talk, murmuring unclearly.
> Facing the mirror stand, they compete equally with their blue-glinting silk-thread hair.
> Opposite the moon, they vie in showing off their white jade hairpins.
> In the midst of the Lesser Existence Grotto (Xiaoyou dong), pine dew drops;
> Above the Great Veil Heaven (Daluo tian), willow mist is contained.
> If only they were able to tarry on account of the rain,
> They need not fear that matters of "blowing the syrinx" are not yet understood.
> How many times has the Amah scolded them for talking beneath the flowers?
> Lord Pan [Pan Yue]consulted them once in a meeting in a dream.
> When I temporarily grasp their pure sentences, it's as if my cloud-soul were cut off;
> If I were looking at their pink faces, even dying would be sweet.

Despondently I look from afar for those delightful people: where are
  they?
Traversing the clouds, I return home to the north while they return
  to the south. (*QTS* 9055–9056)

This is clearly a same-sex erotic poem. Chinese male poets regularly
used male voices to declare their passions for beautiful women, and
women's voices to express their conceptions about women's responses
to men. Poems by men speaking in women's voices, often describing
the suffering of a grieving victim at the hands of her faithless lover, have
been read as political commentary. The powerless, abandoned woman
makes criticisms that the abused official does not dare to utter. In a departure that seems as shocking today as it must have seemed in the Tang
dynasty, Yu Xuanji turns these conventions upside down. She uses her
own woman's voice to express her romantic responses to other women.
She may also be advertising their beauty and talent to male literati.

The introduction identifies the orphaned sisters with Xie Daoyun,
a fourth-century aristocratic poet, who as a child showed her preco-
cious literacy by besting her father's guests in a poetry competition on
the subject of snow. As the poem begins, Yu Xuanji compares the three
southern girls to luxurious pet birds described in the "Rhapsody on
the Parrot" by Ni Heng of the second century C.E. They remind her
of famous beauties of old. Lady Cai Wenji was a Han dynasty noble-
woman and poet married to a Xiongnu chieftain as a result of a war
treaty. She grew to admire her husband and is traditionally considered
the author of "Nineteen Songs from a Nomad Flute," a Tang poetic
cycle. Little Xi Shi, whom Yu claims is no match for the three sisters,
was herself a notorious "state-toppling beauty," the tempting center of
a plot by one Warring States' ruler to overthrow a rival, and the subject of another poem by Yu Xuanji ("At the Temple of Washing Silk
Gauze," *QTS* 9048). Yu identifies Xi Shi, to whom she compares herself, with sexuality and power.

The breathtaking loveliness and apparently supernatural talent of
the three sisters make the poet exclaim that they must formerly have
been attendants of the Queen Mother of the West (Xiwangmu) at the
Turquoise Pond in her paradise on Mount Kunlun. Xiwangmu's entourage of goddesses was known for their beauty and musicianship.
Yu Xuanji also places the sisters in a spot associated with the Queen
Mother's cult: the Lesser Existence Grotto on Mount Wangwu, where
the poet had also traveled. The actual guest house that was the setting
for the poem may be nearby. The sisters' comfortable familiarity with

the goddess is expressed in the intimate form of address, "Amah," that they use for her. She is their teacher who scolds them for chattering idly in the garden when they are supposed to be studying their lessons. The poet may wish the Queen Mother would serve as matchmaker for herself and the girls, a role the goddess often fulfilled in heterosexual unions between a divine teacher and a human student.

For Yu is powerfully attracted to the sisters: she says their words make her feel "as if my cloud-soul were cut off." That is: they take her breath away. She wishes they could tarry to make love: rain and blowing the syrinx are regular metaphors for sexual expressions of love. "Blowing the syrinx" also refers to techniques of ascending to transcendence by means of music, as did the pre-Qin immortals Xiao Shi and his wife, Long Yu. The mixture of divine and worldly love is a commonplace in Shangqing Daoist literature. The four women enjoy an evening of wine, music, and poetry together, and then must part. Yu Xuanji heads north, while the three sisters head back south.

The zither is one of several musical terms in this poem (four-strings, syrinx, tune, song), which also mentions divine musicians (jade girls in the Queen Mother's entourage, Xiao Shi) and musical heroines (Lady Wenji). But the zither is outstanding among them, for it contains three essential meanings for our author: it is a means of self-disclosure, communication, and seduction. Although it is indistinct, the sisters' song tells the speaker who they are and ravishes her. Music parallels the self-expression the sisters and Yu Xuanji share in the words of their exchanged poems. According to Yu Xuanji's response, they are compatible in erotic and literary gifts.

One of Yu Xuanji's most evocative uses of the zither to express her longing to communicate appears in "Sending Someone My Innermost Feelings":

> My sorrow is sent on vermilion strings;
> Holding in passions, my thoughts have become unbearable.
> Early on, I knew meetings of cloud and rain,
> Before arousing my orchid mind.
> Gleaming and shining, peach and plum trees
> Do not obstruct a statesman's pursuits.
> Gray-green pines and cinnamon trees
> Still long for the praise of worldly people.
> In the moon's color, my moss-covered staircase seems clean;
> In my song's resonance, the bamboo close deepens.
> Before my gates, the ground is covered with red leaves;
> I don't sweep, waiting for one who recognizes my sound. (QTS 9052)

From beginning to end, this poem concerns the search for a friend who will understand her. In the opening line she plays her zither to express her feelings, hoping to reach someone who will, as she says in the last line, "recognize my sound." She refers to Bo Ya, the great Warring States' musician who played his zither for his friend, Zhong Ziqi.

Here Yu Xuanji also uses images that go back to the shamanistic hymns of the *Chuci* and to the *Luoshen fu* and *Shennü fu* in the *Wenxuan*. The orchid, a worthy and virtuous plant, recalls her name: "Tender Orchid." "Clouds and rain" refer to sexual intercourse, originally the union of a goddess and a king. The author was notorious for sexual as well as literary precocity: here she suggests her mind was aroused only after her body's awakening. Peach and plum blossoms, standing in for the transient beauty of young girls, shine for a day and bring pleasure to men. But serious men only toy with young women; they will not risk careers or swerve from the path to their goals for the sake of love. Even elder statesmen, those eminent old pines, care about their reputations and need the approval of their peers. The poet waits and sings in her room in the shady bamboo grove at the end of a mossy staircase, hoping for a real friend who will hear her tune and know exactly what it means.

Conclusion

The language of material culture in her poetry opens a window into Yu Xuanji's thought, helping us move beyond sensationalist versions of her life. Simple language describing textiles, boats, and zithers carries a complex array of meanings in Yu Xuanji's writing. A small number of images from material culture occupy a surprisingly large place in the world of meaning in her poems. Nineteen of her fifty surviving poems mention clothing or woven goods, eleven poems mention boats, and at least nine poems mention the zither.

Some images, such as white patterned tabby-weave and netted-gauze silk, have more than one meaning, depending on the context. Clothing identifies the social class of the wearer. A man's perfumed clothes may arouse her scorn or admiration. A sheer silk sleeve can be the target of her rage and frustration over intellectual opportunities lost or serve as an ineffective shield against public humiliation. Yu Xuanji's language of clothing reveals a self-conscious, often lonely, and isolated person, living for much of her life on the margins of Tang society, with few economic or social resources. She expresses her envy of a recluse's prestige and power in the vision of garments cut from auroral clouds, like those of the great goddesses. That divine garment embodies her longing for the contemplative life. Yu Xuanji's textile images show her desire for the gifts, powers, and unfettered lives of divine women. She enacts the self-discipline and asceticism of the Daoist adept when she rejects robes of the finest woven silk. Her own white silk duster, tangled up in her books and papers, expresses the freedom and ease she attains as a Daoist nun.

Yu Xuanji's poetic image of the untied boat also allows several interpretations. The little boat is clearly herself. A drift in mid-ocean, it can seem disoriented and at a loss, lonely and isolated like the poet in her life and times. In other poems that express a more resigned and positive attitude toward her fate, her boat drifts peacefully along the river. Like a boat flowing with the current, she naturally and easily relies on the Dao to bring her back home where she belongs. The boat represents life changes and transformations as well as alterations of place.

The zither, the final image of material culture from Yu Xuanji's poetry, represents her desire to communicate and find a true companion. The zither is an instrument of self-expression. Yu Xuanji uses it to convey her feelings to both men and women friends. Her messages are sometimes both religious and erotic at once. Some readers believe a Chinese poem may express either sexual or spiritual feelings, but not both together. There is also an old tradition of interpreting erotic images in Chinese literature, such as those found in the first section of the *Shijing* (Book of Songs), as political or ethical in intent. In the poetry of Yu Xuanji, however, just as in parts of the *Chuci* and Shangqing Daoist mystical corpus, there is no meaningful distinction; sensual and divine love mingle. The language is both erotic and religious. Images of sensual attraction and sexual union provide a way to try to describe the ineffable Dao.

Expressing herself, using her talents, following the Dao, and finding companions may all have motivated Yu Xuanji to enter the convent. We may never be able to interpret her religious vocation fully or determine her guilt in the murder of her maid. Although many specific facts of her life may never be recovered, Yu Xuanji's poetry, using the language of material culture, speaks in a powerful individual voice that, despite her conflicts and limitations, praises the Dao and the life of the recluse. Her poetry reveals her Daoist identity.

Notes

1. This chapter is part of a longer study of Daoist holy women of the Tang. I thank Stephen Bokenkamp, Victoria Cass, Michael Chang, Susan Fernsebner, Marta Hansen, Donald Holzman, Terry Kleeman, Dorothy Ko, Livia Kohn, Paul Kroll, Liu Lu, Susan Mann, Mabuichi Masaya, Mitamura Keiko, Sherry Mou, Charles Orzech, Hal Roth, Audrey Spiro, Stephen West, Victor Xiong, Yao Ping, and Ye Wa for their suggestions.

2. Accounts of Yu Xuanji's life began to appear a few decades after her death and continue to be produced up to now. Dieter Kuhn (1985) discusses the sources with unusual thoroughness. The earliest account was written around 910 by Huangfu Mei in his *Sanshui xiaodu* (see Kelly 1978). His sensationalized and critical account is the source of nearly all subsequent versions. These include the *Beimeng suoyan* of Sun Guangxian, written around 940–960 (Sun 1939), the *Tangshi jishi* (Recorded Anecdotes Concerning Tang Poetry) of Ji Yugong (Ji 1962), the *Tang caizi zhuan* (Transmissions Concerning Talented Masters of the Tang Dynasty) by the Yuan writer Xin Wenfang, and the Qing anthology known as the "Complete Tang Poetry." In the twentieth century, Mori Ogai (1862–1922) wrote a novel on Yu Xuanji's life (Mori 1951), and Robert van Gulik imagined an episode between her arrest and execution in *Poets and Murder* (van Gulik 1968). Most recently, the Shaw Brothers' studio in Hong Kong made an unusually strong movie on her life, *Tangchao haofang nu* (A Wild Woman of the Tang Dynasty), which combines elements of martial arts, soft porn, and tragedy (1984).

3. Maureen Robertson discusses how poetic convention limits what we can discover about female authors as well as the pitfalls involved in interpreting conventional and occasional poetry (Robertson 1992). My approach to reading poetic texts by women authors is indebted to Professor Robertson, but my conclusions about how much we can discover are more optimistic.

4. Poems by Yu Xuanji are cited by the abbreviation *QTS* followed by the page number in the edition of the *Quan Tangshi* published by Zhonghua shuju (Beijing, 1960).

Bibliography

Bray, Francesca. 1997. *Technology and Gender: Fabrics of Power in Late Imperial China*. Berkeley: University of California Press.

Cahill, Suzanne E. 1993. *Transcendence and Divine Passion: The Queen Mother of the West in Medieval China*. Stanford: Stanford University Press.

Dowland, John. 1968 [1604]. "Flow My Tears." Song Recorded on *Dances of Dowland* by Julian Bream. New York: RCA.

Karashima Takeshi. 1964. *Go Genki-Setsu Tō*. Tokyo: Shūeisha.

Kelly, Jeanne. 1978. "The Poetess Yü Hsüan-chi." In *Traditional Chinese Stories: Themes and Variations* ed. by Y. W. Ma and Joseph S. M. Lau, 305–306. New York: Columbia University Press.

Kuhn, Dieter. 1985. "Yü Hsüan-chi: Die Biographie der T'ang Dichterin, Kurtisane und taoistischen Nonne." Inaugural Lecture, University of Heidelberg: Private publication.

Mather, Richard B. 1976. *A New Account of Tales of the World*. Minneapolis: University of Minnesota Press.

McGarrigle, Anna. 1973. "Heart Like a Wheel." Song Recorded on *Heart Like a Wheel* by Linda Ronstadt. Hollywood: Capitol Records.

Mori Ogai. 1951. *Go Genki*. In *Ogai zenshū*. Tokyo: Iwanami.

Peng Zhixian and Zhang Yan. 1994. *Yu Xuanji shi bian'nian yizhu*. Urumqi: Xinjiang University Press.

Rexroth, Kenneth. 1972. *The Orchid Boat: Woman Poets of China*. New York: Seabury Press.

Robertson, Maureen. 1992. "Voicing the Feminine: Constructions of the Gendered Subject in Lyric Poetry by Women of Medieval and Late Imperial China." *Late Imperial China* 13 1:63–110.

Rotours, Robert de. 1968. *Courtisanes chinoises à la fin des T'ang entre 789 et le 8 janvier 881. Pei-li tche (Anecdotes du quartier du Nord)*. Paris: Presses Universitaires de France.

Schafer, Edward. 1973. *The Divine Woman: Dragon Ladies and Rain Maidens in T'ang Literature*. Berkeley: University of California Press.

Shaw Brothers' Filmstudio. 1984. *Tangchao haofang nü*. Hong Kong: Shaw Brothers'.

Van Gulik, Robert. 1961. *Sexual Life in Ancient China*. Leiden: E. J. Brill.

———. 1968. *Poets and Murder*. Chicago: University of Chicago Press.

Walls, Jan W. 1972. "The Poetry of Yü Hsüan-chi: A Translation, Annotation, Commentary, and Critique." Ph.D. diss., Indiana University, Bloomington, Ind.

Wimsatt, Genevieve B. 1936. *Selling Wilted Peonies*. New York: Columbia University Press.

Yokoyama Eisan. 1968. "Go Genki ni tsuite." *Chūgoku ronsetsu shiryō* 10:218–225.

6

A Mid-Ming Reappraisal of the *Laozi*
The Case of Wang Dao

MABUCHI MASAYA

In current scholarship on Chinese thought, the early Ming is seen as a time when Neo-Confucianism predominated, especially the study of principle (*lixue*) in the wake of the teachings of Zhu Xi (1130–1200). Hardly anyone proposes differently (Sano 1972). When it comes to the mid-Ming, a new line of Neo-Confucianism began with Wang Shouren (Yangming, 1472–1528), and different strands of the teaching arose, leading to a multiplicity of views and various debates in the late Ming (Araki 1972). Among scholars, the consensus is that the tendency to unify the three teachings dominated the latter half of the Ming dynasty (Sakai 1960, ch. 3), and within this framework, scholar-officials variously paid attention to ancient Daoist texts, notably the *Laozi*.[1]

To understand the reception and interpretation of *Laozi* better and pay more attention to alternative and new trends in Ming thought, in the following pages I present the life and work of Wang Dao (1487–1547), a disciple of Wang Yangming who developed his own take on both Daoist and Confucian thought. A proponent of the unity of the three teachings, Wang Dao placed particularly high value on the *Laozi* and wrote a commentary on it, the *Laozi yi* (Meaning of the *Laozi*). To understand his thought and its role in Ming thinking better, I would like to ask three questions: What was the motivation underlying Wang's high esteem of the *Laozi*? What new philosophical ideas did he express through his interpretation of the text? And how is his thought related to the dominant philosophical tendencies in the later Ming? I begin with an introduction of Wang and his life.

Wang Dao's Life and Work

Wang Dao came from Wucheng in Shandong province. His agnomen was Chunfu, his sobriquet Shunqu. As described in his biography in Yan Song's *Wanggong shendao bei* (Stele on the Spiritual Path of Lord Wang), he passed the advanced scholar (*jinshi*) examination in 1511 and began a career as an official, becoming one of the elite scholar-officials of his time. He began at the Hanlin Academy, then moved to the prefectural school at Yingtian. He later became an administrative aide and served in a variety of official positions before retiring on grounds of illness. After spending thirteen years in semi-seclusion, he took another post, becoming an assistant to the Nanjing Chamberlain for Ceremonies in 1546 and advancing as far as the Ministry of Rites, which he joined shortly before his death.

As for his person, the biography relates that he was "elegant and pure," "of rotund looks and a warm disposition, learned and of great foresight," a man who "never acted for personal profit." Despite spending a long time in office, he remained "simple and pure in lifestyle" and, in his oratory, "did not bend to conform to that of his contemporaries." Huang Zongxi in his *Mingru xue'an* (Records of Ming Scholars; Ching 1987) says:

> When [Wang] argued about how to evaluate people of today and people of antiquity, he did not follow what previous Confucians had already developed. His high degree of understanding is illustrated by this fact. (42.1038)

The text also praises his extensive learning, explaining that he deeply involved himself in all areas of study, including yin-yang and calendrical science, medicine and divination, agriculture and sericulture, law, geography, and many others. He also tried to write poetry at the outset of his career but found it a "rather useless" exercise and so moved on to the study of principle, or philosophy, of standard Neo-Confucianism in the wake of Zhu Xi's teachings. He read the *Lunyu* (Analects) with enjoyment and found himself awakened to the "beauty and simplicity of the way of the sages." After this, he faulted contemporary proponents of the study of principle for their promotion of exclusive schools, contending that there had also been excellent people in the Han and pre-Han periods. In addition, he developed an interest in Buddhism and Daoism, not remaining ignorant of any of China's major traditions.

Wang Dao's name has been the focus of very few studies in Ming intellectual history (e.g., Mizuno 1979; 1980). But experts on Wang

Yangming know his name because he was Wang Dao's teacher in his youth, and several letters have survived, dating from 1511 to 1514. Even as early as 1512, however, a split between the two became apparent, leading to Wang Dao's separation from his first teacher. Wang Yangming says:

> In your earlier letter, you say: "To study to awaken to goodness and become sincere is sound. But I am not sure what is meant by goodness, where it originally comes from, where it is now, how to perceive it, how to encounter it, whether it should be put before sincerity or after, and when sincerity is true sincerity. All these may be points of detail and seem minute, but I really wish to delve into them, gradually resolving my doubts. I hope you can help me do so." . . .
>
> Now, your tendencies seem to show that you have not yet examined the original teachings of the sages and are still confused by the explanations of later generations. In every single object and every single being, there is utmost goodness, and it must be from every single object and every single being that one must begin to seek utmost goodness. Only then may one reach the stage of "clear understanding" and that is why earlier I spoke of "where it originally comes from, and where it is now." (*Wang Wencheng gong quanshu* 4, Second letter to Wang Chunfu)

Wang Dao thus harbored doubts about Wang Yangming's notion that goodness could be found by searching for it in one's mind. These were points to which he would return again and again in his later works (see also *Mingru xue'an* 42.1038).

After separating from Wang Yangming, Wang Dao turned to Zhan Ruoshui (1466–1560). Wang Dao describes Zhan, in a 1525 letter to Wei Xiao, as having a strong influence on his thought, but eventually Wang developed a position of his own that went beyond the teachings of all his masters. Still, he is classified as a member of the school of Zhan Ruoshui (*Mingru xue'an* 42.1039).

Wang Dao wrote many and varied works, including a number of commentaries and historical studies, the most important of which was the *Laozi yi*.[2] His essays are contained in his collected works, the anonymously edited *Shunqu xiansheng wenlu* (Record of Works of Master Shunqu, 12 juan, abbr. *Wenlu*, ed. 1932).

Wang Dao's Adoption of the *Laozi*

Replying to Wei Xiao, Wang Dao writes, "From middle age on, I have been especially fond of reading the writings of Laozi" (*Wenlu* 4), showing when his liking for the *Laozi* began. In a letter to Hua Zhushi, he also expresses the high value he places on the thought of the text and of its author, the ancient sage Laozi, by speaking of "Laozi, the great sage of old" (*Wenlu* 4), while in an essay on Han Fei he notes, "The way of Laozi, above joining [the mythical sage-emperors] Fu Xi, Yao, and Shun, below linked with the [historical sages] Yu and Confucius, is unparalled in its brightness" (*Wenlu* 4). In these instances, he puts Laozi and his work on a par with the Confucian tradition.

Nevertheless, on closer inspection, there is a gulf between the way he speaks of Confucius and the way he speaks of Laozi. This can be seen in the following passages:

> The words of Laozi are the ultimate in simulaneously grasping the ancient while controlling the modern. The learning of the disciples of Confucius is the constant warp of nurturing and adjusting the age. Although they are different, these two approaches truly emerged together. Later Confucians did not grasp the full scope of the ancients, and rashly drew distinctions. Their division of the Dao is a late phenomenon. . . .
>
> Laozi concentrated on clarifying the Dao, and so depended on the ultimate, while Confucius from time to time used a lower level of doctrine, gearing his teachings to each individual. This may be compared to the notion that Sākyamuni and Laozi specialized entirely in pursuing the highest vehicle, while Confucius was not shy to speak with the simple and basic. (*Wenlu* 3, *Laozi yi*, ch. 38)

Thus as opposed to Confucius, who was willing to bring the vocabulary of his teachings down a notch in the interest of education, Laozi used only the highest language to speak of the Dao. In the end, their difference lay merely in the way they spoke about the very same Dao. At the time of the ancient sages, Wang says, people of the world had forgotten the root of the Dao and its virtue, instead engaging in the minor points of benevolence and righteousness, ritual and music, thereby falling into a false sense of goodness. He criticizes this and calls for a return to the root of morality, at the level of the Way and its virtue. Thus individual and personal goodness, the concrete goodness of ordinary life, to him was the same as the benevolence and righteousness of the Confucians. But deeper than this was yet another level, at the deepest roots of morality, the true source of goodness in the Dao. As a result, Wang Dao actively valued the ideas of the *Laozi*—to him, they advocated the return from individual and concrete goodness to original morality, to the Way and its virtue at the source of everything (*Wenlu* 3, "On Robber Zhi"). This is the prime reason why Wang values the *Laozi*, and his commentary in the *Laozi yi* explicates the text from this point of view.

Wang's emphasis on the Dao as a source of a deeper goodness is clear in his exposition of chapter two of the *Laozi* in the *Laozi yi:*

> Among all the beings that come forth from the Dao, there is none that is not beautiful, yet their beauty was present in the Dao even before they began—this is the sense in which it is eternally beautiful. Among all the things that proceed from the Dao, there is none that is not good, yet their goodness was present in the Dao even before they began—this is the sense in which it is eternally good. It is only when the names "beauty" and "goodness" appear that the human mind grows more contentious every day. Then style defeats substance, and falsehood corrupts truth. It is in this way that "the beautiful is ugly and the good is no good." (*Laozi yi* 2)

In such passages from the *Laozi yi,* besides the high value obviously placed on the *Laozi* and the *Zhuangzi,* there is also a great esteem for Buddhism.[3] This is expressed in Wang Dao's statement that Śākyamuni, just as Laozi, was striving for the attainment of the highest vehicle to salvation. Wang saw both as pursuing the absolute and explicitly states that all the major thinkers, including Zhuangzi and Confucius, were describing different paths that, nevertheless, ultimately led to the same goal (*Wenlu* 3, "Zhuangzi"). He says:

> Life after life is an ongoing transformation. Whether one lives long or is beyond all life, the main characteristic of both states is still the ongoing transformation of everything. Thus, if one can attain a state beyond life, one will live long; and if one can attain a state of long life, one can attain mastery of life after life. In this, the teachings of the sages of all three traditions converge, even if the explanations they offer to the world differ. Superficial students will never quite grasp this. (*Wenlu* 5, "A Hundred Streams Meet at the Sea of Learning")[4]

What he means by "superficial students" are people attached to an individual and concrete notion of goodness, which he sees as similar to benevolence and righteousness in being nothing but counterfeit goodness. As he says:

> When people do not see the Dao, even if they choose to walk in goodness, they will end up going in some direction, and once there a direction, attachments will follow. This is why their movements cannot escape others' traces, and their theories cannot escape others' fabrications. (*Laozi yi* 27)

Here the basic structure of Wang Dao's thinking becomes clear. He inherits the major philosophy of his time, the standard Neo-Confu-

cianism of Zhu Xi, then goes off in a different direction and uses the
Laozi's criticism of the goodness of ordinary people to criticize it.

He is also critical of its practice, and here follows Wang Yangming,
who says in his *Chuanxi lu* (Instructions for Practical Living):

> The Master [Mencius, 7A26] said: The center is nothing but Heaven's
> principle, nothing but change. Changing along with the times, how can
> one hold on to anything? When trying to make the best response to
> changing times, it is difficult to set up a set of rules ahead of time. Later
> Confucian thinkers established the notion of the principle of the Dao,
> moving along in change yet in unity. Once they set this up as a rigid
> model, they were doing exactly this "holding to one extreme." (1,
> sect. 52)

Here Wang Yangming criticizes the standard Confucian notion that
one should examine things one by one to reach their specific principle and then act in accordance with it. The kind of goodness thus
achieved is characterized as a false goodness, a formalism that posits
a danger to true inner nature. His criticism, however, seems to be limited to Zhu Xi's followers' self-cultivation practices rather than their
ideas.

Wang Dao is more radical than that. For him, once Neo-Confucians
undertake the specific examination of phenomena and follow a set of
rules and patterns, they become enmeshed in particularism and lose
their philosophical strength: they embrace a counterfeit goodness instead of the real thing. Wang Dao recognizes this as a fallacy and over-
comes it by returning to the deepest roots of morality in the Dao. Here
his positive reading of the *Laozi* enters his thought.[5]

He begins by stating that the Dao, the nameless, is the unchanging
substance of the universe and also the Eternal Nonbeing or the
Nonultimate. It is, furthermore, the source of virtue, the named, which
is also called the Great One or the Great Ultimate (*Laozi yi* 42). From
this level, heaven and earth, yin and yang, and the world of myriad
beings arise. Virtue, therefore, stands between the eternally unvary-
ing substantial level of the Dao, the Eternal Nonbeing, and the ever-
changing phenomenal world of myriad beings—maintaining a creative
and productive relationship among them. Therefore, Wang Dao's cos-
mogonic theory says: "Dao [through virtue] is in the human mind just
as it is in heaven and earth" (*Laozi yi* 1). In this way, he shifts the entire pattern of the discussion toward the nature of the mind. His prem-
ise here becomes the structure: Dao—virtue—myriad beings, the lat-

ter with their counterfeit virtues of benevolence and righteousness.
He says:

> Dao and virtue were originally one thing, but the Dao was nameless,
> while virtue was named. The Dao could not be spoken of [*dao*], but
> virtue could be attained [*de*]. Thus, by descending one level from the
> Dao, then one enters into virtue. Benevolence and righteousness are
> the answering traces of virtue. Righteousness is a means to repair that
> which benevolence does not fully reach. Thus, by descending one level
> from virtue, then one enters into benevolence. By descending one level
> from benevolence, then one enters into righteousness. (*Laozi yi* 38)

Dao and virtue are the fundamental substance of the human mind,
and the myriad things are its function. The goal of cultivation practice, then, has to be the attainment of this level of finding "the wonders of Dao and virtue as represented by the sages" (*Laozi yi* 1). Again,
Wang Dao says:

> Dao is in the human mind just as it is in heaven and earth. If one is
> without desires, then one will be true and pure, with mental states ab-
> solutely serene, as clear as the bright sky without a single cloud, as bril-
> liant as a bright mirror without a single speck of dust. This state is the
> basic substance of the mind. If, on the other hand, once there is a de-
> sire, one just follows impulses and moves along in perfect response to
> other beings, then one will be as radiant as a clearly patterned starry
> constellation, as clear as a river flowing along without pause. This state
> is the great function of the mind. (*Laozi yi* 1)

Here the activity of the mind is described as the background for a
Dao-based cosmogony in which virtue creates the myriad beings.[6] Key
points are the equation of individual and concrete goodness with
benevolence and righteousness at the level of the subtle traces of the
mind in its function, and the equation of the Dao and virtue with the
mind in its substance. This indicates the basic direction of his thinking, modified further by several other notions. In one respect, he follows Zhu Xi and promotes the idea that one should overcome the level
of concrete action, of benevolence and righteousness as the mere
traces of a higher purity. He, too, wishes to go beyond the dimension
of concrete things and affairs and immerse himself in the formless
world of the Dao, which at the same time he must deny. He says:

> As people of the world hold on to being, they see only outer things and
> do not immerse themselves in the Dao, follow other beings but are un-
> able to undergo proper transformations. Cultivating themselves in this

way, they become lascivious and greedy and by their wasteful desires squander their life. Pursuing outer rewards, they do things that will bring them fame and lose their true self. . . .

Even if one wishes to transform oneself and the world using the ideas of Laozi, one has yet [to confront the fact that] people wallow in vanity and persist in shallowness, are immersed in phenomena and destroyed by them. They are devastated by rites and rules, submerged in darkness by benevolence and righteousness. They lose themselves and bring destruction upon the state. With ordinary people like this, how could they ever be helped with the teachings of Laozi? (*Laozi yi* 11)

Wang Dao, therefore, wishes to go beyond the level of concrete goodness and operate on the profound depth of the mind, with the goal of grasping the root of the Dao and suffusing the mind with it. At the same time, he acknowledges that he cannot just create a different universe for himself, in which to live in peace and quiet, but has to remain in the real world of people, rulers, and states. Finding a way to maintain true, inner goodness even in the real world, then, must be understood as the prime motivation of his thought. He expresses this in the words "Return from phenomena to nonbeing, then use nonbeing to act upon phenomena" (*Laozi yi* 40). He explains further with an allusion to the concepts of the "mind of the Dao" and "the mind of humanity" from the *Shangshu* (Book of History):

In the midst of phenomena, there is still nonbeing; there is nothing called nonbeing outside of phenomena. The wonder of nonbeing is active throughout phenomena; there is no way one can dispense with nonbeing and be able to function among phenomena. The unity of nonbeing and phenomena is very wondrous—big, it is heaven and earth; minute, it is every individual being; condensed, it is part of every human mind—it pervades them all. (*Laozi yi* 11)

This, in turn, lays the foundation for Wang's basic understanding of existence. He states:

The Dao cannot but bring forth the One, the One cannot but bring forth the Two, and similarly the Two bringing forth the Three, the Three bringing forth the myriad beings—all these circumstances exist on their own without any input. Similarly heaven and earth cannot but be regular—how much more should this apply to human beings? Thus uncarved material cannot but be broken up and made into vessels, just as the sages cannot just keep the Dao to themselves and never apply it. And as they apply it, they use nonbeing to control phenomena; holding on to the old, they manage the present. (*Laozi yi* 28)

As Wang, therefore, thinks about going beyond ordinary, concrete phenomena to reach the Dao at the depth of the mind, he yet finds that he cannot entirely let go of concrete objects. To find a bridge between the two, he again turns to the *Laozi*.[7]

The Aims of the *Laozi yi* and Wang's Overall Thinking

Throughout his *Laozi yi*, as well as in certain other works and essays, Wang Dao tries to capture both the moment of transcendence when one leaps from concrete phenomena to the Dao within the mind, and the moment of attachment when one is involved with concrete phenomena. His main foci are the pursuit of transcending the mind's individual and concrete morality and the search for the underlying, unchanging mental substance at its base. He grapples with this issue by reflecting on and criticizing theories of mind that had gone before him. For example, about Mencius's thesis that human nature is good, he says:

> Mencius says that human nature is good, and places it on a higher level than do Xunzi and Yang Xiong. But Mencius never approaches an explanation of why human nature is good, and when he says that it is, he merely points to inherent human feelings. Now, human nature may be basically good and without evil, yet one's inherent feelings are a combination of both good and evil. Here, then, is the reason why the two masters [Xunzi and Yang Zhu] dared to voice a contrary position and disagree with Mencius. . . . (*Wenlu* 4, "Zisi")

Mencius's error is in generalizing about nature when he is really talking about feelings. Along the same lines, he also criticizes the concept of the "pure knowledge of the good" (*liangzhi*) of Wang Yangming. He states:

> Using the idea of "pure knowledge of the good" and applying it to Confucius would be as erroneous as looking at the sun when it is partly obstructed by clouds. [For Wang Yangming,] "Pure knowledge of the good" is no more than the activation of one's personal feelings, but its existence at the moment before that activation remains doubtful. For Mencius, the "pure knowledge of the good" was his concept of the Four Sprouts [of virtue], which he located in the place where the feelings were first activated. . . . [Wang] Yangming similarly suggests this is the basic substance of the sage, entirely missing the point. (*Wenlu* 6, "Yangming")

Here, the feelings that arise from Mencius's "Four Sprouts" and the power of moral judgment deriving from Wang Yangming's concept of the pure knowledge of the good are both criticized for operating at the level of a mind already developed. The level of nature's response to external objects is not that of the deepest substance of the mind. The most fundamental basis of human nature, on the other hand, is the pre-active, quiescent, soundless, and formless substance, which Wang sees as the quality of "utmost good" (*zhishan*) on which all humans must depend.

Attaining this quality is a matter of practice, and accordingly, Wang Dao's cultivation begins with immersion in the depth of a tranquil and restful mind. This approach stands in stark opposition to the standard Neo-Confucianism of Zhu Xi with its emphasis on the "investigation of things" (*gewu*), a more outside focused inquiry that involved an active mind. Yet Wang Dao's cultivation is also different from the notion of the utter mental immersion associated with Wang Yangming (see *Wenlu* 6, "Response to Zhu"). He finds both outside inquiry and sole reliance on the inner mind insufficient.[8] Instead, practitioners of self-cultivation should give up their grasp on principle as it resides in concrete, individual things and affairs and instead depend on their quality of utmost good as the basic substance of the mind. At the same time, without separating from concrete affairs, they should accord with the Dao in the mind and find principle there. They should not "from their minds proceed to affairs, from principle proceed to the mind." Rather, they should "use the basic substance of the mind to echo outside things, and use affairs to penetrate principle" (*Wenlu* 7, "Preface presented to Zhou Daotong").

Just as principle follows the "pathways of vital energy" (*qi*), and as the Dao is linked to the "never ending movement of vital energy," so too human nature is explained through the concept of vital energy. In this way, Wang Dao's thought is intimately linked with the tradition of "vital energy centered thinking." This also explains his strong focus, again and again, on outside things and affairs. However, the same pattern as it applies to principle, Dao, and human nature is not related with complete consistency to his overall cosmology, which proposes the unity of humanity's basic substance with that of the universe and demands that people transcend external things to attain this basic substance.

Wang Dao himself was conscious of this inconsistency and tried to resolve it by resorting to two notions: the oneness of Dao and vital energy as found in the commentaries to the *Yijing* (Book of Changes), and the transcendence through the Dao as proposed in the *Laozi*. He tries to clarify his position in this way:

The theories of the sages and worthies are not identical; they may be direct or remote, shallow or profound. "One yin, one yang—that is the Dao" is a way [for the *Yijing*] to speak about the flow of the Dao. *Laozi,* on the other hand, says: "The Dao brought forth the One, the One brought forth the Two." Master Zhou [Dunyi] states: "There was the Non-Ultimate, and then there was the Great Ultimate. The Great Ultimate moved and created yang." . . . Yet all these different formulations point to the moment of origin of the Dao. . . .

Laozi says one thing, and Master Zhou says another. When the "Great Commentary" [to the *Yijing*] says how the Dao relates to yin and yang this is the same as [when Laozi speaks of] the two coming from the One. When the [*Yijing* says] that "goodness comes from these," this is the same as [when Laozi speaks of] the two bringing forth the three. When the [*Yijing* says] that "nature comes from their completion," this is the same as [when Laozi speaks of] the three bringing forth the myriad beings. Putting them all together like this, their various levels of direct and remote, shallow and profound can be clarified in one system. (*Wenlu* 4, "Xun Qing")

This means that Wang Dao took the notion of the Dao as presented in the *Yijing* and linked it with the idea of virtue in the *Laozi* to explain the structure of things on the lower level of ordinary affairs, but maintains that this Dao is on a lower level than the deep and remote Dao in the *Laozi*. The problem of the inconsistency in his thought is resolved by his proposal of two different levels and understandings of the Dao. Presenting the term in these two ways, he tries to preserve the unity and integrity of his philosophical system, but is not ultimately successful. In the end, to resolve the tension between the two tendencies of either transcending through the Dao or working with outside things and affairs, he does not give up on either, but rather emphasizes one or the other in different parts of his writings.

Wang Dao's Thought Relative to Confucianism and Daoism

In what category, then, should Wang Dao be placed? As with Xue Hui, Wang Dao's social position was such that he passed the civil service examination, and while serving as a high offical he advocated the harmony of the three teachings. Should he be called a Confucian, a Daoist, or a Buddhist? Or, alternatively, simply an advocate of the integration of the three teachings?

There are several classical perspectives from which one may approach questions of categorization or identification of thought or religion. First, we may categorize people according to the terms they themselves use to describe their thought or religion. Another perspective relies on the standard way in which those around them, in their society or country, categorize or identify their thought. A third perspective is that of outside observers, who may establish standard categories based on the content of their thought. These three perspectives are sometimes used in tandem but, ideally, should be kept separate.

Wang Dao was not exclusively dedicated to any one of the three teachings, so it is not possible to categorize his thought on such grounds. On the other hand, we do have the evaluations of his contemporaries and heirs. For example, Lin Wenjun said that he was "one who talked about the Sage's [i.e., Confucius's] learning" (*Fangzhai cungao* 3, "Preface presented to Mr. Wang"); Yan Song said he "deeply immersed himself in the Study of Principle"; and You Qi called him "the Confucian founder of the generation." To be sure, these are evaluations of people whose basic research was into Confucian thought.

At the same time, the epilogue to the *Ronghui sanjiao* (Merging the Three Teachings) describes Wang Dao as a theorist who tried to unify the three teachings. From the perspective of content, it is indeed possible to see his establishment of Buddhism and Daoism at a level as high as Confucianism as an effort to integrate the three teachings. However, standard Neo-Confucian concepts such as principle, vital energy, mind, and nature framed his thought. Thus it seems most appropriate to approach Wang Dao's ideas as if they were a development and transformation of Confucian thought.

Pursuing the question in this manner, it is not easy to reconcile the various perspectives on Wang Dao into one coherent identification, mainly because the labels of the contemporaneous schools are problematic in themselves. Conventional wisdom has it that the standard Neo-Confucianism of Zhu Xi, the Wang Yangming school, and the School of Evidentiary Scholarship (*kaozheng xue*) are all part of Confucianism, and they certainly all identify themselves as such. When thinkers like Wang Dao enter the picture, however, the lines blur, and demarcation becomes complicated. Therefore, if the question of what is Confucianism—or, for that matter, Daoism—is to be answered historically, then self-identifications, identifications made by those surrounding them, and identifications made according to their essential doctrinal elements all need to be taken into account. It will then be possible to carry out new investigations, with new perspectives and criteria, into the question of categories.

Similarly, one can find suggestions here regarding the difficulties inherent in deciding what it is that we call Daoism. In short, deciding what is and is not Daoism necessitates straightening out the complexities and contradictions inherent in the various perspectives from which identification is approached. The term "Daoism," once such an approach is used, turns out to capture a number of vaguely formed entities. This holds especially true in the case of the two categories of *daojia* and *daojiao.* Regarding the perspectives of self-identification and identification by state and society, there was no way to identify what was and was not called Daoism in the Song and later periods because no sect or school became the exclusive basis for a definition. Daoists were additionally subject to the pressure of Confucian officials, and it was the latter who generally wielded the power to recognize divisions of thinking. So even for the Daoists' own statements with regard to the question of what is Daoism, the gaze of the high officials and the state was decisively influential. That was the case for the majority of people who identified themselves as Daoists in traditional Chinese society. Thus, based on the contradictions inherent in such a self-identification, especially in terms of how the high officials and state defined "Daoism," pursuing this issue in order to decide on the reality of the "Daoism" that existed in Chinese society at the time may be said to be important work. However, it seems that few people have concentrated on the importance of the perspectives of the "non-Daoists" in questions of Daoist identity. Therefore, I think the issue of what *daojia* and *daojiao* are, once three-dimensional work on it begins to progress further, is a question that should be answered inductively.

Wang Dao's Thought among His Contemporaries

The dual nature of Wang Dao's thought is a characteristic that sets him apart from his Ming-dynasty contemporaries. Unlike him, early Ming thinkers and scholar-officials were entirely focused on the study of principle in the wake of Zhu Xi, following him in different formulations yet without any real modification in ideas. Among mid-Ming philosophers there were more thinkers opposed to Zhu Xi, and in the early sixteenth century the study of the mind of Wang Yangming began. Wang Dao has points in common with both these currents. To begin, he does not follow Zhu Xi's emphasis on reverence and pursuit of principle but criticizes his methods as a fossilization of personal activity and sees in them an invitation to the development of counterfeit goodness. In contrast, he proposes a focus on the mind within and a search for the true nature that links human beings with the single vital energy, the basic substance of the cosmos.[9] His main method here is transcendence through the Dao, by which one's unwavering concrete nature can be found. From this position, then, people are able to suitably go along with all manner of circumstances and outer affairs. In the latter perspective, Wang Dao shares a perspective begun by Chen Xianzhang and Wang Yangming,[10] maintaining a strong focus on outside things while at the same time emphasizing their ultimate oneness with the underlying Dao. The latter's concept of the unity of knowledge and action, Zhan Ruoshui's categorization of the investigation of things as a form of action, and the various proposals of the study of vital energy as represented by Wang Tingxiang and Luo Qinshun all exerted a certain influence on Wang Dao's thought.

Rather than listing all the different perspectives of Ming thinkers reflected by Wang, I would like to focus on the specific notions that he has in common with the philosophy of Wang Yangming and Zhan Ruoshui, his two main teachers. We begin with the points shared by all three. Starting with Wang Yangming's doctrines of pure knowledge of the good, I find that his ideas are clearly present in the two tendencies of Wang Dao's thought discussed above. In *Mingru xue'an* 42, Huang Zongxi has shown how Wang Dao's concept of transcendence through the Dao is linked directly with that of Wang Yangming. While little is known of the intellectual influences on Wang Dao prior to his studies with Wang Yangming, it is clear that the latter was the major influence on the former in the early part of the development of his ideas.

Another major influence on Wang Dao was his later teacher Zhan Ruoshui, a thinker with significantly different ideas from those of Wang Yangming (see Qiao 1993). A student of Chen Xianzhang, Zhan was critical of his teacher's practice of quiet-sitting and of the notion that one could find the basic substance of the mind in it, but was also strongly influenced by him. Part of that influence was a strong rejection of Zhu Xi's idea of the universality of principle to be discovered in all things, as well as the understanding that upright principle manifested itself in the mind when it corresponded with affairs. Zhan Ruoshui developed a theory of self-cultivation he described as "pursuing suitable embodiment to recognize heaven's principle" (see *Mingru xue'an* 37). Zhan here finds a solution to the basic questions concerning self-cultivation by referring to the experience of the basic substance of the mind within oneself, but he also links this introspective approach with Zhu Xi's investigation of things, stating that "investigation means attainment" and that it "points to reaching creation, . . . proceeding together in study and reflection." Thus knowing and acting (in Zhan's thought, inseparable yet distinct) are being cultivated together as two sides of the same Dao, and it is by being "in good accordance with the times and the circumstances" that one attains heaven's principle. In other words, when affairs and beings are dealt with at their proper time, then heavenly principle is attained in the mind, and one is able to follow the right path. This is how, through the investigation of things, one can attain heaven's principle.

This reading follows Zhu Xi and also encompasses the idea of the unity of knowledge and action; it includes the intellectual penetration of principle as proposed in Zhu Xi's investigation of things, and at the same time includes a guide to active practice as proposed in Wang Yangming. Goodness here is reached by constantly maintaining close contact with outside things yet never getting too involved in or attached to them. Zhan also states that "the ancients did not set up a contrast between human nature and principle or energy"—which is correct because "the nature of Heaven and Earth is never outside of vital energy or matter" (*Mingru xue'an* 37). Here he makes clear that principle and inner nature are seen through the concept of vital energy, which makes Zhan Ruoshui a follower of the school of the study of vital energy within the Neo-Confucian tradition. Like Wang Dao and Wang Yangming, he finds the thought of Zhu Xi insufficient and wishes to add to it a sense of transcendence through the Dao, a way for the mind to grasp the basic substance of everything, and the intuitive practice that will lead there.

At the same time, all three also wish to maintain the close contact to outside things proposed by Zhu Xi, hoping to establish models for people to relate to the concrete, real phenomena of the world. In this respect they have much in common. Wang Dao's thought is more consistent with Zhan Ruoshui's when it comes to issues like the relationship between the ordinary mind and the transcendent mind, and the reliability of people's innate powers of judgment. For Wang Yangming, as pointed out before, the innate knowledge of the good meant that the human power of judgment was inherent and complete from the beginning and could be fully relied upon. It manifested clearly in a moral conscience that all people shared and would only be minimally diminished by their attachment to outside things. As soon as one engaged in self-reflection, the clear radiance of one's pure knowledge would come shining forth, bringing with it a pure power of judgment. Following its guidance, people would inevitably come to do good and refrain from evil, and through this in turn the latent knowledge of the good would come forth even more brightly. This, for Wang Yangming, was the transcendence of the mind's original substance. It manifested in the moral conscience of ordinary people and was a part everybody had to hold on to firmly and rely upon solidly.

Zhan Ruoshui approaches the issue of innate power of judgment rather differently. In his idea of "pursuing suitable embodiment to recognize heaven's principle," he emphasizes the notion of "cultivating reverence for things" originally taken from the *Lunyu*. This is the notion of a conscious effort at mental collectedness, a necessary awareness in dealing with all things. To reach mental collectedness, a conscious practice is necessary—and here Zhan is closer to Zhu Xi than to Wang Yangming, who was rather critical of Zhan's notion of the pursuit of suitable embodiment, since he saw in it a pursuit of principle on the outside.

The issue of innate judgment is important for Wang Dao. As the *Mingru xue'an* points out, he doubts people's power of judgment and believes that it can go wrong quite often, finding a strong reliance on personal intuition dangerous rather than uplifting. It is here that his position differs most fundamentally from that of Wang Yangming. For Wang Dao, it is insufficient to rely on one's innate knowledge of the good, because it is already activated and reaches out to the concrete situations and things of the world. He thinks that there must be a level beyond and beneath this innate knowledge, on which the human mind is founded and which is its proper substance.

In many ways, this position is close to that of Zhan Ruoshui. Both share the notion that the original matter of the human mind is its original substance, and that this is the most basic goodness of human nature, where alone principle can be found and held on to. This original substance of the mind, however, does not manifest naturally among all human beings, whose mental power of judgment or inherent knowledge can easily go wrong. In a letter to Wang Yangming, Zhan Ruoshui insists that the pure knowledge and pure abilities spoken of by Mencius and then Wang Yangming require effort to access. For him, the mind of people in this world is "hidden by matter and habits"; they are covered by things, ignorant of the true principle within. If they try to rely on this covered-up mind in their judgments, they think themselves right and proper but have in fact fallen into falsehood and error. Here study and investigation are to be pursued assiduously, and reflection on the proper principles of external things has it place. To judge the idea of the pure knowledge of the good, then, Zhan suggests that it lies in the raw material of the mind deep within. He contrasts the *Zhongyong*'s notion of the preemergent with that of the pure knowledge of the good. The former, he says, is what cannot be seen nor heard, while the latter has already unfolded its secrets (*Ganquan wenji* 23). The pre-emergent is used as a metaphor for the level of the mind prior to the pure knowledge of the good.

Seen from this perspective, Wang Dao's thought is indeed closer to Zhan Ruoshui's than Wang Yangming's. First, the notion of the basic substance of the mind, which is also the underlying nature of the world, is common to all, but the presence and activity of this mind in people of the world is evaluated differently. Instead of having people rely on their intuitions, as Wang Yangming would have it, Wang Dao and Zhan Ruoshui see a necessity to uncover and explore the inner mind before these intuitions can shine forth in everyday affairs. Zhan Ruoshui's influence on Wang Dao is most obvious here. Also, both distance themselves equally from the thinking of Zhu Xi, who sees the most important method of understanding principle as being the study and investigation of outside things.

In contrast, Wang and Zhan's focus is on the inner mind and its deeper workings, which may be activated but not found in outside affairs. Still, the inner mind must relate to external things, and its true workings can be best experienced by interacting and corresponding with external things. Thus Wang says that one should search the true way of being "not in the mind but in affairs, not in principle but in the mind," that one should use "the original mind to go along with affairs, and so reach the point where one can use things to observe affairs." This aspect of Wang Dao's thought resembles Zhan's goal of "pursuing suitable embodiment to recognize heaven's principle." In this respect Zhan's thought had an enormous influence on that of Wang Dao.[11] He and Zhan differ in their attitude to the *Laozi*. Wang pays particular attention to Laozi and Buddhism and finds ways to integrate their teachings into his basically Confucian outlook, thus creating his own version of the harmony of the three teachings. Influenced by the religious thinkers, he places a much stronger emphasis than Zhan on the need to transcend all in favor of the original substance of the world and the mind. Zhan Ruoshui, in contrast, has a section in which he criticizes Laozi (*Ganquan wenji* 25), finding his philosophy lacking in benevolence and righteousness and causing harm as a result. This is significantly different from Wang Dao's position and suggests the latter was the more integrative and religious thinker.

Conclusion

The mid-Ming thinker Wang Dao, although trained in a thoroughly Confucian environment, held Laozi's thought very dear and followed it substantially in his own conceptions. While basing some of his ideas strongly on the standard Neo-Confucian thought in the wake of Zhu Xi, and though influenced significantly by the Confucian thinkers Zhan Ruoshui and Wang Yangming, Wang Dao went directly back to the *Laozi*—the demand that people transcend their ordinary consciousness and attain the Dao, defined as the basic substance of the mind, without rejecting or ignoring the importance of concrete affairs and worldly phenomena. His position, developed under the influence of the *Laozi*, moreover, played an increasingly important role in later Ming thought. This can be seen, for example, in the thought of the late-Ming philosopher Liu Zongzhou, who similarly polarizes outward involvement and inner transcendence. To understand Wang Dao's thought properly, one must, therefore, also evaluate and appreciate the thinkers that follow and not focus only on his masters and personal ideas.

Similarly, while Wang Dao is properly and officially a member of the Confucian tradition and his thought plays a most important role therein, his understanding and interpretation of the *Laozi* in his *Laozi yi* also makes him a relevant voice in the history of Daoist thought. The text has received intepretations from all sorts of traditions, especially in the Song-Ming period, and the complexities of Wang Dao's understanding cannot be overlooked when one tries to understand them properly (see Li 1997). This impact of Wang Dao on later thinkers and the appreciation of his problematizing of the *Laozi* is an important issue that will require further study.

Translated and edited by Mark Csikszentmihàlyi and Livia Kohn

Notes

1. Daoism in this context indicates what the Ming thinkers themselves understood by the term. For example, for the early Ming philosopher Liang Qian, it was the tradition of "emptiness, nonbeing, serenity, and ease," the basic substance of the "refinement of energy and the transformation of spirit," and a way to "summon the wind and the rain, order demons and spirits about, and pray for heat and cold" (*Po'anji* 3, "Donghui guanji"). That is, to him, Daoism encompassed three distinct areas, which can be described in modern terms as the thought of Laozi and Zhuangzi, the practice of alchemy and

longevity techniques, and various forms of interaction with the spirit world. For more on the Ming thinkers' understanding of Daoism, see Mabuchi 1998.

2. Among commentaries were notably the *Daxue yi* (Meaning of the Great Learning), *Zhouyi yi* (Meaning of the Book of Changes), *Shuyi* (Meaning of the Book of History), *Shiyi* (Meaning of the Book of Songs), and *Chunqiu yi* (Meaning of the Spring and Autumn Annals). Historical studies include the *Dushi lunduan* (Readings and Evaluations of History), *Daxue yanyi lunduan* (Readings and Evaluations Expanding on the Meaning of the Great Learning), *Pidian liuzi shu* (Critical Issues in the Writings of the Six Masters), as well as a certain number of shorter essays on the writings of Han Yu, Liu Zongyuan, Ouyang Xiu, and Su Shi.

3. In the passage here, Wang Dao refers to Laozi and Zhuangzi in the same breath, placing an equally high value on both. About the *Liezi*, on the other hand, he says that is was rather confused and not a good representative of the Dao, quite unlike the works of the other two early Daoist thinkers. See *Wenlu* 3, "Liezi."

4. One key passage on Buddhism is the letter to Zhou Daotong in *Wenlu* 7. In addition, he also criticizes the behavior and teaching methods of Mazu, as recorded in the "Transmission of the Lamp," calling him a "sinner of a perfected" (*Wenlu* 6, "Kanlin"). In contrast to this, he lauds Daoist immortality as a form of sagehood, and immortality methods as the way of the sages (3, "Yangzi") yet remains critical toward inner alchemical techniques, which he finds "full of delusion" (3, "Qiansui"). He also sees breathing exercises as a "lesser method" (4, "Yanzhou") and criticizes the obscure ways of using trigrams and alchemical ingredients to describe meditative processes as "no different from the magical ways of the world" (5, "Wuzhen"). Similar statements are also found in the commentary to chapter 10 in his *Laozi yi*.

5. Nonetheless, even the fallacy of the traditional Neo-Confucians, when seen from the perspective of the realized mind of the Dao, becomes but one "limb on the body of the sage." Ultimately, all ideas and methods "have their place, and none should be discarded" (*Wenlu* 3, "Chuanxi lu").

6. On the mind as the basic substance of the Dao in human beings, he also says: "The trigrams *qian* and *kun* may tumble, the world may end, but the deepest foundation of my pure, radiant enlightenment is bright forever and will alone survive" (*Wenlu* 5, "Daxue"). Again, he says: "Buddhists also have a doctrine of the end of the kalpa, yet even they claim that one's wonderful original enlightenment is there from the beginnings of all and will not end" (*Wenlu* 3, "Liezi"). Saying this, Wang develops a vision of eternal life beyond time and space.

7. A similar position, expounded in relation to official duty, is also found in the works of the late-Ming thinker Li Zhi, who criticized officials for imposing their personal notions of right and wrong on the populace (see Mizokuchi 1981, ch. 2), as well as in those of the Qing scholar Dai Zhen, who thought Confucian thinkers should pay closer attention to the benefits of others instead of only looking at their own personal feelings (Mizokuchi 1981, chs. 3–4).

8. In this and similar passages (e.g., *Wenlu* 6), Wang Dao contrasts the meth-

ods of Wang Yangming with the necessity to pursue the truth both within and without. However, as Mizuno (1980) has shown, Wang does not maintain this position firmly throughout his works.

9. In contrast to Zhu Xi's position, which claims that humans and other beings all share the same inner nature, Wang finds them completely different and claims that only humans have inner natures similar to those of other humans (see *Wenlu* 1, "Xingshuo"; 4, "Xingli"). See also Mabuchi 1990.

10. He also follows Xue Hui, author of the *Laozi jie* (Interpretation of the *Laozi*). Not a direct student of Wang Yangming and Chen Xianzhang, he is a thinker like Wang Dao who pursued a similar direction. Wang says about him: "Lord Xue's explanation of the *Laozi* is excellent, there is nothing quite as clear as his" (*Wenlu* 6, "Da Wei Zhuangqu"). See also Mabuchi 1998.

11. A different perspective is presented in *Wenlu* 6 ("Yangming"), where he criticizes Lu Jiuyuan, saying: "His teaching encourages empty, prideful, confused, and vain forms of learning; it does not have the beauty of leading back to what is central, proper, and peaceful." The expression "central and proper" also appears in the same chapter, section "Lun Xiangshan," where it describes the traces of Zhan Ruoshui's ideas.

Bibliography

Araki Kengo. 1972. *Mindai shisō kenkyū*. Tokyo: Sōbunsha.

Ching, Julia, ed. 1987. *The Records of Ming Scholars*. Honolulu: University of Hawai'i Press.

Li Qing. 1997. *"Mingdai de Laozi yanjiu."* *Gongo bunka ronsō* 1:279–306.

Mabuchi Masaya. 1990. *"Min-Shin jidai ni okeru jinseiron no tentaku to kyokō."* *Chūgoku tetsugaku kenkyu* 1:34–57.

———. 1994. *"Mindai kōki jugaku no dōkyō sesshu no ichi yōsō."* In *Dōkyō bunka e no tenbō*, ed. by Yamada Toshiaki, 99–128. Tokyo: Hirakawa.

———. 1998. *"Mindai goki jukyō shidaifu no dōkyō shoyū."* In *Dōkyō no rekishi to bunka,* ed. by Yamada Toshiaki and Tanaka Fumio, 275–296. Tokyo: Hirakawa.

Mizokuchi Yūsō. 1981. *Chūgoku zenkindai shisō no kussetsu to tenkai*. Tokyo: Yūzankaku.

Mizuno Minoru. 1979. *"Ō Junkyo no Daigaku oku ni tsuite."* *Firosofia* 67:93–121.

———. 1980. *"Ō Junkyo no kufū setsu."* *Chūgoku koten kenkyū* 25:149–169.

Qiao Qingquan. 1993. *Zhan Ruoshui zhexue sixian yanjiu*. Beijing: Wenjin.

Sakai Tadao. 1980. *Chūgoku zensho no kenkyū*. Tokyo: Kōbundō.

Sano Kōji. 1972. *"Mindai zenhan ni okeru shisō dōkō."* *Nihon Chūgoku gakkai hō* 26:112–126.

Part III
Lineages and Local Culture

7

Arms and the Dao, 2
The Xu Brothers in Tea Country

EDWARD L. DAVIS

Since the mid-1980s, many American and Japanese scholars of Daoism have begun to shift their attention from the period of Daoism's formative development in the late Han, Three Kingdoms, and Six Dynasties to the period when it became the religion of the court in the Tang, Song, and Ming dynasties. This shift in focus has brought with it another change. The pioneers in the systematic study of the early Daoist scriptural traditions were burdened by a legacy of prejudice and ignorance about the religion itself, which for decades, if not centuries, had been viewed as either a degenerate form of what is misleadingly called "philosophical Daoism" or a jumble of magic and popular superstition. It was, therefore, both necessary and understandable that these pioneers would focus, sometimes obsessively, on questions of Daoist identity and self-definition—what, exactly, was the Daoist religion, and how did it distinguish itself from the *Laozi* and *Zhuangzi,* on the one hand, and from village cults and popular religion, on the other? Thanks to these pioneers and many of their students, now leaders in the field, these questions have largely been answered, and a younger generation of scholars is able to revisit the relation of the Daoist religion to classical texts and popular cults without fear of reviving old prejudices.

For historians of middle-period China, when Daoism became something of an imperial religion that was made to serve, on occasion, dynastic ambitions or nativist projects, understanding its complex relationship with local temple-cults is of central importance. The old problem of the identity and self-definition of the Daoist religion, meanwhile, has been subsumed by a new set of questions. These concern the variety of identities and self-definitions of Daoist priests; their multiple functions in local and metropolitan society; their interaction with other religious practitioners, such as spirit-mediums, Buddhist monks, and Confucian literati; and the precise relation of their rituals to the festivals, processions, and theatrical performances of village and urban temple-cults.

This chapter examines some of these questions as part of my ongoing work on one such temple-cult that is often seen as existing within a Daoist framework. This is the cult to the Xu brothers in what we call

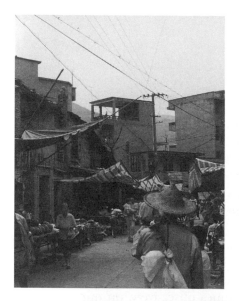

Figure 7.1. The Lingji gong in Qingpu today: its location near the local market, its gate, and its main altar, dedicated to the Xu brothers.

Minbei (Northern Fujian), but what the more localized consciousness of their contemporaries referred to as Minnan or Henan, that is, the southern portion of Min County across the river from the capital Fuzhou. The Xu brothers were two princes of the tenth-century kingdom of the Southern Tang who found themselves at the time of their deaths defending the rural population around Qingbu (modern Qingpu), a market-town twenty-three miles south of Fuzhou, where they are still actively venerated in their main temple, the Lingji gong (Palace of Spiritual Succor), today (see figure 7.1). For their efforts, Xu Zhizheng and Xu Zhi'e were worshiped in life as local heroes and in death as Daoist transcendents—the "Perfected Lords of Abundant Mercy and Spiritual Succor" (Hong'en lingji zhenjun). Temples were built for them on Aofeng (Turtle Peak), three miles to the east of Qingbu, and their cult flourished, especially in the Southern Song, Yuan, and early Ming dynasties, when the Yongle emperor had a replica of the Lingji gong built in the northwestern corner of the Forbidden City in his new capital of Beijing. Because of official and imperial patronage, thousands of pages of scripture, liturgies, and historical documents related to the cult received a prominent position in the Ming-dynasty Daoist canon. Among major historical compilations are the *Xuxian hanzao* (Elegant Writings of the Xu Immortals, HY 1456), the *Xuxian zhenlu* (True Record of the Xu Immortals, HY 1458), and the *Zanling ji* (Collection of Praise for the Numinous, HY 1457).[1]

The Perfected Lords: Between Region and Empire

In my earlier work on the Xu brothers (1985), I devoted my efforts to the explanation of the origin of their cult in Fujian and of the Yongle emperor's unprecedented attention to these obscure local gods. The first of these explanations seemed particularly demanding, since there is no evidence that the Xu brothers ever went to Fujian. Returning to my research after more than a decade, I am more convinced than ever of their absence from Fujian, as well as of my earlier explanation for their divinization in Min County. Disinherited by their family and disenfranchised from political power, these two Southern Tang princes became the cynosure for the aspirations of the landowners of rural Min County precisely at the time when Fuzhou and its environs were being ravaged by civil war and invasion and were absorbed within the Southern Tang state. Among these landowners' aspirations was the preservation of their hard work, because many of them had migrated to the region from the middle and lower Yangzi during the ninth and tenth centuries. Another was to harvest the fruits of their labor on a regional and ultimately national scale. One of the ways this was expressed was in the hagiographical revision of Southern Tang history, placing these marginalized princes at the very center of a state, the Southern Tang, that self-consciously viewed itself as the inheritor of the Tang ecumene and the guardians of a literary-aesthetic culture that would pass on to the Song. And one of the ways in which their aspirations were acted upon was by placing the cult to the Xu brothers at the center of the social order and examination success of rural Min County and by extending their fame through the combined efforts of local and bureaucratic co-regionalists from the Southern Song through the early Ming (see Davis 1985).[2]

Like the relation between *dao* and *fa*, or substance and function (*ti/yong*), the aspirations of these ninth- and tenth-century pioneers in Fujian remained latent until they congealed in the literary consciousness of several Southern Song lineages. This was a point I have made earlier with respect to the Xu brothers, almost as an afterthought (1985). Since then, Robert Hymes and others have driven this point home. In contrast to their Northern Song predecessors, members of the Southern Song elite derived status from their identity as local gentlemen based on strategies of local marriage, defense, and the patronage of local institutions (Hymes 1986, 210–214). The compelling conclusions of Hymes's study of the elite of southeastern Jiangxi are still being debated, and their implications for other regions of Southern-Song China have yet to be assessed (for a contrasting view, see Bossler 1998).

I prefer—and it is only a preference—to paint with a broader brush and would merely suggest that the land- and office-holding elite of the twelfth century finally had to come to terms with a brute fact whose possibility they had already anticipated with dread—a dynasty without an empire. While the provincial elite of the eleventh century could count on their links to the court to maintain their local status, those born at the end of the century could no longer be so confident. This does not mean, however, that the provincial elites of the Southern Song merely substituted horizontal ties for vertical ones. Rather, it means that in a world of shrinking horizons, new links to the transcendent had to be forged out of local institutions—shrines, abbeys, monasteries, and academies. This is true also of the beleaguered court, which to reconstitute itself had now to pay tribute to these same local sources of transcendence. Such, anyway, is one way to read the sharp incline of titles granted to local gods and religious institutions by the court (see Hansen 1990, ch. 4).

There is certainly evidence that the literary and institutional impresarios of the cult to the Xu brothers were members of the local elite in southern Min County from the twelfth century on. The construction of the first "Patriarchal Temple" (*zumiao*) in the late tenth century is identified with a landlord named Fang Jue, and succeeding generations of his descendants organized the institutional and ideological expansion of the cult (*Xuxian zhenlu* 1.6; *Xuxian hanzao* 1.2a, 1.6b). Nine individual Fangs are named, and their activities center on the late twelfth, the first and second halves of the fourteenth, and the early fifteenth centuries.[3] Two members of another lineage, Zhou Yue and Zhou Sui, whose ancestors and descendants were also linked to the cult, picked up the slack in the thirteenth century.[4] The Zhou and the Fang are not the only landed families involved by any means, but they are the ones whose prominence is consistently revealed over the centuries.

While the identity and role of the Zhou lineage will be, as we shall see, easier to account for, the Fangs appear nowhere else but in the literary legacy of the cult to the Xu brothers. With a little armchair legwork, I have come up with one hypothesis as to their provenance.

The Fangs of Putian

In Putian, Xinghua Commandary, a couple days' journey south of Fuzhou, a large lineage named Fang was flourishing in the Southern Song. We know about it—or rather, about the most important of its three branches, the "Purple-Robed Fangs" (Zhuzi Fang)—from the genealogical essays of one of its members, Fang Dacong (1183–1247), an early-thirteenth-century "presented scholar," one of three in his generation alone (*Tie'an ji* 31, 32). These essays were the literary accompaniment to Fang Dacong's reconstruction of the ancestral "Sacrificial Hall" (*citang*)—or what is now called a "Sacrificial Hall"— near the suburban residences of the Fang lineage on Wushi shan (Blackstone Mountain).[5] This temple, which was actually a Buddhist merit cloister, was dedicated to the six tenth-century sons of the founding ancestor of the Purple-Robed Fangs and appears to have fallen into disuse and disrepair. The reconstructed Sacrificial Hall now became the focus of the ancestral rites of all branches of the Fang lineage, placing as it did a first-century Fang named Fang Hong at the apex of an ancestral tree in which the Purple-Robed Fangs constituted the trunk (*Tie'an ji* 32). By 1269, it is said, several thousand Fangs were annually attending the ancestral rites here (*Houcun xiansheng quanji* 161).

We can certainly find in the activities of the Purple-Robed Fangs some of the localist strategies Robert Hymes has identified among the elite of southeastern Jiangxi, especially the preference for marriages within a circumscribed region and social circle. But even here, as the historian Kobayashi Yoshihiro has discovered, the Purple-Robed Fangs showed a marked preference for those families that had as much literary and bureaucratic success as they had (Kobayashi 1995, 508–511). By the time of Fang Dacong, the three descendant groups of his lineage could boast more than 120 officials since the late Tang dynasty and approximately 60 living degree-holders, no doubt nurtured in the schools, the lecture halls, and the library of 40,000 volumes that the lineage maintained throughout the eleventh and twelfth centuries (Kobayashi 1995, 517). Along with their charitable lands, the thirteenth-century Fangs of Putian more closely resembled the Northern-Song Fangs of suburban Suzhou. The Sacrificial Hall was meant to top off two centuries of examination success, bureaucratic office, and literary accomplishment, goals quite explicitly celebrated in the sources as *the* strategy of the Fang lineage. The Sacrificial Hall, in fact, was precisely one of those local religious institutions through which a larger vision was maintained. It celebrated not merely the Fangs' role in an imperial system but also quite explicitly a family tradition of seeking and occupying high positions in the censorate, of steadfastly opposing the appeasement policies of the eleventh and twelfth centuries, and, throughout, of speaking the "plain truth," as they put it, to the powerful (Kobayashi 1995, 507–508).

In one of Fang Dacong's genealogical essays, he mentions very briefly the other two branches of his lineage—the Baidu pai and the Fangshan pai. I am interested in the latter, the Fangs of Fang Mountain. According to Dacong's brief notice, these Fangs, before they took up literary pursuits, moved from the city of Putian to the villages around Wushi shan and from there—still, perhaps, in the tenth century—"away in other directions" (*Tie'an ji* 32.3.ll3–6). Fangshan was in Min County, sixty-four miles north of Putian. This range, which became known as Wuhu shan (Five Tiger Mountain) in the Qing and is so designated on maps today, sits on an east–west axis parallel to the river that separates Fuzhou from southern Min County (*Mindu ji* 14.14–15). In the hagiography of the Xus it is identified as one of the Sanshan Three Mountains—the famous appellation by which the region around Fuzhou was known. More importantly, the Xu brothers refer to themselves as the tutelary spirits of Fangshan, the eastern portion of which includes Aofeng, the exact site of their Patriarchal Temple and of the Lingji gong (*Xuxian hanzao* 2.11a, 3.1a). Now, if the impresarios of this temple-cult, the "South-of-the-River Fangs" (Henan Fangshi), were descendants of the Fangshan Fangs, as some believe they were (see Clart 1998),[6] some interesting conclusions can be drawn.

The Perfected Lords: Between Elites and Commoners

The Xu brothers of the Lingji gong were the patrons, among other things, of a tradition of primary school education established south of the river since the end of the Tang dynasty, a tradition that had allowed even peasants and artisans to aspire to scholarship and culture. This tradition culminated in the "Hall of Purification" (*zhaitang*), a Confucian lecture hall within Lingji gong (*Xuxian hanzao* 1.16b–19a). While peasants and artisans were certainly free to come here and be purified by philosophy, it is clear that the local elite made greater use of it. And none benefited more from its use than the Fangs. In 1198 and again a few years later, the South-of-the-River Fangs produced their first and second "presented scholars"—Fang Jie and Fang Ce, respectively—and their success is directly attributed to the patronage of the Xu brothers following a session of "dream divination" (*mengbu*) (*Xuxian hanzao* 1.3a–b).

Now, what appears to be a common example of the elite practice of "temple incubation" from the twelfth century would become, and perhaps already was, something else entirely. The relationship between the supernatural patrons of the Lingji gong and their clients, the residents of the twenty-odd villages around Aofeng and not just the Fangs, was one of unabashed mediumism. It was not exactly the spirit-possession of the "divination youths" (*tongji*) of village Fujian, nor was it exactly the visionary transmission of texts of the lower gentry around fourth-century Maoshan, but something in between, sharing characteristics of both. Its primary mechanism was the "phoenix basket" (*luanji*), the planchette, or sand table, on which the invoked spirits spell out a message (*Zanling ji* 1a). The first account dates from 955: "The Perfected Lords lowered the brush (*jiangbi*), marking talismanic remedies to help people, and news of this spread far and wide" (*Xuxuan zhenlu* 1.30a). This is only ten years after the death of the Xu brothers, purportedly at Aofeng, and twenty-eight years before Fang Jue sponsored what would become known as the "Ancestral Temple of Spiritual Succor" (Lingji zongmiao), suggesting that the composers of one of these texts' prefaces were correct in identifying the origin of temple worship in a village spirit-medium cult (*congci*) (*Zanling ji* 1.4a). Subsequent descriptions of it waver between divination (*bu*) and possession (*pingfu*), depending on the passage, but it was this mechanism that produced everything from the graded doggerel based on the sixty-four hexagrams (*qianshi*) through linked verse and prose poems to the encomia, exorcistic writs, liturgical documents, stelae, and all the historical records of the temple complex itself. The fourteen volumes and five hundred printed pages of the *Xuxian hanzao* is nothing but the literary residue of these mediumistic sessions, at various degrees of remove and refinement to be sure, but always self-consciously spoken in, and interrupted by, the first-person pronoun of the gods.

I will not trouble with the niceties of this process, which would require a difficult and tedious analysis of the textual language. The supernatural and terrestrial producers of this discourse, some of it inscribed in stone before printed on paper, do not seem troubled by it, though they do feel the need for a justification. What they want to justify, however, is not the process itself, but rather its suitability for public consumption. To do so they must search for a literary precedent, and they find it in an epigraphic genre first introduced to the literati world by the spirit of Liu Zongyuan (773–819): inscriptions on the reverse side of funerary tablets (*beiyin*). The textual reproduction of the Xu brothers' own "reverse tablet" is preceded by a discussion of the practice, which the editors of the *Xuxian hanzao* distinguish from those tablets that record such things as music, moral learning, history, mourning, and biography (1.9a–10a). The contrast drawn is between tablets by living descendants to commemorate the dead and reverse tablets that were intended, quite literally, to embody and prolong a personal relationship after death. The subtext of this difficult passage is, first, Liu Zongyuan's own composition of a reverse tablet for a reclusive monk and, second, the reverse tablet marking Liu's own tomb, in which he or his spirit identified the names of his disciples and clients (his "fellows") (*Liu Zongyuan quanji*, chs. 6, 7, and supplement).

The problem that is being addressed by both text and subtext is the persistence of nonaffinal, hierarchical relationships such as those between a master and disciple or patron and client. Having identified a precedent, the editors of the *Xuxian hanzao* feel no need to elaborate: "Since Liu [Zi-]hou," they say, "there have been reverse tablets; since the Xu [Immortals], Princes of the Yangzi, have begun [to do the same], who dares argue with this?" (1.10a). In the reverse tablet of the

Xu brothers, the gods only hope that they will be blessed with disciples who have half the talent of Liu Zongyuan and of the chronicler of Liu's temple-cult, none other than HanYu (768–830) (*Xuxian hanzao* 1.10a–b). Who dares to argue, indeed!

The vast literary output of the Xu brothers was a product of the thirteenth, fourteenth, and early fifteenth centuries, a period that broadly coincides with the very public patronage of the Zhou and Fang lineages. The members of these lineages, who are specifically identified as the benefactors and press agents of the cult, were not, however, the ones responsible for this literary output. This was the work of a wider array of residents of Jishan li, the administrative unit that comprised several villages on or around Aofeng. Amazingly, we have all the names of these villagers and rural gentlemen (*cunren, liren, xiangren*), though a few may have belonged to the Zhou lineage in particular. From a maze of cross-references I can identify at least two groups, defined by their activities. One group of seven individuals, representing seven surnames, was responsible for those mediumistic sessions that resulted in the historical records of the gods and their temple complex (*Xuxian hanzao* 1.19ab, 8.1a–3a). Another group of five individuals represents four surnames, three of which overlap with surnames of the first group. This second group of five formed a kind of club or society— what in secular sources might be called a *rushe.* Their sessions produced a lot of poetry. They were given floral titles: "Fellow Plum," "Fellow Bamboo," "Fellow Orchid, "Fellow Pine," and "Fellow Chrysanthemum" (*Xuxian hanzao* 5.4ab).[7] This group was also in charge of the "kitchens" (*chu*) of the gods, village feasts that have an ancient history (*Xuxian hanzao* 5.3a–4b, 6.1a–b; see Stein 1971; also Feuchtwang 1992, 85–87).

The temple also appears to have been the center of other literati activities, including painting, *Yijing* studies, Buddhism, and geomancy (*Xuxian hanzao* 6.1b–4b, 6.5b–7a), but the Lingji gong was what we would identify as a "community temple" and not a temple-cult that appealed exclusively to the local elite. The gods responded to the needs and requests of the commoner households of Jishan (*Xuxian hanzao* 5.5a). These are recorded in loving detail and were often the occasion for lengthy memorials. Moving beyond personal requests, we see that the peasants, artisans, and petty merchants of Jishan participated together with the elite in confessional and votive ceremonies that defined and reinforced a rigid social and occupational hierarchy, even as they envisioned a rural order of benign paternalism and harmony. We have the texts of these communal rites (*Xuxian zhenlu* 2.16–43; *Hou-*

cun xiansheng daquan ji), which need to be compared with what we know about the rural order and ideology that was evolving in the Yuan and early Ming dynasties. Looking ahead, these texts embody the world into which the first Ming ruler Zhu Yuanzhang very much wanted to tap with his system of tax captains. Looking back, they are exemplary of the vision condensed in the great Neo-Confucian Zhu Xi's feeble blueprint for rural compacts (Hymes and Shirokauer 1993, 22–25).

Moving beyond these rites, we can also see that the Lingji gong served as the structuring center for the religious and liturgical traditions of the entire region south of the river. Large-scale multivillage "offerings" (*jiao*) were performed here (Luotian jiao, Huanglu jiao, and Yulanpen hui/Ullambana) for the legions of hungry ghosts (*Xuxian hanzao* 11.1a–8a, 11.8a–16b, 11.26a–34b). Exorcistic rituals directed against the many infectious diseases of this subtropical region have roots deep in the past of Chinese and non-Han Fujian, as do the special rituals for women, the Xuepen hui (Bloodpool Gatherings), which reveal themselves here in a largely Buddhist framework (*Xuxian hanzao* 4.7b–14b, 11.16b–19b; see Seaman 1981). The relation, in fact, between the Lingji gong and the Buddhist institutions of the region is profound and complex. Within its purview was drawn a Buddhist Yuqing tang (Hall of Blessings), presided over by Dingguang fo (Skt.: Dīpimkara; Ch.: Randeng), the most important Buddha among commoners in Fujian and a significant object of worship in Jiangxi and Zhejiang as well. Here he is called "The Holy Lord in White Clothing, Dingguang of Mount Pangu" (Baiyi shenggong Pangu Dingguang) (*Xuxian hanzao* 1.20a–22b).[8] The Xu brothers, in fact, claimed a special relationship with this Buddha, as clients to patron, just as the literati and literate clients of the Xu brothers maintained an ongoing intellectual and social relationship with the Chan monks of the region.[9]

In all this I have barely touched on the diverse ways in which the many temple-cults of the region were drawn into the religious orbit of the Lingji gong and Patriarchal Temple.[10] For the moment let me underscore the fact that the complex religious structure I have adumbrated formed the base from which the Zhou and Fang launched their campaign to bring their supernatural patrons to the attention of provincial and metropolitan officials. This campaign was wildly successful, in part, I believe, because the law of avoidance did not apply to Fujian. What this meant, of course, was that if one sought the ear of a prefect, that ear often belonged to a relative. This was particularly the case with respect to the Zhou, who counted many officials and "presented scholars" among their numbers. However, even the lesser Fangs could be assured that their well-placed connection hailed from Min County. In Fujian, the bureaucratic and the personal were not in opposition (Hymes 1997, 130).

The Fangs of Min County

When we examine the role that the Lingji gong played in the lineage consciousness of the Fang and the Zhou, we might say that it functioned much like the Sacrificial Hall did for the Purple-Robed Fangs of Putian. This analogy is intended to suggest that the former were seeking an alternative way to distinguish themselves from their increasingly hegemonic cousins in Putian, who, by the way, had instituted a series of tomb sacrifices from which the throngs attending the Sacrificial Hall were excluded. In this scenario the Fangs of Min County were acting like the second, Baidu branch of the Putian Fangs, who devoted their ritual efforts to the patronage of the gods of the Xiangying miao (Auspicious Response Temple) in Putian, despite the inclusive claims of the Sacrificial Hall (Dean 1993, 35–37; 1998b, 27–28).[11] However, even if the Fangs of Min County were quite conscious of the ritual activities of their relatives farther south, they also had competitors much closer to home. At the end of the Song and beginning of the Yuan dynasties, a second-generation disciple of Zhu Xi named Xiong Qufei had built the Aofeng shutang (Turtle Peak Study Hall), in which he taught and worshiped before images of the "Five Worthies of the Orthodox Transmission of the Dao," whose names I need not enumerate (*Minzhong lixue yuanyuan kao* 37.4a–9a). No one in Xiong's circle had anything to do with the Xu brothers, and vice versa. The Fangs of Min County, as we have seen, had their own orthodox transmission, so to speak, which derived from Liu Zongyuan and Han Yu.

At the very least, then, we can conclude that the three descent groups of the Fang lineage in Minbei constructed their identity along very different lines. And where the Purple-Robed Fangs supplemented their annual celebrations at the Sacrificial Hall with a tomb-cult to the pioneer ancestors of their descent group, which seemed only to emphasize their hegemony over the former, the Fangs of Fang Mountain turned to the "death site" of two other immigrants to Fujian to serve as stand-ins for their own pioneering ancestors and as foci for the accomplishments and aspirations of their own descent group. The analogy between the temple-cult to the Xu brothers and a cult to ancestors is strengthened by the fact that in the thirteenth century the cult to the Xu brothers absorbed the nearby temple-cult to an actual pioneering ancestor, Weng Chengzan, a man who had come to Aofeng in the late ninth century and was recognized as the one responsible for converting the area to productive use (*Xuxian hanzao* 1.30–31; see Davis 1985, 48).[12]

Now, if the patronage of the Xu brothers was analogous to an ancestor cult, we might entertain the notion that it also represented an alternative way of constructing such a cult, and a way that was more in tune with the popular tradition of Fujian. Too much is often made of the categorical distinctions between gods, ghosts, and ancestors. In Fujian, at least, whose history can be traced in the single and multi-surname settlements of Chinese immigrants since the Han dynasty, the cult to gods and the cult to ancestors were often conflated. This combination of temple (*simiao*) and ancestral hall (*jiaci*)—a persistent characteristic of many areas of Fujian from the Song through the Late Imperial and even Republican periods—was designated in genealogies as "household temples" (*jiamiao*). They were dedicated either to one of the several salvific deities characteristic of Fujian (Mazu, Guanyin, Baosheng dadi, Qingshui zushi, etc.) or to an ancestor identified as a celestial emperor or lord (e.g., Wu[xing] dadi), but in both cases the temple might also include altars to other ancestors. Other, more complex forms of combining territorial and ancestral cults were to be found in multisurname settlements (Lin and Peng 1993, 38–46). In Fujian, moreover, commoners regarded the most significant pre-Song temple-cults—to the three divinities of Mount Wuyi, for example, or to the four rulers of the early Han kingdom of Min-Yue—as both protectors and founding ancestors (Xu 1993, 141–160). These gods had secured the peace and prosperity of Northern Fujian while guaranteeing its independence, such that the people of Fujian could absorb and enjoy the benefits of the civilization of the Central Plain on their own terms. The Fangs, too, were expressing their own lineage consciousness through two gods that had protected Min County from internal tyrants and invading states, that had made the region safe for landownership and study, and that had allowed these landlords and their studious descendants to make a serious mark on the larger world without having to give up their own. As such, the cult to the Xu brothers allowed this descent goup and others like them to negotiate, on the one hand, between the local and the global and, on the other, between the perspective of the commoners who worked for them and the perspective of their elite cousins who excluded them.

This said, we must nonetheless insist that the temple-cult to the Xu brothers was not a "household temple," nor for that matter should it be referred to as a Daoist temple or abbey. It was a community temple that served the illiterate peasants and petty merchants of the region as much as the literate commoners and self-conscious descent groups such as the Fang and Zhou. All strata, moreover, participated in the large-scale rituals performed at the temples by Daoist priests and Buddhist monks. And if it were the literati of the area who "composed" the commemorations of these rituals or even gathered in exclusive groups to perform their own, they did so in ways that were nothing but more-refined versions of the mediumism of their less-educated co-regionalists. That such commemorations achieved such a prominent place in the Daoist canon, along with a vast array of historical and Daoist liturgical texts, should not distract us from the largely ecumenical identity of the temple-cult.

Notes

1. Liturgical texts include HY 468–475, while divination texts include HY 1291–1292. The Lingji gong on Aofeng has been under reconstruction since 1976, while the Lingji xinggong (Auxiliary Palace of Spiritual Succor) in the Forbidden City no longer survives. For evidence that the cult to the Xu brothers persists in some fashion on Taiwan as well, see Banck 1985, 191–192. The cult to the Xu brothers is discussed briefly in Boltz 1987, 91–93, 195–197; Lagerwey 1987, 260–264. See also Xu 1993; Liu and Peng 1993 on Fujianese religion.

Other original sources include: *Houcun xiansheng daquan ji* by Liu Kezhuang (1187–1269), ed. *Sibu congkan* 69–70 (HY 474); *Liu Zongyuan quanji*, ed. Guangzhi shuju in Guangzhou; *Mindu ji*, compiled by Wang Yingshan in 1612; *Minzhong lixue yuanyuan kao* by Li Qingfu, dat. 18th c., ed. *Siku quanshu zhenben erji* 131–136; and *Tie'an ji* by Fang Dacong (1183–1247), ed. *Siku quanshu zhenben erji* 305–306.

2. Xu tentatively suggests that the cult to the Xu brothers derived from, or was modeled on, a cult in northwestern Fujian to two other generals of the southern Tang named Zhang and Chen (1993, 193–194). I would argue, rather, that the contemporaneity of the two cults and the similarities pointed out by Xu suggest that the cult to Zhang and Chen, like the cult to the Xu brothers, should be understood as a creative response to the Southern Tang's absorption of northern Fujian.

3. Fang Xun, Fang Xian, and Fang Zhong for the late twelfth; Fang Zhuangyou, Fang Fengwu, and Fang Ciweng for the early fourteenth; Fang Huan and Fang Wen for the late fourteenth; and Fang Wenzhao for the early fifteenth centuries.

4. Zhou Ruli for the eleventh; Zhou Yi, Zhou Shixiu, and Zhou Chong for

the late twelfth; and Zhou Dinglai, Zhou Yue, and Zhou Sui for the thirteenth centuries.

5. See *Houcun xiansheng quanji* 93. Liu Kezhuang's son was married to a daughter of Fang Dacong's brother, just as Liu himself was married to women of two lineages, the Chen and the Lin, who customarily provided wives for the Fangs. The Purple-Robed Fangs are a good example of the Southern Song's "national elite" as described by Bossler 1998, 204.

6. Hugh Clark, who is working on the Fangs of Putian among other descent groups, assures me that they were, though I have yet to see the document that confirms this. In the meantime, see Clark 1998.

7. See also *Xuxian hanzao* 6.1ab for a short meditation on the meaning of "fellowship" and on the Confucian symbolism of their floral titles. Helen Siu (1990) describes one such elite social club from late-imperial Guangdong. The Chrysanthemum Festival in Xiaolan in the Pearl River Delta involved floral displays, drinking, and poetry competitions. It was held in front of an ancestral hall and formed an elite supplement and counterpoint to the *jiao*-offerings performed at the community temples, in which the elite also participated, but which were open to all. The floral displays and poetry competitions were closely related: "These poetry couplets centered on Tao Yuanming, a fourth-century official who retired to the life of a hermit in his chrysanthemum gardens because he refused to serve another master at a time of rapid dynastic transition" (Siu 1990, 777). This might warrant an interpretation of the festival as a confirmation of the identity of the participants as "local gentlemen." As Helen Siu points out:

> The chrysanthemum, together with the plum, orchid, and bamboo, was a popular topic of artistic representation among scholars in Xiaolan and elsewhere. Since the Song period, the flower was seen as expressing the ideals of the hermit, the elevated distance of the scholar from mundane political affairs. However, retreat continued to affirm attachment to the imperial order. Participation in literati culture, even at a distance from the court, was an important asset in local politics, where the authority of the imperial bureaucracy was often brought to bear. (1990, 777–778)

In other words, the symbolic capital of the floral symbol, its linking of the user to a literati culture that extended far in time and space, trumped the content of the symbol and could bring its users influence with the magistrate and other officials, as Siu demonstrates, because these also recognized the value of such symbols. The same might be said for elite patronage of cults to immortals, which had come to form an integral part of high literati culture since the Six Dynasties. For a well-argued alternative viewpoint, see Hymes 1997.

8. These titles refer to facts in the life of Zheng Zichan, who was thought to be the last incarnation of the Buddha Dingguang fo. Zheng was born in Tong'an County in 934. In 1004 he moved to Mount Pangu in Nankang, Jiangxi, where he became the abbot of a Chan cloister. While there he was also thought to have fulfilled a prophecy concerning the appearance of a "white-clothed bodhisattva." See Lin and Peng 1993, 281–293. The authors

also present a short, but quite commendable, introduction to the Xu brothers (1993, 204–216). For the most recent, in-depth study of the cult to Dingguang fo, see Lagerwey 1998.

9. Dingguang fo, along with another prominent god of the region, the Great Emperor of the Eastern Peak, memorialized the Jade Emperor in the early months of 995, bringing to the latter's attention the meritorious deeds of the Xu brothers. As a result, the Jade Emperor granted the Xu brothers the titles "Perfected Lord of the Jade Portal" and "Perfected Lord of the Golden Portal," titles that were actually conferred on them during the performance of a Yellow Register Retreat later that same year, i.e., 995 (*Xuxian zhenlu* 1). The prominent role of Dingguang fo is subsequently reflected in the *Hong'en lingji zhenjun miaojing* (HY 317), a fifteenth-century text.

10. See *Xuxian zhenlu* 1.8a for an indication of the geographical extent of this orbit. These temple-cults, the result of a "division" or "borrowing" of incense, are discussed at length in Davis 1985, 17–21, citing *Xuxian zhenlu* 1.7: "Each year the elders would escort the gods [of these temples] to have an audience in the Ancestral Temple [of Spiritual Succor]. They would sacrifice and hold *zhai* to demonstrate that they had not forgotten their origin." This clearly refers to the processions on the anniversaries of the Perfected Lords when the large-scale *jiao*, mentioned above, would be performed by Daoist priests and Buddhist monks.

11. A *Xiangying miaoji* (Record of the Temple of Auspicious Response) was composed in 1138, after the completion of a major restoration, by two officials of the Baidu line, Fang Lue and Fang Zhao. The Xiangying miao was also known as the "Temple to the Great Official," whom Dean, following Hugh Clark, has tentatively identified with Fang Jun, an eleventh-century "presented scholar" of the Baidu Fangs (Dean 1998b, 27–28*n*23).

12. Aofeng was also the site, in 1600 and 1637, of two successive Three-in-One temples, for which see Dean 1998a, 131, 134–135.

Bibliography

Banck, Werner. 1985. *Das Chinesische Tempelorakel, II*. Wiesbaden, Germany: Harrassowitz.

Boltz, Judith M. 1987. *A Survey of Taoist Literature: Tenth to Seventeenth Centuries*. Berkeley: Institute of East Asian Studies, China Research Monograph 32.

Bossler, Beverly. 1998. *Powerful Relations: Kinship, Status, and the State in Sung China*. Cambridge: Harvard University Press.

Clark, Hugh. 1998. "The Development of the Ancestral Offering Hall in the Kinship Tradition of Minnan (Southern Fujian) in the 10th–13th Centuries, and the Family Rituals of Zhu Xi." Paper Presented at the Annual Meeting of the Association of Asian Studies, Washington, D.C.

Davis, Edward L. 1985. "Arms and the Tao, 1: Hero Cult and Empire in Traditional China." In *Sōdai no shakai to shūkyō*, ed. by Sōdai kenkyūkai, 1–56. Tokyo: Kyūko shoin.

Dean, Kenneth. 1993. *Taoist Ritual and Popular Cults of Southeast China*. Princeton: Princeton University Press.

————. 1998a. *The Lord of the Three-in-One: The Spread of a Cult in Southeast China.* Princeton: Princeton University Press.

————. 1998b. "Transformations of the *She* (Altars of the Soil) in Fujian." *Cahiers d'Extrême-Asie* 10:19–75.

Feuchtwang, Stephan. 1992. *The Imperial Metaphor: Popular Religion in China.* London: Routledge.

Hansen, Valerie. 1990. *Changing Gods in Medieval China, 1127–1276.* Princeton: Princeton University Press.

Hymes, Robert. 1986. *Statesmen and Gentlemen: The Elite of Fu-Chou, Chiang-Hsi, in Northern and Southern Sung.* Cambridge: Cambridge University Press.

————. 1997. "A *Jiao* Is a *Jiao* Is a ? Thoughts on the Meaning of Ritual." In *Culture & State in Chinese History: Conventions, Accomodations, and Critiques,* ed. by Theodore Huters, R. Bin Wong, and Pauline Yü. Stanford: Stanford University Press.

Hymes, Robert, and Conrad Shirokauer, eds. 1993. *Ordering the World: Approaches to State and Society in Sung Dynasty China.* Berkeley: University of California Press.

Kobayashi Yoshihiro. 1995. "Sōdai Fukken Pūten no Hōshi ichizoku ni tsuite." In *Chūgoku chūseishi kenkyū zokuhen,* ed. by Chūgoku chūseishi kenkyūkai, 503–526. Kyoto: Kyōto daigaku gakushu shuppankai.

Lagerwey, John. 1987. *Taoist Ritual in Chinese Society and History.* New York: Macmillan.

————. 1998. "*Dingguang gufo:* Oral and Written Sources in the Study of a Saint." *Cahiers d'Extrême-Asie* 10:77–129.

Lin Guoping and Peng Wenyu. 1993. *Fujian minjian xinyang.* Fuzhou: Fujian renmin.

Seaman, Gary. 1981. "The Sexual Politics of Karmic Retribution." In *The Anthropology of Taiwanese Society,* ed. by Emily Ahern and Hill Gates, 381–396. Stanford: Stanford University Press.

Siu, Helen. 1990. "Recycling Tradition: Culture, History, and Political Economy in the Chrysanthemum Festivals in South China." In *Comparative Studies in Society and History* 32.4:765–794.

Stein, Rolf A. 1971. "Les fêtes du cuisine du taoïsme religieux." *Annuaire du Collège de France* 71:431–440.

Xu Xiaowang. 1993. *Fujian minjian xinyang yuanliu.* Fuzhou: Fujian jiaoyu.

8

Identity and Lineage
The *Taiyi jinhua zongzhi*
and the Spirit-Writing Cult
to Patriarch Lü in Qing China

MORI YURIA

The *Taiyi jinhua zongzhi* (Great Unity's Instructions on [Developing] Golden Florescence), ever since its translation by Richard Wilhelm and C. G. Jung under the title *The Secret of the Golden Flower* (1929), has been one of the best-known Chinese religious classics in the West. However, as Daoist historical studies grew, it received less attention from scholars, because they tended to concentrate more on the formative period of the religion in the middle ages. Also, the text was thought spurious. As the late Dr. Anna Seidel remarked, "The text of this movement [of inner alchemy] translated by Richard Wilhelm is unfortunately of a rather recent date and of doubtful transmission" (1995, 26–27).

However, this is not entirely true if one takes the trouble to look at the editions and transmission of the text within the activities of popular religious cults in Qing China. The fact that the text is of comparatively recent date makes it interesting for an entirely different area of Daoist studies, and its religious role can be better understood, especially in the light of Monica Esposito's recent analysis of extant versions and their lines of transmission (1998). She explored the following six texts:

1. *Xiantian xuwu taiyi jinhua zongzhi* (Instructions on [Developing] Golden Florescence by the Great Unity of Former Heaven, Emptiness and Nonbeing). In *Lüzu quanshu* (Complete Collection of Patriarch Lü), edited by Shao Zhilin, 1775.
2. *Fuyou shangdi tianxian jinhua zongzhi* (Instructions on [Developing] Golden Florescence by the Celestial Immortal, the Highest Lord Fuyou). In *Quanshu zhengzong* (Complete Collection of the Orthodox Lineage), edited by Jiang Yupu, 1803.

3. *Xiantian xuwu taiyi jinhua zongzhi*. In *Lüzu quanshu zongzheng*
   (Complete Collection of the Orthodox Lineage of Patriarch Lü),
   edited by Chen Mou, 1852.
4. *Jinhua zongzhi*. In *Daozang jiyao* (Repository of the Daoist Canon),
   edited by Jiang Yupu, ca. 1796–1819.
5. *Lüzu shi xiantian xuwu taiyi jinhua zongzhi*. In *Daozang xubian*
   (Supplement to the Daoist Canon), edited by Min Yide (1758–
   1836), 1834.
6. *Changsheng shu* (Book of Long Life), originally entitled *Taiyi
   jinhua zongzhi*. In *Changsheng shu xuming fang hekan* (Integrated
   Edition of the Book of Long Life and Its Longevity Techniques),
   edited by Dan Ranhui, 1921.

Through comparison of these texts, Esposito has shown that the *Jinhua zongzhi* was first formed as a spirit-writing scripture in the Jingming
(Pure Brightness) tradition and was subsequently accepted by several
different sects (see Esposito 1996; 1998a; 1998b). The lines of transmission of the text can be clearly asserted by tracing various factors
that were eliminated—or added—at the various stages of acceptance.
As a result, it becomes evident that the text was appropriated in a rather
disrespectful manner from one sect to another. They each tried to
make use of the text as proof for their own legitimacy, showing that it
had come down in none other but their tradition or lineage. This appropriation of the text implies not only the presence of a common
need for a unifying and legitimating document among these sects, but
also the existence of common structure to their faith. Interestingly,
the sects involved in the appropriation of the *Jinhua zongzhi* were also
deeply engaged in spirit-writing, and especially spirit-writing linked
with Lüzu, Patriarch Lü, the poet and immortal Lü Dongbin (see
Baldrian-Hussein 1986).

The following discussion of the text will present the process of
formation of several of its versions, concentrating on the way each
sect represented the relationship between Lüzu and themselves
through spirit-writing. This then, it is hoped, will shed a little light
on the ways in which spirit-writing functioned, or at least was expected to function, in each sect that used it to assert its legitimacy. I
will begin by focusing on the formation of Shao Zhilin's version, then
examine the development of Jiang Yupu's text, and finally look at
Min Yide's edition as contained in his *Gu shuyinlou cangshu* (Collected
Books from the Ancient Pavilion) and in the *Daozang xubian* listed
earlier.[1]

The Formation of Shao Zhilin's Version

The oldest extant version of the *Jinhua zongzhi* is the text included in *juan* 49 of the sixty-four-*juan* version of the *Lüzu quanshu*, edited by Shao Zhilin in 1775, a revised and enlarged edition of the thirty-two-*juan* version, prefaced by Liu Tishu in 1742. The *Jinhua zongzhi* is not included in the latter, but Shao Zhilin's version contains fifteen prefaces, two appendices, and one postface (see Mori 1998a, note 5; Esposito 1998, 93–94).

Through these prefaces, we can trace the formation of the text. As half of them were eliminated from most later versions, they undoubtedly give the most important extant account of the formation of the *Jinhua zongzhi*. According to them, around 1666 there was a group of at least seven participants who came together at the spirit-writing altar of Zhou Yehe in Piling (Changzhou, Jiangsu). There, Lüzu descended, together with the ancient patriarchs of the Quanzhen (Complete Perfection) school, Tan Changzhen and Qiu Changchun, and two years later the revelation of the *Jinhua zongzhi* began. At this time the altar was said to be located in the Bailong jingshe (White Dragon Chapel) in Piling. This is probably the same place as Zhou's altar, but there are no records that explicitly make the identification. At first, the revealed characters could not be decoded, so the seven members requested further explanations from Lüzu, to which the immortal responded. Pan Yi'an describes how the members gathering at Zhou's altar developed Lüzu's spirit-writing:

> As I remember, it was in the *wushen* year [1668] that our holy patriarch Chunyang [i.e., Lüzu] began to transmit the "Instructions." The seven people who made a commitment [to Lü] bowed deeply and obtained [his teachings]. None but these seven were given this transmission. The most profound teaching was [expressed in] no more than one or two words. It could not be put into words and letters. Afterwards, the seven questioned [Lü] in detail. As our holy patriarch spared no mercy in giving clarifications, [his teachings were] compiled for days and months. Eventually they composed a volume. (*Lüzu quanshu* 49, pref. 9a)

Through such communication between the members and the deity, the text was gradually compiled over a period of months (see Mori 1998a, 45–47). According to Shiga (1999), who studies spirit-writing cults in contemporary Hong Kong, the founders of the Xinshan tang, an altar community also centered on the spirit-writing of Lüzu, had a similar experience in 1935. They, too, initially could not understand the characters the immortal drew and had to ask him for an interpretation. Thus they were gradually trained to understand his teachings (Shiga 1999, 214).

Although all questions from disciples have been omitted in the extant versions of the *Jinhua zongzhi*, we can still find some passages that bear the marks of a question-and-answer situation, especially when the immortal patiently explains teachings he has already transmitted (for example, *Lüzu quanshu* 49.9a, 17b). The *Jinhua zongzhi*, therefore, began as a compilation of the dialogues between Lüzu and the spirit-writing disciples, for whom the most important fact, I think, was their belief that the teachings had come to them directly from the immortal himself.

However, according to a preface by Zhang Shuang'an (1692), it was little more than twenty years later that the next revelation started at the altar of Tu Yu'an, in a place known as the Old Red Plum Hall (Gu hongmei ge). Here, another group had been formed, which comprised seven members initiated under Tu's instruction. After the *Jinhua zongzhi* was transmitted to them, Tu and Zhuang Xing'an chose the proper words of the immortal and asked Zhang Shuang'an to edit them into a scripture (*Lüzu quanshu* 49, pref. 18a–19b).

While a prototype version of the text probably came into existence in this way, it is not extant today. According to the preface by Shao Zhilin (1775), the version he received from a certain Mr. Wu of Sumen consisted of twenty chapters, including the words of the immortals Tan Changzhen and Qiu Changchun. But Shao, finding them redundant, removed the other immortals' words and included them as appendices to Lü's teachings. As a result, the *Jinhua zongzhi* was reduced to thirteen chapters. This is the version included in Shao Zhilin's *Lüzu quanshu* of 1775. Although it is impossible today to reconstruct the contents of the prototype version, it is safe to say that it was less organized than the extant version.[2]

The Dual Sense of Lineage
Seen in Shao Zhilin's Version

On the face of it, Shao Zhilin's version appears to be a scripture of the Jingming school, but the situation is not that simple because this version contains certain facets of the text that cannot be explained in these sectarian terms. The Jingming school was a tradition from Yuzhang (Nanchang, Jiangxi) and its environs, which claimed to come from the immortal Xu Xun (also known as Xu Jingyang, Xu Zhenjun, or Xuzu). It emerged in the late Tang dynasty as a popular cult and flourished in the twelfth to fourteenth centuries as the Jingming zhongxiao dao, or the Way of Pure Brightness, Loyalty, and Filial Piety (see Akizuki 1978; Schipper 1985). In the *Jinhua zongzhi*, the teaching of Jingming is claimed as a revelation from the three immortals Lü, Tan, and Qiu, granted in order to recover the transmission of Jingming. According to the *Jingming yuanliu* (Sources and Currents of Pure Brightness), contained in an appendix attributed to the immortal Tan (*Lüzu quanshu* 49.25b–26b), the transmission had been lost after Liu Yuzhen (1257–1308), the school's Yuan-dynasty founder, and his successor, Huang Zhonghuang (1271–1328), had led the school to its apogee.

> The partiarch [Tan] said: The source [of this line] is the Shangqing [Highest Clarity] lineage. Lord Mao is regarded as the first generation. After ten generations of transmission, it gradually began to lose its truth. At the beginning of the Jin dynasty, Lan'gong transmitted it to Chenmu; Chenmu transmitted it to Xuzu; Xuzu transmitted it to the ten great disciples.
>
> After seven more generations, Masters Yuzhen and Zhonghuang succeeded to the lineage. Today, the transmission has been lost. That is why we have brought it, that is, the instructions [of Golden Florescence]. (*Lüzu quanshu* 49.25b)

The preface of Tu Yu'an (1692) shows how he came to respect Jingming teachings. At the time when Tu was first shown a scripture entitled *Jingming zhongxiao lu* (Record of Pure Brightness, Loyalty, and Filial Piety) by his master Pan Yi'an, he was inspired by the school's teachings. Later, he asked Pan whether it were possible to enjoy the direct instruction of Xu Xun, a thousand and more years after the immortal had ascended to heaven. Pan replied, "It is not difficult" and explained to him that Xu Xun, who now dwelt in heaven, a few years previously had asked Shangdi, the Highest Lord, to order Lüzu and Tan Changzhen to administer the great teaching of Jingming and to bring it down to Zhou Yehe's altar. Tu, in great surprise and joy, went to this altar with Pan to be a disciple of Lüzu (*Lüzu quanshu* 49.15b–17b).

According to this description, Lüzu and the Quanzhen patriarchs held celestial ranks lower than that of Xu Xun, serving as messengers who mediated betweeen Xu Xun and Lü's disciples. Although they called themselves disciples of Jingming, the members of the spirit-writing cult who assembled at the altar of Lüzu do not seem to have had as much direct communication with Xu Xun as they had with Lüzu.

This indirect relationship between the disciples and Xu Xun seems to correspond to their dual sense of lineage. According to the "Instructions from the Immortal Tan Changsheng" (an appendix of Shao Zhilin's version), the original seven members of the Bailong jingshe also claimed that they belonged to the Taiyi lineage, which traces directly back to Lüzu. As the *Jingming yuanliu* says:

> The Patriarch Tan said: In the transmission of Jinhua Taiyi [Lord of the Great Unity of Golden Florescence], there is another lineage. Chunyang shengzu [i.e., Lüzu] is regarded as the great founding master of the first generation. This is the main doctrine included in the three teachings, the genuine backbone of the teaching of the immortals and buddhas. Each disciple at the altar belongs to his own generation whose name is determined in the order of [the names of eight trigrams,] *qian, kan, gen, zhen, xun, li, kun,* and *dui.*
>
> [Those who belong to the first generation are] Pan Yi'an named Qiande, Tu Yu'an named Qianyuan, Zhuang Xing'an named Qianwei, Cheng'an named Qianxin, Zhou Yehe named Qianlong, Liu Du'an named Qianshan, and Xu Shen'an named Qianheng. Henceforth, disciples initiated under those seven should start with the generation of the character *kan.* When you finish making a round of all the letters, you will come back again to the first. (*Lüzu quanshu* 49.26b)

This shows clearly that those assembled at the Bailong jingshe came to be listed as members of the Taiyi lineage. Taiyi, it is likely, was the name given to this specific spirit-writing cult of Lüzu.[3] However, it is difficult to ascertain the precise relationship between the lineage and the Jingming school on the evidence of this statement. On the one hand, the Taiyi lineage seems to be regarded as a suborder of Jingming; on the other hand, it is interesting that the lineage is referred to as a line distinct from the mainstream of the school, a line with Lüzu as its initiator. The Jingming tradition and Lüzu were not merged into one, in the usage of this text.

The Negative Attitude Toward the Quanzhen School

In Shao Zhilin's version, Lüzu and the Quanzhen patriarchs are given slightly lower positions than Xu Xun. In the very beginning of the text, the Quanzhen tradition is even referred to rather critically:

> The Quanzhen could flourish in its ultimate bloom. It had a prosperous time among its followers but declined in the mind-transmission un-

til it reached extreme disorder and confusion, reaching the replacement and decline seen at present. (*Lüzu quanshu* 49.1ab; see Miyuki 1967).

This attitude is not surprising if one looks upon this version as a product of the Jingming school. However, the situation is not so simple. Given that Zhuang Xing'an was one of the coeditors of the prototype version of the *Jinhua zongzhi* and had some connections with the Longmen lineage, the major sect of Quanzhen in the Qing, it appears very strange to find expressions so offensive to the Quanzhen school.

Interestingly, the name "Zhuang Xing'an" is found in the preface of a text called *Qiuzu yulu* (Recorded Sayings of Patriarch Qiu). He is cited here with the recommendation that the text—claimed to be transmitted through the Longmen lineage—be handed down to the Longmen Master Zhu Yunyang for publication to a wider audience. It seems a natural assumption to identify this Zhuang with the Zhuang Xing'an who appears as a member of the Bailong jingshe. Evidence pointing into this direction is as follows:

1. Longmen Master Yunyang was Zhu Yunyang, known as an editor of *Wuzhen pian chanyou* (Clarifying Unclear Points in the Tract on Awakening to Perfection), who also lived in Piling around the 1660s (see Mori 1998, 260–261).
2. One of the main topics dealt with in the *Qiuzu yulu* is "circulation of the light" (*huiguang*), which is similar to a meditation method mentioned in the *Jinghua zongshi* (Mori 1998, 268).
3. According to Pan Jingguan's preface to the *Qiuzu yulu*, the text was shown to disciples of Zhu in the *dingwei* year (1667), and soon afterward Zhuang asked Zhu to publish it (Mori 1998, 258–261).
4. In a note to chapter 8 of the *Jinhua zongzhi,* the words of Zhu Yunyang are quoted (see *Lüzu quanshu* 49.18b).

On the basis of these factors, it seems safe to assume that the Zhuang Xing'an who recommended the transmission of the *Qiuzu yulu* to Zhu Yunyang was the same person who engaged in editorial work on the *Jinhua zongzhi*. Accepting this supposition, one should also consider the possibility that the method of "light circulation" was brought from Zhu Yunyang's school to the Bailong jingshe around 1667–1668.

Considering the degree of communication between Zhuang and the Longmen lineage, why do we find such a critical attitude to the Quanzhen sect in the *Jinhua zongzhi*? One supposition is that there was a disagreement within the sect among those who insisted on the importance of the Jingming lineage and those who did not. Interestingly,

Zhuang Xing'an, unlike Tu Yu'an, does not refer to Jingming in his preface (1693). Instead, he wrote that both he and his mother recovered from a fatal illness with the help of Lüzu, who came down to Zhou Yehe's altar. It seems that Zhuang's respect focused on Lüzu himself rather than on the Jingming immortals, while Tu and Pan strongly identified themselves with the Jingming lineage. The assumption then becomes possible that it was only after 1692, when the center of the cult shifted to Tu's altar, that the power of Jingming became overwhelming. It appears that people eager for succession to the Jingming lineage appropriated the Lüzu cult in Piling and the teachings attributed to him, just around the time the text was compiled.

Jiang Yupu's Version

More than one hundred years after the compilation of the first version, Jiang Yupu (1756–1819), an elite official at the Qing court, adopted the *Jinhua zongzhi* as a scripture of the Tianxian lineage. According to the *Guochao qixian leizheng chubian* (Initial Collection of Categorized Documents on Servers of the Dynasty, ch. 94) and its supplement (see Li 1890), he filled the post of chief minister in the Office of the Imperial Stable in 1802, became vice director of the Ministry of Works in 1806, and served in the Ministry of Revenue in 1808. His involvement in elite society is also attested by the fact that two celebrated ex-officials of the time, Zhu Gui (1731–1806) and Zai Quheng (1755–1811), wrote postscripts (dated 1803) to the *Quanshu zhengzong*, the anthology of Lüzu's revelations compiled by Jiang. According to Zai Quheng's preface, Zhu Gui once instructed Zai in the Dao by means of "Lüzu's words of instruction" (*Lüzu xunyu)* when both of them were in Yuedong. Apparently, there was a network of believers in Lüzu among high officials around Jiang Yupu, and Jiang's work provides some concrete information about one of its centers.

The process by which the *Jinhua zongzhi* changed from Shao Zhilin's version to Jiang Yupu's is complicated. Monica Esposito suggests that Shao Zhilin's text was first included in an anthology called *Quanshu zhengzong*, possibly a former version of the text Cheng Mou restored in 1852, and was then revised and appropriated into Jiang's edition (1998a, 104).[4] Jiang Yupu's version is also found in the more familiar anthology *Daozang jiyao*. The editor of this anthology can be identified as Jiang Yupu himself on the basis of two prefaces attributed to the immortals Zhongli Quan and Su Lang. They contain a reference to Lüzu giving an order to publish the *Daozang jiyao,* addressed to the disciples of a certain Jueyuan tan (Altar of the Source of Awakening) or Diyi kaihua tan (First Altar of Opening Transformations; see later), the names given to an altar of Jiang Yupu (Zhongli's Pref. 5a; Su's Pref. 6b). The following discussion, however, is based on his version as contained in the *Quanshu zhengzong* because it has more prefaces to clearly reflect Jiang's religious background than the *Daozang jiyao.*

Jiang Yupu's and Chen Mou's versions of the text share remarkable features that differentiate them from Shao Zhilin's. They no longer contain the prefaces written in the names of Jingming disciples; they preserve Tu Yu'an's preface but omit or change important references to the Jingming lineage. For example, the passage cited earlier, which describes how Pan Yi'an informs Tu about Lüzu's descents to Zhou Yehe's altar, is eliminated completely; Tu Yu'an's "disciples of the successor to the Jingming lineage" is changed to "disciples of the successor to the Jinhua lineage." Similarly, the prefaces written in spirit-writing by various immortals are preserved in both of Chen's and Jiang's versions, but all references to the Bailong jingshe, Piling, and all indications of a connection with the Jingming lineage are no longer present.

If one assumes that the text used in Chen Mou's version originally preceded Jiang's, one can claim that Jiang followed his predecessor in rejecting the traces of the Jingming lineage. However, as Esposito has pointed out (1998b, 10), Chen's and Jiang's versions differ in that the former still follows the Jingming lineage, preserving an appendix very similar to the *Jingming yuanliu* found in Shao Zhilin's version. On the other hand, Jiang's version clearly denies the exclusive relationship between the Jingming lineage and the *Jinhua zongzhi.* In his introductory remarks to the *Quanshu zhengzong,* he asserts:

> The *Jinhua zongzhi* is an independent transmission from a direct successor to the Tianxian [celestial immortals]; it is not a scripture only of the Jingming school like the *Zongjiao lu* and others. (*Quanshu zhengzong,* "Fanli" 2a)

Here, he emphasizes the close relationship between the text and the celestial immortals, that is, the Tianxian lineage. This is described in more detail by Zhiqiu (= Fan Ao, a disciple of Jiang Yupu) in a postscript of this version of the *Jinhua zongzhi:*

> I believe that when Lord Fuyou [Lüzu] named the Tianxian lineage, a phrase of the verse must have been transmitted. When I asked Huijue about this, he told me modestly, "Once I heard that there was [a verse composed of] twenty characters which goes:

> In complete silence without existence,
> You and the Former Heaven will be unified;
> The original yang is back to its proper position,
> When you walk alone into the Jade Castle of the Immortal."

He also told me: "Our Lord Fuyou is the founder of the Tianxian, and Hongjiao enshi [Liu Shouyuan] is his second. You must remember this with respect." (*Quanshu zhengzong* 2.67b–68a)

Huijue is one of Jiang Yupu's pseudonyms found in the *Quanshu zhengzong* and *Daozang jiyao*.[5] This shows that the Tianxian lineage worshiped Lüzu as their first master immortal and Hongjiao enshi (or Liu Shouyuan; *Quanshu zhengzong*, Pref. 40a) as the second, and that Jiang held a responsible position in the lineage because he taught Zhiqiu their secret verse. According to the same postscript, the teaching of the *Jinhua zongzhi* could never be properly clarified without transmission of the Tianxian lineage. He says:

> The *Jinhua zongzhi* contains many expressions on the subtle teaching of the Dao, but only a few people could acquire the central teaching of the school. This will never be clarified without the transmission of the Tianxian. There is no one who can show this wonderful text but the founder of the Tianxian. This has been transmitted to this world only by Lord Fuyou. (*Quanshu zhengzong* 2.67a)

It is obvious here that the text was now appropriated by the Tianxian lineage.[6] However, despite their negative attitude toward its original editors, the new line undeniably held highly similar beliefs in Lüzu and was also a spirit-writing cult venerating the immortal.

Jiang Yupu's Altar

Jiang Yupu's engagement in spirit-writing is more than obvious. In one preface attributed to Liu Shouyuan, he was ordered by Lüzu and Liu to compile this anthology (*Quanshu zhengzong*, Pref. 38b). As a matter of fact, the *Quanshu zhengzong* is an anthology compiled at Jiang Yupu's altar, where they revered Lüzu and Liu Shouyang as their principal deities. Regrettably, despite the numerous messages from the immortal, there is only little information on the organization and history of the cult. Still, a few glimpses can be gained. According to Jiang's preface, Lüzu says:

> There are places inspired with my spirit-writing, and there are no phrases that have not been transmitted [in those places.] Here, at the

Original Altar of the Source of Awakening, you [Jiang et al.] have compiled the old characters as previously transmitted separately, put them
together with some additions, and recorded them. . . . This is the au-
thentic proof [of enlightenment] that has been transmitted from era
to era for thousands and hundreds of years at thousands and hundreds
of altars. Now I name it "the orthodox lineage" [*zhengzong*]. (*Quanshu
zhengzong*, Author's Pref., 33b–34b)

Attributed to Lüzu, this preface was addressed to Jiang Yupu and
his cooperators.[7] It shows that the *Quanshu zhengzong* was thought to
contain the essence of Lüzu's teachings transmitted to innumerable
altars in the past, and it was compiled at an altar called "Original
Altar of the Source of Awakening" (Jueyuan bentan), also known by
various other, similar names,[8] which was considered the main and
central site of all of Lüzu's transmissions anywhere. Also, according to
some documents in the *Quanshu zhengzong*, Lüzu had opened seven
"Awakening" altars, among which this one was regarded as the highest. This is why it is often called the "first" altar.[9]

The origin of the Altar of Awakening is as vague as that of the Tianxian lineage. A tantalizing, if detailed, description of its history is found
in Enwu's postscript to the *Quanshu zhengzong*. The text says:

[Among the many altars in the world], the seven [altars of] Awakening
are most prominent. At the capital, in the best location, the Altar has
widely opened up and provided instruction to numerous followers.
There were six founders who all received a decree [from Lüzu] to en-
lighten the world and came to supervise the Altar. Previous supervisers
included Guangji zhenjun and my master Huang, Xianyou zhenjun. In
the winter of the *wuwu* year [1798], the great altar was rebuilt, when,
by the decree [of Lüzu], Hongjiao zhenjun held the teaching and
opened the secret to the people. (*Quanshu zhengzong*, "Juanshou" 62a)

In spite of the vagueness caused by an utter lack of context, this description implies that Jiang's Altar of Awakening was located in Beijing. It also shows that it was after 1798, the year it was rebuilt, that Liu
Shouyuan began to exercise power over the cult. As we have seen, he,
in his role as the immortal Liu, was believed to be the second founder
of the Tianxian lineage, which therefore should have begun around
1798.

Min Yide's Version

Min Yide was a priest of the Longmen lineage, the largest branch of
the Quanzhen school under the Qing.[10] He criticizes Jiang Yupu's ver-

sion of the *Jinhua zongzhi* in the *Daozang jiyao* as spurious and contrasts it with the originality of a version transmitted through the Longmen lineage on Mount Jin'gai ever since 1688. He says:

> The text appeared in the *wuchen* year of the Kangxi era [1688] and was transmitted in the hermitage of Longqiao on Mount Jin'gai. A wise man of the past, Tao Shi'an, printed it. During the Jiaqing era [1796–1820], the vice director Jiang Yuanting [Yupu] obtained a false text by mistake and included it in his *Daozang jiyao*.
>
> Later, he received our text in Zhejiang. He hoped to substitute it for the false one, but the wood blocks were in Beijing. When [someone tried to] get them back [from there], the vice director also went back to the capital, where he passed away. Thus, the project [of substitution] was interrupted and left incomplete. In spite of that, how could my heart forget it even for one moment?
>
> Recently, when I went to Moling [Nanjing], I found a popular copy of the text which was a little different from Tao's edition [Tao Shi'an's text]. It had one or two more sections than Jiang's. The latter seems to have derived from Tao's version, but some parts must have been added and some removed. Words are different from person to person. Here, I will emend and revise it [Jiang's edition] solely on the basis of that by Tao. (*Gu shuyinlou cangshu* 5; *Jinhua zongzhi* 3a)

Tao Shi'an (d. 1692) was a Longmen priest who lived on Mount Jin'gai from 1645 onward. Min Yide asserts that the original *Jinhua zongzhi* first appeared on his mountain and was edited by Tao Shi'an. In his commentary to the text, he further asserts that it was created by means of spirit-writing, giving a description that he attribtues to Tao Shi'an. He says:

> Having come to this part, the phoenix pen stopped all of a sudden. Although it was before the new moon, a great light that was neither the sun nor the moon unexpectedly began to shine, and nothing could hide beneath the light. The air was filled with an unusual fragrance; in the sky you could hear the solemn sound of music of heaven. After a few moments, the phoenix began to move at last to write: This was the comment of the light by Amitābha. . . . Now, in the mountain library on Mount Jin'gai, Yan [Lüzu] has preached the essential doctrines of the Golden Florescence of Great Unity in the emptiness of Former Heaven. I resolved that I should practice and attain the result in order to change the eastern land into Sūkhavati.
>
> How wonderful! When my great wish was declared, the great fortune corresponded. When something begins, an omen comes beforehand. The light of the essence [Amitābha] reaches even from the fur-

thest place. Now I could move Amitābha to bring down the radiant commentary of the primary essence that gives me infinite happiness and protection. (*Gu shuyinlou cangshu* 5; *Jinhua zongzhi* 20a)

According to this, the Buddha Amitābha suddenly interrupted Lüzu's phoenix pen while it had descended to the mountain library on Mount Jin'gai and gave his radiant commentary. Following this revelation of this light, or radiance, Lüzu explained that it was an auspicious response from Amitābha to his resolution to change the eastern land into Sūkhavati, the Pure Land paradise (*jingtu*). The same event is also noted in Tao Shi'an's commentary, inserted immediately after the previous passage. He comments:

On this occasion, many immortals assembled and gave verses [to praise Lüzu's resolution.] Although it is impossible to describe the event in more detail, here is the outline of this important lesson. It was truly a meeting only once in eighty thousands kalpas. Who would have expected to have this at Longqiao? Those who have an opportunity to read this text should never lose their confidence. (*Gu shuyinlou cangshu* 5; *Jinhua zongzhi* 20b)

Following this insertion, Min Yide explains why he put it there:

This was what Shi'an wrote. Now, the text that Jiang [Yupu] has relied on belongs to the line of the Central Lineage. They appropriated the text [*Jinhua zongzhi*] and tried to oppress the Northern Lineage. Thus they eliminated this [Tao Shi'an's commentary]. The same things can be said about the most popular copies. Here, I make this supplemental comment [to attract the reader's attention]. (*Gu shuyinlou cangshu* 5; *Jinhua zongshi* 20b–21a)

Min Yide, therefore, alleges that some of the original commentary by Tao Shi'an was deliberately removed from Jiang's version because the Central Lineage (of Jingming) tried to suppress the Northern one (of Longmen). His account, however, completely contradicts all evidence on the formation of the text in Piling. The problem, it appears, is largely on the side of Min Yide—a supposition supported by his preface to the *Jinhua zongzhi*. It says:

The founder, the Heavenly Worthy Lord Fuyou, resolute in his demand for salvation of the people, has a great wish to save the world. Thus he attained the profound teaching of the Great Unity of Former Heaven, Emptiness and Nonbeing, the Jinhua zongzhi, and expressed it in thirteen chapters as a basic teaching for saving the world. (*Gu shuyinlou cangshu* 5; *Jinhua zongshi* 1ab)

This account of Min Yide describes the original text of the *Jinhua zongzhi* as consisting of thirteen chapters, the same number as still found in the extant texts. As shown above, however, the text had twenty chapters before Shao Zhilin reduced it to thirteen in 1775. Following his reduction, all extant texts have had the same arrangement. On the other hand, it is quite possible that members of the Lüzu cult in Piling expanded the thirteen chapters to twenty. Yet if this had happened, Shao Zhilin would have known about the existence of a thirteen-chapter text and would probably have mentioned it, but he never refers to it, instead emphasizing that he reduced twenty chapters to thirteen. Then again, it is very strange that Min Yide himself did not use Tao Shi'an's text, which, as he asserts, had been transmitted on Mount Jin'gai. In spite of his fierce criticism, what he included in his anthology was a revised version of Jiang Yupu's text taken from the *Daozang jiyao*. It seems, therefore, that a text attributed to Tao Shi'an existed on Mount Jin'gai, which was in fact composed after the reduction of the *Jinhua zongzhi* to the edition in thirteen chapters, and that the originality of this text was fictitious, its revelation on Mount Jin'gai in 1688 being an imaginary story.

Why, then, would the Daoists around Min Yide fabricate such an imaginary transmission? Maybe they desired it, feeling the need for a direct transmission of the text to their own mountain. As Min notes in his commentary, Tao Shi'an's description of Lüzu's descent was removed from Jiang's text in order to suppress the Longmen lineage— which suggests that the descent of the immortal had something to do with this group. The same is also apparent in Min's account of a meeting between the Longmen leader Wang Kunyang (Changyue) and Tao Jing'an. He says, again in attribution to Tao Shi'an:

> In the autumn of the *wuchen* year of emperor Kangxi's reign [1688], the precept master [Wang Kunyang] came down to the south and rested at the Zongyang gong. The hermit patriarch [Tao] Jing'an went to meet him. When he offered this text, the precept master treated him very politely, and after reading it with a bow, he said, "The heart of the Highest Lord's transmission is fully expressed here." (*Gu shuyinlou cangshu* 5; *Jinhua zongzhi* 23b)

That is to say, in the very same year when the *Jinhua zongzhi* was supposedly revealed on Mount Jin'gai, Tao Jing'an met Wang Kunyang in Hangzhou and showed him the text. Tao Jing'an (1618–1673) was an uncle of Tao Shi'an, known as one of the founders of the Longmen lineage on Mount Jin'gai with the title "founding master of Mount Jin'gai"

(*Jin'gai xindeng* 2.9a). On the other hand, Wang Kunyang was a leading Longmen patriarch at the Baiyun guan in Beijing, who, from 1656 onward, ordained thousands of people with the permission of the Qing court (see Chen 1988; 1990). He is considered the leading representative of the Quanzhen school in Qing times. His meeting with a master of Mount Jin'gai was, therefore, of great importance, because Wang was their master and a major leader of the great tradition of the Quanzhen. The anecdote of Wang's praising the *Jinhua zongzhi* as the perfect expression of the transmission of Lord Lao shows that the text was admitted as proof for the legitimacy of the Longmen lineage on Mount Jin'gai. Although fictitious, the episode shows how important the text was.

At the same time, the Daoists on Mount Jin'gai were also concerend with losing proper contact with the great tradition. According to a note of Min Yide in his *Huangji hepi xianjing* (Immortals' Scripture on the Creation of the Universe for Imperial Rulers), there were many restrictions on the transmission of precepts, not only because the government had banned all personal ordinations of Buddhists and Daoists, but also because of restraints in their own lineage. To transmit the precepts, one had to possess *lü* (statutes, a code of transmission), *shu* (scriptures given with the precepts), and *juan* (a scroll with a lineage tree and an imperial edict). Being afraid to divulge the content to those not properly qualified, Daoists used to burn them when they could not find anyone deserving transmission. Consequently, as Min says,

> three generations after the master of the precepts [Wang Kunyang], the way [of transmission] no longer existed. Today, during the Jiaqing era [1796–1820], when a precept transmission is held, Patriarch Qiu's text [of the transmission] of the precepts is lost. What is being transmitted nowadays is what we learn from the *Jingming zongjiao lu*, which is not at all like the transmission of Patriarch Qiu. Earlier masters on the mountain [Mount Jin'gai] had burned the text to follow the rule. Fortunately, the scripture survives in copies, but both scroll and code are lost. (*Gu shuyinlou cangshu* 6; *Huangji hepi xianjing* 28ab)

The direct transmission of the precepts from Wang Kunyang was of the greatest importance to Min Yide's Longmen lineage. In spite of that, they had already lost the way of transmission at that time. In such a cornered situation, it must have been a great relief for them to possess a text praised by Wang himself as the direct transmission of the Highest Lord. The Longmen sect on Mount Jin'gai thus seems to have gained a guarantee of legitimacy from the spirit-writing of Lüzu.

The revelation of the *Jinhua zongzhi* was not an exceptional event for Daoists living on Mount Jin'gai. According to Min Yide, the place had a long history as a holy site of Lüzu—sporting a bronze statue of the immortal that had been placed in the Song and being claimed as Lüzu's fundamental altar, having seen the compilaton of his spirit-writings (*Jin'gai xindeng* 2a, 9b, *Shanlue fu*). In addition, it is evident that Min Yide himself was deeply engaged in the spirit-writing activities of Lüzu. The *Gu shuyinlou cangshu* contains several texts providing direct instructions from Lüzu through spirit-writing, one entitled *Sanni yishi shuoshu* (Explaining the Cure of the World by the Three Saints), another called *Du Lüzu sanni yishi shuoshu guankui* (Narrow Insights into Lüzu's Revelation of the *Sanni yishi shuoshu*). The former is said to be Lüzu's a commentary on a celestial scripture that did not survive; the latter is a record of Min's own self-cultivation practiced on the basis of Lüzu's revelation. Here, Min directly asks Lüzu himself how to meditate properly and in response receives a detailed interpretation of the immortal's teachings (see *Gu shuyinlou cangshu* 5; *Yishi shuoshu guankui* 25ab, 31a).

Very likely it was this aspect of their religious tradition that allowed the Daoists on Mount Jin'gai to accept the *Jinhua zongzhi* as a holy scripture. It might have been difficult, or even impossible, for them to separate their sense of identity as Longmen Daoists from their belief in Lüzu, because Lüzu was one of the five founding patriarchs of the Quanzhen school. However, considering that the belief in Lüzu combined with the activity of spirit-writing was widely shared among many groups and cults, independent of the Quanzhen school, his veneration and descents on Mount Jin'gai may also be seen as a religious activity that cannot be entirely reduced to the Longmen tradition. The Longmen tradition was a master–disciple lineage, developing as time passed and generating, or at least imagined to generate, an irreversible, straight, and direct line. Spirit-writing, unlike this lineage, made it possible for believers to skip its mediation and communicate directly with one of their founding patriarchs, reinforcing a feeling of belonging and ultimately strengthening the sense of lineage.[11]

Conclusion

The *Jinhua zongzhi* was first completed as a text of the Jingming lineage, but as it was transmitted to later editors, the exclusive relationship between the text and the Jingming lineage was denied. As new editors received the text, it was linked to different lineages through the arbitrary insertion of personal commentaries that served to establish a desirable relationship between the text and the various editors' lineages. However, contrary to the fierce insistence of those competing editors, the *Jinhua zongzhi* was not transmitted along each lineage but was passed along a stratum running across them, the stratum of the spirit-writing cults of Lüzu.

Two facets of the religious identity of those who transmitted the *Jinhua zongzhi* become clear. On the one hand, they were members of one or the other spirit-writing cult of Lüzu, and thus each had a very basic sense of identity as the immortal's disciple. On the other hand, they acquired a sense of lineage by placing the text and its transmission into a desirable sectarian context. In other words, the various prefaces and notes attached to the words of Lüzu correspond to the editors' sense of lineage, while the words of Lüzu in the scripture match their common identity as the immortal's disciples, an identity that underlies their lineage identity. It is difficult to explicitly point out this dual structure in just one text, but by comparison of those different versions, the distinction of the levels becomes perceptible.

Nevertheless, this does not necessarily mean that there is no sign of the two levels and phases of formation within each text. Especially as and when each version is linked to the past, to historical lineages such as Jingming or Longmen, it is easy to see indications of the two facets of the editors' religious identities. Thus in Shao Zhilin's version, the position of the cult to Lüzu is described as if it belonged to a different lineage than the Jingming or, at least, to a sublineage of it. In Min Yide's case, the situation is more complicated. However, one can still extract an indication of both facets by pointing out that the traditions of both spirit-writing and the veneration of Lüzu had a base in the religious history of Mount Jin'gai and that it could not be reduced to the Quanzhen tradition. In both cases, the spirit-writing cult served to revitalize or reinforce its members' sense of lineage, even though the foundation of the lineage depended on the members' imaginative interpretation and pragmatic adoption of historical events rather than on an institutional transmission solidly established in history.

As Terry Kleeman has argued, from Song times onward, spirit-writing provided "improved access to the sacred realm" with which "men and women without the status of religious professionals came to have a direct relationship with exalted levels of the sacred realm" (1993, 63). In the cases presented here, spirit-writing not only constituted a method to relate people to Heaven but also provided them with a lineage on earth, that is, a device that connected them with their preferred lineage context, where religion and history are not differentiated.

Notes

This paper is based on my presentation at the Tōyō tetsugakkai (Society for the Study of Eastern Philosophy), June, 1997, where I compared the versions listed as numbers 1, 2, and 4 with Min Yide's edition contained in his *Gu shuyinlou cangshu*. Here I first suggested that the text was originally edited by the Jingming school and that it was then taken over by the Tianxian school and the Longmen sect.

I have also touched upon similar issues in a recent article (Mori 1998). My special thanks go to Dr. Monica Esposito, with whom I have exchanged notes and opinions since December, 1997. She has given me most coherent advice, especially on the existence of certain versions of the *Jinhua zongzhi* I did not know previously.

1. *Lüzu shi xiantian xuwu taiyi Jinhua zongzhi*, in *Gu shuyinlou cangshu*, ch. 5 *Zangwai daoshu* 10, 327–343. The extant version of the *Gu shuyinlou cangshu* as included in the *Zangwai daoshu* does not contain any publication information, but recent research suggests that the text was first published in 1904 (Hu 1995, 232). However, the constitution of the text itself suggests an earlier date. That is to say, most of the texts preserved in the anthology seem to have been completed by the end of the Daoguang era (1821–1850). Of its thirty-eight titles, those that have datable prefaces are no later than 1839 or 1840 (that is, those by Xue Yanggui, a disciple of Min, and his friend Li Wenyuan). In his 1834 appendix to the *Tianxian xinzhuan* (Heart Transmission of the Celestial Immortals), moreover, Min Yide mentions that he himself was the publisher of the basic edition of the *Gu shuyinlou cangshu* (8.35).

2. In fact, Shao Zhilin confesses that he was embarrassed by the appearance of the former version that could be regarded as *Jinhua keyi* (Rules and Observances of Golden Florescence) by future readers (Pref., 1.2a).

3. It was probably no coincidence that both this lineage and the scripture shared the name "Taiyi," but it is not clear what exactly the connection was to the deity.

4. I am deeply indebted to Monica Esposito for providing information on Chen Mou's text.

5. We can identify them because he referred to himself in several combinations as follows: Guanghuazi Huijue, in in the commentary to the *Jinhua zongzhi* (see *Quanshu zhengzong, Jinhua zongzhi* 63a); and Huijue dizi Jiang Yupu shouzhong shi, in the postscript to the *Shiliu pinjing* (see *Quanshu zhengzong* 1; *Shiliu pinjing*, 108a).

6. It is not entirely clear why the members of the Tianxian lineage call themselves by this name. However, it seems that they regarded *tianxian* (celestial immortals) as the highest rank among the *xian* and found in Lüzu and his teacher Zhongli Quan masters who would teach people the way to attain this exalted level. Enhong (a member of Jiang's altar group) in this context refers

to the significance of the transmission of the "celestial immortal" (*Zhong-Lü chuandao ji,* afterword; *Daozang jiyao,* Weiji 2.58a). In the first chapter of the same work, moreover, the first five ranks of the immortals are discussed, with *tianxian* at the top.

7. At the end of this preface, the names of nine members of Jiang Yupu's cult are given: Huijue (Jiang Yupu), Enhong, Dagu, Zhiqiu, Tongren, Deming, Daqi, Zhixi, and Zhizhuo. See *Quanshu zhengzong,* Pref. 35ab.

8. On the expression "Jueyuan tan," see *Quanshu zhengzong* 9.14a, 25ab. Other variations are Jueyuan baotan (Precious Altar of the Source of Awakening), Juetan (Altar of Awakening), and Jueyuan jingshe (Chapel of the Source of Awakening). See *Quanshu zhengzong* 9.2b, 13.18b.

9. As this type of variations there are Diyi tan (First Altar), Diyi juetan (First Altar of Awakening), Diyi kaihua tan (First Altar of Opening Transformations). See *Quanshu zhengzong* 13.15b, 19b, 26a; Pref., 38a. On the superior position of the Jueyuan bentan (Primary Altar of the Source of Awakening), see *Quanshu zhengzong* 13.23a.

10. On the development of the Longmen lineage, see Chen 1988 and 1990; Tsui 1991; Esposito 1993; Mori 1994; and Wang 1995a and 1995b.

11. I have not been able to fully describe Min Yide's spirit-writing in this section. For more details on his ideas and practices, see Mori 1999.

Bibliography

Akizuki Kan'ei. 1978. *Chūgoku kinsei dōkyō no keisei.* Tokyo: Sōbunsha.

Baldrian-Hussein, Farzeen. 1986. "Lü Tung-pin in Northern Sung Literature." *Cahiers d'Extrême-Asie* 2:133–170.

Chen Bing. 1988. "Qingdai Quanzhen dao Longmen pai de zhongxing." *Shijie zongjiao yanjiu* 1988/2:84–96.

———. 1990. "Ming Qing Daojiao liang da pai." In *Zhongguo Daojiao shi,* ed. by Ren Jiyu, 627–682. Shanghai: Renmin.

Cleary, Thomas. 1991. *The Secret of the Golden Flower: The Classic Chinese Book of Life.* San Francisco: HarperCollins Publishers.

Esposito, Monica. 1993. "La Porte du Dragon—l'école Longmen du Mont Jin'gai et ses pratiques alchimiques d'après le *Daozang xubian* (Suite au canon taoïste)." Ph.D. diss., Université de Paris VII, Paris.

———. 1996. "Il Segreto del fiore d'oro e la tradizione Longmen del Monte Jin'gai." In *Conoscenza e interpretazione della civiltà cinese,* ed. by P. Corradini, 151–169. Rome: Ubaldini Editore.

———. 1998a. "The Different Versions of the *Secret of the Golden Flower* and Their Relationship with the Longmen School." *Transactions of the International Conference of Eastern Studies* 43:90–110.

———. 1998b. "Longmen pai yu *Jinhua zongzhi* banben laiyuan." Paper Presented at the Research Meeting on Daoist Culture, Waseda University, Tokyo.

Hu Fuchen, ed. 1995. *Zhonghua daojiao da cidian.* Beijing: Zhonggou shehui kexue chubanshen.

Kleeman, Terry. 1993. "The Expansion of the Wen-ch'ang Cult." In *Religion and Society in T'ang and Sung China*, ed. by Patricia Buckley Ebrey and Peter N. Gregory, 45–74. Honolulu: University of Hawai'i Press.

Miyuki, Mokusen. 1967. "The Secret of the Golden Flower: Studies and Translation." Diploma Thesis, Jung Institute, Zürich, Switzerland.

Mori Yuria. 1994. "Zenshinkyō ryūmonha keifu kō." In *Dōkyō bunka e no tenbō*, ed. by Dōkyō bunka kenkyūkai, 180–211. Tokyo: Hirakawa.

―――. 1998a. "Taiitsu kinke shūshi no seiritsu to hensen." *Tōyō no shisō to shūkyō* 15:43–64.

―――. 1998b. "Kyūso goroku ni tsuite." In *Dōkyō no rekishi to bunka*, ed. by Yamada Toshiaki and Tanaka Fumio, 257–273. Tokyo: Yūzankaku.

―――. 1999. "Ryo Dōhin to Zenshin kyō: Shinchō koshū kingai-san no jirei o chūshin ni." In *Koza: Dōkyō*, vol. 1, ed. by Sunayama Minoru, Ōzaki Masaharu, and Kikuchi Noritaka. Tokyo: Yūzan kaku.

Needham, Joseph, and Lu Gwei-djen. 1983. *Science and Civilisation in China* vol. 5.5. Cambridge: Cambridge University Press.

Schipper, Kristofer M. 1985. "Taoist Ritual and Local Cults of the T'ang Dynasty." In *Tantric and Taoist Studies in Honour of Rolf A. Stein*, ed. by Michel Strickmann 3:812–834. Brussels: Institut Belge des Hautes Etudes Chinoises.

Seidel, Anna. 1995. *Taoïsme: religion non-officielle de la Chine*. Trans. by Farzeen Baldrian-Hussein. *Cahiers d'Extrême-Asie* 8:26–27.

Shiga Ichiko. 1999. *Kindai chūgoku no shamanizumu to dōkyō: Hongkong no dōdan to fūji shinkō*. Tokyo: Bensei shuppan.

Wang Zhizhong. 1995a. "Lun Mingmo Qingchu Quanzhen jiao 'zhongxing' de chengyin." *Zongjiao xue yanjiu* 28:32–38.

―――. 1995b. "Quanzhen jiao Longmen pai qiyuan lunkao." *Zongjiao xue yanjiu* 29:9–13.

Wilhelm, Richard. 1984. *The Secret of the Golden Flower: A Chinese Book of Life*. Harmondsworth: Penguin Books.

9

Manifestations
of Lüzu in Modern
Guangdong and Hong Kong
The Rise and Growth
of Spirit-Writing Cults

SHIGA ICHIKO

Introduction

The mention of Daoism in Hong Kong usually brings to mind territorial temples (*miaoyu*), Daoist temples (*daoguan*), or large-scale *jiao*
festivals and Daoist priests performing rituals in such festivals. The religious organizations called *daotan* or *daotang*, discussed in this article,
are also one form of Daoism in Hong Kong, or they can be described
as occupying the most important place in the Daoist community of
Hong Kong. However, only a few studies have so far been made of
them, perhaps because most of them are inconspicuously located in
buildings in urban areas.

A *daotan* or *daotang* (hereafter referred to as *daotan*) is a religious
organization centered on spirit-writing and the worship of Daoist
deities. Its beliefs arc primarily based on Daoism but also include various elements of other religious traditions such as Confucianism, Buddhism, and folk religion. In this sense, a *daotan* is highly syncretistic.
Its main ritual activities include spirit-writing séances, annual festivals
to celebrate the birthdays of gods, and large-scale ritual celebrations
called *fahui*. The *daotan* also provides death-related services, such as
merit rites (*gongde fashi*), services for worshiping spirit tablets (*lingwei*),[1]
and the spaces to deposit ashes of the dead (*kanwei*). In addition, several *daotan* undertake social-welfare activities, such as running schools,
nursing homes, and clinics and helping victims of natural disasters in
mainland China. Most *daotan* are registered as non-profit, charitable
associations with the government (Shiga 1995).

In Hong Kong, the term "*daotan*" is usually used for a small Daoist
organization with only an altar and for spirit-writing in a cramped room

185

of a residential or commercial building. The term "*daoguan*," on the other hand, is commonly associated with Daoist organizations that maintain great shrines in large suburban sites. But such *daoguan* were also originally small organizations called *daotan*, and they are substantially the same. I will use the folk term "*daotan*" to refer to the Daoist organizations with these features regardless of their size. It is not clear precisely how many organizations like these there are in Hong Kong today, but according to my research, it can be conservatively said that there are more than fifty.

From a historical point of view, *daotan* originated from spirit-writing cults that arose in Guangdong, particularly in the Pearl River Delta, since the mid-nineteenth century. Table 9.1 lists spirit-writing cults established in Guangdong and Hong Kong before the 1950s.[2] As it indicates, since the oldest group, the Yunquan xianguan, was established in Nanhai County in 1848, many cult groups arose and spread from Guangdong through Hong Kong in the beginning of the twentieth century. Although the cults listed show some variation in scale, social background of their members, and choice of emphasis in activities, there is one common feature. As I shall examine in more detail, their activities consisted largely of relief work, such as providing free medical services, funeral services, and self-cultivation based on the moral and religious ideas of the three teachings, particularly Daoism. It is also clear that most of them worshiped Lüzu, that is, Lü Dongbin, as their patriarch. Some of the associations in the list have grown and adapted to the social changes in modern Guangdong and Hong Kong and are still active today. Others were more short-lived and have vanished again. In other words, *daotan* today are the successors of religious movements that began in the latter half of the nineteenth century in Guangdong. The purpose of this chapter is to consider how the *daotan* movement developed in modern Guangdong and Hong Kong.

In the late nineteenth century, not limited to Guangdong and Hong Kong, spirit-writing cults emerged in various places on an almost country-wide scale, spreading to such a degree that scholars studying the same phenomenon in Taiwan speak of "the nineteenth-century spirit-writing movement" (Fan 1996, 116; Clart 1996, 16). Various movements, emerging in different areas of China, provide fragmentary but significant information about nineteenth-century spirit-writing movements. For example, the first spirit-writing cult in Taiwan was the Puquan she (later renamed Yixin she), established in 1853 by the local elite of Magong, the capital of the Penghu Islands. Their founding medium had learned a spirit-writing technique in the Gongshan she, a charitable society in Quanzhou (Fujian), and their main activities were spirit-writing séances, public lecturing sessions (*xuanjiang*), and the publication of morality books (*shanshu*). Following their founding, other spirit-writing cults were organized in Magong, while similar organizations also sprang up in northern Taiwan, soon leading to their spread throughout the island (Wang 1996; Clart 1997, 4–5).

In Sichuan, in the *gengzi* year of the *Daoguang* reign (1840), divine revelations were received in the Longnü si (Temple of the Dragon Maiden), leading to the revelation of more than ten spirit-writing texts, such as the *Guansheng dijun mingsheng jing zhujie* (Explanation of the Holy Scripture of the Imperial Lord Guandi). This shows that spirit-writing cults not only spread gradually through southwestern China, but that they were also influential among sectarian groups (Wang 1996, 124–127; Takeuchi 1990). It is fair to say that the Cantonese spirit-writing movements of the nineteenth century form part of this overall tendency.

To understand these movements of the nineteenth century properly, one should know that they were inseparably linked with an eschatological sentiment, involving the idea of salvation from the "kalpa catastrophe" (*jie*) that had arisen especially among local elites in response to the rapid social change of the time. Yamada Masaru, a specialist in the settlement history of Sichuan, points out that in certain new settlements, the local elites established social-welfare societies often associated with spirit-writing. One example is the Shiquan hui (Society of the Ten Perfections), which was established after a spirit-writing séance revealed that goodness needed to be practiced in order to escape the coming great catastrophe (Yamada 1995, 249–251). Local elites worried about social and moral disorder in the time and not only actively practiced goodness as a group but also encouraged the masses to do so by establishing charitable societies or publishing morality books. As Phillip Clart points out in his study of Taiwanese spirit-writing movements, local elites "shared a consciousness of belonging to a religious movement that had as its aim the moral reformation of a decadent age by means of instructions and exhortations handed down by the gods" (Clart 1996, 16). Such consciousness was shared not only by the local elites in Sichuan and Taiwan but also by the majority of elites in other parts of China, including that of Guangdong.

However, each spirit-writing movement had its specific beliefs, organizations, and developments. For example, Taiwanese and Cantonese spirit-writing cults differ in their beliefs, liturgies, and activities, with the former being heavily Confucian in flavor. Often beliefs

TABLE 1
DAOTAN IN HONG KONG AND GUANGDONG, 1840-1949

Name	Year	Location	Deity
Yunquan xianguan 雲泉仙館	1848	Mt. Xiqiao	Lüzu
Changchun xianguan 長春仙館	1851	Mt. Aoxiu	Lüzu
Xiaopeng xianguan 小蓬仙館	1855	Guangzhou, Fangcun	Lüzu
Cuiyun dong 翠雲洞	1862	Qingyuan	Eight Immortals
Taoyuan xianguan 桃源仙館	1873	Qingyuan	Lüzu
Chunyang xianuan 純陽仙院	1881	HK Lantan island	Lüzu
Shenggong caotang 省躬草堂	1894	Guangzhou	Guangchengzi
Qingyun dong 慶雲洞	1898	Chashan	Lüzu
Puji tan 普濟壇	1899	Guangzhou, Fangcun	Huang Daxian
Puqing tan 普慶壇	1901	Suirui cun	Huang Daxian
Yushan tang 與善堂	1902	Huangshan xiang	Lüzu
Cunzhen xianguan 存真仙館	1907	Guangzhou, Guanshan	Lüzu
Yuquan xianguan 玉泉仙館	1910s	Foshan zhen	Lüzu
Baiyun xianguan 白雲仙館	1910s	Guangzhou, Dengfeng lu	Lüzu
Guangye xiantan 廣業仙壇	1920s	Shunde xian	Lüzu
Jinlan guan 金蘭觀	1932	Guangzhou	Lüzu
Shanbao shanshe 善寶善社	1930s	Dongyuan xian	Taiyi zhenren
Huichun shanyuan 回春善院	1930s	Guangzhou	??
Zuile shantang 最樂善堂	1930s	Guangzhou	??
Xinshan tang 信善堂	1935	Guangzhou, Fangcun	Lüzu
Qiuxin she 求心社	1930s	Dabu xian	Lüzu
Guangji shantang 廣濟善堂	1940	Meizhou	Lüzu
Zhibao tai 至寶台	1941	Guangzhou	Lüzu
Jueshan jingshe 覺善精舍	1940s	Qijiang	Lüzu
Guanben yuantang 關本源堂	1940s	Nanhai, Jiujiang	Lüzu
Lüyuan daotang 呂苑道堂	1940s	Shunde, Longjiang zhen	Lüzu
Rencheng caotang 仁誠草堂	1945	Guangzhou	Lüzu
Kangji hui 康濟會	1946	Guangzhou	Jigong
Hongdao jingshe 宏道精舍	1947	Guangzhou	Lüzu

involve the worship of the Three Benevolent Masters (*san enzhu*), that is, Guansheng dijun (Guandi), Fuyou dijun (Lü Dongbin), and Siming zhenjun (Ruler of Fates). Or again, they might venerate the Five Benevolent Masters (*wu enzhu*), the above three plus Yue wumu wang (King Mu) and Xuantian shangdi (Dark Warrior). Among them, Guandi is preeminent.

Another difference among the groups is that Taiwanese spirit-writing cults are strongly influenced by sectarian traditions worshiping the Eternal Mother, variably called Wusheng laomu (Unborn Venerable Mother) or Yaochi jinmu (Golden Mother of the Jasper Pond). By contrast, Cantonese spirit-writing cults are more Daoist in character: the word "*daotan*" literally means "Daoist shrine," many cults worship Lüzu as the main deity, and some identify themselves as descendants of the Quanzhen school. Unlike Taiwanese cults, they show little influence of Mother worship, although in Guangdong and Hong Kong there are some groups that engage in it, such as the Xiantian dao or the Tongshan she, which both also have considerable power in the Hong Kong Daoist community.

In addition, there is a subtle difference with respect to activity. On the whole, Taiwanese spirit-writing cults tend to emphasize the publication of morality books and the holding of public lectures, while Cantonese spirit-writing cults have given priority to medical services. It is possible that these differences arose from differences in the cultural and historical background of the two areas (Shiga 1998). This is why I give special attention to the religious and socio-economic background in Guangdong, such as the condition of the Daoist community and the spread of Lü Dongbin worship.

Furthermore, I would like to present an argument against the theory that *daotan* in Hong Kong are direct descendants of the Quanzhen tradition. According to this theory, the Longmen subsect of the Quanzhen school had spread to Guangdong province by the end of the seventeenth century, as is apparent in the fact that the Daoist temples established or rebuilt on Mount Luofu at that time all belonged to the Longmen subsect. Daoists training on Mount Luofu spread to Guangdong, especially to the Pearl River Delta, and established Daoist temples there. During this process of expansion, some changes occurred in the original Quanzhen tradition, including the decline of monasticism, the amalgamation of Quanzhen patriarchs and popular religious deities, a greater emphasis on rituals, and the introduction of spirit-writing. These changes were a response to popular religious demands. At the beginning of the twentieth century, the Quanzhen sect was introduced into Hong Kong by Daoists trained at the official Quanzhen monasteries, while in the Pearl River Delta, "Lüzu centers," spirit-writing cults devoted to Lüzu, arose one after another. Even though these Lüzu centers did not belong to the Quanzhen school, their founders had rich Daoist knowledge, learning from the activities of Quanzhen monks. The centers were, therefore, not directly part of the Quanzhen tradition but strongly influenced by it (see Tsui 1991).

Contrary to this view, as I plan to show, the rise and development of the *daotan* movement has many aspects left unexplained by this theory. In fact, even the Daoist temples in Hong Kong that identified themselves as part of the Quanzhen school were originally the Lüzu centers or spirit-writing cults in the guise of Quanzhen liturgy. In addition, the spirit-writing movement was not led by Daoist priests as professional religious practitioners but by laymen with Daoist knowledge and financial ability.

To clarify these points, the following describes the development of the *daotan* movement, focusing on these questions. What was the religious and socio-economic background of the *daotan* movement? Which social strata and what occupational groups participated actively in it? What was the driving force behind it? How had they come to form a "Daoist identity"? The relevant time span is the period from the rise of the movement in the latter half of the nineteenth century to 1949, when most of the cults in Guangdong were forced to close and move to Hong Kong because of the new religious policy enforced by the communist government.

Daoism in Pre-Modern Guangdong

The condition of Daoist temples and practitioners in pre-modern Guangdong is not well documented, and the key source is the *Guangdong nianjian* (Guangdong Yearbook) of 1942. According to this, there are four major Daoist temples on Mount Luofu: Chongxu guan, Huanglong guan, Baihe guan, and Sulao guan, housing several hundred Daoists. In the Qing dynasty, anyone belonging to one of them had to pay twenty taels every year; after he had lived there for three years, he was allowed to remain for the rest of his life, but he was still required to donate money for oil and incense (*xiangyou qian*). Wealthy men were allowed to build cottages and could live by themselves on the mountain (*Guangdong nianjian* 6.166–167).

Another early source is the *Changchun daojiao yuanliu* (Origins and Development of the Daoism Lineage of [Qiu] Changchun) by Chen Minggui of the Qing. It states that under the Qing, most Daoist temples in Guangdong belonged to the Quanzhen school, as disciples tracing their descent from the Quanzhen master Ceng Yiguan had spread all over the area. Ceng Yiguan, a tenth-generation disciple of the Quanzhen master Li Qingqiu, came from Shandong to Mount Luofu in the late seventeenth century. During the reign of Kangxi, he became the abbot of the Chongxu guan and other Daoist temples (*Changchun dao-jiao yuanliu* 7.38).

How were the Daoist temples on Mount Luofu managed? Was a strict monastic system maintained, and were all members required to renounce the world? No direct records remain today, but extraneous evidence suggests that the system was rather loose and that the temples were like high-grade hermitages for the upper classes. The English traveler A. M. Henry who went hiking on Mount Luofu in the late nineteenth century, for example, notes that the Sulao guan was the wealthiest temple there because it was "largely patronised by rich merchants from Hong Kong and elsewhere, who come to spend a few months or weeks in what they call religious retirement, living on vegetable diet" (Henry 1886, 320–322). Another Westerner, the English vice consul, made an excursion to Mount Luofu in 1892 and visited the Sulao guan. He was welcomed by two men speaking English. Both of them had stayed in the United States for many years as a cook and a merchant. After they retired, they came to the Sulao guan to quietly pass the remainder of their lives (Bourne 1895). The Sulao guan as an upper-class hermitage is succeeded by spirit-writing cults with the name of *xianguan*, which literally means "lodge of the immortals," such as the Yunquan xianguan, which arose in the first stage of the *daotan* movement.

Aside from Mount Luofu, the various local areas of each prefecture also had Daoist temples, whose organization usually followed the model of those on the mountain and which belonged to the same sect. Daoist priests residing there were usually called *daoshi;* they lived on mountains and practiced physical and spiritual cultivation, earning their living by performing rituals for people (*Guangdong nianjian* 6.167). Daoists from Mount Luofu established or rebuilt most of the local temples in Guangdong. In these temples Lüzu was always worshiped, and in some temples spirit-writing séances were also performed.

Let us consider Daoist temples in the city of Guangzhou as an example. Here we have several institutions, for example the Sanyuan gong (Temple of the Three Primes), located at the foot of Mount Yuexiu, in the northern part of the city. Its long history can be traced to the Yuegang yuan, established by Bao Jing in the fourth century. At the end of the Ming dynasty, it fell into ruin, but during the reign of Shunzhi (1644–1661), it was repaired. In 1706 it was restored further by the Daoist Du Yangdong, who had been an abbot of the Chongxu guan (*Guangdong tongzhi* vol. 229; *Gujilue* 14, *Siguan* 1; *Luofu zhinan;*

23). The Sanyuan gong was one of the official monasteries of the Quanzhen school (Yoshioka 1989, 181).

At the foot of Mount Yuexiu was another Daoist temple called Yingyuan gong (Temple of Accordance with the Primes), which was also one of the official monasteries of the Quanzhen school (Yoshioka 1989, 181). It was established by Ke Yanggui, a disciple of Ceng Yiguan (*Changchun daojiao yuanliu* 7.38). John Henry Gray, a missionary who lived in Canton in the late nineteenth century, visited it and found dozens of priests in residence there. They worshiped at three major shrines, one dedicated to the Three Pure Ones (Sanqing), one to the Dipper Mother (Doumu), and one to Lü Chunyang, that is, Lü Dongbin. In the latter, Gray says, stood a bowl with holy water, used by the faithful to cure ailments (1875, 382).

In addition, nineteenth-century Canton had at least four Daoist temples centered on the worship of Lüzu. There was first the Chunyang guan (Temple to Chunyang), located on Mount Shuzhu in the southern suburb across the Pearl River. It was founded in 1824 by a Daoist named Li Mingche. Then there was the Xiuyuan jingshe (Pure Lodge for Cultivating the Prime), located in Huangsha in a western suburb. It was originally a shrine of Lüzu built in 1854. Receiving income from two fish ponds, it was managed by Daoists invited from the Chongxu guan (*Nanhai xianzhi* [1872], vol. 5, *Jianzhi lue* 2.51). A governor general, Rui Lin, was one of the patrons because his deformed son recovered after drinking a medical tea prescribed in a séance performed there (*Nanhai xianzhi* [1910], vol. 26, *Zalu* 51). The wife of John Henry Gray observed one such séance in 1872 in a Lüzu temple. She writes:

> We saw the monk and the petitioner kneeling before the altar. The monk was kneeling in front of the devotee. Our attention now became absorbed in another monk, who had before him on a table a large wooden board covered with sand. He was standing by the altar. A second monk was by his side, with pen and paper, to write down the message supposed to be delivered by the god whose image stood on the altar. A third monk joined the other two, whose duty, we learned, was to explain the message when written.
>
> . . . The chief performer now took his instrument, which was a piece of stick about a foot in length, into his hand, or rather he balanced it on his two forefingers. It resembles a long pen-handle, and is made of white wood. From the centre below projects a small piece of wood, which writes on the sanded board. It altogether reminded me of the planchettes so much in fashion a few years ago in England.
>
> In a few minutes the wooden instrument began to move, as was sup-

posed, without the help of the monk who held it. It moved up and down on the board, tracing large characters on it; and when the board was marked all over, that part of the message was transcribed on paper by the monk, the sand was shaken, and the board placed again on the table ready for the continuation of the writing. This happened three times, the petitioner looking on all the while with rapt attention. The fourth time the lightly-balanced wooden instrument refused to move, and the monk said the god had retired. (I. Gray 1880, 109)

The above description makes it clear that the spirit-writing procedures used in the Xiuyuan jingshe were very similar to those employed in Daoist cults in Hong Kong today.

The third temple was the Chunyang guan located near the Bridge of Huanzhu in the southern suburb across the Pearl River. It also had a spirit-writing séance for ordinary believers, which was observed by John Henry Gray (H. Gray 1875, 85–86). The fourth temple of Lü Chunyang was located at the foot of Mount Baiyun in the northern suburb—close to this famous abode of immortals (Kerr 1904). There were, therefore, more than a few Daoist temples worshiping Lüzu in nineteenth-century Guangzhou, and most of them had spirit-writing séances or provided talisman water with medical effectiveness for ordinary people. These Daoist temples were established prior to the *daotan* movement, and it is likely that they supplied a model for the latter.

In addition to these major religious institutions, there were also rather secularized temples called "Daoist lodges" (*daoguan*), found both in urban areas and in the countryside. People called their priests *Nah mouh louh*, indicating a religious practitioner specialized in chanting scriptures, exorcising ghosts, and averting disasters.[3] Such priests were highly popular, and as a result the "lodges" spread widely among the common people. Typically today, a *Nah mouh louh* handles rites of marriage, death, birth, growth, transition, and construction, as well as the selection of the appropriate days and the healing of diseases. Established Daoists, such as those on Mount Luofu, however, consider these priests deceitful and bothersome and reject their activities as heterodox (*Guangdong nianjian* 6.167).

The *Guangdong nianjian* also describes other Daoist organizations, so-called "charitable societies" (*shanshe*), which have a looser connection with religion, encourage their members to practice goodness, and work for the salvation of all. They worship Laozi, Lüzu, Guandi, and the Monkey God and tend to be middle-class or rich merchants (6.167). This description, though not detailed, shows that the popular discourse on the hierarchy and role division of Daoist temples, organizations, and practitioners was already shaped in the Republican period. In fact, the differences among them cannot have been so clear. However, as spirit-writing cults claimed to be Daoist, they were necessarily involved in this discourse. As a result, *daotan* had to take a stance that tried to approach the lifestyle of Daoist literati on Mount Luofu while also claiming differences between themselves and the *Nah mouh louh* to avoid being identified with the low-ranking priests.

Manifestations of Lüzu in Different Social Groups

Lüzu or Lü Dongbin is a figure of multiple characteristics and attributes. As Baldrian-Hussein has pointed out, in tales of the Northern Song, he appears as a Daoist, a calligrapher, a poet, an alchemist, a healer, a soothsayer, a drug peddler, and an ink seller, relating to all these diverse groups of people. Even in the early Song, Lü Dongbin was already an object of widespread cults among them (Baldrian-Hussein 1986, 134, 139). The Pearl River Delta under the Qing reveals a similar situation in that Lü Dongbin was worshiped among various social groups, most notably medicine merchants and children.

Guangzhou and Foshan, the core cities of the Pearl River Delta, were both famous for their pharmaceuticals, being trading centers where herbal medicine from all over the country were gathered and distributed. Drug merchants and peddlers constantly came and went, mainly by boat over the riverways and canals. The two cities were also famous for pharmaceutical manufacturing, and in Foshan medicine production was a chief industry, ranking equal with that of pottery, iron, silk, and cotton (Luo 1994, 213–214). According to the *Foshan zhongyi xiangzhi* (Gazetteer of Foshan District) of the year 1923, there were many pharmacies, including about twenty shops that primarily made pills, powders, and salves (6.13). In addition, there were about forty shops that provided boiled medical teas made from herbs as prescribed by doctors often employed by the shop, and ten or more shops that sold unprocessed medical materials. Some of the shops were founded as early as the late Ming (6.24).

Pharmacies often advertised their products as being based on the mystical prescriptions of immortals. Similarly, medicine peddlers, when they sold goods at marketplaces, often advertised the efficacy of their medicines with mysterious tales of having met an immortal or Daoist, in the mountains or in a dream, and having received a book of prescriptions from him. Medicine merchants, therefore, felt special veneration for immortals and Daoist priests, while consumers viewed pharmacies and drug peddlers with both awe and suspicion. The close relationship between pharmacies and immortals or Daoists appears all over China but seems to have been particularly strong in the Pearl River Delta, where drug traders came and went, medicine production flourished, and sacred mountains with immortals' legends were nearby.

One example is a shop called Chen-Li Ji, an old pharmacy established in the Ming dynasty. According to its founding legend, an unspecified immortal, who might be Lü Dongbin, helped create the original shop and later acted variously to preserve and support it (see Yu 1929, 94–96). A similar story, told in the morality book *Yinzhiwen tushuo* (Illustrated Explanation of the Text of Secret Blessings; dated 1899), notes that one day Chen Tiquan, the shop's founder, climbed Mount Xiqiao to pick herbs to make a medical tea for his sick mother. He prayed on the mountain for forty-nine nights. One morning he met an old man picking herbs, who understood his situation and gave him a drug and a book. Chen made his mother take the drug, and then she recovered. The old man's book contained prescriptions for pills or powders, and Chen realized that the old man must have been an immortal. He followed the prescriptions for his drugs, all of which were very effective, and opened a pharmacy (*Yinzhiwen tushuo*, 417–418).

The same relationship between a pharmacy and Lü Dongbin is also found in the foundation legend of the pharmacy Li Zhongsheng Tang, which was famous for the Pill of Protecting and Curing (*baoji wan*). According to the *Foshan yaoye zhi* (Record of Foshan Pharmacies; dated 1992), its founder, Li Zhaoji, came from Xinhui County in Guangdong Prefecture and in the early years of Guangxu moved to Foshan to do business. He believed in Daoism so deeply that he practiced cultivation of mind and worshiped Lü Dongbin every day. According to the legend, one day Li dreamed that he was given one copy of a prescription by Lü Dongbin and told to make drugs to cure people. When he awoke, he still remembered the prescription and made the drugs accordingly (*Foshan yaoye zhi*, 332).

The connection with Lü Dongbin is not limited to these two pharmacies, and drug merchants may have played an important role in promoting the *daotan* movement. This is suggested by the fact that more than a few founders and members of *daotan* had experience dealing in herbal medicines both as drug merchants and doctors, or were born in a family of drug merchants. For example, the founder of Puji tan, the predecessor of Wong Tai Sin, was born into a drug-trading family located in a village at the foot of Mount Xiqiu in Nanhai (see Lang and Ragvald 1993). Similarly, *daotan* members often had highly developed medical knowledge and the technical expertise to make medicines. They often made up their own prescriptions, and many morality books they published contain "prescriptions of immortals" gained through spirit-writing. Then again, several charitable associations, including spirit-writing cults that provided free prescriptions, established relationships with drug merchants in order to buy medicines at discount rates. Sometimes drug merchants provided the capital to run charitable associations, often because the latter received special tax benefits (Li 1982, 202–210). Some spirit-writing cults, like Shenggong caotang, also ran pharmacies.

As well, drug merchants often donated money for publishing morality books. It was not unusual to find the names of drug shops in a book's list of sponsors, and sometimes books also printed ads for drugs. Zhao Fenliang, one of the patrons of a Lüzu cult called Baodao tang, is a good example. A pharmacist with a large business in Guangdong and Hong Kong, he placed ads for his medicines in the morality book *Fuyou dijun jueshi jing* (Scripture on Enlightening the World by the Imperial Lord Fuyou; 1922), which was published through his donation. For pharmacies, publishing morality books thus was also one method of advertising their products. All this suggests that the drug merchants' capital, technical expertise, and networks may have been among the driving forces that promoted the *daotan* movement. Another major group involved with Lü Dongbin worship was children. In pre-modern Guangdong, during the Mid-Autumn Festival, many places had a folk custom in which groups of boys and girls would play shamanistic games by moonlight. Some girls' games were variants of the cult of Zigu, widespread in southern China since about the fifth century and an antecedent of spirit-writing.

One game is particularly related to Lü Dongbin and spirit-writing: the "Descent of the Eight Immortals" (*jiang baxian*) or the "Invitation of the Master" (*qing shifu*). First, one boy lies on the ground under the moon, while others hold incense and walk around him, chanting an incantation. The prostrate boy then enters a trance and the others ask him: "Master, are you a literary immortal or a military immortal?" If he answers "literary," that is, Lü Dongbin, he will stand up and write with a spirit-writing pen (*jibi*) in a tray of sand. Getting tired, he is asked whether he wants a disciple. If so, a boy of twelve or thirteen takes on this role. Eventually, the medium is awakened by having water sprinkled on his face; he does not usually remember anything of the sequence (Chao 1944, 634–637; Liu 1993, 634–637).

While this is only a game, some *daotan* started just like this, the Xinshan tang, for example.[4] Established in 1935 in Fang Village, a northeastern suburb of Guangzhou, it goes back to two young men working in a lumber shop, one aged thirty, the other sixteen or seventeen. Both were from the country around Nanhai and had no formal education. In the fall of 1935 they and their friends often played mah-jongg together in the lumber shop. One day, because they got tired of mah-jongg, they tried to play spirit-writing. They referred to a book called *Wanfa guizong* (Manual of Ten Thousand Methods), full of incantations and talismans with which to invite the deities to descend. They took a willow twig to use as a spirit-writing pen and covered the square mah-jongg table with incense ashes to use as a spirit-writing board. The youngest shop boy became the medium. The events are recounted in detail in the *Weishan zuile* (Doing Good Is Utmost Happiness), a compilation of spirit-written oracles from 1934 to 1939. It says:

> Since the fall of 1934, we had talked about spirit-writing, but we had no information about talismans [to call deities to descend]. After a while we got a book called *Wanfa guizhong*. We read it enthusiastically and tried to have a séance in several ways as prescribed in it. One day it happened, and the great immortal Lüzu was manifested himself. At that time what had been drawn on a table was a picture of a sword. We were filled with rapture and cried, "the immortal has come!" (*Weishan zuile*, 1)

They believed that the picture of the sword represented Lüzu, because he was usually portrayed wearing a sword. After that, whenever they played spirit-writing, Lüzu descended. In the beginning, they sometimes could not understand what the writing meant; some messages were drawn in pictures like the sword, other messages were written in characters. When they could not understand them, they asked Lüzu to provide a redrawing. One day someone brought a book called *Lüzu zhenjing* (Perfect Scripture of Patriarch Lü). After referring to it, the writing gradually became clearer. In the twelfth moon, they asked Lüzu to take them as his disciples and establish a spirit-writing cult. Lüzu agreed, and they set up the Xinshan tang on the second floor of the lumber shop.

The Xinshan tang thus originated with a spirit-writing experiment by two young men who were neither literati nor professional Daoists and who engaged in spirit-writing as a casual amusement—reminiscent of the shamanistic game of the Mid-Autumn Festival. What began as a playful entertainment soon became a serious cult, and the barely literate men turned into students of Lü's sacred writings. The cult is thus also an example of how the written tradition and preliterate shamanism were integrated in to the *daotan* movement.

The Early Stages of the *Daotan* Movement

The earliest detectable *daotan* cult was founded in 1848 at a scenic place on Mount Xiqiao, Nanhai, known as the Baiyun dong (White Cloud Cavern). Mount Xiqiao had been an academic center from Ming times onward, the site of many Confucian academies, called "study halls" (*shuyuan*) or "houses of refinement" (*jingshe*), established by literati fond of scenic beauty (Luo 1994, 81–88).

During the Qing dynasty, new Confucian academies and poetry societies (*shishe*) were established here, and the popularity of the place continued until the end of the eighteenth century, when it fell into decline. As the introduction to the *Xiqiao Baiyundong zhi* (Gazetteer of the White Cloud Cave in Xiqiao, dated 1838) explains, "Nowadays most buildings and gardens have fallen into ruin and are covered with growing thickets. It is quite a regrettable situation" (3). It proposes to reconstruct some temples and have them maintained by a resident Daoist priest. Following this proposition, on the site of the former Gongyu Academy, a new temple dedicated to Lüzu was constructed in 1840 and named Canhua gong. This was a precursor of the Yunquan xianguan (Guan 1985, 6).

Mount Xiqiao was not only a center of Confucian academies but also a sacred mountain that attracted Daoists interested in alchemy and drawn to the mountain's abundant springs and herbal medicines. Lü Dongbin appeared among them and came to occupy an important place in the local cult of immortals even before the establishment of the Yunquan xianguan, leaving a footprint on a rock in the Baiyun dong and becoming venerated in a statue owned by He Baiyun (*Baiyundong zhi* 1.13, 2.13). Later, the first abbot of the Yunquan xianguan, Li Zongjian, was a famous calligrapher. He passed the lower examination but did not hold a government appointment, coming rather to live in the Yunquan xianguan as a Daoist (*Nanhai xianzhi* [1872], 20). His attitude and background matched those of the Daoist literati on Mount Luofu, and he too was focused on physical and spiritual cultivation in a place of scenic beauty.

As regards the organization of the Yunquan xianguan on Mount Xiqiao, the *Xiqiao yunquan xianguan shiji* (Historical Record of the

Cloud Spring Hermitage in Xiqiao), a short memoir written by early members, is one of the few available sources of information. According to this, the Yunquan xianguan was a hermitage that housed a voluntary association for the practice of goodness, merit-making, and self-cultivation. To obtain membership, one had only to pay a membership fee of twenty (later sixty) taels and bring the recommendation of two members. This effectively limited membership to the affluent classes and to acquaintances of previous members. Once a person was admitted, he or she was given a Daoist name decided through spirit-writing. There was no monastic system; the members did not wear their hair in Daoist fashion or dress in Daoist robes, nor did they observe a vegetarian diet, chant scriptures, or meditate. Three years after becoming members, they could stay for their entire lives. The Yunquan xianguan, therefore, was a kind of retreat for the wealthy.

Members held three large-scale celebrations every year: the birthday of Lüzu on the fourteenth day of the fourth moon; the Hungry Ghost Festival on the fifteenth day of the seventh moon; and the birthday of the Jade Emperor on the sixth day of the twelfth moon. During the Hungry Ghost Festival, merit services were held for deceased members, dead relatives, and friends of members; at that time a variety of Confucian, Buddhist, and Daoist scriptures were chanted for seven days and nights. The cantors were sometimes members, but mostly professional priests hired from outside.

Spirit-writing séances and public lecturing sessions were also important activities. The morality book *Shanyu rentong lu* (Record of Being Good to the Human Community) was a collection of spirit-written oracles received from 1879 to 1890. In addition, the Yunquan xianguan was famous for its efficacious *Lüzu yaoqian* (Medical Fortune Slips Prescribed by Lüzu), which gave prescriptions for men, women, and children (*Nanhai xianzhi* [1910] 26.49). The organization was composed of a director, an accountant, an auditor, a receptionist, and a general manager. The director was elected by the members once every three years, and operational expenses came mainly from membership fees, donations, and money offerings made in the annual celebrations. The association purchased a great deal of real estate, including houses and shops, which in turn provided a significant income. In the early years, members typically belonged to the local elite, that is, they were local gentry, literati, doctors, teachers, wealthy merchants, and so on. Soon after the establishment of the group, the Governor General Qi Ying sent a tablet in his own calligraphy, demonstrating the support of the Yunquan xianguan by the upper classes.

Another prominent institution of the early phase was the Chang-chun xianguan in Guangzhou City, established around 1850 by the Governor General Ye Mingchen, a spirit-writing fanatic who allegedly commanded his troops during the Second Opium War (1856–1860) on the basis of orders received from the divine. The Changchun xian-guan served as a residence for Daoist literati without kin but fell into decline after the Opium War. In the late 1860s the general Jiang Liyi established the Jupo Academy on its site (Huang 1994, 81; Gray 1875, 413). In the meantime, Ye Mingchen and his father in 1855 established another association, called Xiaopeng xianguan in the western suburb of Guangzhou City. According to Gray, they worshiped Lüzu as their main deity and provided efficacious medicine prescriptions that be-came very popular among the people (Gray 1875, 662–666).

Several associations named *xianguan* also arose in the Guangdong countryside, in Qingyuan County. In 1854 the Taihe Cavern was opened on Mount Huajian in 1873, and the Taoyuan xianguan was established here as a center for the worship of Lüzu and the immor-tal Wei Ruyi. According to a local gazetteer, three provincial governors sent tablets with their own calligraphy in celebration of its establish-ment, lauding its provision of charitable services, such as burying war victims without kin. All these *xianguan* of the mid-nineteenth century were in isolated locations with scenic beauty and relied heavily on the support of the upper classes. They offered charitable services and morality books and were a venue for retired upper-class people to prac-tice self-cultivation.

The *Daotan* Movement after the Reign of Guangxu

Around the turn of the century, local elites were caught up in an es-chatological sentiment and the hope of salvation from "the great catastrophe" in response to the social disorder caused by frequent disasters, epidemics, and wars. Responding to these conditions, the *daotan* movement began to lean more toward charitable activities and spread further into the lower classes. Traditionally, *xianguan* had been hermitages for the upper classes, but now many began to shift their concern from esoteric Daoist knowledge and individual cultivation to moral reformation and the practice of goodness.

It was a general belief at the time that moral decline caused "great catastrophes," such as natural disasters and epidemics. There was no way to escape these catastrophes other than to restore moral order (Yamada 1995), an idea also expressed in the Lüzu oracles as recorded in the *Shanyu rentong lu* (256, 274–275). To escape the great catastrophes, the text advises its followers to confess sins, be without fault, act with charity, and appeal to the Emperor of Heaven (286). As a result, the local elites at this time focused on helping others rather than cultivating themselves; they thought that only good deeds could prevent the great catastrophes that were beyond human knowledge. They believed that while the goodness practiced by one person might be small, the collective practice of goodness would be significant. However, another passage states that "in the case of large-scale disasters, you cannot escape unless you do great good and earn great merit" (134). If the small goodness and merit of an individual cannot avert great catastrophes, what can people do? The oracles answer that establishing charitable societies is a very effective way to escape the great catastrophes.

Heaven is not fair or humane, the *Shanyu rentong lu* points out, and there is no way to be always prosperous and forever escape the great catastrophes. Thus, every year people become victims of wars, floods, droughts, epidemics, and famines. Seeing these things happen, Heaven is grieved but cannot bring relief to people immediately. To make up for this insufficiency, human beings must take action.

> I propose to establish charitable societies in many places such as the Aiyu Charitable Society in Guangzhou and the Tongwa Hospital in Hong Kong. These are large scale societies. But regardless of the size, big or small, you should set up such societies. Next time a disaster happens, charitable societies can rescue more people. (218)

The rise of charitable societies in Guangdong province peaked during the reign of Guangxu (Fuma 1982, 42). Members of the Yunquan xianguan were deeply affected by this trend and took an active part in it. Similarly, most spirit-writing cults arising during the Guangxu reign tended to take on the character of charitable societies; their growth was frequently triggered by epidemics, beginning with the plague of 1894 (Benedict 1996). Three cults serve as pertinent examples.

First, the Puji tan, the predecessor of the Wong Tai Sin group in Hong Kong (see Lang and Ragvald 1993), arose in direct response to the 1894 plague. The founder, Liang Ren'an, was born in a village near the foot of Mount Xiqiao in 1861. His father was a merchant of herbal medicines. When he was in his early twenties, he joined the Customs Service, but the plague changed his fate and he began to perform spirit-writing séances to ask for divine protection and prescriptions. Receiving messages from Wong Tai Sin, he and his friends continued to have spirit-writing sessions and eventually set up a formal altar in Guangzhou City in 1897. In 1899 they built a shrine called Puji tan in a western suburb across the Pearl River, worshiping Wong Tai Sin as their main deity together with Lüzu and Wei Zheng. In 1915 Liang moved to Hong Kong, rented a flat in Wanchai, and set up an altar for Wong Tai Sin in his room. In the following year he opened a medicine shop near his apartment. In 1921 he received a message from Wong Tai Sin that a new shrine should be built; he duly erected one in the village of Zhuyuan at the foot of Lion Rock Mountain. This small shrine developed into the most popular temple in Hong Kong after World War II (Lang and Ragvald 1993).

The second example is the Shenggong caotang. It, too, began during the plague of 1894, as documented in their main morality book, the *Shenggong lu*. A statue of Guangchengzi[5] had been set up in the rear of a study hall near the government seat of Fanyu County in the eastern part of Guangzhou City. This became renowned for its miraculous efficacy, and many people came to worship. When the plague broke out, people held a spirit-writing séance in front of the statue, and Guangchengzi descended on the twenty-third day of the fourth moon, preaching that people should practice goodness to avoid the plague and widely distribute talismans to cure people. After several sessions, followers decided to establish a charitable society, supported by the local gentry and officials of Fanyu County as well as by a government land grant. This was the beginning of the Shenggong caotang. They worshiped Guangchengzi as their main god together with other immortals, including Lüzu (*Fanyu xianxu zhi* vol. 5.26; *Shenggong lu* vol. 1 and vol. 2).

Their main activity was to provide medical services, including prescriptions through spirit-writing, free medicines, and consultations with doctors of traditional Chinese medicine. Sometimes following Guangchengzi's instruction, they produced their own pills. After the establishment of the Republic, they ran a medicine shop to make money and provided vaccinations, funeral services, and aid for disaster victims (*Shenggong caotang dashi jiyao,* ch. 7).

The third example is the Yu shantang, which began during the cholera epidemic of 1902 with a series of spirit-writing sessions performed at the Huixing Charitable Institute. The institute was one of nine big charitable societies in Guangzhou; it had been established in New Town in 1900 and contained an altar for Lüzu. During the cholera outbreak, its member Zhao Zunsi performed spirit-writing there to ask for prescriptions. Zhao held a *juren* degree and earned his living by teaching. He made pills to treat cholera according to Lüzu's instruction and distributed them widely. The pills were so efficacious that followers increased day by day. Eventually, he and his followers set up a new shrine worshiping Lüzu called Yihe lou; this was located in Huangsha, a western suburb of Guangzhou City. The following year, they established a new charitable society called Yu shantang next to the Yihe lou, whose main activity was to provide free medicine and assistance to the poor. They had twenty-four branches in Guangdong and, with the support of local merchants, also developed charitable activities in Hong Kong, Macao, and Singapore. Baodao tang, the Hong Kong branch, was established in 1921 (*Baosong baohe ji*, 385–387; *Fuxing* 5:11–13).

All these three *daotan* had a number of things in common, aside from the fact that they were all founded at times of plague. First, they emphasized medical services, such as receiving prescriptions through spirit-writing, producing pills, consulting with doctors, and so on. Second, they published morality books edited from spirit-writing oracles, including prescriptions given by immortals and talismans to cure diseases. Third, they were located not in isolated places of scenic beauty but in urban or suburban areas. *Daotan* as charitable societies and helpers in distress became mainstream during the Republican period and were succeeded by Hong Kong's present-day groups.

The *Daotan* Movement in the Republican Period

The Republican period saw two major changes in the *daotan* movement. First, the range of members' social strata gradually expanded. The Yunquan xianguan is a good example. According to an old member's memoir, in the early days most members belonged to the upper classes, including local gentry, literati, and wealthy merchants. However, in the Republican period, more members were businessmen engaging in commerce and industry

In the late 1920s the leaders were the director of the Chamber of Commerce and Industry, an overseas Chinese, and a politician. They replaced the traditional elites who had passed the imperial examinations, reflecting the general power shift from the local gentry to merchants. In addition, common people—farmers, shop keepers, and retail salesmen—gradually joined in greater numbers (*Xiqiao yunquan xianguan shiji*, 55). The same trend is also apparent in new foundations, such as that of the Xinshan tang, which arose in 1935 and whose members were ordinary young men working in a lumber shop, neither wealthy merchants nor literati nor religious specialists.

A second major change was that the *daotan* movement extended throughout Hong Kong and Macao. For example, the Yunquan xianguan established branches in all these places; the Yushan tang set up a branch in Hong Kong; some Shenggong caotang members started businesses in Hong Kong and built a new temple there in 1934. This change in location reflects the population expansion of Hong Kong, which had an estimated 840,473 people in 1931 as opposed to 456,739 in 1911 (Fan 1974, 2). Many Cantonese looking for business opportunities and jobs were moving to Hong Kong; refugees from disasters and civil wars found a new home there—bringing new religious impulses and encouraging the establishment of local *daotan* branches.

After the Japanese army invaded China in 1937 and occupied Guangzhou and Hong Kong, most spirit-writing cults were forced to stop their activities, returning to their customs only after 1945. Among the most prominent groups then was the Zhibao tai (Establishment of Utmost Treasure), founded by He Qizhong.[6] According to his biography written by a follower, he was born in 1916 as the illegitimate child of a silk merchant in Shunde County. In 1930, when he was in middle school, he visited a spirit-writing cult and received prophecies that turned out to be true. From then on he believed in spirit-writing and began to learn it, becoming a medium, while working in a silk shop. Between 1937 and 1940 he went to the Chongxu guan on Mount Luofu and studied under a Daoist master of the Longmen subsect. After 1941 he returned to Guangzhou to support his family, living in his friend's silk shop. The shop had been a pharmacy before the fall of Guangzhou, and on the second floor there was an altar for Lüzu. He Qisheng started a spirit-writing cult there and named it Jishan xiantan; later he moved it to Xiguan in the western part of Guangzhou City. This was the beginning of the Zhibao tai.

Like the shop clerks who started the Xinshan tang, He was young and of a low social class, but unlike them he had great talent for spirit-writing, a strong interest in Daoist knowledge, and ambition. The medicines prescribed by his spirit-writing séances were renowned for their miraculous efficacy, so the number of followers gradually increased. After he returned to Guangzhou, he continued to study rituals under the Quanzhen Daoist Ye Zongmao, an abbot of the Yingyuan gong and a resident of the Xiuyuan jingshe. Finally, he got an ordination certificate from the Yingyuan gong as a member of the twenty-fourth generation of the Quanzhen sect. He seems to have had a large circle of acquaintances. Besides Quanzhen Daoists, he kept company with

Buddhist priests, leaders of the Xiantian dao and the Tongshan she, and traditional Chinese doctors. Through these exchanges, he acquired a wide variety of religious knowledge. Later he encountered Lu Yinfang, a wealthy Hong Kong merchant, and greatly expanded his activities, establishing in 1945 the officially accredited Chinese Daoist Charitable Society of Zhibao.

He Qizhong claimed that the Zhibao tai was a successor to the Quanzhen school in two ways. First, he himself became a follower of the school and received ordination. Second, he created a genealogy that linked the Zhibao tai with the Quanzhen school. In the Zhibao tai's original certificate, there is the following passage:

> It began with Donghua dijun. . . . The teaching was then transmitted to Patriarch Qiu of the Longmen subsect. . . . Eventually the teaching was transmitted to the patriarch of the fourth generation of Longmen subsect.
>
> His family name was Huang and his Daoist name was Xuanxian. He was a native of Chen County in Guangdong. He was born on the eleventh hour of the 22nd day of the seventh moon. He descended on the spirit-writing board and established teachings in the Zhibao tai in Guangzhou after the model of Lüzu. He enlarged the gate of salvation and showed the right way. His teaching was called the Zhibao school. (*Baosong baohe ji* 159–160)

Huang Xuanxian was a fictional Daoist created by spirit-writing, who allegedly founded the Zhibao tai as a new branch of the Longmen subsect of the Quanzhen school, in effect becoming the pivot of a new genealogy. He Qizhong thereby legitimized the Zhibao tai as an orthodox Daoist organization in the Quanzhen tradition, elevating it above the status of a spirit-writing cult.

According to a report, the number of members of the Zhibao tai was more than seven hundred in the beginning and increased to several thousand after a while (Liu 1992). Most traditional *daotan* did not admit women members, but the Zhibao tai clearly stated that women could also join, possibly contributing to the popularization of female spirit-writing mediums and scripture cantors. However, their prosperity did not continue for long. In 1949, when the communist government was established, spirit-writing cults were regarded as a "feudalistic superstition," and like other spirit-writing cults, the Zhibao tai was forced to cease its activities. He Qizhong and his company fled to Hong Kong and set up a new Lüzu altar and planchette in a downtown building, which in due course developed into the Qingsong guan, one of the most powerful Daoist organizations in Hong Kong today.

Conclusion

The rise and growth of *daotan*, as we have seen, is a complex and multilayered phenomenon that cannot be explained only by the traditional view that sees them as a result of the transmission and spread of the Quanzhen tradition. This is not to deny that the Quanzhen school had some influence on the *daotan* movement. In nineteenth-century Guangdong, many Daoist temples belonged to the Quanzhen school and had close ties to the Daoists of Mount Luofu. Most worshiped Lüzu and were renowned for some folk medicines, such as spirit-written prescriptions and talisman water. It is likely that those temples supplied a model for the later *daotan* movement.

However, Lüzu worship and spirit-writing, the most important elements of the *daotan* movement, were not limited to the spread of Quanzhen temples. The practice of communicating with Lüzu by spirit-writing was popular among different social groups, from the upper to the lowest classes, and even to children—a phenomenon that cannot be explained only by the popularization of elite culture. Cantonese folk customs, such as the shamanistic games played by children at the Mid-Autumn Festival, show that ancient folk religious practices—antecedents of spirit-writing—were continuously handed down and formed a religious foundation underlying local culture.

Another important aspect is the sociology of *daotan* members. They were lay believers with Daoist knowledge and financial ability, not professional Daoist priests belonging to the Quanzhen sect. Especially in the early stages of the *daotan* movement, it was bureaucrats, local gentry, and wealthy merchants who became active participants. Their power, wealth, and strong devotion to Daoism and spirit-writing became driving forces in the movement. In the second stage, when the *daotan* began to take on the character of charitable societies, it was the drug merchants' capital, technical expertise, and networks that formed the primary driving forces behind the movement's development. Although their movements developed outside official Daoist circles, they identified themselves as "Daoist" on the basis of their own idea about what Daoism was.

In the Republican period, the range of people involved in *daotan* expanded. The young founders of Xinshan tang, which originated in the folk shamanistic game, volunteered to be Lüzu's disciples, that is, to be Daoist through communications with their master by spirit-writing. The founder of the Zhibao tai, the most famous *daotan* in postwar Guangzhou, was also originally only a young spirit-writing medium but had the amibition to become well known and wealthy. He obtained rich Daoist knowledge and funds through a Quanzhen priest's guidance and a large circle of acquaintances, allowing his ambition and imagination not only to make Zhibao tai popular and powerful in Guangzhou but also to create a new genealogy linking it with the Quanzhen school. One may see all this as part of the popularization of an originally pure Quanzhen tradition, but I do not share this view. I would rather see the *daotan* phenomenon as the lay people's movement toward the orthodoxy of Daoism, as their way of working toward their religious ideals and advancing their social prestige. The movement indicates, to borrow Kristofer Schipper's words, "the upgrading and emancipation of local power structure, and not the downgrading or popularization of Taoism" (1985, 834).

To conclude, the *daotan* movement began and grew through the integration of elements from various social groups, merging their ideas and lifestyles. It gained momentum around the turn of the century, when social disorder and unrest led to strong eschatological sentiments, then settled down to become a strong and supportive part of Hong Kong society today.

Notes

This paper is a conflation, revision, and expansion of ideas and materials discussed in Shiga 1999, chs. 4–6. The main field research for this study was done from May of 1992 to August of 1993 when I was a research student of the OISP program of the Chinese University of Hong Kong, receiving support from the Rotary Foundation, and from January to April of 1994, when I was a visiting scholar at the Center of Asian Studies, University of Hong Kong, supported by a grant from the Niwano Peace Foundation. I am deeply indebted to both supporters and to the academic programs that helped me in my studies.

1. *Lingwei* literally means the space where a spirit tablet of the dead is placed. Most *daotan* sell a *lingwei* including a spirit tablet made from white tile. On the tile, the name, place of birth, and photograph of the dead person are printed.

2. Table 1 is based on data collected from local gazetteers, morality books, and my interviews with senior members of *daotan* in Hong Kong and Macao.

3. *Nah mouh louh* is a Cantonese transliteration. The romanization is based on the Huang-Kok Yale system.

4. The early history of the Xinshan tang is based on manuscripts written by one of the founders, my interviews with the founders' descendants, and a spirit-written text entitled *Weishan zuile*.

5. Guangchengzi is an immortal who instructed Huangdi (Yellow Thearch) on longevity.

6. The materials in this section are derived mainly from *Baosong baohe ji,* edited on the basis of records and articles concerning four *daotan,* which He Qizhong had a part in founding.

Bibliography

Baldrian-Hussein, Farzeen. 1986. "Lü Tung-pin in Northern Sung Literature." *Cahiers d'Extrême-Asie* 2:133–170.

Benedict, Carol. 1996. *Bubonic Plague in Nineteenth-Century China.* Stanford: Stanford University Press.

Bourne, F. S. A. 1895. *The Lo-Fou Mountains: An Excursion.* Hong Kong: Kelly & Walsh.

Chao, Wei-pang. 1944. "Games at the Mid-Autumn Festival in Kuangtung." *Folklore Studies* 3:1–16.

Clart, Phillip. 1996. "The Ritual Context of Morality Books: A Case-Study of a Taiwanese Spirit-Writing Cult." Ph.D. diss., University of British Columbia, Vancouver, Canada.

————. 1997. "The Phoenix and the Mother: The Interaction of Spirit Writing Cults and Popular Sects in Taiwan." *Journal of Chinese Religions* 25:1–32.

Fan Chunwu. 1996. "Qingmo minjian cishan shiye yu luantang yundong." M.A. thesis, Zhongzheng University, Taipei.

Fan, Shuh Ching. 1974. *The Population of Hong Kong.* Hong Kong: Swindon Book Co., Ltd.

Fuma Susumu. 1983. "Shindai engan rokushō ni okeru zendō no fukyū jōkyō." *Toyama daigaku jimbungakubu kiyō* 7:15–45.

Gray, Isabella. 1880. *Fourteen Months in Canton.* London: Macmillan and Co.

Gray, John Henry. 1875. *Walks in the City of Canton.* Hong Kong: De Souza & Co.

Guan Xiang. 1985. *Xiqiao lansheng.* Canton: Guangdong lüyou.

Henry, B. C. 1886. *Ling Nam or Interior Views of Southern China.* London: S. W. Partridge.

Huang Shiqing. 1983. "Xiqiao yunquan xianguan huiyi." *Nanhai wenshi ziliao* 3:56–59.

Kerr, John G. 1904. *A Guide to the City and Suburbs of Canton.* Hong Kong: Kelly & Walsh.

Lang, Graeme, and Lars Ragvald, eds. 1993. *The Rise of a Refugee God: Hong Kong's Wong Tai Sin.* New York: Oxford University Press.

Li Huichuan. 1982. "Guangzhou gongyi shetuan gaikuang." *Guangzhou wenshi ziliao* 12:195–210.

Liu Xiangming. 1992. "Minguo shiqi guangzhoude daojiao." *Yangcheng jingu* 5:44–45.

Liu Zhiwen, ed. 1993. *Guangdong minsu daguan.* Canton: Guangdong lüyou.

Luo Yixing. 1994. *Ming-Qing foshan jingji fazhan yu shehui bianqian.* Guangzhou: Guangdong renmin.

Schipper, Kristofer M. 1985. "Taoist Ritual and Local Cults of the T'ang Dynasty." In *Tantric and Taoist Studies* 3, ed. by Michel Strickmann, 3:812–834. Brussels: Institut Belge des Hautes Etudes Chinoises.

Shiga Ichiko. 1995. "Hongkong no dōtan—kindai minshū dōkyō no ichi keitai toshite." *Tōhōshūkyō* 85:1–23.

————. 1998. "Saikin no Taiwan randō kenkyū no dōkō to kongo no tenbō." *Tōhō shūkyō* 92:31–42.

————. 1999. *Kindai chūgoku no shamanizumu to dōkyō: Hongkong no dōtan to fūji shinkō.* Tokyo: Bensei shuppan.

Takeuchi Fusashi. 1990. "Shinmatsu shisen no shūkyō undō." *Gakushūin daigaku bungakubu kenkyū nempō* 37:59–93.

Tsui, Bartholomew. 1991. *Taoist Tradition and Change: The Story of the Complete Perfection Sect in Hong Kong.* Hong Kong: Christian Study Centre on Chinese Religion and Culture.

Wang Jianchuan. 1996. *Taiwan de zhaijiao yu luantang.* Taipei: Nanten shuju.

————. 1997. "Zhuanbian zhongde shenqi: Taiwan guandi dang yuhuang chuanshuo de youlai." In *Xingbie shenge yu Taiwan zongjiao lunshu,* ed. by Li Fengmao and Zhu Ronggui, 121–139. Taipei: Academia Sinica.

Yamada Masaru. 1995. *Ijūmin no chitsujo—Shindai shisen chiiki shakaishi kenkyū.* Nagoya: Nagoya University Press.

Yoshioka Yoshitoyo. 1952. *Dōkyō no kenkyū.* Kyoto: Hōzōkan.

Yu Min. 1929. "Lü Dongbin de gushi." *Minsu* 41/42.

Part IV
Ritual Boundaries

10

Fang Yankou and Pudu
Translation, Metaphor,
and Religious Identity

CHARLES D. ORZECH

The Problem of Religious Identity
and the Poverty of Syncretism

Over the years, students of Chinese religion have struggled to understand and articulate the encounter between South Asian and Chinese religions, variously depicting this encounter as "conquest," "sinification," and "transformation." Recent work on the interaction between indigenous Chinese traditions and the traditions originating to the west and south of China (Zürcher 1980; Bokenkamp 1983 and 1990), as well as work on so-called apocrypha have begun to render such simplistic characterizations of this encounter problematic. In the course of my study of the *Renwang huguo boruo bolomiduo jing* (Scripture for Humane Kings, T. 245/246; Orzech 1998) I found myself struggling to articulate the sophisticated hermeneutical "play" between Confucian and Buddhist religious concepts that signaled the emergence of a new Chinese Buddhist religious identity, and which later characterized the reception of Esoteric Buddhism during the Tang dynasty. My problem was that the language of "mixture," "hybrid," or syncretism was vague and imprecise and provided little help in understanding what was going on, particularly with regard to new notions of religious identity.

The Daoist *pudu,* or ritual of "universal salvation," is often held up as a case of syncretism, a Daoist imitation of the Esoteric Buddhist *fang yankou,* or "release of the flaming mouths," in which the ritual elements of both traditions have been blended. The ritual has received relatively little and superficial analysis.[1] Indeed, the scholarship on these rituals can be seen as emblematic of the approach that many analyses of Chinese religion have taken. Like the *pudu,* Chinese religion has often been and continues to be characterized as a mixture, a pragmatic concoction, a melange, a hybrid, or a syncretic blend of religions.

Just what do we mean when we say that something is "syncretic"? In its simplest form, syncretism presupposes that two hitherto distinct religions, rituals, or what have you become mixed together, and that if circumstances were changed, the mixture would naturally separate. The conglomeration is unnatural, a kind of miscegenation. Carston Colpe has attempted to provide a more precise and, therefore, more analytically useful definition in his article "Syncretism." But Colpe concludes, "All that can be done is to point out constellations in the general history of religions that have made possible what historians may, under certain conditions, call 'syncretism'" (1987, 220a). To label a religion "syncretic" or "hybrid" (even with a hyphen, as in the term Buddho-Daoist) implies that there are two sorts of religions: the purebred and the bastard. But since all culture and religion are constituted in a continual process of encounter and mixture, to go on using such terms seems to me counterproductive, and the politics of this are more than a little problematic.[2] This is not to say that some Chinese did not regard certain forms of religious and cultural interaction as miscegenation. Many, including the famous cleric Huiyuan, did.[3] But we are not playing the same game as they are, and we should try to disentangle their prejudices from our prejudices. At best, the language of mixture, even when couched in the technical-sounding terminology of syncretism, is sloppy and analytically useless. At worst, it is biased and pernicious. Recent work on metaphor and translation offer a more nuanced approach to the problem of religious identity. As I see it, the *pudu* is a Daoist translation of the Esoteric Buddhist *fang yankou* ritual, and Daoists who perform it in no way confuse the two traditions.[4]

Ritual and Translation

Translation theory is not, of course, alien to the Chinese situation. The theory of "matching" or "extending" meanings (*geyi*) was articulated as a method of translating Buddhist technical vocabularies in the early Six Dynasties.[5] *Geyi* brought together indigenous Chinese terms and notions from the *Daode jing*, the *Zhuangzi*, and the *Yijing* as analogues in the service of communicating South Asian Buddhist ideas. Although *geyi* supposedly ended as a technique of translating with the advent of Kumārajīva in the early fifth century, the *hermeneutic reality* of using

Chinese culture to communicate Buddhist notions did not abate; rather, it became more sophisticated, and I have argued elsewhere that it reached a very advanced state in the work of the Esoteric *ācāryas* (masters) of the Tang court, especially Amoghavajra and his immediate Chinese disciples (Orzech 1998, 169–174).[6]

In contrast to the simplistic and misleading rhetoric of syncretism, theories of translation not only articulate that things come together but also afford a way to articulate *how* things come together, following the trail from initial encounter to forms of mutual accommodation, borrowing, or transformative development.[7] In short, recent work on translation and metaphor afford us a more nuanced approach to the complexities inherent in the construction of religious identity.

In a fascinating essay on the use of Hindu metaphors and terminology in early Bengali Muslim literature, Tony K. Stewart observes,

> Religious encounter seen as translation . . . is not just an act of utterance followed by the emotional, political, and ideological conflict of conversion, but ultimately reveals a movement of *accommodation* by the receiving or target language and the culture it represents, which when sufficiently pursued eventually becomes an act of *appropriation*. The target language incorporates fully the new terms and concepts that result from this encounter, a process which is patently different from syncretism. The act of incorporating what is alien ultimately changes its host . . . (2001, 276)[8]

Moreover, "when the 'translation' is successful, the new term becomes a part of the target culture's extended religious vocabulary, and carries with it, or at least points to, another conceptual world" (2001, 276). Stewart demonstrates that the Hindu terminology and conceptions present in early Bengali Muslim texts does not reflect an ad hoc mixture. Rather, these texts are witness to a process of religious encounter in which new *Muslim* identities were constructed by a careful appropriation of indigenous religious concepts and vocabulary. In laying out his argument, Stewart presents a typology of translation theories that, for the sake of convenience, I will summarize here. He terms these "formal equivalence," "refracted equivalence," "dynamic equivalence," and "metaphoric equivalence." "Formal equivalence" involves a one-to-one match of terms and is, for all intents and purposes, an ideal. Even when it occurs, immediate clarification is needed. Indeed, early translation "committees" attempting to render Sanskrit and Pali in Classical Chinese often produced a wooden or literal word-for-word rendition that then served as the basis for a cleaned-up, more palatable end product. No one assumed the literal version was an end in itself.

"Refracted equivalence" offers us a more down-to-earth picture of what goes on in translation. André LeFevre conceptualizes translation metaphorically as a "mirror" reflection of the original, but the "glass" of the "mirror" not only reflects but also refracts or distorts (LeFevre 1982, 3–19; 1975). For instance, an author might equate such high-level terms as "*bodhi*" and "Dao," often knowing full well that while they can play vaguely similar roles in Buddhism and Daoism (to attain *bodhi*, to attain the Dao), they are not the same. Having discovered the inevitable "refraction," we are still afforded little analytic leverage with regard to the distortion in question. The "dynamic equivalence" theory propounded by Eugene Nida (1964; 1969) and theories of "intersemiotic" or "metaphoric equivalence," as articulated by Stewart and inspired by the work of Jakobson (1971) and Johnson and Lakoff (1980; 1999) are more useful.[9]

By emphasizing *how* a term functions in its new social and linguistic universe, Nida shifts the focus away from equivalence to the contours and deployment of the distortion caused by translation. Nida sees the translator's choice of terms as part of a wider strategy that takes into account parallel functions of the terms in their own social and textual context. For example, when the Tang dynasty Esoteric master Amoghavajra praised emperor Daizong as a *mingwang* (Skr. *vidyārāja*), it is unlikely that he meant that Daizong was a *vidyārāja* in the same sense that Acala (Budong) is, and he would not bother to invoke Daizong in ritual as he did invoke Acala. Rather, in his capacity as "protector of the Law," Daizong functions *like* a *vidyārāja*. Thus, in a letter written by Amoghavajra to Daizong thanking him for a gift of incense, we read,

> Already you have showered me with gifts. When can I ever repay you? It is proper that I reverently bathe the statues at the appointed times and that I perform the *homa* rites at the half moon in order that the thirty-seven worthies [of the Vajradhātu mandala] may protect the state of the brilliant king and that the sixteen protectors might augment the awesome spirit of the sage thearch, so that you may live as long as the southern mountain, eternally, without limit. [827c24–828a24]

As is evident in his correspondence with Daizong, Amoghavajra's use of the term "*mingwang*" expanded previous Chinese use of the phrase "brilliant king" found in the Confucian classics like the *Great*

Learning, for now a "brilliant king" finds his proper role in protecting the Dharma. Conversely, the equation *mingwang = vidyārāja* changes the semantic scope of *mingwang* in its Buddhist setting by adding to it connotations involving the Chinese ideology of the sage-king. In their correspondence, Amoghavajra and Daizong deployed the term "*mingwang*" dynamically to suit particular contexts (Orzech 1998, 191–198). There is no need to assume that either man "converted." Indeed, it is important to note that such a dynamic translation makes it possible—even probable and strategically desirable—for two participants to understand the equivalence differently, deliberately construing the term to suit the immediate context (Sangren 1987, 185; Orzech 1998, 95, 99–107).[10]

When key terms of a religious ideology are brought into play, the interaction often goes beyond the limited mapping of one term to another. Each term carries with it a broad range of metaphorical "entailments" and coordinate terms that can also be mapped. In other words, sophisticated translators may deliberately bring entire alien metaphorical complexes into play and through careful choice enrich both worlds. Stewart calls this "metaphoric equivalence." One extended and elaborate example of this strategy involves the fifth-century *Renwang jing,* which I have explored elsewhere (Orzech 1989; 1998). In that scripture the translation of the Buddhist "kings of forbearance" (*renwang*[a]) by the Confucian "humane kings" (*renwang*[b]) becomes the starting point for a comprehensive engagement of Confucian and Buddhist religious worlds and the emergence of a new religious identity: Chinese Buddhist (1989, 17–24; 1998, 99–107).

George Lakoff and Mark Johnson's work on metaphor throws considerable light on such broader mapping. During the last quarter of a century, Johnson, Lakoff, and their students have carried out a systematic exploration of how metaphoric mappings between a source domain and a target domain are fundamental to our ability to think complex thoughts (1980; 1999).[11] According to Johnson and Lakoff, metaphor involves more than mere linguistic equivalence. Rather, metaphor is the basis of thought itself. It begins in early childhood as sensory-motor development is mapped onto judgments to produce a fund of largely unconscious "primary" metaphors. Examples include MORE IS UP, SIMILARITY IS CLOSENESS, STATES ARE LOCATIONS, and so on (Lakoff and Johnson 1999, 48–56).[12] Later, this primary act of translation from one domain to another is extended in new ways. For instance, in referring to the common contemporary metaphor LOVE IS A JOURNEY, Lakoff explains,

> The metaphor involves understanding one domain of experience, love, in terms of another domain of experience, journeys. More technically, the metaphor can be understood as a mapping (in the mathematical sense) from a source domain (in this case, journeys) to a target domain (in this case, love). The mapping is tightly structured. There are onto-logical correspondences, according to which entities in the domain of love (e.g. the lovers, their common goals, their difficulties, the love re-lationship) correspond systematically to entities in the domain of a journey (the travelers, the vehicle, destinations, etc.). (Lakoff 1993, 207)

Metaphor is, in effect, a form of translation, and it gives us a way to articulate what takes place in cultural encounter. In such encounters we can often see an entire source and target complex from one cul-ture being mapped onto a source and target complex in another cul-ture. For instance, in Buddhism, acts are "seeds," and the consequences of acts are referred to as "fruit" (MORALITY AS AGRICULTURE). An agricultural metaphor has been mapped onto a moral domain. Thus, through karma and reincarnation, one "reaps" reward in heaven or suffering in hell. Buddhism's most far-reaching contribution to Chi-nese religion may have been its notion of individual karmic retribu-tion that in some arenas displaced indigenous corporate theories of retribution (such as *chengfu*). But the translation of this South Asian metaphoric complex was itself appropriated and transformed by Chi-nese metaphors involving morality and bureaucracy. Just as this world is governed bureaucratically, so too are heaven and hell (COSMOS AS BUREAUCRACY). Thus there are "magistrates" arrayed in various "courts" with "secretaries" who must handle the paperwork. Just as in a *yamen*, protocol must be followed and justice must be meted out as punish-ment. Indeed, the central role of documents in Daoism and the very notion of "registers" (*lu*) attests to the pervasive structuring power of this metaphor.[13] In this "metaphoric equivalence" we find more than mere borrowing, the translation of one term by another, or even the enrichment of one vocabulary by another. We have, instead, two com-plex metaphoric worlds rendering, reflecting, and expanding one an-other in an intersemiotic pas de deux. An entire metaphoric world (and its subcomplexes and entailments) has been mapped onto another metaphoric world, which is in turn transformed by this new mapping.[14]

The *Fang Yankou* and the *Pudu*

Ever since ethnographers and historians of religion began to describe the ritual life of the Chinese, the complex of "ghost rituals" has been a primary exhibit for the syncretic character of Chinese religion. Indeed, if we examine performances by Buddhists and Daoists during the ghost festival, we find striking similarities. A five-pointed crown is worn by the Daoist during the *pudu,* and a similarly patterned five-pointed crown is worn by the Buddhists in performing the *fang yankou.* Both Daoists and Buddhists use "vajra-handled" bells, both employ "mudras" (*yin*), and both chant "mantras" (*zhenyan; shenzhou*). Scholars of Daoism such as Duane Pang and Michael Saso point out the "Buddhist-inspired" elements of the ritual while they note that the "essence" of the performance is Daoist (Pang 1977, 98–99). John Lagerwey also repeatedly notes the Buddhist influence on the hell-busting rituals deriving from the Lingbao corpus. Yet little has been done to articulate just what role the Buddhist material plays in the Daoist ritual. One is left with the distinct impression that we are witnessing some sort of ad hoc ruse, a religious fraud perpetrated solely in the interest of market share. As Lagerwey observed,

> Taoists who do such services have to compete with Buddhists for clients, for Buddhists traditionally have done and still do both Rituals of Merit and of Universal Salvation. Indeed, important elements in these Taoist rituals are clearly of Buddhist origin, the paintings of the ten hells which line the side walls of the altar during these rituals, for example, and the dates after death in which the Ritual of Merit should be done. There is considerable overlap between Buddhist and Taoist Rituals of Merit, more even, at least in Taiwan, than De Groot's essay on "Buddhist Masses for the Dead at Amoy" (1884) would suggest. The only real difference, a Taoist priest once told me, is that the Buddhists bring the soul to a paradise in the west, the Taoists to one in the east! And even this distinction would seem to be contradicted by the soul-banner inscription used by Master Ch'en which places paradise in the west. (Lagerwey 1987, 172)

But as the anthropologist A. M. Hocart once cautioned, we would do well to proceed with caution when evaluating statements by native informants (1973, 46). Perhaps something more than ad hoc attempts to garner market share is going on here; perhaps the borrowing reflects a sophisticated encounter between two ritual systems, a translation that is dynamic, metaphoric, and intersemiotic. Maybe we are missing something important concerning the construction of Daoist religious identity.

So let us look more closely at these apparently "identical" rituals. For the purposes of this chapter, I will limit my examination of *pudu* ritual to the manual contained in fascicles 60–62 of the *Lingbao lingjiao jidu jinshu* titled *Xuandu daxian yushan jinggong yi* (HY 466), the description by Duane Pang of a *pudu* in Honolulu based on a related manual, my own observations of *pudu* at the conclusion of a *jiao* in Lam-tsuen Valley in the New Territories of Hong Kong in 1981 and one performed during the "ghost festival" the same year, and the brief manual *Lingbao dalian neizhi xingchi jiyao* (HY 407), translated by Judith Boltz (1983). I will also be drawing on my own previous work on the *fang yankou* (particularly of T. 1320 *Yuqie jiyao yankou shishi yi* [Orzech 1989; 1994]). I will proceed by noting some general similarities and then lay out the ritual programs in some detail.

Generally speaking, the similarities between the Daoist *pudu* and the Buddhist *fang yankou* may be outlined as follows:

1. Material details, that is, Taoist use of "vajras," five pointed "crown," etc.[15]
2. Similarities involving terminology and ideas (vajra, karma, sweet dew, ghosts).
3. The use of "Brahmā-language."
4. The use of "mantras" and "mudras."
5. Complex metaphorical similarities in overall ritual structure or conception.

These do not exhaust the similarities, but they will do for a start. The Daoist *Xuandu daxian yushan jinggong yi,* like other Lingbao texts, shows considerable influence from Buddhism both in terminology and in its overall program. As I noted above, Erik Zürcher and Stephen Bokenkamp have examined borrowings of Buddhist vocabulary in the Lingbao corpus and the complex of ideas surrounding Brahmā-language. Each of these would take considerable time to unpack, so instead I will focus here on the key terms on which the broader metaphoric mapping depends.[16]

Any careful observer of these performances will note that the overall program of the *pudu* and the *fang yankou* are similar. Both follow the same pattern of invocation/visualization of the ritual world, transformation of the adept into a savior, hell-busting, feeding of the beings, preaching of merit, and dismissal. Both employ mantra and mudra, or "secret gesture" (*shoujue*). Both rituals adapt individual soteriological programs to communal salvation. In both, salvation takes the form of an initiation. Both are based in macrocosm–microcosm homologies. Both can be linked to alchemical and sexual imagery. Both rituals exhibit the same sort of sequencing, concluding abbreviation, and so on of the sort noted by Staal (1980) and Payne (1985; 1991). And the list could be lengthened.

Here we need to think about "metaphoric equivalence," for at this level of generality Buddhist and Daoist rituals have no distinguishing characteristics and might be viewed as interchangeable if not wholly identical. However, if we look closely at the metaphors central to each ritual, a more nuanced picture emerges. The Buddhist ritual involves the feeding and salvation of hungry ghosts (*egui*), those *preta* who in Buddhist lore are condemned to wander about starving and whose mouths burn (and thus the term "*fang yankou*," release of the "flaming mouths"). The Daoist ritual refers instead to wandering souls as *guhun* or orphaned *hun* souls. The different terms used to refer to the "ghosts" is the key to understanding that the *pudu* is a sophisticated Taoist "translation" of the *fang yankou*.

The Buddhist *Fang Yankou*

The Buddhist *fang yankou* involves a ritual peregrination to assemble beings from all of the six *gati*. Its dramatic core involves an assault on hell followed by a banquet for hungry ghosts (*egui*, Skr. *preta*). The rite unfolds with the use of mantra to assemble the ghosts, to open the hells and the ghosts' constricted throats, to eliminate their karmic obstructions, and to multiply the offerings of "sweet dew" (*ganlu*, Skr. *amṛta*) to slake their thirst. The five Tathāgatas are then invoked, and the assembled beings are given consecration (*guanding*, Skr. *abhiṣeka*) and then escorted off to rebirth in the Pure Land. The ritual is structured according to well-established templates stemming from the *Sarvatathāgatatattvasaṃgraha* (T. 865, 866, 882, etc.) and its related cycle of texts. The earliest versions of the ritual are found in T. 1313–1315 and 1319 and date from the eighth and ninth centuries. A later, more elaborate manual (T. 1320), which probably dates from the Yüan dynasty, incorporates the key mantras of the earlier Tang manuals and fills out the ritual in the fashion of the Buddhist tantras, complete with accompanying mudra and instructions for visualization. This manual is the basis for all later known manuals.[17]

This salvific "banquet" exhibits a highly regular structure based on the metaphor—harkening back to the Vedas—of inviting a guest for dinner. "At the most fundamental and overt level, both Vedic and Tantric rituals are banquets in honor of the gods" (Wheelock 1989, 111).[18] In Vedic ritual, the gods are first invited to the banquet with an appropriate mantra; they are provided seats, water to wash with, flowers, and so on. They are praised and then fed, often with *soma,* an ambrosia (*amṛta*) identified with the "seed" of the sacrificer and the intoxicating drink of the gods that conferred both immortality and fertility. The offerings are transmitted to the "guests" by pouring them into the sacrificial fire. In turn, the Vedic worshiper could expect a variety of boons: health, wealth, fertility and sons, and immortality. The entire performance hinged on the proper execution of the hymns and mantras. This "banquet" metaphor and its entailments are present to this day in *pūjā* ("offering"), which characterizes popular Hindu worship, and in the various rites of the tantras. Indeed, if we examine the sixteen traditional *upacāra*s, or "attendances," of household and temple *pūjā,* we find remarkable correspondence with *homa* and other esoteric rites (Falk 1987, 12:83a–85a). Not surprisingly, one mainstream tradition in Japanese Shingon (Chūinryū of Koyasan) divides most rituals into five modules based on the guest metaphor: purification, construction, encounter, identification, and dissociation (Payne 1985, 219–222).[19]

Tantric ritual continues this banquet metaphor and maps several further metaphoric complexes onto it. As exterior ritual, the process of invoking and feeding the gods of the mandala and the use of the sacrificial *homa* fire, all conducted with the proper mantra, remain in place. Already in Vedic practice we see the metaphoric complex of the *soma*/seed of the sacrificer that has been mapped onto the banquet (SOMA IS AMṚTA, IS SEED). In yogic and tantric practice a further metaphoric layer involving the internalizing of the Vedic fire has been added. Thus, the sacrificial fire is identified with yogic "heat," or *tapas,* and in this interior "yogic" banquet the altar, mantras, offerings, and so on are mapped onto the body of the adept (BODY AS ALTAR, THE FIRE AS TAPAS). While the Vedic banquet with the gods transformed the sacrificer into an immortal ("We have drunk *soma;* we have become immortal") tantric ritual transforms the adept into a divinity, a bodhisattva, or a Buddha.[20] In short, tantric ritual is a palimpsest of many metaphoric analogues. It is a rich complex of source domains and targets, and the evocation of one metaphoric layer can activate others.

Buddhism, and particularly the Buddhist tantras, extend these metaphors yet further. In typical practice the adept confesses transgressions (a process often accompanied by *homa*), arouses the "seed of enlightenment" (*bodhicitta*) through external and internal offerings, is consecrated (*guanding,* Skr. *abhiṣeka*), and, using the very seed syllables (*bīja, zhongzi*) of the divinities previously invoked and worshiped, generates himself as a Buddha or bodhisattva. The tradition makes the analogy between the interior banquet and the exterior banquet quite explicit, with the external consumption of fuel and offerings for the benefit of a community paralleled by an internal incineration of the adept's karmic obstructions or defilements. Extending the metaphor, it is said that the "exterior *homa*" is the fire altar, the sapwood, and so on, while in the "adamantine inner *homa* total enlightenment is the flame and my own mouth is the hearth" (T. 867; 18.266a).

Most tantric Buddhist rituals focus not only on the identification of the worshiper with a Buddha or bodhisattva, but also on the *effect* of such identification in the world. Thus most rituals are apotropaic, and the adept, acting as the divinity, secures various sorts of blessings for a community.[21] The *fang yankou* deploys this metaphoric richness in the execution of a sequence in which the adept first arouses "the vast and great mind" (the mind of enlightenment, or *bodhicitta*), visualizes and invites the Buddhas and other divinities of the mandala/altar, repents transgressions, and then begins the banquet with visualized offerings of "sweet dew" (*bodhicitta, ganlu*). Next the adept generates him- or herself as the bodhisattva Avalokiteśvara (Guanyin) through the yogic transformation of the sonic and photic "seed-syllables" (*bīja, zhongzi*). With eyes closed, the adept visualizes a clear and pure lunar disk in the heart.

> Shining brightly on the disk is a *Hrīḥ bīja* which transforms into an eight-petaled lotus. On this lotus throne is Guanzizai [Avalokiteśvara]. . . . The Bodhisattva thinks thus: "each being has this flower of enlightenment. The pure Dharmadhātu is without stain. . . ." One then visualizes this eight-petaled lotus gradually expanding to fill up limitless space and thinks, "On behalf of the ocean-like assembly of Tathāgathas illuminated by this flower of enlightenment I vow to complete the great offering. If my mind is steadfast in this concentration then limitless creatures will arouse compassion, and all those who are illuminated by this enlightenment blossom's light will be completely liberated from all suffering and have the same marks as Guanyin bodhisattva [Avalokiteśvara]." (T. 1320; 21.476b)

The lotus vision now shrinks into the adept's own body. The adept makes the Guanzizai mudra "empowering" (*adhiṣṭhāna, jiazhi*) the four places: the heart, shoulders, throat, and top of the head. At each place the mudra touches there appears a *Hrīḥ*. Once the adept recites the mantra OM VAJRA DHARMA HRĪḤ, the body of the adept becomes that of Guanzizai (T. 1320; 21.476b–c).

Having assumed the guise of Guanyin and having donned the crown of the five *Tathāgatas* indicative of his or her consecration (*abhṣeka, guanding*), the adept recites the vow of Dizang (Kṣitigarbha) to save all beings in the hells and thereupon makes the round of the six paths (*gati*), summoning beings to the banquet. On reaching the gates of hell the adept looses an attack employing mudra and mantra. Making the Vajra-fist, the adept advances, visualizing the opening of hell while chanting the hell-smashing spell (*po diyu yinzhou*). A fiery light streams from the mudra, and from his mouth (pronouncing the mantra) there comes a fiery brilliance. The adept visualizes a red *hrīḥ* syllable shining on the lunar disk in his heart. The light of his mouth, that from the mudra, and that of the syllable in his heart together illuminate the *Avīci* hell. The chanting of the mantra thus three times unlatches the locks on the gates of hell and opens the doors, and all of the suffering beings come out. Recalling the vow of Dizang not to attain Buddha-hood until all the hells are emptied, the adept moves on to the next realm of rebirth (that of the hungry ghosts) to summon them to the Dharma assembly. Making the mudra of "opening the throats" and chanting the mantra of the Tathāgata of Expansive Spirit, the adept opens his hand like an opening Lotus blossom, and above the white lunar disk one visualizes the syllable *A* pouring forth sweet dew, which condensing into a vapor, falls like a gentle rain on the bodies of the ghosts and spirits, extinguishing their flames and purifying and cooling them (summarizing T. 1320; 21.476c–478a). Now sated, the assembled beings are led in worship of the Three Jewels, arouse the "essence of enlightenment" (*fa puti xin*), and receive the "seal of the discipline" and consecration, and they too make offerings (T. 1320; 21.478b–480b).[22]

Thus the intertwining of inner and outer banquets based on metaphors of inner and outer fires and the oblations put into the fires are key to understanding the *fang yankou* ritual. First, in basic Buddhist terms, "moving the mind to make offerings" to others results in the arousal of *bodhicitta* (the "seed" of enlightenment) in oneself (OFFERING IS SEED, IS ENLIGHTENMENT). This nourishing "seed" quenches the fire of the passions and releases one from the "hell" of samsara (PASSIONS ARE FIRE; ENLIGHTENMENT IS CONSECRATION). In Esoteric ritual these offerings are the genesis of one's own enlightenment. In the *fang yankou* (and in other apotropaic applications of Esoteric ritual) the same metaphoric complex is then extended to all beings. The sound and light of the *bīja*/seed loose the gates of hell and unbind all fetters (karmic defilements) so that the "flaming mouths" (*yankou*, MOUTHS ARE HEARTHS) of the liberated ghosts can be watered with the sweet dew (ganlu, *amṛta*, SWEET DEW IS BODHI-CITTA, IS CONSECRATION) of the teaching! Thus the *fang yankou* is a symbolic abrogation of karma and the banquet a "sweet rain" of Dharma. Both are based on the Buddhist metaphoric complex of internal yogic practice and external *homa,* or fire sacrifice. The emblems of this metaphoric complex are the terms "*yankou*" and "*egui*"—the flaming mouth of the hungry ghost that must be fed with the sweet dew of the teaching.

The Daoist *Pudu*

Turning now to the Daoist *pudu,* we at first see the obvious similarities, then some striking differences. As in the *fang yankou,* the adept summons and assembles the "Heavenly Worthies of the Ten Directions" and along with his assistants he intones the "Great Talisman for Mobilizing the Brahmā-*qi*" (*daxing fanqi fu,* HY 466; 60.5ab). Then through a meditative program that merges the Three Pure Ones into the One, the adept is transformed into a "savior." He directly invokes the Three Pure Heavenly Worthies and an additional four Heavenly Worthies (the Heavenly Worthy of the center, completing the eight, is not mentioned in the manual, 5b–12a), and he dons the five-pointed *wulao* crown and assumes the identity of Taiyi jiuku Tianzun, the Heavenly Worthy Who Saves the Suffering. His descent to the world is followed by deployment of the hell-busting talisman (*poyu fu*) and the removal of fetters (14a–16b). This is followed by a circumambulation of the cosmos, during which a variety of *guhun,* or orphaned *hun* souls, are rounded up and shepherded to the feast, led now by Bamen kaidu Tianzun, the Heavenly Worthy Who Opens the Way to Salvation Through the Eight Gates (17b–23a).[23] These cosmic peregrinations parallel the visit to the six paths in the Buddhist ritual and even include the "six paths" as one of the ten locales on the itinerary. Clearly, the basic structure of the ritual mirrors that of the *fang yankou!*

Nonetheless, the metaphoric complexes and entailments of this banquet for *guhun* are overwhelmingly Daoist. While mantra-like spells (*zhou*) are chanted, it is not the oral mantra but the written word that takes center stage as each event in the ritual drama involves the deployment of a *fu*—a written talisman. While Buddhist ritual manuals can be (and often are) pared down to a series of mantras, the scaffolding of the *Xuandu daxian yushan jinggong yi* consists of a string of *fu* whose core metaphors are unmistakably Daoist. Take, for example, the "Enunciation of the Hell-smashing *Fu*" (*xuan poyu fu*):

> In boundless Fengdu
> with range on range of Vajra mountains
> the illimitable brilliance of the Numinous Treasure
> illuminates and cauterizes the pool of trouble
> and lights up the bodies of the departed.
> With the rites of audience at the Altar of the Occult Origin
>   (*xuanyuan tan*)
> the advancing spirits ascend the blue sky
> as the acolyte guides them with the Numinous Banner. (16ab)

And again, in the "Enunciation of the *Fu* Which Bursts Open" (*kaipi fu*):

> The light of the Numinous Treasure of Jade Clarity shines into the
>   three roads.
> In every detail it lays open the karmic road.
> Penetrating everywhere,
> it reaches to the very throne of the East Flower.
> Suddenly without leaving a trace,
> the spirits transcend heaven
> and journey to the banquet with the three primordial officers.
>   (*you yan san guan,* 16b)

Beyond the obvious borrowing of the outline of the Buddhist *fang yankou* there are "Buddhist" details here (vajra mountains, karmic road), but "Fengdu," the "brilliance of the Numinous Treasure," the "audience at the Altar of the Occult Origin," the "three primordial officers," and the notion of the *fu,* or written talisman, themselves alert us to a decidedly Daoist root metaphor, THE BODY IS A STATE. The "entailments" of this metaphor are those of the Chinese bureaucracy. The country is administered by "officials" whose salvific knowledge is deployed in the creation and use of written documents. This "banquet," for orphaned souls, is an official banquet, a banquet that takes its form from official audiences (THE BANQUET IS AN AUDIENCE). Once the Daoist takes on the identity of Taiyi jiuku tianzun, he becomes an officer (THE PRIEST IS AN OFFICIAL), at each step using *fu* to "summon" the *guhun,* to open their throats, to feed, clothe, and transform them. While we might argue that Buddhist Esoteric tradition homologizes the human body to the fire altar, the cosmos, and the divine body, the notion that the body is a state with its own terrain and its own gods and officials is certainly *not* present.

The *fang yankou* lavishes considerable attention on the opening of hell and the eradication of karma, and relatively little space to the clothing and feeding of the spirits. Conversely, the *Xuandu daxian yushan jinggong yi* hell-busting sequence is brief, while the enumeration of the many types of *guhun* souls, their feeding and clothing, goes on for more than eighteen double pages (61.4a–22b). In a series of rites parallel to but more extensive than the Buddhist program, the Heavenly Worthy Who Nourishes (beings) uses a spell to produce "sweet dew" (*ganlu,* again) that calls the *hun* souls, opens their throats (another Buddhist detail), and feeds, unbinds, clothes, and cleans them. Here the metaphors and their entailments point to a Daoist symbolic universe of communal responsibility, miraculous fountains, and sympathetic relationships between nature and physiology, once again based in the body of the Daoist. Thus, for example, in "Enunciating the *Fu* for Opening the Throats" (*xuan kai yanhou fu*) we read:

> Vast and obscure, Heaven's Numinous Fountain
> moistens the withered and nourishes the beings.
> It flows in accord with nature,
> and thus the saliva of the gods (*shenjin shengye*) flows forth.
> The clear [water] of the Great Occult
> enlivens the *hun* and shrivels the *po.*
> The Numinous [Treasure] provides continuous relief
> and the Clear Numinous protects [them] from
> the fierce flames and dense smoke [of Fengdu].
> The flower pool is boundless,
> no one can fathom its source.
> The withered infants blossom forth
> and the three *qi* fly to heaven. (61.11ab)

Both the assault and the banquet are cast in a Daoist key, based on an occult interior world that resonates to the external world and is guided by divine officials. Moreover, the constricted throats in the title of the *fu* are not present in the text of the *fu,* which speaks instead in terms of nourishing "withered" infants (ORPHANED SOULS ARE INFANTS). The only throat found here involves that of the gods and of the Daoist whose saliva is deployed to salvific effect. The presence and primacy of this interior bodily locale with its extensive pantheon is most directly indicated in the *Xuandu daxian yushan jinggong yi* by the "Enunciation of the *Fu* of the Food of the Teaching of the Secret Brahmā Which Opens the Bowels" (*Xuan bifan kai zangfu fashi fu zhuan* 61, 29). Judith Boltz has translated a related manual that gives us some of the distinctive flavor of this metaphor and its entailments:

> Visualize next the myriad savants and thousand perfected as they come
> drifting through space and enter the pearl en masse . . . after the per-
> fected have assembled the [supreme Monarch] of primordial com-
> mencement releases the propitious rays of the white hairs between his
> eyebrows, casting them down to illuminate all the purgatories of the
> Nine Abysses of Fengdu, that is, they shine down from Nirvana [*niwan,*
> the nine palace-grottos in the cranium] to beneath the navel. With each
> ray . . . the Celestial Worthies who Relieve Suffering . . . enter into all
> the purgatories . . . all the incriminated *hun* souls are pardoned and for-
> given and they exit forthwith from the purgatories . . . join in the
> chanting and descend, pacing the phosphoresent clouds. They [the sav-
> ior worthies] sprinkle all the *hun* souls with sweet dew and ritual rains,
> by which they are able to cool and clarify their minds and bodies and
> open wide their throats. (Boltz 1983, 500–503)

As the *Xuandu daxian yushan jinggong yi* continues, it is evident that
the cleansing and nourishing of the *guhun* is based not on the metaphoric complex of Vedic and yogic *homa* fire found in the *fang yankou*
(the presence of the ostensibly "Buddhist" term *niwan* notwithstanding) but on the Daoist metaphor of the body as a state. This bureaucratic metaphor itself had long before been mapped with Daoist
metaphors of internal alchemy (*neidan:* THE BODY AS COSMOS; HEAVEN
AS CRANIUM, HELL AS BOWELS, etc.). The "sweet dew" of this banquet
indicates not the Vedic/yogic *amṛta/ bodhicitta* but rather the divine
saliva or pearl of "jade yang" and the elixir of the immortals of Daoism that is synthesized in the fiery crucible of the Daoist master's body
(*lianhua fa,* THE BODY AS CRUCIBLE; 61.31b–32a). The orphaned *hun*
souls are "criminals" who must "undergo the procedure of refinement"
(*shou lian fa;* 61.8b) or undergo "refining and transformation" (*lianhua,* PURIFICATION IS RECTIFICATION; 61.20a), and so on. The *pudu*
"banquet" is based on the bureaucratic, physiological, and alchemical
metaphors of Daoism and its salvific program, and its "sweet dew" elic-
its the entailments of those metaphors.

It should be quite clear at this point that "syncretism" is totally inadequate as a framework for understanding what is going on in the
pudu. We do not have here an ad hoc throwing together of elements
properly a part of two separate systems. Rather, in the *fang yankou* we
see Buddhists utilizing ritual programs and metaphoric complexes (a
language of mantra, *dhāraṇī,* and *bīja*—the potent sonic seeds of reality in the *Yogatantras*) of South Asian origin with many layers of
"source" and "target" domains to address a particularly Chinese need
(the annual mopping-up of the cosmos). The Daoist *pudu* rituals ap-

propriate the overall idea and plan of the Buddhist program and even many of its details. But this is a "translation" in which the many-layered South Asian metaphoric complex is mapped as a whole onto a similarly many-layered East Asian metaphoric complex involving orphaned *hun* souls and the bureaucratically orchestrated process of their salvation through alchemical transformation in the Daoist's body. The *pudu* is properly a case of "metaphoric equivalence."

Given the fact that both the Buddhists and the Daoists held communal banquets on behalf of departed souls long before the advent of Esoteric Buddhism, and given the fact that both religions deployed banquet metaphors that entail "sweet dew" (albeit of very different metaphoric provenance), it is no wonder that observers consider the *pudu* and the *fang yankou* "indistinguishable." But there is a coherent difference. The *pudu* does not copy the *fang yankou*. It translates its ritual program—a descent to hell and a salvific shepherding and nourishing of the beings of the universe—in a coherent Daoist performance based on distinctively Daoist metaphors.

There are, however, a few loose ends, and this takes us back to the apparent identity between the *fang yankou* and the *pudu* propounded by some native and scholarly observers. Have the two rituals interacted for so long that they are interchangeable? Many laypeople who hire the priests and monks care little about the matter. But they certainly are not interchangeable for the Buddhists and Daoists who perform the rituals! Michel Strickmann has argued that the idea of a banquet itself is of Buddhist origin. Yet Chinese culture seems to be organized around food and banqueting, so convergence on this matter is not surprising. Perhaps Buddhist ritual inspired the notion of using the symbolism and techniques of alchemy in a communal setting, but this is probably true of the Lingbao movement as a whole.

One dimension of Daoist *pudu* that may be "intersemiotic" is the relationship between the Daoist's own salvific intitiation and his or her ability to "save" or initiate others, for the alchemical sublimation of the adept is played out as a sublimation/initiation of the suffering souls (Lagerwey 1987, 210). As already noted, a similar structure occurs in the *fang yankou,* and consecration/initiation of the *egui* is found in the Tang manuals. The association was played out at large Buddhist ordination centers that held *fang yankou* at times of mass ordinations (Strickmann 1996, 373–378). The longstanding association between wandering monks and wandering *preta*—both of whom must be fed— is of decidedly Buddhist provenance.

There are a number of areas in which Daoist rituals may have influenced the Buddhist *fang yankou* and vice versa. The Buddhist manual refers to the beings according to their appropriate *gati* and uses the term "*egui*." The addition of the "Writ on the Ten Types of Lonely *Hun*" (*Shilei guhun wen,* T. 1320; 21.483b–484a) would appear to address decidedly Daoist expectations.[24] Also peculiar is the mantra for ghosts who are obstructed from the distribution of food (*zhangshi gui,* 480a). Given the elaborate evocation and destruction of karma that follows the hell-busting sequence, this seems superfluous. Or maybe here we have an echo of the "obstructed" souls (*zhihun*) of the Daoist tradition? Perhaps more striking is the final bonfire in which Dizang Wang, along with offerings of hell money, is consumed. Strick-mann conjectured that this represented not a *homa* but a Daoist-styled incineration of documents (Strickmann 1996, 407). He is, I think, cor-rect. What he seems to have overlooked is that the *homa* fire is present in the Buddhist rite in the "flaming mouth(s)" (*yankou*) that must be fed "sweet dew."

Notes

1. For an overview, see Orzech 1994, 51–72. Bemoaning the lack of stud-ies, Michel Strickmann has recently considered this material (1996, 403–411). Actually, Yoshioka (1959, 369–432) has a substantial treatment of the complex.

2. Syncretism remains a widely used category in religious studies and an-thropology. For a look at the politics of its use in anthropology, see Stewart and Shaw (1994). See also T. K. Stewart and C. W. Ernst (forthcoming).

3. Huiyuan inveighed against the mixing of Chinese and Buddhists in cer-tain roles as "mutual interference of different species." See Orzech 1998, 108.

4. I will be using "translation" in three senses. First, as actual translation from one language to another. Second, as the representation of the sounds of one language in another (more precisely, transliteration). Finally, as the process of transferring ideas, complexes of ideas, and ritual structures between one set of texts and performances and another, whether in the same language or not.

5. On *geyi*, see Ch'en 1964, 68–69; Zürcher 1972, 1:184; T'ang 1951, 276–286; Fung 1953, 2:241–242.

6. The task of interpretation in the context of "sinification" is perceptively treated in Gimello 1978, 52–89; Gregory 1991, 93–114.

7. Zürcher (1980) has distinguished between "strong" and "weak" forms of borrowing, and between formal and complex forms of borrowing of Bud-dhist materials in early Daoist texts (up to the sixth century).

8. I am indebted to two fine essays by Stewart, which introduced me to re-cent translation theory (1999; 2001).

9. For a critique of Nida, see Gentzler 1993, 43–73.

10. Sangren has argued that such differential interpretation is at the heart of the concept *ling* (numinous, efficacious), and the skillful manipulation of social interaction through differential interpretation constitutes *ling*.

11. I would like to thank Glen Hayes, whose paper "The Necklace of Immortality" (1996) introduced me to the work of Lakoff and Johnson.

12. Here I follow the convention in metaphor studies of placing metaphors in small caps.

13. Erik Zürcher advances an argument somewhat similar to this. Thus in his survey of Buddhist elements in early Daoist scriptures, he distinguishes "weak" borrowings from "strong" borrowings, with the former largely emptied of their Buddhist meanings (*kong*, or "emptiness," for example). He argues for three "complexes" that had profound impact in Daoism: karma and retribution, morality (including the notion of precepts and vows), and Buddhist cosmology (1980, 119–122). Stephen R. Bokenkamp, in an analysis of the Buddhist influence on the Lingbao corpus, has explored the impact of the South Asian metaphor of creative language ("Brahmā-language") on the development of Daoist *dhāraṇī* and Brahmā-script, as well as the impact of the metaphor of the "pure-land" on the scriptures of Ge Chaofu. He has done similar work on the impact of the bodhisattva stages (1983, 462–464, 469–476; 1990).

14. Stewart draws on Roman Jakobsen, who has given the label "intersemiotic" to translation from one medium, say speech, to another medium, such as signs (Jakobsen 1971, 261). In other words, an entire signification complex can be "mapped" onto another such complex.

15. We should note that the style of Daoist *vajras* is unique.

16. For the record, the *Xuandu daxian yushan jingkong yi* contains a rather humdrum list of "Buddhist" terms: *Tianzun* (Heavenly Worthy), *ganlu* (*amṛta*, sweet dew), *wu zhuoshi* (five turbulent epochs), *sanjie* (*triloka*, triple world), *sanbao* (*triratna*, triple gem), *moluo* (*māra*, evil), *liudao* (*gati*, six destinies), *zhengfa* (*saddharma*, correct teaching), *fa* (*dharma*, divine law), *falun* (*dharma-cakra*, wheel of the law), *shifang* (ten directions), *shizuo* (lion throne), and Guanyin (Avalokiteśvara). Also present are various permutations of the term "*fan*," or Brahmā.

17. For a treatment of the later manuals, see Orzech 1994.

18. For an introduction to and brief bibliography on the vast topic of Vedic ritual, see Heesterman 1987. For the metaphor of the guest in Vedic ritual, see Heesterman 1993, 36–39 188–189.

19. For my analysis of the modular structure of Esoteric ritual, see Orzech 1998, ch. 6; for the chart "Boiler-plate Sequences," see 1998, 296.

20. This citation is from *Rig Veda* 8:48. See O'Flaherty 1981, 134.

21. The apotropaic dimension of Esoteric and Vajrayāna ritual has not escaped scholarly attention. For a treatment, see Beyer 1973, 254–258; Stablein 1976a, 165–173; 1976b, 55–69.

22. For a more complete treatment, see Orzech 1989, 101–109; 1994, 56–61.

23. "Eight gates" refers to an eight-sided mandala with the eight trigrams, the zenith, and the nadir representing the ten directions of the cosmos.

24. It is obviously an addition, as it follows the statement that "the *Yuqie jiyao yankou shishi yi* is complete" (483b3).

Bibliography

Beyer, Stephan. 1973. *The Cult of Tārā: Magic and Ritual in Tibet.* Berkeley: University of California Press.

Bokenkamp, Stephen R. 1983. "Sources of the Ling-pao Scriptures." In *Tantric and Taoist Studies,* ed. by Michel Strickmann, 2:434–486. Brussels: Institut Belge des Hautes Etudes Chinoises.

———. 1990. "Stages of Transcendence: The *Bhūmi* Concept in Taoist Scripture." In *Chinese Buddhist Apocrypha,* ed. by Robert E. Buswell, Jr., 119–147. Honolulu: University of Hawai'i Press.

Boltz, Judith M. 1983. "Opening the Gates of Purgatory." In *Tantric and Taoist Studies,* ed. by Michel Strickmann, 2:487–511. Brussels: Institut Belge des Hautes Etudes Chinoises.

Ch'en, Kenneth K. S. 1964. *Buddhism in China: A Historical Survey.* Princeton: Princeton University Press.

Colpe, Carsten. 1987. "Syncretism." In *Encyclopedia of Religion,* ed. by Mircea Eliade, 14:218–227. New York: Macmillan.

Falk, Nancy E. Auer. 1987. "Pūjā." In *Encyclopedia of Religion,* ed. by Mircea Eliade, 12:83–85. New York: Macmillan.

Fung, Yu-lan. 1953. *A History of Chinese Philosophy* 2 vols. Trans. by Derk Bodde. Princeton: Princeton University Press.

Gentzler, Edwin. 1993. *Contemporary Translation Theories.* London: Routledge.

Gregory, Peter N. 1991. *Tsung-mi and the Signification of Buddhism.* Princeton: Princeton University Press.

Gimello, Robert M. 1978. "Random Reflections on the 'Sinification' of Buddhism." *Bulletin of the Society for the Study of Chinese Religions* 5:52–89.

Hayes, Glen A. 1996. "The Necklace of Immortality." Unpublished paper presented to the Tantric Studies Seminar of the American Academy of Religion.

Heesterman, Jan C. 1987. "Vedism and Brahmanism." In *Encyclopedia of Religion,* ed. by Mircea Eliade, 15:217–242. New York: Macmillan.

———. 1993. *The Broken World of Sacrifice: An Essay in Ancient Indian Ritual.* Chicago: University of Chicago Press.

Hocart, A. M., ed. 1973 [1952]. *The Life-Giving Myth and Other Essays.* London: Butler and Tanner.

Jakobson, Roman. 1971. "On Linguistic Aspects of Translation." In *Selected Writings II: Word and Language,* ed. by Roman Jacobson, 260–266. The Hague: Mouton.

Johnson, Mark, and George Lakoff. 1980. *Metaphors We Live By.* Chicago: University of Chicago Press.

———. 1999. *Philosophy in the Flesh: The Embodied Mind and Its Challenge to Western Thought.* New York: Basic Books.

Lagerwey, John. 1987. *Taoist Ritual in Chinese Society and History.* New York: Macmillan.

Lakoff, George. 1993. "The Contemporary Theory of Metaphor." In *Metaphor and Thought,* ed. by Andrew Ortony, 202–251. Cambridge: Cambridge University Press.

LeFevre, André. 1975. *Translating Poetry: Seven Strategies and a Blueprint.* Amsterdam: Van Gorcum.

————. 1982. "Mother Courage's Cucumbers: Texts, Systems, and Refraction in a Theory of Literature." *Modern Language Studies* 12:3–19.

Nida, Eugene. 1964. *Towards a Science of Translating.* Leiden, The Netherlands: E. J. Brill.

Nida, Eugene, and C. Taber. 1969. *The Theory and Practice of Translation.* Leiden, The Netherlands: E. J. Brill.

O'Flaherty, Wendy Doniger, trans. 1981. *The Rig Veda: An Anthology.* Harmondsworth, England: Penguin Books.

Orzech, Charles D. 1989a. "Puns on the Humane King: Analogy and Application in an East Asian Apocryphon." *Journal of the American Oriental Society* 109:17–24.

————. 1989b. "Seeing Chen-yen Buddhism: Traditional Scholarship and the Vajrayāna in China." *History of Religions* 29:87–114.

————. 1994. "Esoteric Buddhism and the *Shishi* in China." In *The Esoteric Buddhist Tradition,* ed. by Henrik H. Sørensen, 51–72. Copenhagen: Seminar for Buddhist Studies Monograph.

————. 1998. *Politics and Transcendent Wisdom: The Scripture for Humane Kings in the Creation of Chinese Buddhism.* University Park: Pennsylvania State University Press.

Pang, Duane. 1977. "The *P'u-tu* Ritual." In *Buddhist and Taoist Studies,* ed. by Michael Saso and David Chappell, 94–122. Honolulu: University of Hawai'i Press.

Payne, Richard K. 1985. "Feeding the Gods: The Shingon Fire Ritual." Ph.D. diss., Graduate Theological Union, Berkeley.

————. 1991. *The Tantric Ritual of Japan: Feeding the Gods: The Shingon Fire Ritual.* New Delhi: Aditya.

Sangren, P. Steven. 1987. *History and Magical Power in a Chinese Community.* Stanford: Stanford University Press.

Staal, Fritz. 1980. "Ritual Syntax." In *Sanskrit and Indian Studies,* ed. by M. Nagatomi et al., 119–142. Dordrecht, The Netherlands: D. Reidel Publishing.

Stablein, William. 1976a. "A Descriptive Analysis of the Content of Nepalese Buddhist *Pūjās* as a Medical-Cultural System with References to Tibetan Parallels." In *In the Realm of the Extra-Human: Ideas and Actions,* ed. by Agehananda Bharati, 165–173. The Hague: Mouton.

————. 1976b. "Tantric Medicine and Ritual Blessings." *The Tibetan Journal* 1:55–69.

Stewart, Charles, and Rosalind Shaw, eds. 1994. *Syncretism/Anti-Syncretism: The Politics of Religious Synthesis.* London: Routledge.

Stewart, Tony K. 1999. "The Language of Equivalence: Interpreting Bengali Muslim Literature from the Middle Period." In *Essays in Memory of Momtazur Rahman Tarafdar,* ed. by Perween Hasan and Mufakharul Islam. Dacca, Bangla Desh: Dacca University Centre for Advanced Research in the Humanities.

————. 2001. "In Search of Equivalence: Conceiving Muslim-Hindu Encounter through Translation Theory." *History of Religions* (February) 40, no. 3.

Stewart, Tony K., and Carl W. Ernst. forthcoming. "Syncretism." In *Encyclopedia of South Asian Folklore,* ed. by Margaret Mills and Peter J. Claus. New York: Garland.

Strickmann, Michel. 1996. *Mantras et mandarins: Le bouddhisme tantrique en Chine*. Paris: Gallimard.

T'ang, Yung-t'ung. 1951. "On *Ko-yi*, the Earliest Method By Which Indian Buddhism and Chinese Thought Were Synthesized." In *Radhakrishnana: Comparative Studies in Philosophy*, ed. by W. R. Inge et al., 276–286. London: Allen and Unwin.

Wheelock, Wade T. 1989. "The Mantra in Vedic and Tantric Ritual." In *Mantra*, ed. by Harvey P. Alper, 96–122. Albany: State University of New York Press.

Yoshioka Yoshitoyo. 1959. *Dōkyō to bukkyō* vol. I. Tokyo: Nihon gakujutsu shinkōkai.

Zürcher, Erik. 1972. *The Buddhist Conquest of China: The Spread and Adaptation of Buddhism in Early Medieval China* 2 vols. Leiden, The Netherlands: E.J. Brill.

——. 1980. "Buddhist Influence on Early Taoism: A Survey of Scriptural Evidence." *T'oung Pao* 66:84–147.

11

Daoist Hand Signs
and Buddhist Mudras

MITAMURA KEIKO

Daoist hand signs (*shoujue*) have been used in personal and communal rites since the Six Dynasties for a variety of purposes, including the exorcism of evil forces, control over spirits, and healing of diseases. They developed formally in the medieval period under the direct influence of Buddhist mudras (literally, "hand seals," *shouyin*) yet also continued to unfold in their own distinct way. Since most of their practice was esoteric and their transmission predominantly oral, only few early sources remain. In fact, it is only from their mention in the *Datang liudian* (Six Classics of the Great Tang), in a section entitled "Palm Signs" (*Zhangjue*), that we can presume their existence and use in the early middle ages. From less direct indications in Tang texts, moreover, it appears that hand signs were actively used in Daoist rituals at least toward the end of this dynasty.

Besides the standard *shoujue* (hand sign), words used for secret gestures and finger signs in Daoism include *tao* (twist), *qia* (pinch), *jue* (sign), *zhangjue* (palm sign), *zhijue* (finger sign), *taozhi* (finger twist), *jieyin* (knot seal), *jiefa yin* (dharma knot seal), and *shouyin* (hand seal, or mudra). Each of these might refer to signs made by both hands, by one hand, or by some hand movement. The terminology is vague and multivalent, again mainly because the predominant form of the signs' transmission was oral rather than textual.

There are only few studies on Daoist hand signs to date. Some examine the relation between Buddhist mudras and Daoist hand signs,[1] others focus particularly on late sources of the Ming and Qing dynasties.[2] Although relatively few in number, hand signs used in ritual today have also received some scholarly attention.[3] The numbers of signs have declined continuously through history, down from several hundred in the Tang and at least several dozen in the Yuan and Ming, as documented in the *Daofa huiyuan* (A Corpus of Daoist Ritual, HY 1210).[4] Among the latter, thunder styles (*leiju*) and sword signs (*jian-jue*) were especially common, hand symbols that played a key role in the then-popular thunder rites. Unlike their rather high ritual specialization, it seems that before the Song, hand signs served a large variety of purposes and were thus a great deal more numerous.

In general, two main groups of Daoist hand signs can be distinguished: those that developed in direct imitation of Buddhist mudras, and those that can be described as uniquely Daoist finger techniques. Hand signs deriving from Buddhist mudras include signs signifying "lotus," "bridge," "sword," and so on.[5] They are the same in name and execution, yet their specific description in Daoist texts makes it clear that they were given an additional significance. Here, unlike in Buddhism, each finger segment was linked with the larger cosmos by being associated with the eight trigrams, seven stars of the Dipper, or twelve zodiac positions.

Hand signs deriving directly from Buddhist mudras raise the question of how and when certain patterns were taken over and reinterpreted to fit the specifically Daoist worldview. By extension, this brings up the larger issue of the interaction between the two religions. Scholars have examined this issue variously, comparing scriptures and ritual manuals, relating ethical and cosmological systems, and analyzing different statements made by religious leaders. In all cases, key problems involve the identification of significant characteristics of Buddhism and Daoism in the various periods of Chinese history; the question of whether any of these characteristics were special enough to belong uniquely to one or the other; and—for those characteristics that were shared—the huge problem of religious interaction, that is, which religion produced the characteristics first and how were they taken over and transformed (or not transformed) by the other. These questions have often been related to the phenomenon of "syncretism," which implies the conscious mixture of two religious creeds or ritual systems. The term, as Charles Orzech discusses at length in this volume, is highly problematic and does not suit the Daoist-Buddhist situation very well. Following his lead, I will, therefore, discuss Daoist hand signs in terms of the adaptation, borrowing, and translation of Buddhist techniques.

Then again, there are uniquely Daoist finger techniques, best found in the Ming-dynasty ritual compendium *Daofa huiyuan* as well as in the Song-work *Tianxin zhengfa* (Proper Methods of the Heavenly Heart, HY 566) by Deng Yougong (1210–1279; see Boltz 1987, 35; Andersen 1991, 81–85). These uniquely Daoist signs emerged historically later than mudra-inspired patterns, and again we have to ask the question of the process of adaptation, change, and development and try to identify where a uniquely Daoist technique begins and the translation from Buddhism ends. Many problems remain open, as, for example, dating and context: when exactly what kinds of sacred gestures and finger signs were applied in which kinds of Daoist rituals; or where the specific Daoist technique came from that involves thumb pressure to be executed on either the tip or the central section of a finger.

Daoist rituals, in themselves, present a huge area of unexplored territory, and many of them have grown and been formed through the interaction with Buddhism—but Buddhist ritual, too, has done its share of adapting Daoist forms. From the perspective of the application and forms of sacred hand gestures, three types of Daoist ritual emerge, from the middle ages onward: the formal practices of the *fangshi* and longevity seekers; the techniques of inner alchemy (with their related thunder rites); and the communal rituals of Daoist groups, both lay and monastic. In all cases, the transformation of the body into a locus of contact with, and merging into, the otherworldly realm of the Dao is a key element in the rites, and sacred hand gestures serve to empower and enhance this transformation. They became especially prominent in the early eleventh century with the rise of the school of Divine Empyrean under Emperor Huizong of the Song and continued to flourish in the manifold thunder rites of succeeding dynasties until they were streamlined and began to decline in the Ming. The following discussion presents their basic patterns and historical unfolding.

Hand Signs and Spells in the Middle Ages

A clear statement about the purpose of Daoist hand signs is found in a classic on the subject, the *Tianhuang zhidao taiqing yuce* (Jade Volume of Great Clarity on the Utmost Way of the Heavenly Sovereign, HY 1472), henceforth abbreviated *Tianhuang yuce*. This text is a three-*juan* compendium on how to attain political harmony and the ideal rulership in the Dao, with a preface dated 1444 by the royal Ming prince Zhu Quan, who was an eager supporter of Daoism and an important editor of Daoist material in the early Ming (see Ren and Zhong 1991, 1172–1173). The text says:

> The Master said: Twist signs are used to communicate with the perfected, control malicious sprites, summon protective generals, and effect the healing of diseases. (3.1a)

A similar text is the *Zhuguo jiumin zongzhen biyao* (Secret Essentials of the Assembled Perfected on How to Aid the State and Save the People, HY 1217), henceforth abbreviated *Zhuguo biyao*. It, too, is a basically political compendium, but of an earlier date, bearing a preface of 1116 by the compiler Yuan Miaozong. He was a renowned Daoist under the Song emperor Huizong, who had studied with many masters and dedicated himself to proposing valuable Daoist rituals for the realization of political stability (see Ren and Zhong 1991, 968–969). The text says:

> You must deploy a suitable twist sign whenever you undertake ritual perambulation, question a sick person, exorcise malicious sprites, enter the sanctuary, cross a river, enter a mountain, or draw a talisman. (8.19a)

In other words, hand signs were associated with protection from disasters, especially when engaging in sacred acts, with the exorcism of demons or evil influences, and with the healing of diseases.

While these general statements, together with more detailed information on the formation and application of the signs, are found in later texts, Daoist works of the middle ages have very little to offer on hand signs and their uses. The earliest mention of something possibly akin to the later hand signs occurs in the Lingbao texts *Qianzhen ke* (Regulations for the Thousand Perfected, HY 1399) and *Wulian jing* (Scripture of Fivefold Purification, HY 369; see Bokenkamp 1983, 481, 483) of the Six Dynasties. They sporadically mention sacred hand movements, such as the "sword hand" (*jianshou; Qianzhen ke* 27ab) and the "snapping fingers" (*tanzhi; Wulian jing* 2b). These hand movements, in my estimation, are not yet like mudras but are merely fundamental gestures that accompany certain rituals. The fact that there is practically no information about them shows the power of the oral tradition, which protected the secrecy of Daoist activities. At the same time, magical gestures do appear in various other (shamanic) arts, thus suggesting a gradual evolution of the Daoist sacred gesture, about which written documents keep conspicuously silent.

It is only in the late Tang that a truly valuable source appears: the *Xuanpu shan lingkui bilu* (Secret Register of the Numinous Casket of Mount Mystery Garden, HY 580), abbreviated *Xuanpu shan bilu*. Although not entirely reliable in its dating, the text has a preface by Huangfu Peng, which is dated to the year 860 and gives a long line-

TABLE 11.1
PURPOSES AND PATTERNS OF HAND SIGNS
IN THE *XUANPU SHAN BILU*

Sect.	Sign	Purpose	Hand	Spell
1.1	Dipper Bowl	control things	L	*cuanyu lieyu aotuo shenyu*
1.8	Soaring Dragon	assemble clouds	L	*yun luomo weimo yuyu xuan*
2.8	Flying Matter	walk on water	L	*yumo yumo xuyu*
3.2	Giant Scabbard	become invisible	L	*yuan luohu*
3.3	Mystery	transform things	R	*ana xuanyu*
Bie.1	no name	remove obstructions	R	*xuanluo huiyu poli*
Bie.2	Brahma Knot	control spirits	L	*yulun sulu mo youli*
Bie.13	Soaring Dragon	entering gourd	L	*xuanyu xuanyu youli*

age of masters that transmitted its contents, most importantly Lin Ziyao, from whom Huangfu Peng claimed to have received it, and the fifteenth Celestial Master Zhang Gao, who allegedly presented some of the rituals to the Tang emperor Xuanzong. Again, the work is mainly concerned with the establishment of political stability through Daoist rituals (see Ren and Zhong 1991, 417–418). The work, whose title indicates that it was stored in the Hanging Gardens on Mount Kunlun and is fundamentally of celestial origin, is an extensive and rather formalized list of Daoist hand signs, including the seals of the Dipper Bowl (Tiangang yin), the Soaring Dragon (Tenglong yin), the Giant Scabbard (Jutao yin), the Flying Matter (Feizhi yin), the Mystery (Xuanyin), and the Brahma Knot (Pozhuan yin). The purpose of these signs, usually called by the Buddhist appellation *yin* (seal), was to enable practitioners to move heaven and earth, call down thunder, assemble clouds, walk on water, become invisible, and transform things. Each of them, moreover, went hand in hand with the application of a certain talisman (*fu*) and with the formal chanting of an incantation or spell (*zhou;* see table 11.1).

To give one example, the first hand sign, the Seal of the Dipper Bowl, was formed with the left hand by straightening the index and middle fingers, with the other fingers and the thumb curled into a fist. In conjunction with different talismans, the hand sign was used to either dissolve or consolidate the shame of things (see figure 11.1). The spell that went with it was *"cuanyu lieyu aotuo shenyu."* As Liu Zhongyu has demonstrated (1993), this and similar spells were not Chinese but, in imitation of Buddhist *dhāraṇī* or esoteric mantras, used Sanskrit or pseudo-Sanskrit phrases as their base. The seals of the Divine Tiger (Shenhu yin), the Heavenly Sovereign (Tianhuang yin), and the Brahma Knot come with spells that are immediate replicas of mantras used in Tantric or Zhenyan Buddhism. They entered Daoism in the eighth or ninth century, after this school of Buddhism had been transmitted to China (see Orzech 1989), and are clearly found on Buddhist statues of the late Tang. Unlike Liu, I find the source of Daoist spells used with hand signs not entirely in Buddhist mantras, even though in some cases they may be identical. Rather, I would propose a more indigenous development of the signs used in both traditions and growing in an environment of intense Buddhist-Daoist interaction in the mid- to late-Tang dynasty. The spells may have a Sanskrit origin in their wording to begin with, but they were thoroughly indigenized by the Daoist religion and do not ultimately represent a simple imitation of Buddhist techniques.

More specifically, like Buddhist mantras, the spells in the *Xuanpu shan bilu* were all basically phonetic in nature and did not attempt to

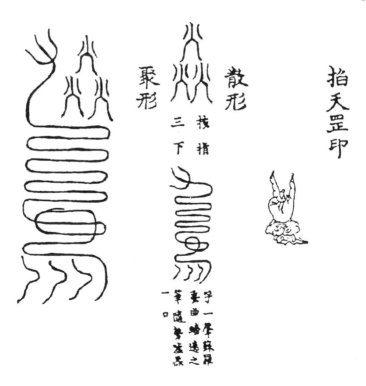

Figure 11.1. The hand sign of the Dipper Bowl and its talismans. (Source: *Xuanpu shan bilu* 1.20a.)

make any meaningful sense. They are, moreover, highly similar to those found in the Buddhist *Yujia jiyao* (see note 1), and in general, one can say that the relation of mantras to mudras in Esoteric Buddhism was close to that of spells to hand signs in Daoism. The statement of a ritual supplement to the *Yujia jiyao* (T. 1320, 21.473b–484a) thus applies to both: "Effort and wisdom are matched in the fingers" (478a).

On the other hand, there were also mudras that made use of techniques unique to China and not found in India. Some, for example, involved exerting thumb pressure on one or the other part of the fingers; others, such as those described in the *Changqu lidu nü tuoluoni zhoujing* (Sūtra of Fearful Dhāraṇī Spells for Benefits and against Poison, T. 1265, 21.294–295), by an unknown monk named Quduo and probably dating from the eighth or ninth century, have specific techniques linked to each finger segment, such as "to expel and suppress demons" with the tip of the index finger, "to heal diseases" with the root of the ring finger, and "to worship and gain merit" with the top joint of the pinkie.[6] Both these characteristics can be described as distinctly Daoist, and their appearance in Buddhist sources suggests that certain aspects in the practice of sacred gestures evolved from Daoism into Buddhism, and not vice versa.

Overall, therefore, we see a close and intimate interaction between the two religions in the practice of sacred gestures, mudras inspiring hand signs to begin with, hand signs undergoing adaptations and developing next and influencing Buddhist patterns again in certain ways. A classic example here are mudras such as the one designated as "sword"; these major secret gestures in Buddhism also played a key role in Daoism from the Six Dynasties onward. They appear variously in Daoist texts, such as the *Xuanpu shan bilu*. Their functions changed as they were adapted into Daoism, then expanded again in Buddhism under Daoist inspiration.

Classifications and Patterns in the Song

The *Tianxin zhengfa* of the thirteenth century lists thirty-six different hand signs, beginning with those for the three highest heavens and deities: Jade Clarity and the Heavenly Worthy of Primordial Beginning; Highest Clarity and the Worthy of Numinous Treasure; Great Clarity and the Worthy of the Dao and the Virtue (see table 11.2). They comprise signs of a number of celestial and stellar gods together with those used to establish command over the spirit world and gain easy access to the realms of heaven. Destroying and exorcising demons also play

TABLE 11.2
THE THIRTY-SIX HAND SIGNS
OF THE *TIANXIN ZHENGFA* (6.19AB)

1. Jade Clarity	19. Moon Lord
2. Highest Clarity	20. Dipper Bowl
3. Great Clarity	21. Opening Heaven's Gate
4. Jade Emperor	22. Closing Earth's Door
5. Great Ruler	23. Staying Humanity's Gate
6. Northern Emperor	24. Blocking Demons' Road
7. Heavenly Ding Gods	25. Piercing Demons' Heart
8. Original Master	26. Destroying Demons' Gall
9. Dipper	27. Containing Demons
10. Exorcising Evil	28. Five Thunders
11. Perfected Lords	29. Golden Knife
12. Sword	30. General Overseer
13. Sun Constellation	31. Persecuting Demons
14. Opening Seal	32. Transforming Spirit
15. Summoning Seal	33. Six Ding Gods
16. Entering Seal	34. Purple Tenuity
17. Three Treasures	35. Heaven's Gate and Earth's Pivot
18. Sun Lord	36. Dipper

a key role, as well as blocking off their paths and closing the doorways of earth and the underworld.

Another work of the same period is the *Zhuguo biyao*. It is the most complete collection of Song-dynasty signs, both those involving thumb pressure and those using hand movements, that are not specifically linked with the thunder rites. Here a total of eighty hand signs are listed, thirty-nine to be executed with the left hand and ten with the right hand, plus eight used for the seven stars of the Dipper and fifteen for mastery over the five phases (see table 11.3). Among the left-hand signs, eighteen are identical with those listed in the *Tianxin zhengfa*, largely those associated with heavenly deities and constellations. Only one, the Persecuting Demons Sign, is the same among the right-hand signs, and none at all match the signs listed in the other categories. While most signs here are specified according to execution with the right or left hand, there are yet a number that can be done with either or both hands.

In each case, the text specifies the fingers to be used and the positions they take. Typically, one forms a sign by exerting thumb pressure on one or more joints of the other fingers, as, for example, in the case of the Seven Dippers, or again that of the seven stars of the Northern

TABLE 11.3
HAND SIGNS IN THE *ZHUGUO BIYAO* (CH. 8)

1. Left-Hand Signs

All Heavens
Dharma Master
*Jade Clarity
*Highest Clarity
*Great Clarity
*Northern Emperor
Celestial Master
*Original Master
*Purple Tenuity
*Sun Lord
*Moon Lord
Hall of Light
*Dipper Bowl
*Heavenly Ding Gods
Heavenly Jia Gods
*Five Thunders
Ding and Jia Gods
*General Overseer
*Transforming Spirit
*Exorcising Evil
Meritorious Officials
Containing Pestilence
*Dipper
Punishing Demons
Forestalling Demons
*Golden Knife
Raising Troops
Four Mountains
*Sun Constellation
Chasing Demons
Golden Ding Gods
*Opening Seal
*Entering Seal
Pushing Demons into the
    Underworld
Golden City
Expelling Strange Phenomena
Expelling Locusts
Riding on Clouds
Killing Demons

2. Right-Hand Signs

Entering Sanctuary
Destroying Sanctuary

Expelling Disease
Binding Demons
White Tiger
Green Dragon
Guiding Souls
*Persecuting Demons
Establishing the Sword
Liberating the Dragon

3. Signs for Flying to the Five Dippers

Southern Dipper (L)
Northern Dipper (L)
Western Dipper (L)
Eastern Dipper (R)
Central Dipper, yang (L)
Central Dipper, yin (R)
Thunder Fire, yang day (L)
Thunder Fire, yin day (R)

4. Signs for the Seven Stars of the Dipper (L)

Gui Star, press second segment of index finger
Gou Star, press first segment of index finger
Fan Star, press first segment of middle finger
Shou Star, press third segment of middle finger
Bi Star, press second segment of ring finger
Pu Star, press second segment of little finger
Piao Star, press third segment of little finger

5. Signs for Controlling the Five Phases

Wood (L)
Fire (L)
Earth (L)
Metal (R)
Water (L)
Demon Knife (L)
Twisting Dragon (L)
Earth Center (L)
Central Earth Knife (L)
Demon Killing Knife (L)
Destroying Knife (L)
Evil Killing Knife (L)
Destroying Five Bad Rebirths Knife (L)
Killing Demons (L)
Summoning Star Gods (L)

*same as in *Tianxin zhengfa*

Dipper (see table 11.3, section 3; also figure 11.2). Unlike the late-Tang *Xuanpu shan bilu,* in which hand signs were static and strictly symbolized certain deities, concepts, or objects, the Song materials have a wide variety of signs that are executed with thumb pressure or hand movements and work more according to specific functions than symbolism. A clear development can thus be discerned between the Tang and the Song, a movement away from mudra-inspired, static symbols and toward more indigenously Daoist hand movements and cosmic functions.

The Origins of Daoist Finger Techniques

Using hands and fingers in a sacred or ritual context can first be linked with the ancient techniques of shamanism, which also involved dances, chants, and other practices later adapted into the methods of the *fangshi,* or magical practitioners, and through them into Daoism. An early text documenting the use of hand signs among the *fangshi* is Ge Hong's (283–341) *Baopuzi* (Book of the Master Who Embraces Simplicity, HY 1177), a key work on the understanding and practice of alchemy and early ritual methods. Here we have

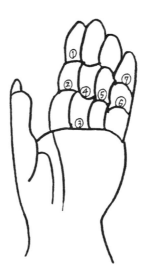

Figure 11.2. The position of the seven stars of the Dipper in the fingers. (Source: *Zhuguo biyao* 8.16a.)

[Upon entering the mountain] if you happen to see a poisonous snake, face the sun and, taking three mouthfuls of breaths from the left, confine it. Press your tongue against the roof of your mouth and place a hand upon your Central Barrier point. Next, close the Gate of Heaven and shut the Door of Earth [nose and mouth] and press something against the snake's head while making a circle about it with your hand, drawing a prison on the earth to confine it. You may also take it up and play with it. Even if you place it around your neck, it will not dare bite you. As an automatically unremovable charm, blow upon the snake with your exhalations, and it will never again leave the prison you made.

When others have been bitten by a snake, take three mouthfuls of breath from the left and blow upon the wound; it will immediately get better and cause no more pain. If you and the patient are separated by a dozen or so miles, you may do the breath procedure from a distance and shout the name of the patient. For a male, the spell is to be said over your left hand; for a female, over your right. (17.8a; Ware 1966, 290)

Clearly, in the early stages of Daoism, hand signs were used in conjunction with spells, or incantations, and talismans to afford protection and exorcise evil. What exactly practitioners did with their hands, however, is not described in the text. Still, the protective and exorcistic spells mentioned in the *Baopuzi* again appear in the early Tang, when Sun Simiao (601–693) cites a text called *Jinjing* (Scripture of Prohibitions) in his *Qianjin yifang* (Additional Medicines Worth a Thousand Pieces of Gold, chs. 29, 30; see Liu 1984; Sakade 1989). Here, in addition, more than twenty palm signs are given, among them several that involve pressing the thumb against one or the other finger. A different variation of the same idea is also described in the *Sandong zhunang* (A Bag of Pearls from the Three Caverns, HY 1131), an encyclopedia of Daoist materials compiled by Wang Xuanhe in the mid-seventh century (see Reiter 1990). It has

The *Taiyi dijun dongzhen xuanjing* (Mysterious Scripture of Perfection Cavern of the Imperial Lord of Great Unity) says: Close your eyes, clap your teeth five times, and take the middle finger of your left hand to press seven times against the nostril. Then take your right index finger and press nine times against the area between your eyebrows. This will expel all malicious influences of the three, five, seven, and nine as well as close the gates against the multitude of spirits. (3.18a)

Once done with the finger pointing, clap your teeth three times again and, in a soft voice, recite the following spell:

> The luminants above fly through the net,
> May vermilion and yellow spread their haze,
> May their energy surround all the numinous and nasty
> And let their corpses rot in depth and darkness.
> Harmonize my spirit souls, purify my material souls,
> Let me join my body with the Great Spirit above!
> Cause me to live forever and not die,
> Remain whole for myriads of years!
> May I be bright and perceptive, of penetrating vision,
> Forever joyful, beneficent and exuberant.
>
> Having concluded the recitation, clap your teeth three times again, then swallow the saliva three times and with your right index finger press below the left eye seven times. This will allow all yin energy to be completely at rest—at least while you don't raise your hand too high. (5.6ab)

Here exorcistic and life-preserving effects are gained by applying finger pressure to certain key points of Daoist anatomy, notably the gate of energy at the entrance of the nostrils and the "Hall of Light" (*mingtang*) point between the eyebrows. The idea is very similar to that found in the later practice of hand signs in which, too, certain positions in the fingers have cosmological significance and the application of pressure is used to activate protective or exorcistic powers.

Another relevant passage on the same issue is found in the *Daodian lun* (On the Classics of the Dao, HY 1122), another early-Tang encyclopedia by an unknown author, which has also partly survived in Dunhuang manuscripts (see Ren and Zhong 1991, 879–880). It has

> The *Ciyi jing* (Scripture of the Female One) says: The Perfect Lord of Great Simplicity has an efficient technique to avoid nightmares, especially useful to beginners. It goes as follows.
>
> Whenever you have a series of nightmares, understand that they are either caused by soul sprites, serve as tests for your heart/mind, or are attempts to snatch your corpse. In all cases, you need to apply the following technique for the dissolution of bad influences. As soon as you wake up, take your left hand and press your nostril area twice times seven, then clap your teeth twice times seven and chant the following incantation. . . . (4.4b)

Again, the main purpose of the finger technique is exorcistic, and it involves other ritual and purificatory activities, such as clapping the teeth, swallowing the saliva, and reciting an incantation. Closely related to other forms of purification, exorcism, and ritual acts of protection, hand and finger methods like these served to ensure safety for the whole person and were later integrated into a more extensive ritual context. Combined with spells and talismans, Daoist hand signs engaged the good spirits of the otherworld and banished the bad. Originating in finger techniques that activated certain cosmic points in the body, they are deeply rooted in ancient indigenous practice and only secondarily evolved into their formal patterning under the influence of Buddhist mudras. This development is evident first in the *Xuanpu shan bilu,* or about two hundred years after the *Sandong zhunang* and *Daodian lun.* Here the term "hand seal," or "mudra," first occurs in a Daoist context; here also the techniques of thumb pressure against certain fingers are described for the first time; and here we have the first mention of specific names of hand signs—all inspired by the Buddhist model and adapted actively into an already well-prepared Daoist environment.

Sacred Hand Movements

Besides hand positions that indicate certain symbolic patterns and are used in ritual contexts, there are also various sets of sometimes complex hand movements, usually undertaken while facing a specific direction and accompanied by an incantation. For example, the *Shangqing lingbao dafa* (Great Rites of the Highest Clarity and Numinous Treasure Traditions, HY 1211), by Wang Qizhen (Boltz 1987, 43–44) of the late twelfth century, lists five sacred sounds to be uttered seven times each in the different directions when entering a ritual chamber and burning incense in preparation for ritual. They are

> *ling*—north-northeast, press the *chou* pattern
> *mo*—east-northeast, press the *yin* pattern
> *lü*—east, press the *mao* pattern
> *tao*—east-southeast, press the *chen* pattern
> *ni*—south-southeast, press the *si* pattern (7.10b)

With each utterance, the hand should move in the direction indicated. More specifically, as described in the section "Hand Pattern of the Golden Wheel to Control Demons,"

> When moving from west to east, the hand needs to form the pattern shown below [see figure 11.3]. (*Shangqing lingbao dafa* 7.11a)

Then again, the *Duren shangjing dafa* (Great Methods of the Highest Scripture of Universal Salvation, HY 219) has this spell:

"gold"—west, press the *you* pattern
"wheel"—east, press the *mao* pattern
"control"—west, press the *you* pattern
"demons"—east, press the *mao* pattern
"pattern"—west, press the *you* pattern (40.16b)

This links the efficacious formulation with the ritual position, showing which direction the hand movements are supposed to follow. The hand movements, moreover, are linked with the specific directional and zodiac positions marked on the fingers (see figure 11.4). The purpose of the integration of rituals, chanting, and finger positions is to purify the entire body in all its cosmic positions and directions and to make sure that the good energy stays within the body and circulates correctly.

Another set of hand signs that involve movements is found in the *Zhuguo biyao,* especially in relation to methods of flying to the five Dippers. Many signs associated with these constellations are used to help

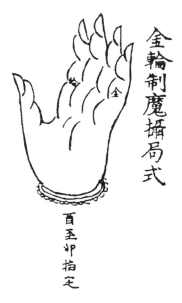

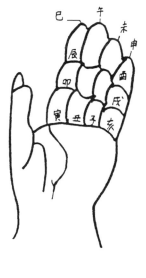

Figure 11.3. The "Golden Wheel to Control Demons." The character for "gold" is on the pinkie; that for "wheel" is on the index finger. (Source: *Shangqing lingbao dafa* 7.11a.)

Figure 11.4. Zodiac positions as marked in the fingers. (Source: *Duren shangjing dafa* 40.16b.)

in healing diseases and exorcise demons. They are activated by first mentally chanting the names of the Dipper gods, praying for their protection during the ecstatic ascent to their palaces, and then pressing certain spots in the fingers with the thumb. The text says:

> Press your fingers following the enclosed illustration, clap your teeth three times, envision the Dipper, and hold your breath. Then silently recite the names of the stars and fly off to meet them. (8.13ab)

The text does not specify how exactly the combination of visualization, chanting, and hand movements is supposed to work. However, it makes it clear that hand signs are ultimately connected to the protection of the body.

A similar description of the same method, with a list more attentive to meditative details, is found in the *Daofa huiyuan*. Here, in the section "Jade Master's Precious Way to Catch Evil Spirits," certain points on the fingers are identified with the eight trigrams and twelve zodiac positions. Practitioners move their hands in a particular way while chanting spells and practicing visualizations. For example, to fly to the Southern Dipper, they activate each star in turn:

> For the Chi Star, visualize cinnabar fire and execute the *si* [SSE] pattern
> For the Zhi Star, visualize yellow fire and execute the *chen* [ESE] pattern
> For the Huo Star, visualize red fire and execute the *li* [S] pattern
> For the Fu Star, visualize purple fire and execute the *wu* [S] pattern
> For the Zun Star, visualize dark fire and execute the *kun* [SW] pattern
> For the Sheng Star, visualize golden fire and execute the *wei* [WSW] pattern (198.16b–17a)

Again, the exact meditation is not completely spelled out, but the hand patterns are more specific than those mentioned in the *Zhuguo biyao*. Another section, also of the *Daofa huiyuan*, entitled "Jade Master's Spreading the Net to Catch Malicious Influences," has instructions on how to activate the finger positions of the eight trigrams and twelve zodiac constellations in order to summon the thirteen thunder gods. They are as follows:

> Heavenly Thunder: *Tianlei yinyin*, press the *hai* pattern (NNW)
> Spirit Thunder: *Shenlei honghong*, press the *wu* pattern (SSE)
> Dragon Thunder: *Longlei juanshui*, press the *chen* pattern (ESE)
> Water Thunder: *Shuilei pofan*, press the *zi* pattern (N)

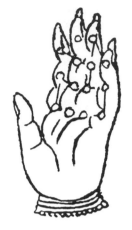

子雷五
寅速滅邪精熱大雷大卯雷二寅雷三丑雷四
波翻子社令雷火寅霹靂交橫巽神機一變
天雷隱隱亥神雷轟轟午龍雷捲水辰水雷

Fig. 11.5. The position of the thirteen thunders on the fingers together with their names and description. (Source: *Daofa huiyuan* 198.13a.)

Fire Thunder: *Sheling leihuo,* press the *yin* pattern (ENE)
Clapping Thunder: *Pili, jiaoheng,* press the *xuan* pattern (SE)
Spirit Pivot: *Shenji yibian,* press the *yin* pattern (ENE)
Swift Destruction: *Sumie xiejing,* press the *daji* pattern (center)
Great Thunder: *Leida,* press the *mao* pattern (E)
Second Thunder: *Lei'er,* press the *yin* pattern (ENE)
Third Thunder: *Leisan,* press the *chou* pattern (NNE)
Fourth Thunder: *Leisi,* press the *zi* pattern (N)
Fifth Thunder: *Leiwu,* press the *hai* pattern (NNW)
(198.13b–14a; see figure 11.5)

Another set of thunder-related hand signs, also found in the *Daofa huiyuan*, is used specifically to expel demons, cure diseases, and pray for rain. They are cited from the *Shenxiao zishu dafa* (Great Methods of the Purple Book of Divine Empyrean, HY 1209). Here we have

> The Five Thunder Signs:
> Heavenly Thunder: in both hands, press *yin*, while the little finger remains on *jia*
> Spirit Thunder: index and middle fingers are bent, while the thumb presses on *zi* and the ring and little fingers press on the thumb
> Dragon Thunder: index, middle, and ring fingers are bent, while the thumb is curved over them and holds the position *hai;* the little fingers pushes on the others, with the thumb in *jia*
> Water Thunder: the index finger is bent, while the thumb presses on *chou* and the remaining fingers press on the thumb
> Magic Thunder: index, middle, and ring fingers are bent, while the thumb presses on them without yet locking on *jia* (11.10ab)

These five hand signs do not involve finger movements but represent a combination of mudras and finger-pressure techniques. This is also evident from another passage on thunder rites found in the same text. It says:

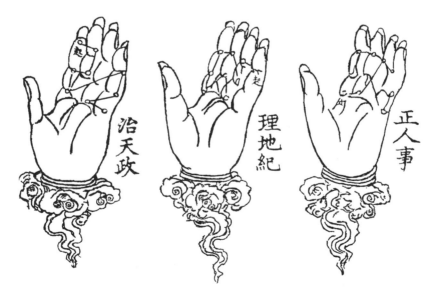

Fig. 11.6. Hand signs to support cosmic order on the levels of heaven, earth, and humanity. (Source: *Daofa huiyuan* 106.17b–23a.)

> Press the position *chen* with your left hand and take in the energy of
> the trigram *xun* while facing its matching direction. . . . Then press the
> position *zi*, again facing the direction of *xuan* and ingesting its energy.
> (4.1a)

To support and maintain cosmic order, yet another set of talismans
and hand signs is applied, among them specifically those used to "order the heavenly government" (*zhi tianzheng*), to "straighten the earthly
mainstays" (*li diji*), and to "rectify human affairs" (*zheng renshi*). Where
to press in each case is evident from the accompanying illustration (see
figure 11.6). Patterns activated here are easily connected with those
hand signs that involve movements; they are variously described in ritual Daoist texts found in the canon, first the *Zhuguo biyao* and many
more in the Ming and Qing.

Conclusion

In the Ming dynasty, when the *Tianhuang yuce* was compiled, leading
hand signs were those symbolizing jade, the sword, the nine palaces,
the seven stars, the Jade Clarity, the Northern Emperor, the eight trigrams, and the three terraces. Using the three joints of the four fingers,
they matched also the four mainstays and the eight directions (3.9a).
This group represents a much reduced repertory if compared to the
hand signs in earlier materials. The ritual use of hand signs typically
accompanied incantations or ecstatic excursions to the cosmic net. In
the context of this practice, it was acceptable to use one hand to make
finger signs or apply pressure to relevant spots, such as those symbolizing the eight trigrams, the seven stars of the Dipper, or the twelve
zodiac positions. In addition, cosmic patterns laid out on the palm of
the hand played a role similar to that of the diviner's compass and
could be used in a large variety of contexts and functions. Only later
were finger patterns linked with the bowl of the Dipper and applied
to larger cosmic control.

This discussion has focused on ritual texts contained in the Daoist
canon that present hand signs, describing their historical unfolding
and different typologies. It has become clear that Daoist hand signs
in their formal presentation and ritual use developed under the
influence of Buddhist mudras but were by no means a simple imitation of the latter. Rather, beginning with the Tang dynasty, Daoists combined the formal symbols and styles used in Buddhist mudras with their
own finger techniques and cosmological systems. As the terminology

changed from the Buddhist-based *yin* (seal) to the Daoist *jue* (sign), so the tradition adapted and integrated the Buddhist patterns into its own worldview, signifying a shift toward a uniquely Daoist practice that had its roots in medieval techniques of pressing certain sacred spots in the body for greater spiritual efficacy.

Beginning with the Northern Song and the flourishing of thunder rites, hand signs were no longer used only in meditative and exorcistic practices but were reoriented to playing an active role in the summoning of the Five Thunders, as documented in the *Daofa huiyuan*. Here many varieties of thunder styles and sword signs appear, used in the different thunder rites and becoming more intensely linked with them over time. In the ritual texts, finger techniques recorded both before and after the Song tend to be described as central for establishing the bodily integrity and harmony of the practitioner. They are also essential in increasing and maintaining the Daoist's cosmic powers and protection. They are intimately connected to methods of guarding the body against baleful influences that were already important in ancient times. The various ways of exerting finger pressure and/or pressing important spots in the body underlie the Daoist tradition of hand signs, assuring that, despite massive Buddhist influence, the signs and their usages remain firmly embedded in the indigenous religion.

To conclude, I would like to emphasize two points. In Buddhist mudras, the right hand is seen as the pure and the left hand as the impure one. This order of things is completely reversed in Daoism, in which the left hand, being of yang nature, represents cosmic purity.[7] Above and beyond this basic cosmic distinction, Daoist ritual texts pay close attention to the exact function and purpose of a given hand sign and assign a specific hand in proper accordance with the talisman used and the incantation chanted.

The other point I would like to make is that in certain extra-canonical texts, such as the *Longhu shan bichuan shoujue* (Secretly Transmitted Hand Signs from Mount Longhu; see Saso 1978), numerous hand signs are immediately patterned on Buddhist mudras.[8] In materials contained in the *Daozang*, and those discussed in this study (which date from the Tang through the Ming dynasties) on the other hand, signs different from Buddhist mudras tend to dominate. The exact relationship between these two kinds of sources and/or traditions within Daoism is yet to be determined.

Translated by Livia Kohn

Notes

1. See Yoshioka 1952; Misaki 1991; Xiao 1991; 1992. The latter especially examines the Buddhist influence on Daoist rites and signs, examining in particular the *Yujia jiyao jiu anan tuoluoni yankou guiyi jing* (Sūtra of Ānanda's Salvific Dhārani and Rites for Feeding Flaming Mouths, Contained in the Essential Collection of Yogic Practices, T. 1318, 21.468–472) by Amoghavajra, renowned Tantric master of the eighth century.

2. Yoshioka (1952) in this context studied especially the *Qiankun yizhang tu* (Charts of Palm Signs of the Trigrams of Heaven and Earth), a text of the mid-Ming; the *Fengxue jiaozi shu* (Book on Teachings of Wind and Snow) of the late Ming; and the *Jilian keyi* (Rules and Observances for Sacrifices and Purifications) of the Qing. He also considered the *Liujia feishen shu* (The Six Jia Gods' Art of Flying), the *Bamen yanqin shenshu* (Divine Book of the Beasts of the Eight Gates), and the *Wanfa fanzong* (Tradition of the Myriad Methods) of late imperial origin. In addition, Michael Saso (1978) undertook a study of these and similar materials.

3. See Ōfuchi 1983, 1:11–19, 221–225; Liu 1984, 2:80–98. Liu found that in present-day Taiwan, redhead Daoists of the north have a repertoire of fourteen hand signs, while blackhead Daoists of the south commonly use eleven. Each sign symbolizes one particular deity, object, movement, or ritual action. They apply the same term, independent of whether the sign is made by two hands, one hand, or only certain fingers.

4. On the text, see Boltz 1987, 30, 47; Loon 1979; Yoshioka 1961, 60.

5. On these, see Saudern 1960; Kokusho 1987; Nan 1990; 1992.

6. Another text that has the same phenomenon is the *Gongyang yishi* (Ritual Observances of Rites of Nurturing, T. 859, 18.177–181).

7. This is clearly spelled out in the *Tianhuang yuce* (ch. 3) and in the *Zhuguo biyao,* the latter linking the left hand with the sun (yang/purity) and the right hand with the moon (yin/impurity). See Yoshioka 1952.

8. The text contains seventy-five hand signs, most of which are basically mudras, executed either by one hand or two. Texts in the Daoist canon, on the contrary, have more signs involving finger pressure. Why this difference? Who was using which? How did they evolve historically? How do they appear in late-imperial materials? All these are unanswered questions that await further study, for which a good resource may be the recently published ritual collection by Wang Qiugui (1997).

Bibliography

Andersen, Poul. 1991. "Taoist Ritual Texts and Traditions with Special Reference to *Bugang,* the Cosmic Dance." Ph.D. diss., University of Copenhagen.

Bokenkamp, Stephen. 1983. "Sources of the Ling-pao Scriptures." In *Tantric and Taoist Studies,* ed. by Michel Strickmann, 2:434–486. Brussels: Institut Belge des Hautes Etudes Chinoises.

Boltz, Judith M. 1987. *A Survey of Taoist Literature: Tenth to Seventeenth Centuries.* Berkeley: University of California, Center for Chinese Studies.

Kokusho Kankōkai, ed. 1987. *Kaitei zuin taikan.* Tokyo: Kokusho kankōkai.

Liu Zhiwan. 1984. *Chūgoku dōkyō no matsuri to shinkō.* Tokyo: Ōfūsha.

Liu Zhongyu. 1993. "Qiajue chutan." *Daojia xue tansuo* 10:166–185.

Loon, Piet van der. 1979. "A Taoist Collection of the Fourteenth Century." In *Studia Sino-Mongolica: Festschrift for Herbert Franke,* ed. by Wolfgang Bauer, 401–405. Wiesbaden: Franz Steiner: Münchener Ostasiatische Studien.

Misaki Ryōshū. 1991. "Chūgoku, Nihon no mikkyō ni okeru dōkyō teki yōso." In *Nihon, Chūgoku no shūkyō bunka no kenkyū,* ed. by Sakai Tadao, Fukui Fumimasa, and Yamada Toshiaki, 115–154. Tokyo: Hirakawa.

Mitamura Keiko. 1998. "Kagisho ni mieru shuketsu no henyō." *Tōhō shūkyō* 92:15–30.

Nan Huaijin, ed. 1990. *Mijiao tuyin ji* vol. 1. Taipei: Laogu wenhua.

———, ed. 1992. *Mijiao tuyin ji* vol. 2. Taipei: Laogu wenhua.

Ōfuchi Ninji, ed. 1983. *Chūgokujin no shūkyō girei.* Tokyo: Fukutake.

Orzech, Charles D. 1989. "Seeing Chen-yen Buddhism." *History of Religions* 29.2:87–114.

Reiter, Florian C. 1990. *Der Perlenbeutel aus den drei Höhlen: Arbeitsmaterialien zum Taoismus der frühen T'ang-Zeit.* Asiatische Forschungen vol. 12. Wiesbaden, Germany: Otto Harrassowitz.

Sakade Yoshinobu. 1989. "Son Shibaku ni okeru iryō to Dōkyō." In *Senkinhō kenkyū shiryōshū,* ed. as *Tōyō igaku zenpon sōsho* 52–65. Osaka: Orient Publishing.

———. 1992. "Dōkyō no jyufu ni tsuite." *Kansai daigaku bungaku ronshū* 42.3:59–92.

Saso, Michael R. 1978. *Dōkyō hiketsu shūsei.* Tokyo: Ryūkei shosha.

Saunders, E. Dale. 1960. *Mudra: A Study of Symbolic Gestures in Japanese Buddhist Sculpture.* Princeton: Princeton University Press.

Wang Qiugui. 1997. *Zhongguo chuantong keyi benhui pian Fujian sheng Long Yan shi Dongxiao zhen Lüshan jiao Guangji tan keyi ben.* Taipei: Xinwenfeng.

Ware, James R. 1966. *Alchemy, Medicine and Religion in the China of A.D. 320.* Cambridge, Mass.: MIT Press.

Xiao Dengfu. 1991. *Daojiao xingdou fuyin yu fojiao mizong.* Taipei: Xinwenfeng.

———. 1992. *Daojiao shuyi yu mizong dianji.* Taipei: Xinwenfeng.

Yoshioka Yoshitoyo. 1952. "Dōkyō no tōketsu inkei ni tsuite." *Taishō daigaku gakuhō.* Reprinted in *Yoshioka Yoshitoyo chōsakushū* 3:2–18. Tokyo: Satsuki shobō.

———. 1961. "Bukkyō jukai shisō no Chūgoku teki shūyō." *Shūkyō kenkyū* 35.1:51–72.

12

Documents Used in Rituals of Merit in Taiwanese Daoism

Maruyama Hiroshi

There are many different angles from which one can approach the study of Daoist ritual, but my specific interest focuses on the contents and structure of the written documents used in them, and I try to understand their meaning within the larger religious worldview and practice of Daoism. The use of written documents is unique to Daoist ritual and is one feature that distinguishes it from Buddhist, Confucian, and popular rites. It is essential in defining Daoist ritual as Daoist and thus carries an important weight in the formation of Daoist identity. Rites in general serve to restore and reinforce identity by allowing commitment and belief to be strengthened through repetitive and securely predictable actions. A clearly structured and systematic interaction with the otherworld in this context serves to create a sense of belonging and meaning for the Daoist follower. Written documents, both through their high formality and legal jargon as well as through the various rites, divine personages, and priestly empowerment associated with them, function to establish a formalized system of universal order. The predefined ritual pattern of interacting with a hierarchically structured and bureaucratically organized otherworld grants Daoists a sense of control over their destiny and a firm position in the larger universe. Written documents are central to this self-definition of Daoists as members of the celestial organization, serving as the main means by which they communicate with the otherworldly powers and as the key to understanding the role of the ritual Daoist master as acting celestial official.

By presenting written documents in a ritual context, Daoists convey their wishes, intentions, and even orders to the otherworld. As there are multiple situations in which divine intervention is desirable,

Daoists have developed a large repertoire of different forms and formats of written documents. There are, for example, the announcement (*biao*), the memorial (*shu*), the mandate (*die*), the invitation (*tie*), the accusation (*zhuang*), the talisman order (*fuming;* also "symbol order"), the petition (*zhang*), and the placard (*bang;* see Lagerwey 1987). Each of them is uniquely used in certain specific contexts to convey particular content to deities of specific positions.

Written ritual materials of these various types are summarily referred to as "ritual documents" (*wenjian*). They are indispensible for any successful ritual performed by a Daoist of High Merit (Gaogong daoshi) and are collected variously. For our purposes, I would like to focus particularly on documents used in rituals of merit as they are performed by Daoists of southern Taiwan, beginning first with a description of the materials, then looking at their historical antecedents in and/or relationship with ritual manuals of the Song and Yuan dynasties that have come down to us in the Ming Daoist canon. Certain key issues emerge from the study of these different collections. They include the problem of standardization, the questions of historical continuity, and the varying views of the otherworld and differing rituals among local lineages. Although the Daoist sense of identity and order in all cases depends on the formal, written interaction with the deities, it is far from standardized and allows for variations both in location and over time. Examining these variations gives us further insight into the developments and tendencies Daoist identity has undergone in the past several centuries and where it is headed today.

Previous Research and Available Sources

The study of the use and function of memorials and other documents in Daoist ritual is highly specialized; therefore, only few previous works have been published on the subject. Most important are Kristofer Schipper's studies of the Prayer for Peace Offering (*qi'an jiao*) and the presentation of the memorial and the role of the immortals' ledgers in it (1974; 1977). They are, however, only indirectly concerned with rituals of merit, which are my main focus. More pertinent are chapters 10 through 13 of John Lagerwey's work (1987), which discuss liturgies undertaken on behalf of the dead and, therefore, also rituals of merit. Beginning with the placard that is posted at the site of the ritual, he explains the various documents involved in some detail.

Among Japanese studies, there is foremost the pioneering collection on Chinese ritual by Ōfuchi Ninji (1983). Here the various documents involved in rituals of merit are given detailed attention and thorough presentation (1983, 650–677). The purpose is primarily to make the documents accessible to the scholarly world, and thus the collection has ample reprints of original sources. True to its purpose, the work leaves the materials to speak for themselves or to be analyzed in the future and does not delve into their historical provenance or importance.

Beyond these specialist studies, there is the work of the Taiwanese folklorist Liu Zhiwan, who deals mainly with the Prayer for Peace Offering and the Wangye Offering (1983). However, Liu has, at least so far, not published any study that particularly treats the rituals of merit of southern Taiwan. Then there is the collection of the sacred texts used by the Xinzhu Daoist Master Zhuang, collected and edited by Michael Saso (1974). But this does not contain complete materials pertaining to rituals of merit. Most recently, there is the work by Lü Chuikuan (1994), but it too has nothing much to say about our topic. My main focus lies in the written documents used in rituals of merit more so than in the Prayer for Peace Offering, and within that framework I am primarily concerned with the relationship of presently used materials to those transmitted in ritual manuals since the Song, notably those that deal with the tradition of Yellow Register Rites (*huanglu zhai*). I find this study both relevant and highly accessible, given the present state of the sources.

As regards the sources, my own fieldwork has provided me with two sets of ritual texts used by the Daoist priest Du Yongchang. A resident of Yong'an village in Gaoxiong County, he is a representative of the Zhengyi tradition and regularly uses the materials he kindly made accessible to me. The first set of texts is a collection that the officiant keeps by his side for reference when he writes out the formal memorial for the ceremony. Entitled *Gongde wenjian* (Ritual Documents for Rites of Merit), this collection goes back to the arrangement by the Tainan Daoist Zeng Chunshou and consists of two volumes of fifty-nine and fifty-seven pages, respectively. Within the catalog published by Kristofer Schipper (1966), manuscript number 180 should be used in rituals of merit, especially in the context of underworld rites, going back to the same tradition as this collection. I will, in the following, refer to it as the *Zeng Collection.*

The second set of texts I was fortunate to receive from Master Du contains the materials he actually used in a ritual of merit, which was held in December, 1992, at the Huang family residence in Zhongxiao Street of the Hamlet of Yong'an. It involved the tenfold liberation of the souls of the dead, celebrated on the second day of the Offering. Giving in to my pleading, Master Du transcribed the documents he used in a separate volume, which I will here call the *Du Collection*. The two sets of materials form the backbone of my research.

Beyond that, there are the various ritual texts assembled in the collection by Ōfuchi (1983). His materials go back to the well-known Tainan Daoist Chen Rongsheng, who uses them in the rites he celebrates. They are comparable in structure and content to the two sets I received from Master Du.

To compare the three sets of materials, I would like to point out their commonalities and differences, using the actual performance of the ritual as I observed it in Yong'an village as my basic standard of judgment. First, the texts collected by Ōfuchi contain fifty-four items that are arranged according to the order of the ritual program, each of them explained. They include items necessary for all stages of the rite, such as the opening of the road to the netherworld, the presentation of the memorial, the preparation of the writ of pardon, the writ of pardon from the Pool of Blood, the setting up of the sacred altar, the delivery of the memorial, the ordering of the talisman lads, the provision of mandates at the audiences, the replenishing of the treasury, the sublimation of the souls, the recitation of the precious litanies, the offering of medicines, the announcement of the Ten Directions, the summoning of the underworld officers, and many more. The materials are presented in an accessible manner and can be easily used as comparative references. The announcement is named and described as consisting of four kinds of mandates and six rectangular envelopes, but its contents are not given; also, the talisman of the talisman order is not given in its original form; and the mandates used in the Division of Lamps (*fendeng*) and Rite of Universal Salvation (*pudu*) are abbreviated because they are the same as used in the ritual of Offering. In some cases, texts that should be partially different are entirely identical, such as the mandate of money transfer for lost souls and to the treasury officers.

The *Zeng Collection* has a number of unique characteristics. First, it is a tremendously practical and clearly arranged manual that allows the priest of High Merit easy access to all the information he needs. It first presents an overview of the various kinds of announcements and mandates used in the preparatory Announcement ceremony and in the formal ritual itself, then details their structure and contents. In the section on the Announcement, it has seven types of announcements, eight kinds of mandates to officials and generals, four forms of written announcements, and two kinds of talisman orders. Following this, the text presents eight models for placards, both large and small, and five formats of memorials. This text also contains certain stylistic patterns and specific information, such as parallel verse, formal titles and insignia, the name of the sponsoring group and family, as well as slogans to be put on banners.

In the section on documents to be used in the formal ritual itself, the collection presents three kinds of memorials, five types of written announcements, twelve kinds of mandates, seven kinds of talisman orders, as well as songs on cherishing the womb. It is particularly noteworthy that the section on talisman orders divides clearly according to the form and style of the talisman involved. The only documents missing here are the basic text of the writ of pardon and the mandate for the replenishing of the treasury. It is thus not entirely complete. The missing sections can, however, be easily supplemented on the basis of Ōfuchi's collection, so that a complete picture of Taiwanese Daoist ritual documents can be gained.

The *Du Collection* differs from the other two sources described so far in that it is clearly a revision of materials used and burned in real rituals. It contains the sacred documents as they were actually used in a recently celebrated rite and specifies the details of the texts down to the type of paper and color of ink employed. This, as well as the unique format it gives for the talisman order, makes it a special and precious collection. Nevertheless, it is not entirely handwritten; areas other than the celebrants' specific names are often typed or copied from handwritten originals. Still, even these have handwritten notes and talismans added by Master Du, which really make the collection invaluable. Listing all the various documents in a table comparing the three sources, it appears that the *Du Collection* has all the different types employed—a grand total of forty-one documents. The total table would come to ninety-two sheets, listing Du's materials as the standard on the right and the comparable materials from Zeng and Ōfuchi on the left.

All three of them, although not complete each in itself, match one another very closely and taken together provide an excellent source of basic materials on Daoist ritual documents in Taiwan.

The Documents and Their Contents

Using the *Du Collection* as the standard and most basic source, the following discussion examines the various documents used in rituals of merit in Taiwanese Daoism and studies some documents of importance both in terms of content and volume. At the same time, I will also try to find matching materials in texts of the Song and Yuan dynasties, as they are now contained in the Daoist canon of the Ming, in an attempt to point out continuities and divergences over the ages.

A standard for the volume used in the rituals, that is, the number of documents dispatched at any given stage, the *Du Collection* includes twenty-three documents used at announcement ceremonies, six documents sent as writs of pardon, thirty used when chanting precious litanies to the underworld kings, and twelve orders to the talisman lads. It also uses highly special materials in the ritual of untying the knots and in the replenishing of the treasury. With this in mind, let us now look at the four main kinds of documents used.

Announcement.

During a two-day ritual of merit, an announcement is made first to the various deities. This begins by sending a message to the Palace of the Three Pure Ones and Seven Treasures (Sanqing qibao gong), dispatching a formal message to the various supervising officials, generals, and deities of the soil who have their offices here. This is known as the three rectangular envelopes (*sanfang han*). In the ritual celebrated by Master Du, he also sent off orders to a number of different deities that served to protect the purity of his altar platform. They included the messengers and troops of the various celestial offices, the city god of Gaoxiong County, the two soul-hunting generals Shenhu (Spirit Tiger) and Heqiao (How Proud), as well as various lesser local gods, including Tudi gong (Earth God). They were all given orders to save the soul of ancestress He Jinmei, who married into the Huang family. There were, then, five different kinds of mandates. Once the three rectangular envelopes and five mandates had been prepared for send-off into the otherworld, a written announcement of this pending delivery was made to the underworld officer in charge of talismans (Xiajie zhifu li). This written announcement of delivery originally consisted of twelve documents, which in the ceremony were joined in one mandate. In addition to this mandate, there were twelve talismans, one for each department of the underworld. In a formal rite of ordering the talisman lads, these were entrusted to be taken below and thus became secondary talismans. We will come back to this later.

The documents used in the preparatory Announcement are also

found in earlier materials. For example, Jin Yunzhong's *Shangqing ling-bao dafa* (Great Rites of the Highest Clarity and Numinous Treasure Traditions, HY 1213) and Wang Qizhen's work of the same title (HY 1211), both of the thirteenth century, contain representative ritual documents used in similar ceremonies and of a highly similar nature. To distinguish the two texts, I will call them *Jin Dafa* and *Wang Dafa*, respectively. They match Master Du's performance, except that they prescribe formal letters to the otherworld to be dispatched three times and that the deities addressed are a great deal more numerous (see also Lagerwey 1987, 174–175). For example, the *Jin Dafa* lists 118 deities (28.17b–20a), and the *Wang Dafa* has even more (62.24a–26b, 63.58b–61a, 64.59a–63a). However, the two texts have in common with Master Du's practice that they begin their announcements with letters addressed to the Three Pure Ones, then proceed to the local city god, gods of the soil, and the various divine officials in the Bureaus of Heaven, Earth, and Water. This shows that, at least in rituals of merit, the organization, ranking, and structure of the Daoist pantheon has remained constant.

As for the actual content of the announcement documents, the *Du Collection* says:

> Respectfully and sincerely, your servant prays for mercy and grace from the Great Dao. I humbly beg that you grant my wish. From now on, day and night, let us receive your radiance of grace and accept our testimony of deliverance and salvation. To this end, I humbly present the various talismans and writs I have here, properly sealed and executed by me. (Line 13)

A comparable phrasing is found in the *Jin Dafa*, in the section that contains the announcement to Jade Clarity, to be dispatched as part of the Yellow Register rite. It says:

> Respectfully and sincerely, your servant prays for the mercy of the Dao. I humbly beg that you let me, your humble servant, open salvation for the deceased and make it known to all the perfected officers in the various departments that we are preparing to perform ceremonies in accordance with the divine order. Let your radiance of grace descend upon us and accept our testimony of cultivation and worship. (28.21a)

These, then, are fundamentally the same and, as a more detailed examination of their contents reveals, present very much the same topics. There are no major differences in the modern documents used by Master Du and those recorded from the Song dynasty.

Writ of Pardon.

The ritual of the writ of pardon, according to the *Du Collection,* involves three talismans: the Perfect Talisman of the Destruction of Purgatory (*Po diyu zhenfu*), the Perfect Talisman to Rescue the Benighted Souls (*Ba youhun zhenfu*), and the Talisman Order of the Nine Dragons of the Eastern Ultimate (*Dongji jiulong fuming*). It begins with requesting their descent from the spirit world, and to this end a written announcement is dispatched, known as the Announcement of the Destruction of Purgatory. This announcement forms a set together with the writ of pardon, written under the authority of the Three Heavens and sent to the underworld, and with the announcement sent to the meritorious officials of the Realm of Earth.

The third of the talismans used here, the Talisman Order of the Nine Dragons, can be traced to the Six Dynasties. Here we have the *Ziran zhaiyi* (Observances for the Rite of Spontaneity, HY 523), a ritual manual of the Lingbao tradition. It says:

> "Humbly bowing, I pray to the Highest Lord, lofty sages, and great spirits, as well as all the many perfected and numinous, wishing that they pour down the richness of the great compassion upon me. May they create numinosity in proper response [to this prayer] and deliver us all to the blessed state of salvation. I pray: Please bring down your limitless grace!"
>
> With this, summon the flying celestials and spirit beings from above, receive the Talisman Order of the Nine Dragons from the Green Palace of Eastern Florescence, and hand them down to the investigative departments of the Ten Directions. (5b–6a)

This explains the celestial location and ritual use of the talisman but does not describe its shape or contents. A somewhat clearer description is found in the *Jin Dafa,* which lists a total of twelve talismans to be used in traditional Lingbao rites (*zhai*). They include all three talismans still used today as well as the Numinous Talisman of Long Life (*Changsheng lingfu*), the Perfected Talisman of Salvation from Suffering (*Jiuku zhenfu*), the Talisman Order of Primordial Beginning (*Yuanshi fuming*), the Talisman Order of Ascension to Perfection (*Dengzhen du fuming*), the Talisman of Teaching the Three Worlds (*Pugao sanjie fu*), the Talisman of Penetrating to All Heavens (*Liguan zhutian fu*), the Talisman of Controlling the Earth Gods (*Chizhi dizhi fu*), the Talisman of Joining the Four Protections (*Sizhen hetong fu*), and the Triple Contract of Ascension to Heaven (*Shentian sanquan*). The three talismans used in Daoist ritual today, therefore, have a long history, but their many companions have not survived in active ritual application.

How about the writ of pardon itself, then? The *Jin Dafa* states that on the evening before the rite proper, three talismans and one register need to be called down. They are the Talisman of Salvation from Suffering, the Talisman to Rescue the Benighted Souls, the Talisman Order of the Nine Dragons, and the Register of Rebirth in Heaven (*Shengtian lu*). The last is described more specifically as the Highest Precious Register of Ordering the Pardon for Rebirth in Heaven (*Tai-shang chishe shengtian baolu*), but it does not play any role in the modern *Du Collection,* which in its stead has the writ of pardon. Still, both are broadly similar in that they are orders issued to the underworld authorities with the aim of gaining the release of the dead from their sins and suffering.

In the *Wang Dafa,* on the other hand, there is a specific document entitled "Writ of Pardon" (44.12b), which contains materials that are almost identical to those used in Daoist ritual today. For example, the writ of pardon as contained in the *Du Collection* begins with a description of the world at the time of creation:

> Then the kalpa Dragon Country (Longhan) commenced, and the perfect pivot of the origin took shape in symbolic writings. (Line 3)

To compare, the *Wang Dafa* has

> The Talisman Order of Primordial Beginnning, since the kalpa Dragon Country, has been transmitted in sacred verse and hidden, symbolic writings. (44.12b)

Highly similar is the description of the emergence of human suffering in the world. Here the *Du Collection* has

> Then there was greed and attachment in the world, and people came to be immersed in an ocean of suffering. (Line 5)

The *Wang Dafa*, in comparison, says:

> Thereupon people were immersed in suffering, and the fate of the world was determined by greed and attachment. (44.12b)

Again, the latter section of the writ of pardon in the *Du Collection* reads:

> Whatever they have done in past generations or in this life, to go against Heaven or put a burden on Earth, all disloyalty, disobedience, and injustice, whatever sins of the three karmic factors and the six senses, whether serious or light: pardon and remove them all! In accord with

the documents of this ritual, deliver them from their suffering and, according to their fruits, cause them to ascend on high.

As for all the other orphaned souls and obstructed souls of the six modes of existence and the four modes of birth, may they ascend in accordance with their destiny and find happiness in a new life.

Let all those in charge of the infernal offices of the Long Night in the Nine Obscurities and the buffalo-headed clerks be promoted one degree in rank. Let the generals and officers who have watched over the altar, their subordinates and assistants, the agents of the symbols [talismans] and officers of merit in charge at the time of the ritual also advance one grade. In future whenever there is a great ceremony of salvation to rescue those in the underworld, carry out [the orders] according to the rules and regulations.

Oh! The Great Dao is formless; it changes as the situation requires. (Line 17; see Lagerwey 1987, 208–209)

A highly similar passage occurs in the *Wang Dafa:*

Whatever they have done in the past to go against Heaven or put a burden on Earth, all disobedience and disloyalty, all inhumanity and injustice, they have wrongly suffered the punishment of death. Whatever sins they have committed through their six senses and six desires, whether serious or light: pardon and remove them all! In accord with the proper talisman order of this ritual, deliver them from darkness and suffering and let them ascend to the realm of bliss. . . .

As for all the other orphaned souls and obstructed souls of the six modes of existence and the four modes of birth, may they ascend in accordance with their destiny and find happiness in a new life. . . .

Let all the numinous officers that hover near the sacred altar, all their subordinates and assistants, all the swift messengers carrying the talismans be promoted one degree in rank. Let the buffalo-headed clerks in charge of the Long Night of Fengdu, the great demon kings, the administrators of the Nine Obscurities, the City God, the Earthgod of the village, and all the many officials and generals who have aided the ritual also be advanced one grade.

From now on and in future whenever there is a great Yellow Register rite or a rite of Universal Salvation, any ceremony geared to save those in the underworld, carry out [the orders] according to the rules and regulations.

Oh! The numinous power of the Great Dao resides in the manifestation and transformation of the gods. (Line 17; see Lagerwey 1987, 208–209)

Comparing these various citations, it is easy to see that there is a close match in wording and content between the modern *Du Collection* and the traditional *Wang Dafa,* a match not found with materials contained in the *Jin Dafa.* This allows the conclusion that the writ of pardon used in Daoist rituals in Tainan today is not part of the tradition of the *Jin Dafa* but follows that of the *Wang Dafa.*

There are some further points of interest regarding the writ of pardon. For example, the *Wang Dafa* has both a writ of pardon and a writ of summons and explains that ordinary ritual manuals do not contain any versions of these documents. According to him, in his day both kinds of documents were often written informally by contemporary practitioners, using a style that did not conform to that of the standard manuals and exerting an increasingly powerful influence on the tradition. He regrets the loss of the less common forms and explains that he has decided to preserve all varieties in his collection, yet edits them in the process.

To understand this historical dimension and editing process somewhat better, certain passages are of particular relevance. There is first, as John Lagerway has pointed out (1987, 209), a critical review of the register used in the talisman enunciation ceremony. Although there is no such register in the modern *Du Collection,* its writ of pardon closely resembles it and, in fact, takes its place in the ritual. For this reason, the criticism also applies to materials still in use today. It was composed by Ning Quanzhen (1101–1181) and is cited in the *Jin Dafa* (32.14b–16a), the *Wang Dafa* (ch. 44), and also in Jiang Shuyu's (1156–1217) *Wushang huanglu dazhai lichengyi* (Highest Observances for Setting Up the Great Yellow Register Rite, HY 508, ch. 44). It can be summarized in five points:

1. The descent of the register from Heaven is described in an exaggerated fashion.
2. The end of the document does not have a proper order of execution; instead, it first needs an order from Heaven, and only then can it be executed.
3. Examples of sins committed are too numerous and too extreme.
4. After the date, the names of the celestial executives are given, which is too much like the order of pardon issued by the earthly authorities.
5. The phrasing and structure of the register is too much like the order of pardon issued by the earthly authorities; this is not suitable for a writ of pardon addressed to the underworld rulers.

The points raised second, fourth, and fifth apply equally to the Song materials and the modern *Du Collection.* As raised in the second point, the *Du Collection* definitely concludes with certain phrases, such as *cunxin* (visualize in your mind) and *chenggao fengxing* (receive orders and properly worship), which indicate that a direct order from Heaven was required for the text's execution. It also, matching the fourth point of the criticism, lists a number of celestial executives (*tianxiang*), such as Messenger Xu, Operator Jia, Supervisor Lu, Celestial Master Zhang, and Nonultimate Spirit Yin. Then again, in accordance with point five, it contains mandates along the very same lines as found in the order of pardon addressed to the rulers of the underworld, as it is included in the *Wang Dafa* (44.13b–16a). All these points, then, suggest strongly that the writ of pardon used by Master Du follows the tradition of the *Wang Dafa.*

The Precious Litany to the Rulers of Darkness.

The *Du Collection* contains ten talisman orders used in combination with ten scrolls of litanies to be chanted to the underworld kings. At the end of the first scroll, it prescribes the issuing of talisman orders to the nonultimate worlds in the ten directions, beginning with the east. These are then joined by announcements issued to the crane-mounted immortal officials and by mandates given to the souls of the dead. This combination greatly increases the numbers of the various documents found in the *Du Collection.* Also, the ten talisman orders each have a different format and shape. Their efficacy, as already pointed out in the ancient *Duren jing* (Scripture of Universal Salvation, HY 1), powerfully dispels all diseases of hearing, eyesight, speech, and movement and does away with chronic ailments and repeated patterns of suffering. They also serve to grant successful growth and development, the discovery of precious objects, and the revival of the dead (ch. 5).

As the talisman liturgy is chanted in the rituals of merit, the power of the talisman orders is activated to effect a kind of bodily resurrection of the dead, their sublimation into a more celestial form. Similar patterns are also found in the traditional ritual manuals of the Song to Ming dynasties. Here we have the *Duren shangjing dafa* (Great Rites of the Supreme Scripture of Universal Salvation, HY 219), which contains a section entitled "Tenfold Reverted Numen" (*Shi zhuanhui ling-pin*, ch. 9), as well as Lin Lingzhen's *Jidu jinshu* (Golden Book of Rescue and Salvation, HY 466), which describes a Rite of Tenfold Return (*shihui zhai*) and the sacred space to be erected for the rites of universal salvation, which too involve the Tenfold Return (chs. 235–236). The same text, furthermore, contains a number of talismans to be used in these rites (270.29ab), but the latter are entirely different from anything contained in the *Du Collection*. In the light of these earlier sources, the idea of the Tenfold Reverted Numen can be described as yet another feature of modern Daoist ritual that has been transmitted from the Song and Ming.

The Talisman-Matching Lads.

According to the *Du Collection*, the ceremony addressed to the Talisman-Matching Lads (Hefu tongzi) involves the issuing of twelve mandates to the Lads, which are parallel to the written announcements that were made on the previous day of the ritual and sent off to the twelve rulers of the underworld. Both serve to effect the release of the dead from purgatory, and both are written in the format of a talismanic half that has to be matched with its proper counterpart in the otherworld. The task of the twelve Lads is to send off the talismans and to see to the proper matching of the talismanic mandates.

The Lads appear first in Six Dynasties texts. The *Mingzhen ke* (Regulations of the Luminous Perfected, HY 1400) has a Lad of Highest Wisdom (Shangzhi tongzi) who resides in the northwestern corner of the universe and addresses questions about the underworld, as he is invited to see it by the Heavenly Worthy of Primordial Beginning (Yuanshi tianzun) (1a). Also, the idea of one or a group of divine Lads assisting in salvation is already present in Lingbao rites of the same period. However, the notion of a separate ceremony that focuses on their role in matching the talismanic mandates appears only since the Song. The expression "Lad Ceremony" (*tongzi ke*) is first found in the *Jin Dafa* (44.19b), but even here it is not described in any detail. In the *Wang Dafa*, on the other hand, there is a brief mention—without detailed explanation—of certain talismanic documents used in comparable ceremonies (64.42b–43a). The ceremony involves twelve mandates entrusted to the Lads as well as twelve mandates directed to the Nine Hells below. Their content largely matches that of the materials found in the *Du Collection* today.

For example, the latter, in its written mandate to the underworld rulers, has:

> The above listed talisman should be transmitted to the Underworld Ruler of Wind and Thunder who resides in the east. It is to be sent through the host of Precious Radiance Lads. They, once arrived in the underworld, will see to the proper matching of the talisman. Then the sins [of the dead] can be pardoned in due accordance with the rules and regulations. May it be executed in proper order!

A very similar statement occurs in its mandate to the Lads:

> The above listed talisman should be transmitted to the Lads of Precious Radiance who reside in the east. Holding the Talisman of the Destruction of Purgatory, they will swiftly go to the Underworld Ruler of Wind and Thunder, and for him see to the proper matching of the talisman. Then the sins [of the dead] can be pardoned in due accordance with the rules and regulations. May it be executed in proper order!

The first of these passages also appears in the *Wang Dafa* in a mandate to be transmitted to the Nine Hells (64.42b–43a), while the second is seen in the same text in the mandate to the Lads. Again, the continuities between the *Wang Dafa* and the modern ritual are striking.

Untying the Knots and Filling the Treasury.

According to the *Du Collection,* at the time of the ceremony of untying the knots (*jiejie*), one mandate of liberation is read to the souls of the dead, then transmitted to them so they can attach it to their bodies. This document serves as formal proof that the loan from the celestial treasury the now-dead person received when he or she was first born into the world has been repaid fully. It also testifies to the sums of spirit-money transmitted to the otherworld by the descendants of the deceased. Later, at the ceremony for filling the treasury (*dianku*), similar mandates are issued to the officials there. They order the officials to properly receive and administer the sums transferred and, on their basis, to remove the names of the dead from the list of debtors. To activate both kinds of mandates, the officiating priest in this world attaches a powerful seal to them, the Seal of the Three Treasures (*Sanbao yin*). Like the talisman orders used earlier, these mandates, too, come in talismanic form and have to be properly matched. It is interesting, then, that they are fundamentally treated as talismans.

Comparable documents in historical sources are not found in either the *Jin Dafa* or the *Wang Dafa*. However, there are some ritual manuals, dated to the Yuan and Ming dynasties, that have similar materials, notably in the context of the Yellow Register Rite celebrated on behalf of the living. One of them is the *Jidu jinshu,* which has a mandate to the underworld treasury that orders the matching of funds and the release of the souls to the living (313.30ab; see Hou 1975, 152); another is Zhou Side's *Jidu dacheng jinshu* (Golden Book of the Great Completion of Rescue and Salvation, *Zangwai daoshu* 17), which has a yang mandate of ritual merit to be issued to the disciples and a matching yin mandate addressed to the supervisors of the ritual (36.17b–

19a). The same text also contains a yang mandate to receive life, which is addressed to the worshiping devotee, and a yin mandate of the same nature, dispatched to the supervisors of the treasury who plan human life (21.22b). The rite of filling the treasury plays an important role in modern rituals of merit. However, it is not very ancient and goes back only to materials of the Yuan or Ming dynasties. Why this would be the case is a question that requires further study.

Conclusion

Let us, therefore, summarize our findings so far. First, it is a difficult task to obtain relevant materials on the various sacred documents that are issued to the gods in the course of a Daoist ritual of merit. There are different versions even today, beginning with the collection undertaken by Ōfuchi, moving on to the standard reference work used by practicing Daoists (the *Zeng Collection*), and finally coming to the texts actually used and burned in a contemporary ritual that were kindly written down by Master Du in what we have called the *Du Collection*. These three are all valid sources, but they differ significantly enough to preclude the establishment of a truly standardized canon of modern ritual documents. The same holds true for the various ritual manuals that have survived from the Song period onward; their texts present the additional difficulty that we cannot know or even reconstruct the actual use the documents were put to at the time. On the other hand, we are fortunate to have all these materials, both modern and traditional, which provide a valuable resource for our studies.

Next, placing the documents and rites contained in the *Du Collection* at the center of the inquiry and linking them with various historical predecessors, we can distinguish three levels of ritual development and lineage. The first of these is the level matching the *Jin Dafa*, the earliest ritual manual that has relevant materials. Here we find mainly documents used in the ceremony of the preparatory announcement, the three talismans employed in the Writ of Pardon ritual, and the format of offerings used. They are important in that they show that at least some section of modern Daoist ritual definitely goes back as far as the Song dynasty.

A second level of ritual is revealed in the materials of the *Wang Dafa*, which was compiled by Daoists of the Eastern Florescence lineage (Donghua pai), which flourished around Mount Tiantai in Zhejiang. Its tradition is later than that represented in the *Jin Dafa* and stands at a certain critical distance to it. It shares the writ of pardon, the announcement to the Department of Earth, and the various mandates issued to the Lads with the practices undertaken today. In addition, the Daoists of Taiwan still use the Talisman Order of the Nine Dragons in their writ of pardon as it was composed by Ning Quanzhen of the *Wang Dafa* tradition; they are conscious of this fact, attributing the talisman to Ning, the Perfected of Great Wisdom Who Rescues from Suffering and Saves All in Great Pity and Great Compassion (Daci dabei jiuku jiudu dahui zhenren Ning; see Lagerwey 1987, 237). It is likely that the tradition was transmitted from Zhejiang down to Fujian, and from there to Taiwan, thus establishing a continuity of ritual practices to the line of Ning Quanzhen. The level of ritual represented by him, in turn, is part of the ritual reorganization under the Southern Song, which transformed and elaborated the ritual patterns of earlier schools.

The third level of ritual found in modern practice can be traced back to the ritual manuals of the Yuan and Ming dynasties. It is apparent most clearly in the mandates issued during the ceremonies of untying the knots and filling the treasury; they are used as part of the litanies sung to the underworld rulers. Just as was the case with the Talisman Order of the Nine Dragons, so some aspects of these documents, notably the Lad of Highest Wisdom who is sent to the underworld, appear in the Lingbao texts of the Six Dynasties period, but their use in that time is not clearly known. The way the mandates are being used today involves a great deal of direct contact with the souls of the dead. In fact, the mandates sent out at the time of the preparatory announcement, those used when the road to the underworld is opened, the various formulaic mandates used as part of the precious litanies, as well as those applied in the ceremony of untying the knots, are all directly addressed to the dead themselves, giving their specific names as the subjects of rescue and salvation. Not only that, the documents are intended to be worn by the dead on whatever spirit bodies they may have in the underworld. Such a concrete understanding of the power of the physical documents themselves is not found so clearly in either the *Jin Dafa* or the *Wang Dafa*. The former, for example, has only one mandate called *Zhengjian gongde die* that addresses the dead (29.6a). This records numerous merits dedicated to the soul and summarized in one single document, unlike Taiwanese mandates that appear in various documents.

Comparing the modern and Yuan-Ming practices to those described in Song-dynasty materials, it becomes evident that the kinds of mandates used later and their particularly concrete application were not yet present in the earlier period. They, therefore, can be said to represent a slightly later stage of Daoist ritual. The same stage already goes beyond the set of nine precepts to be observed by the dead as well as the use of talismans and registers to effect their successful transfer into the heavens. In Taiwan today, rites of sublimation into heaven tend to be rare, and similarly there are only very few documents in the *Wang Dafa* that are pronounced for the dead at the time of sublimation. Rather than using talismans and registers, this work resorts to mandates directly addressed to the souls of the dead. These mandates, then, are increasingly numerous today, a feature that now characterizes Daoism in Taiwan.

The purpose of rituals of merit is ultimately the transfer of the souls of the dead into the heavens of eternal life; they end with a ceremony that signifies their successful transformation. Rites to this same end can be found both in primitive and organized religions, from ancient shamanism to modern religion. However, among this wealth of similar rites, the Daoist practice stands out in that the officiating priest himself takes on the role of an otherworldly bureaucrat, and the rites involve large numbers of highly formalized written documents that have to be issued, transported, and executed with proper formality and great care. As this is a feature unique to the Daoist religion, it is significant in understanding its special nature and the particular identity Daoists express in their ritual practices. Yet this identity is by no means static. Rather, it can best be understood as a continuous process of adaptation, renewal, and change, through which specific rites and their accompanying written documents are transformed to accommodate the varying needs of different communities and different times.

Translated by Livia Kohn

Note

The present study is based on fieldwork conducted in the southern part of Taiwan, beginning in 1987. Districts studied include in particular the city and county of Tainan as well as the area around Gaoxiong. The focus of the fieldwork was the performance and understanding of Daoist rituals, as undertaken in this area by Daoist masters of the Zhengyi (Orthodox Unity) or Tianshi (Celestial Masters) tradition.

Bibliography

Hou, Ching-lang. 1975. *Monnaies d'offrande et la notion de trésorérie dans la religion chinoise.* Paris: Ecole Française d'Extrême-Orient.

Lagerwey, John. 1987. *Taoist Ritual in Chinese Society and History.* New York: Macmillan.

Liu Zhiwan. 1983. *Taiwan minjian cinyang lunji.* Taipei: Lianjing.

Lü Chuikuan. 1994. *Taiwan de daojiao yishi yu yinyue.* Taipei: Xueyi.

Ōfuchi Ninji. 1983. *Chūgokujin no shūkyō girei.* Okayama: Fukutake shoten.

Saso, Michael. 1974. *Zhuang-lin xu daozang.* Taipei: Chengwen.

Schipper, Kristofer M. [Shi Bo'er]. 1966. "Taiwan zhi daojiao wenxian." *Taiwan wenxian* 17.3:173–192.

———. 1974. "The Memorial in Taoist Ceremonies." In *Religion and Ritual in Chinese Society,* ed. by Arthur P. Wolf, 309–324. Stanford: Stanford University Press.

———. 1977. "Tokō no shikinō ni kansuru ni, san no kōsatsu." In *Dōkyō no sōgoteki kenkyū,* ed. by Sakai Tadao, 252–290. Tokyo: Kokusho kankōkai.

13

Offerings in Daoist Ritual

ASANO HARUJI

Offerings, given to a deity for a ritual purpose, form a major element in the structure of ritual. They express the will and wishes of the devotees while also serving to communicate with the deity. All objects presented in formal offerings have symbolic value, just as the act of offering itself should be understood from the perspective of symbolism. While this is of great interest, this chapter is concerned with another question. During my field work in Taiwan, I have observed that offerings in Daoist ritual are similar in kind to those used in popular and Buddhist rites. It seems that objects offered by Daoists do not distinguish this religion from other religious traditions. Offerings are such an important element in the ritual structure—why, then, do they not reveal something unique about Daoism? There should be a unique Daoist identity to both the rituals themselves and the offerings made in them. Studying them and their raison d'être, therefore, will shed light not only on the role of Daoism in Chinese society but also on how Daoism expresses itself.

In the following, I will first introduce the offerings presented in Daoist rituals in Taiwan, then discuss and analyze them in a wider cultural and historical context.

Offerings Currently Used in Daoist Rituals

Daoist rituals in Taiwan are performed by priests associated with the Celestial Masters (Tianshi) or Orthodox Unity (Zhengyi) tradition,[1] while the structure and organization of the rituals themselves go back to the Numinous Treasure (Lingbao) school, which distinguishes *zhai* (purgation ceremonies) and *jiao* (sacrificial offerings). In Taiwan today, *zhai* are generally rites geared to the salvation of the souls of the dead, while *jiao* are used to elicit blessings for the living. Both involve confession of sins and prayers for forgivenness, originally part of *zhai*, as well as the formal offering of wine, food, and other objects in an act of blessing and thanksgiving, which was originally part of *jiao*. Being close in their nature today, they can well be considered the same ritual; for this reason, I refer to them as Daoist ritual in general.

Offerings presented during Daoist rites are specified in the *Yaoyong wupin dan* (List of Essential Goods), given to a trustee (or client) by the Daoist priest in charge. It records the specific objects to be prepared for formal offering on particular days and also provides their classification. In the following, I will present one such list, as obtained from the Daoist master Chen Rongsheng of Tainan in southern Taiwan in preparation for a three-day *jiao* for peace and blessings. It has the following objects and categories (see also Asano 1994a; 1995; 1996).

1. Incense, flowers, and candles
(to be present on every altar table).

(A) Incense includes the different types of Anba, Wushen, Guangdong, and Gongmo incense. The first three kinds are in stick form; the last is powdered.

(B) Flowers have to be fresh. They are presented tied into bundles and placed in vases. Usually they are set out in pairs.

(C) Candles come in a larger and a smaller type. The larger are big, red candles that are both thick and tall; the smaller are red tea-type candles placed on top of the candle stand. All candles tend to be laid out in pairs.

2. Tea, wine, and other drinks.

(A) Tea and other hot-water brews include Wulong tea, four-fruit (*siguo*) tea, licorice soup (*gancao tang*), and the like. Wulong tea and wine are placed on each table in the greater altar area, while four-fruit tea and licorice soup are offered specifically to the high gods of the Three Pure Ones when a ritual is performed that requires the establishment of a special sacred area (*daochang*). To explain these objects, four-fruit tea is made from four dried fruits: *longyan*, white gourd, jujube, and orange. They are soaked, then boiled with rock suger. Licorice soup is made from licorice-root soaked in boiling water.

(B) Wine includes mainly Shaoxing wine and rice wine, which are both placed on the various tables in the altar area and used in other ritual acts.

(C) Water refers to talisman water (*fushui*), created when the ashes of a burned talisman are dissolved in water. It is frequently used to purify the altar and appears specifically in offerings used during the noon sacrifice (*wugong*).

3. Vegetarian foods (no meat
or strong-smelling vegetables [*wuxin*]).

(A) Fruit and preserved fruit. Mostly when fruit is listed, it means the presentation of fresh fruit. Because typically four kinds of fruit are laid out together, this type is also called the four fruits. Preserved fruit is produced by placing fresh fruit into sugar, then letting it dry, either by cooking or setting in the sun. Several pieces of this fruit, as well as of dried *longyan* and white gourd, are then strung together on a bamboo stick, and six to eight are placed on a table as an offering. Often the sticks are arranged to create the shape of a terrace.

(B) Whole grains. This includes fresh rice or millet, cooked rice, rice balls (*zongzi*), and other non-ground grain products. Fresh rice is used in sacrifices to the demons of the five directions as well as in offerings to inferior deities and uncared-for souls. Cooked rice, too, is given to uncared-for souls and used in the noon sacrifice. Rice balls are made from glutinous rice and soda; they are conical in shape and often appear on altar tables together with the *qian* and *yuan* cakes. They are offered to gods and may, therefore, also be considered part of the next category.

(C) Ground grains. These include a number of cakes, buns, and pastries, such as those typically found in a Chinese bakery. There are first flat, round sweet cakes that are baked (*dabing, jiaobing*). Then there are baked buns that are hollow inside (*xiangbing*). Other pastries are made by steaming rather than baking. Here we have first flat steamed cakes with a red-colored surface, called "rice turtles" (*migui*). Then there are also several kinds of steamed stuffed buns. One kind has the character "*jing*" written on it and is accordingly called *jingbao*. Another is a steamed stuffed bun with a red-colored surface (*hongyuan*); the same type also appears in an oval shape (*honggui*). Furthermore, there are high rice-flour cakes wrapped in purple paper (*gaozi*), as well as buns shaped like pigs or goats, made either from rice or wheat flour (*mianzhu, mianyang*). Others include white steamed cakes made from rice flour, sugar, and yeast (*faguo*), steamed light-brown or tea-colored buns made from rice flour and sugar (*ganguo*), slender, oval-shaped red cakes (*qian*), small and round red dumplings (*yuan*), buns shaped like a buddha's hands (*foshou guo*), as well as ordinary biscuits (*bingzi*).

(D) Sugar candies. Offerings here include candies made from sugar and called the "five animals" (*wushou*). They do not have the shape of actual animals, but their name has the same pronunciation as the expression "five excellent ones" (*wuxiu*). One in five of these is shaped like a pagoda and is accordingly called "sugar pagoda" (*tangda*). Four are shaped like cock crowns and are called the "four cock crowns" (*si jiguan*). They are offered to gods of high position. Besides them, there are many kinds of smaller candies, typically used as offerings to the souls of the dead (see figure 13.1).

(E) Food in bowls (*caiwan*). This offering consists of various kinds of grains and vegetables cooked and offered in a number of bowls. Typically, there are six such bowls placed on every table in the altar area; sometimes they may also contain dried foods as well as traditional cookies (*malao, milao, fengpian*).

(F) Delicacies from the sea and the mountains (*shanzhen haiwei*). This group includes sugar, salt, ginger, and peas. Sometimes, especially in Buddhism, ginger is counted among the five strong-smelling vegetables and is, therefore, considered unclean.[2]

4. Meat.

(A) Cooked meat. This includes the meat of the so-called five sacrificial animals—chickens, ducks, pigs, fish, and shrimp—which may

Figure 13.1. Fruit, tea, wine, buns, and candies offered at a Daoist altar in Tainan. (Source: Author's private collection.)

sometimes be replaced by replicas made from dried tofu. Then there are the three sacrificial animals, which are three kinds of meat and fish, typically chosen from creatures of different gestations: mammals, birds, and fish (or shellfish). They, too, can be replaced with tofu replicas.

(B) Raw meat. This group includes meat from three kinds of animals, often arranged together and offered as one set. The animals included vary; their meat is commonly offered to gods of lesser standing. For example, pork chops may be offered to a paper tiger.

(C) Sacrificial animals. Mainly pigs and goats, they are typically paired as one set; they are offered to deities of elevated positions, but pigs—not paired with goats—are also presented to entire groups of uncared-for souls (hungry ghosts) during rites of salvation. Before being presented at the altar, they must be devoid of blood and viscera, which are placed into proper containers, then offered to superior deities, such as the God of Heaven.

5. Money and jewelry.

(A) Gold, silver, money, jewelry, and watches. These are placed on trays and offered specifically during the noon offering, after which they are returned to their owners. Sometimes they are replaced by paper money.

(B) Spirit money. This includes a number of different currencies circulating in the spirit world. Here we have longevity money (*shoujin*), Great Ultimate money (*taiji*), conch shells (*caizi*), ninefold money (*jiujin*), heavenly gold (*tianjin*), gold bars (*chijin*), heaven money (*tianqian*), drafts on the Celestial Treasury (*tianku*), lofty money (*gaoqian*), and others. All these are made from paper and are burned after the sacrifice.

(C) Silver pieces (*yinjiao*). These are coins thrown among the audience during the rites of salvation

6. Writing utensils.

(A) Writing materials, such as paper, ink stones, black and red ink sticks, and brushes. All these are placed on wooden buckets and set up in the five directions of the altar area, in all cases with dragon slips, or dragon cards. Typically, the papers have inscriptions matching the direction in which they are placed, so that the set in the east bears the characters *anzhen dongfang zhenwen*, "Perfected Words for Pacifying the East."

(B) Dragon cards (*xiaolong zipai*). These are papers printed with a dragon design and placed in the same containers as the writing uten-sils (see figure 13.2).

Except for this very last category, all the items listed here are also used in the rituals of Buddhism, Confucianism, and popular religion. This is not to say that these offerings are not characteristically Daoist in nature. For even if the same offering is used, the method and significance of the offering may differ from one religious tradition to another. In other words, if the offering is significant in Daoism, one must not ignore its Daoist features simply because other traditions use it too. Nor must one ignore the factor of commonality. With this un-derstanding, let us now first look at the question of meat.

Figure 13.2. Writing utensils with appropriate signs offered at a Daoist altar in Tainan. (Source: Author's private collection.)

Meat in Daoism and Popular Religion

Meat in Daoist rituals generally also includes the five strong-smelling vegetables (various types of onions and garlic). But in the "list of essential goods" summarized above, the latter are excluded, so that in this discussion I will focus mainly on meat. Historically speaking, the use of meat in offerings violates the Daoist principle of rejecting blood sacrifices, and its use in Taiwan today, therefore, appears to be contrary to the tradition. Why, then, is meat offered? Does this mean that Daoism has become vulgar and enmeshed with popular religion? Has it lost its unique tradition?

To begin, it is a norm in Taiwan today to consider meat as unclean food, an attitude found among all classes of Chinese society. For this reason, in Daoist ritual proper, meat must still be excluded, and in great *jiao* ceremonies, everyone has to observe a meat taboo. Not only the Daoist priests, but all participants, and sometimes even all local residents, are required to eat vegetarian food for a certain period. Meat-eaters are denied access to the altar, since their presence could diminish or destroy the success of the ritual. This is because in order to communicate with the divine, one must have a light and pure body, attained—among other methods—by abstaining from meat. The practice of preparatory meat abstention in a ritual context has long been part of the Chinese tradition and is also documented in Daoism from its early years.

Why, then, is meat included in the list of offerings? It is true that there is some difference between the taboo against meat that participants observe and that taboo applicable for offerings. However, the two often also coincide, and there is a belief that since the participants are forbidden to partake of all unclean food, none such should be allowed on the altar. In other words, no real meat should be used, even in sacrifices of the three or five animals, which are replaced by various vegetarian ingredients such as dried tofu. This shows that any association with uncleanliness should be removed from both the participants in and objects of the ritual. Pigs and goats made from wheat flour, commonly used as offerings, derive from this idea. It should be noted also that even if vegetarian ingredients are used in the sacrifices of the three or five animals, still at some point real meat will have to be offered. Thus sacrificial pigs and goats are used in the presentation of the memorial, and real animals are used as sacrifices to uncared-for ghosts (see figure 13.3). Although there is a difference between the taboo that participants observe and the taboo that is valid for offerings, when traditionally proscribed foods are actually used in the offering, we should look behind the act to the specific motives and purposes.

How can we, therefore, account for the appearance of sacrificial pigs and goats in the presentation of the memorial? In the *jiao* ritual, the memorial is presented to the Jade Emperor as part of a rite called "Worshiping the God of Heaven." The Jade Emperor is considered the supreme deity in popular religion. The god being like a traditional emperor, the offering to him must be formal and highly official, using traditional Confucian forms, which included the sacrifice of live animals at the altar. Thus ancient Confucian and popular patterns resurface here in a Daoist context—actively contradicting Confucian values, which state that the formal sacrifice to Heaven exceeds the powers of ordinary people and is thus not permissible. Nevertheless, the ritual practices of the Confucian tradition are considered the norm for popular practices, and as in Confucian ceremonies so here too, sometimes the meat of the sacrificed animals is given to the participants after the rite. In one way or another, these long-established practices have also made their way into Daoist ritual space.

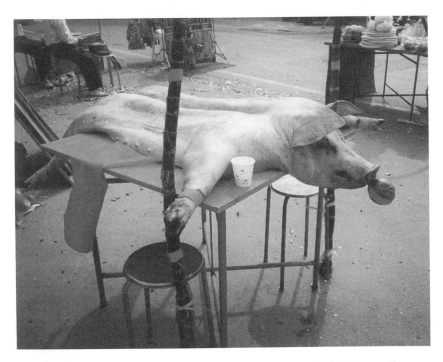

Figure 13.3. A freshly slaughtered pig offered at a Daoist altar in Tainan. (Source: Author's private collection.)

The use of the five sacrificial animals in major Daoist rituals can be explained in the same way as that of pigs and goats in the presentation of the memorial. The same belief pattern demands that animals be sacrificed to deities who are formally entitled to major meat offerings. However, sometimes substitutes are used because, as some scholars believe, these rituals are not so important as the presentation of the memorial. Unlike those scholars, I think that the substitutes appear because the rituals differ. In other words, the presentation of the memorial takes place outside the altar and is different from the rites inside.

Another use of the three sacrificial animals is in offerings to various demons and uncared-for ghosts, geared toward driving off lesser spirits that bring disasters to the people. Here animals are sacrificed because these spirits are believed to like meat and other bloody foodstuffs; meat is offered to satisfy their needs, which alone will make them pliant and responsive to people's wishes. Sacrificial meat here serves as a means of exchange. This contrasts sharply with the use of meat in the presentation of the memorial, where it is considered a token of the people's sincerity rather than a kind of food offering and stands for their wish to sacrifice their own bodies to the high god, who is treated to a banquet like a high official.

Sacrificial pigs used in the salvation ritual have almost the same significance as the meat that appears in sacrifices to demons. The rite is performed for hungry ghosts and orphaned souls who are not cared for by any living relative; they are considered threatening and fearsome. As ghosts and souls of the dead are closer to the living, sacrifices to them should include food typically eaten by people. As a result, cooked foods are often used. On the other hand, because the ghosts are hungry and belong to a different plane of existence, they eat both cooked and raw food; therefore, large quantities of rice and raw pork are also presented. On the surface, in both the salvation ritual and the presentation of the memorial, sacrificial pigs are offered, but the meaning of the two sacrifices is significantly different.

To sum up, both the motive and purpose of meat offerings in Daoist rituals go back to popular religion and mainstream Confucian practice. The meat offered to the highest popular deities meets the demands of the popular belief that animals should be sacrificed to them, as rich meat dishes would be offered to senior officials. Meat is offered to lower-ranking gods because of the popular belief that they need to be given the food they like in order to be responsive to people's wishes. Although motives and purposes differ, both forms of meat offerings go back to popular religion. By allowing meat offerings as and when requested by certain clients, Daoists thus make a concession to popular beliefs. This, however, does not mean that they mix their tradition with popular religion into one system or that they are deluded by the latter.

Daoist rituals are performed at the request of specific clients, whose popular beliefs may influence the way the rites are conducted. Nevertheless, Daoism maintains its own identity and sets itself apart from popular religion, exerting its own power as a distinct tradition. The clients, too, believe it necessary to maintain distinctive Daoist rituals that are considered to be on a higher level than those of the popular cults.

One indication of this is the fact that, although the Daoist tradition proscribes meat, it may be allowed in the Daoist ritual space. Yet it will never be placed in front of the Three Pure Ones. Instead, meat is generally placed on the altar of the Three Worlds, which is located directly opposite that of the Three Pure Ones and honors the variety of beings in the various levels of the cosmos. Meat offerings are, therefore, placed strictly on the periphery of the *jiao* altar. Similarly, the presentation of the memorial is conducted outside the *jiao* altar area, and sacrificial pigs and goats are never placed on the platform where the key rituals are performed. Instead, they are located far away from it, near the table at which preliminary rites are undertaken, before Daoists mount the holy platform proper. Although meat offerings that originate from popular religion, therefore, encroach upon the Daoist ritual space, this encroachment is restricted to the peripheral region and never allowed into its heart.

Properly speaking, unclean food is excluded from the Daoist list of offerings, as it has always been, and Daoism maintains its unique tradition through the exclusion of meat. Having distanced itself from popular religion in its inception and through the middle ages, Daoism now moves closer to it while still maintaining a respectful distance. Although otherwise-taboo food is laid out along with other food offerings in the Daoist ritual space, the religion does not change its unique ritual structure. The main offerings remain tea, soup, and incense, as well as (particularly in the noon offering), flowers, candles, fruit, wine, grains (whole and ground), water, and valuables.

Meat is not a proper Daoist offering. Although it is brought into the Daoist ritual space, it is not received without restriction and control but is subject to specific rules guiding its reception and has been included only to accommodate the needs of clients. In other words,

when a client requests a ritual, he or she may wish to make some offerings in traditional Confucian and popular ways in addition to the
Daoist ritual proper. Daoists will allow this, and in Taiwan, at least, this
has become a tradition.

The Magic of Blood

Meat, as a product that contains the life-giving fluid of blood, has a
distinctly magical aspect. In the land-purification rite, often undertaken by Taiwanese Daoists, a form of redhead magic is practiced, following traditional ways that have long been in existence on the periphery of Daoism. They involve blood from either a chicken or duck
applied to the talisman that is used in the Daoist rite or the feeding
of a small slice of meat into the mouth of a paper tiger. The magical
function associated with meat and blood as used in this sort of rite is
historically described both in the *Baopuzi* (Book of the Master Who
Embraces Simplicity, HY 1177) and the *Daofa huiyuan* (A Corpus of
Daoist ritual, HY 1210). It is important to distinguish between the magical and ritual use of these substances, even though they may look the
same on the surface.

When blood-containing food was proscribed in the rituals, blood
and meat were probably excluded in all circumstances. According to
the "pure covenant" (1b, 8a) described in Lu Xiujing's (406–477)
Daomen kelue (Abridged Codes for the Daoist Community, HY 1119;
see Nickerson 1996), there was no eating or offering of meats and no
use of blood and meat in the magic performance. In addition, according to the Tang-text *Fayuan zhulin* (Pearl Garden of the Dharma
Forest, T. 2122, 53.269–1030), Buddhists criticized Daoists for changing the offering of what should have been "dried deer meat and pure
wine" to "dried dates and fragrant water" (ch. 69). On the basis of this
record, it seemed that meat and wine were excluded for some time
during the middle ages. Also, the *Zhengyi jie'e jiaoyi* (Orthodox Unity
Rites for the Liberation from Peril, HY 793) says that no "dried meat
or impure food" should be allowed. Otherwise, the heavenly officials
will not provide protection (14b). Beyond this, the *Zhengyi jiazhai yi*
(Orthodox Unity Observances for the Protection of Residences, HY
800) and the *Zhengyi jiaomu yi* (Orthodox Unity Observances for the
Protection of Graves, HY 801) have no meat listed among their various offerings.

However, blood and meat have different uses when it comes to the
food consumed by the participants of the rite, the food used as an of-

fering to the gods, and the food applied in magical activities. Thus the *Baopuzi* states that the "five strong-smelling vegetables" and all blood-containing food should not be taken when fasting in preparation for immortality practices (5.6b). In order to concoct an elixir, one must fast and obey purity rules for at least one hundred days, abstaining from the five strong-smelling vegetables and avoiding contact with ordinary people (4.19a). Taking raw vegetables and heavy or fresh foods will render the vital energy in the body too strong, making it hard to contain (8.4a). As a result, if one desires to ascend to heaven, one must not eat meat or blood-containing foods, instead fasting and obeying purity rules for one entire year (15.13b).

The text also says that "wine and dried meat" could be used as offerings, while blood-sealed covenants and the entrails of chickens were used only in magical arts (16.12b). Along the same lines, the *Lingbao wufu xu* (Explanation of the Five Lingbao Talismans, HY 388) states that "all the five strong-smelling vegetables and all food containing pork fat" are taboo as offerings (2.5a); "fat birds" and wine, on the other hand, could be used in offerings (2.4b). Similar statements are also found in other works.[3]

In all cases, participants in the ritual had to observe strict abstentions. The five strong-smelling vegetables and all forms of meat were basically regarded as unclean and could thus be used only under special circumstances. There were some rituals during which dried meat and wine were used together as part of the offerings. Dried meat, considered "cooked" and thus of a different quality than raw, "blood-dripping" meat, was, therefore, not always included in the blood-food list. Thus Tao Hongjing's (456–536) *Zhen'gao* (Declarations of the Perfected, HY 1010), in its "Verse of the Lady Immortal, Wife of Cheng Wei," says: "When preparing to take an elixir of immortality, you must not eat blood food but you can eat dried meat" (10.24a). Just as whole grains are distinguished from ground grains, so it seems a distinction was made between fresh meat dripping with blood and its dried variety.

The same is also obvious in Zhou Side's *Jidu dacheng jinshu* (Golden Book of the Great Completion of Salvation, ed. *Zangwai daoshu* 17) of the Ming dynasty, which notes that wheat flour used in offerings must not be contaminated by any offensive smell (like that of raw meat) and should be handled only with a new bamboo steamer and clean cheese cloth (40.52b). Sometimes, because milk had such a smell, it too was considered unclean. Thus the *Jidu dacheng jinshu* states: "Because it smells offensive, milk in ritual must be treated like raw meat" (40.52b).[4]

It is an undeniable truth that under different circumstances there were changes in the way in which meat was offered or whether it was offered. As recorded in the *Baopuzi* and *Daofa huiyuan,* bloody meat was allowed for use in magical practices. From the point of view of the magicians, it was used because it symbolized the life force and was thus not considered unclean.

Offerings of Fruit and Writing Utensils

Aside from the use of meat, the other notable feature of the Daoist "list of offerings" is the presence of fruit and writing utensils, although tea, soup, wine, and incense also played an important role.[5]

Fruit as offering is described in Jin Yunzhong's (fl. 1224) *Shangqing lingbao dafa:*

> Fresh fruit to be used as an offering for the occasion should be well selected and washed clean. According to the traditional observances for *jiao* rites, it must be changed every day. Excluded from use are pomegranates, sugar cane and other fruits of this type as well as all that contain unclean, muddy substances. Pure fruit growing on branches of trees is best. It should be placed, together with hot tea, before the Highest Emperor and the Three Treasures. Then a formal offering can be made in accordance with the regulations. (17. 22a)

Fruit is also used in the rituals performed by other religions. However, in Daoism it is probably the ideal material for offerings, because its lightness, purity, and origin on the branches of trees match the light and pure energetic power of the high gods of the Dao. Thus numerous ritual texts in the Daoist canon list fruit as a key offering, such as, for example, the *Lingjiao jidu jinshu* (Golden Book of Salvation of the Numinous Teaching, HY 466). Its list of "gifts to be used in the *jiao* ritual" includes dates, nuts, pears, peaches, plums, apricots, lichees, lotus seeds, mandarin oranges, tangerines, and persimmons, with a note that they all could be offered (319.41a). Other texts, not unlike the *Shangqing lingbao dafa,* mention that certain vegetables should not be included among offerings. The *Jidu dacheng jinshu,* for example, decrees that all vegetables should be excluded because they have been fertilized by manure and other human rejects (40.52b). Then again, the *Zhengyi licheng yi* (Proper Observances of Orthodox Unity, HY 1202) records that sugar cane, taro, potatoes, herbs (especially roots), lotus root, and kudzu vines are "unclean substances buried in the mud" and, therefore, must not be used as offerings (26a). The "unclean, muddy substances" mentioned in Jin Yunzhong's work cited earlier thus may well refer to vegetables growing close to the earth or roots, such as taro, potatoes, and lotus root. Fruit can be offered (except pomegranates and lotus seeds), but vegetables cannot.

Fruit is also commonly used as a substitute for other food or as a major form of nourishment in the longevity practice known as "abstention from grain" (*bigu;* see Lévi 1983; Eskildsen 1998). Practitioners avoid eating all grain and heavy food in order to prevent intestinal congestion and render their bodies lighter. In many immortals' hagiographies, the protagonist consumes fruit either during or after the immortalization process—most commonly dates, persimmons, peaches, and pine nuts. Although these are not directly related to fruit used as offerings, the practice probably reflects the same underlying consciousness. Whether to become an immortal, to concoct an elixir, to practice magic, or to communicate with the divine through offerings and sacrifices, in all cases adepts had to keep their bodies light and pure and adjust their vital energies to the purer forces of the Dao. Abstention from grain and eliminating impurities both come from this same basic understanding. Whether it is in the sacrifice from which the "five strong-smelling vegetables" and blood food are prohibited or in the abstention from grain whose purpose is to attain longevity or immortality, "fresh fruit from the branches of trees" plays a major role and is accepted with enthusiasm. It is highly suitable for both deities who were originally transformed from the light and pure energy of the cosmos and practitioners who wished to communicate with or get closer to the gods.

If the same understanding of food is found in both ritual offerings and the abstention from grain, then there might be other common features. One such feature is the distinction made between whole and ground grains. Among ancient immortality seekers, it is recorded in the biography of Tao Yan in the *Daoxue zhuan* (Biographies of Students of the Dao, in *Sandong zhunang,* HY 1131; see Bumbacher 2000):

> Tao Yan, styled Aijing, was from Xunyangin Lujiang. When he was about fifteen to sixteen years old, he changed his diet and began to abstain from grains. At first, he would still eat flour, later he only ate dates. (3.2a)

This shows that ground grains were still consumed in the early phases of grain abstention and that a strong distinction was made between ground and whole grains. To classify the offerings from this angle, one could list ground grains together with fruit, that is, with the purest of offerings. The reason why ground grains are used as offerings may well be due to the fact that they are often considered the equivalent of fruit.

Unlike fruit, writing utensils are more like offerings of meat and can appear as its substitute. The *Shoushen ji* (In Search of the Supernatural) describes the Lord of the Yellow Stones as a deity very fond of purity who would never kill an animal in sacrifice. To honor him, paper, ink, and brushes were offered instead (4.84). Aside from replacing meat sacrifices, offerings of writing utensils also implied that the image of the deity was that of a literati-official. In addition, their offering is related to the Daoist tradition of object-based devotion (*zhenxin*).

A general description of this phenomenon is first found in the *Huanglu dazhai yi* of the Song dynasty. It says:

> People of old were pure and simple, they cherished the Dao and embraced virtue, were free from greed and free from desires, each being sufficient upon himself. By merely using their will and sincerity, they could communicate with the divine and elicit a response; without any material objects or valuables, they could mysteriously harmonize with the perfection of Heaven.
>
> However, in our latter-day age, people's hearts are full of pride and deception, and they only desire riches and material goods, ignoring the law of karma and retribution; they devalue life and honor wealth, forgetting their family and destroying their country. Within, they harbor the myriad evils; without, they accumulate bad fortune and disaster, more and more causing destruction for each other, without ever becoming aware of what they are doing.
>
> For this reason, it is important to teach them to give things up. Then, robbers will no longer arise on the outside, and both within and without will be tranquil and at peace. All bad occurrences will be dissolved. Thus, to prove one's devotion and liberate one's mind, using material objects is primary. If one is able to give them up, the mind will soon follow suit and one will attain the goodness of sages.
>
> As a result, one's mind and intention will be as lofty as heaven, as solid as the earth, reaching out to the sages and perfected above. Then there is nothing that will not be attained by one's faith; nothing that will not respond to one's heart. The ultimate in finding divine responses lies in faith alone—and nothing else. (1.12b)

Object-based devotion thus means the voluntary giving up of material wealth and personal properties as a proof of faith and way of purifying the mind and heart. Only by offering money, valuables, and other material things can one find proper communication with and response to the divine. A list of suitable objects follows:

13 gold dragons
11 rolls of devotional colored silk
10 sets of devotional high-quality paper, ink sticks, brushes, and ink stones
10 bundles of devotional fragrant flowers
2.4 bushels of devotional rice
2.4 dippers of devotional oil
24 pounds of devotional charcoal
14,000 units of devotional money
3 devotional wood tablets
10 devotional jade pieces
3 devotional jades for the casting of dragons
27 gold buttons
(*Huanglu dazhai yi* 1.12b–15b)

Gold dragons are best made of gold, but people lacking the means for providing them can also use other materials, more suitable to their status and financial situation. They appear even today in the form of small cards with dragon designs that are used in piles in Taiwanese rituals. They are placed on wooden buckets filled with rice, the rice representing the devotional rice of the earlier tradition. Similarly, the real paper, ink stone, black and red ink sticks, and writing brushes demanded here are often placed on wooden buckets. Although offerings in Taiwan today are, therefore, not comparable in scale to those prescribed in the *Huanglu dazhai yi*, they are yet part of the same Daoist tradition of object-based devotion.

Why, then, are gold dragons, paper, ink sticks, and ink stones used as offerings? The text explains the presence of the gold dragons as follows:

Dragons are steeds that carry messages up to Heaven. In order to have any communication established and to evoke a powerful response, there is nothing better than a dragon messenger. As soon as the message is put on his back, he is already soaring off. (1.13a)

To convey one's wishes and messages to Heaven as part of the practice of object-based devotion, gold dragons are, therefore, indispensable. Should one try to get one's message across without them, divine retribution from the side of the heavenly officials will inevitably follow.

As for the offering of paper, ink sticks, and ink stones, the *Huan-glu dazhai yi* says:

> Setting up purification ceremonies and conducting rites to the Dao can be done either to rescue the souls of the dead, of one's myriad ancestors and innumerable forebears, to pray for good fortune, or to ask for divine grace in the dissolution of disasters and the prevention of bad luck.
>
> In all these cases, the various officers of the Four [Heavenly] Bureaus, Five Emperors, Three Worlds, and Ten Directions keep a detailed record of all good deeds and merits, noting carefully and in detail the sins committed. In order to do so, they need paper and brushes, to write in the ledgers of merit and good deeds. In offering devotion to the Ten Directions, these must therefore never be missing. (1.13b)

As human beings conduct rites on earth, so the celestial officials will record the merit accumulated in the ledgers kept in the administrative centers of the otherworld. Only through their record keeping does the ritual take effect. To have one's merit, as it is earned through the performance of the ritual, properly recorded, paper, ink stick, ink stone, and brush are indispensable. Without them, the ritual will not be efficacious, and to make matters worse, the divine officials will mete out punishments for the oversight. The *Huanglu dazhai yi* makes no mention of ink sticks or ink stones, but brush and paper alone will not produce records; thus I think they should be part of the discussion. The text has, on the other hand, a number of other devotional objects to be offered, together with a detailed description of which divine official will mete out which punishment when a certain object is missing in the presentation. Modern versions tend to omit the latter, but they include dragon cards, paper, black and red ink sticks, brushes, ink stones, and rice in the list of necessary offerings. These, then, can be understood as belonging to the tradition of object-based devotion.

Daoist ritual imitates the formal rites performed for traditional literati-officials, and Daoist priests are officials in the divine realm. A key component of Daoist ritual is to activate the power of the divine offices through various forms of written communication—memorials, petitions, letters. Writing utensils are, therefore, not only part of the established tradition of object-based devotion, but can be considered representative of the unique self-image Daoism has of its role in the world and the functions of its rituals.

Fruit and ground grain occupy an important position in the offerings, as do paper, ink sticks, writing brushes, and ink stones. Both in traditional rites and in the rituals performed today, they constitute the dominant portion of the offerings, demonstrating the active exclusion of blood food and reconfirming Daoist identity in ritual action.

Conclusion

Daoism fundamentally rejects blood sacrifices as part of its offerings as a way of reconfirming and maintaining its identity vis-à-vis popular religion, pursuing a higher religious goal than the latter. However, in the Song dynasty, when traditional Chinese sacrifice and ritual were in decline and Daoist and Buddhist funeral rites and sacrifices increased in popularity (see Matsumoto 1983), Daoists performed rituals less for their own sake or for that of the nation, focusing more and more on the benefit for the greater populace. At this time, they did not oppose popular religion but developed a position of tolerance.[6] That is to say, while Daoists basically kept their inherent self-understanding and basic characteristics, they moved closer to the practitioners of popular religion. As a result, as the modern list of offerings shows, Daoists today allow meat to be presented in the sacred area.

The purpose of doing so is to integrate offerings typically used in popular religion into the structure of Daoist ritual. The list of essential offerings any Daoist client receives, then, includes meat as a valid sacrifice; it shows that Daoists today accept meat sacrifices without hesitation. This, in turn, raises the questions of whether a Daoist ritual that includes blood sacrifices is still a Daoist ritual? To answer this, the difference in emphasis and importance has to be pointed out. The most important components among Daoist offerings are incense, flowers, candles, tea, wine, and fruit, as well as products made from ground grain, which have the same significance and are used in many forms. In addition, offerings of writing utensils, as based on the tradition of object-based devotion, are also used prominently. Meat or the five strong-smelling vegetables never replace any of them or attain nearly as important a position in the offerings. They are included on the periphery, placed carefully away from the holiest altars, and mainly serve to complement Daoist offerings with popular ones in order to achieve fuller efficacy. Although Daoists, therefore, allow certain aspects of popular religion to enter their realm, the overall ritual structure of the religion has not been altered. There is no merging of Daoism and popular religion but a fruitful coexistence and complementary practice.

In contemporary Daoist rituals in Taiwan, to conclude, specifically

Daoist features may appear rather inconspicuous. This is because they are often performed as part of larger ceremonies at the request of specific clients whose main orientation is popular religion. This is to say that while Daoism is at the core of the ceremony, the ceremony itself is of a popular nature—and this is clearly reflected in the offerings.[7] Examining them, the identity and structure of Daoism in contemporary Taiwan becomes clearer.

Translated by Zhonghu Yan

Notes

The sources on Taiwanese Daoism used in this paper were obtained during field work in Taiwan. In 1980 I did preliminary explorations on a short-term basis. From 1988 to 1990 I undertook more formal field work as a visiting research associate of the Institute of Ethnology at Academia Sinica, Taipei. I am deeply indebted for its generous hospitality. In the past decade, moreover, I have continued to return to Taiwan for more short-term investigations.

1. Daoists in Taiwan are distinguished according to redhead and blackhead (see Saso 1970; 1971). Although both are members of the lineage of the Celestial Masters or Orthodox Unity Daoism, their functions are slightly different. Redhead Daoists are centered in the northern part of the island; they do not perform funerary rites and refer to themselves as Zhengyi while calling their blackhead counterpart Lingbao (Liu 1994, 79; Lu 1994). Since both stand in the Zhengyi lineage, however, I feel the distinction according to these two terms is not properly applicable. I accordingly speak of both of them as Zhengyi priests. Should a distinction be necessary, I use the terms redhead and blackhead. My fieldwork was mostly undertaken among blackhead Daoists in southern Taiwan.

2. Ginger in Daoism is typically not considered one of the five strong-smelling vegetables, which are defined variously. The *Shangqing lingbao dafa* (Great Methods of Highest Clarity and Numinous Treasure, HY 1213) has them as onions, leeks, big garlic, small garlic, and caraway seeds (9.6b); the *Daoxue keyi* (Rules and Observances for Students of the Dao, HY 1118) has them as leeks, big garlic, small garlic, onions, and scallions (1.4b). The latter text, moreover, encourages Daoist priestesses to take ginger honey (1.19a), showing that ginger was not considered unclean.

3. See, among others, *Sanhuang zhai* (Rites for the Three Sovereigns, *Wushang biyao* [HY581], 49.1b); *Toulong bi yi* (Observances for Casting Dragon Disks, *Huanglu zhaiyi* [HY507], 55.3b); *Jijiao fa* (Methods of Offerings, *Lingbao liuding bifa* [HY581], 2b); *Ji tiannü shier xinü fa* (Rites to the Twelve Heavenly River Ladies, *Shangqing liujia qidao bifa* [HY584], 5ab); *Toulong songjian* (Casting Dragons and Sending of Memorials, *Shangqing lingbao dafa* [HY1213], 41.3b).

4. A similar milk taboo is also recorded in the *Huanglu dazhai yi* (Obser-

vances for the Great Yellow Register Rite, HY 508, 2.15b, .49.5b) and in Jin
Yunzhong's *Shangqing lingbao dafa* (HY 1213, 17.22b).

5. Ōfuchi explains the significance of incense by referring to ritual books
used in southern Taiwan, including the *Huanglu zhaiyi* (Observances for the
Yellow Register Rite), *Lingbao duren dafa* (Great Lingbao Methods of Salvation),
and the *Shangqing lingbao dafa* in its various versions. The smoke from the incense, he concludes, serves to convey the people's sincerity and wishes to the
gods (1983, 225–226). In addition, Yamada Toshiaki cites the *Lingbao wufu xu*
on the use of incense when inviting the Five Emperors. He believes that in
early Lingbao scriptures incense was offered as a way to solicit the divine presence, its curling smoke assuming important meaning (see Yamada 1989, 17).

6. Kleeman, in his classification of Chinese religions from the perspective
of blood sacrifices, describes the religious community since the Song as the
"public religious world." He observes that here "Daoism has been most successful in responding to the demands of popular religion" (1996). From what
I have learned in my own studies in Taiwan, I can only agree with him.

7. Furuie and Matsumoto (1991) observed Wangye sacrifices in southern
Taiwan from the perspectives of both Daoist priests and village residents (that
is, clients). They concluded that the nature of the ritual and the demands of
the client are unrelated except for tangential contact.

Bibliography

Asano Haruji. 1994a. "Gendai Taiwan no dōkyō saishi ni okeru sonaemono
    ni tsuite." *Kokugakuin daigaku Nihon bunka kenkyūjo kiyō* 73:157–190.
———. 1994b. "Dōshi to dōshidan: Gendai Taiwan nanbu no jirei kara." In
    Dōkyō bunka e no tenbō, ed. by Dōkyō bunka kenkyūkai. Tokyo: Hirakawa.
———. 1995. "Dōkyō girei no sonaemono." *Tōhōshūkyō* 86:24–55.
———. 1996. "Keidokagi no kumotsu." *Girei bunka* 23:62–89.
Bumbacher, Stephan Peter. 2000. *The Fragments of the* Daoxue zhuan. Frank-
    furt: Peter Lang.
Eskildsen, Stephen. 1998. *Asceticism in Early Taoist Religion*. Albany: State Uni-
    versity of New York Press.
Furuie Shinpei and Matsumoto Kōichi. 1991. "Ōya shōsai no girei kūkan." In
    Kan Chūgoku kai no minzoku to bunka, ed. by Uematsu Akashi, 1:63–83.
    Tokyo: Gaifūsha.
Kleeman, Terry F. 1996. "You jisi kan Zhongguo zongjiao de fenlei." In *Yishi
    miaohui yu shequ*, ed. by Li Fengmao and Zhu Ronggui, 547–555. Taipei:
    Academia Sinica.
Lévi, Jean. 1983. "L'abstinence des céréals chez les taoïstes." *Etudes Chinoises*
    1:3–47.
Liu Zhiwan. 1994. *Taiwan no dōkyō to minkan shinkō*. Tokyo: Fūkyōsha.
Lü Chuikuan. 1994. *Taiwan de daojiao yishi yu yinyue*. Taipei: Xueyi.
Matsumoto Kōichi. 1983. "Sōrei saishi ni miru Sōdai shūkyōshi no ichikeikō."
    In *Sōdai no shakai to bunka*, ed. by Sōdaishi kenkyūkai, 169–194. Tokyo:
    Kyuko shoin.

Nickerson, Peter. 1996. "Abridged Codes of Master Lu for the Daoist Community." In *Religions of China in Practice*, ed. by Donald S. Lopez Jr., 347–359. Princeton: Princeton University Press.

Ōfuchi Ninji. 1983. *Chūgokujin no shūkyō girei*. Tokyo: Fukutake.

Saso, Michael. 1970. "The Taoist Tradition in Taiwan." *China Quarterly* Jan–Mar:83–103.

———. 1971. "Red-Head and Black-Head: The Classification of the Taoists of Taiwan According to the Documents of the 61st Celestial Master." *Bulletin of the Institute of Ethnology of the Academia Sinica* 30:69–82.

Yamada Toshiaki. 1989. "Dōkyō sōkyō shiron." *Chūgoku gaku kenkyū* 8:11–20.

Glossary

Amah 阿媽
Anba 唵叭
anyin 安穩
anzhen dongfang zhenwen 安鎮東方真文
Aofeng shutang 鰲峰書堂

Ba 巴
ba 軷
Ba youhun zhenfu 拔幽魂真符
Ba Yu wu 巴渝舞
Bai yunguan 白雲觀
Baidu pai 白杜派
Baihe guan 白鶴觀
Bailong jingshe 白龍精舍
Baiyi shenggong Pangu Dingguang 白衣聖公盤古定光
Baiyundong zhi 白雲洞志
Bamen kaidu Tianzun 八門開度天尊
Bamen yanqin shenshu 八門演禽神書
Ban Gu 班固
Bandun Man 板楯蠻
bang 榜
banjiao 判教
Bao Jing 鮑靚
Baodao tang 抱道堂
baoji wan 保濟丸
Baopuzi 抱朴子

Baosong baohe ji 寶松抱鶴記
Baoyuan taiping jing 包元太平經
beiyin 卑隱
Bian Jue 扁鵲
Bian Que zhenzhong bijue 邊闕枕中秘訣
biao 表
bigu 避鼓
bing 兵
bingshu 兵書
bingzi 餅子
Bo Ya 伯牙
bu 卜
Budong 不動
busi 不死

Cai Wenji 蔡文姬
caiwan 菜碗
caizi 財子
Canhua gong 晉化宮
Cao 曹
Cao Cao 曹操
Ceng Yiguan 曾一貫
chan 禪
Chang'an 長安
Changchun daojiao yuanliu 長春道教源流
Changqu lidu nü tuoluoni zhoujing 常瞿利毒女陀羅尼咒經
Changsheng lingfu 長生靈符

295

Changsheng shu xuming fang hekan	長生書續命方合刊	*Cuanyu lieyu aotuo shenyu*	爨于烈于澳陀誂宇
Changzhou	常州	*cun*	存
chanhui	懺悔	*cunren*	村人
Chanhui wen	懺悔文	*cunxin*	存心
chen	辰		
Chen	陳	*dabing*	大餅
Chen Minggui	陳銘珪	Dacheng	大成
Chen Mou	陳謀	Daci dabei jiuku jiudu dahui	
Chen Rongsheng	陳榮盛	zhenren Ning	大慈大悲救苦
Chen Tao	陳陶		救度大惠真人寧
Chen Tiquan	陳體全	*Dadao jia lingjie*	大道家令戒
Chen Xianzhang	陳獻章	*Dadong zhenjing*	大洞真經
Chen Zhong	陳仲	Dagu	大固
Cheng'an	誠菴	Dai Zhen	戴震
Chengdu	成都	Daizong	代宗
chengfu	承負	*dalian*	大斂
chenggao fengxing	承誥奉行	Daluo tian	大羅天
Cheng-Zhu	程朱	Dan Ranhui	澹然慧
Chenhou Yinzi dui	陳侯因資敦	Dangqu	宕渠
Chen-Li Ji	陳李濟	*daochang*	道場
Chenmu	諶母	*daode*	道德
chenwei	懺緯	*Daodian lun*	道典論
Chi Daomao	郗道茂	*Daofa huiyuan*	道法會元
Chi Tan	郗曇	*daoguan*	道觀
chijin	尺金	*Daojiao yishu*	道教義樞
Chijingzi	赤精子	*daoke*	道科
Chiyou	蚩尤	*Daomen kelue*	道門科略
Chizhi dizhi fu	敕制地祇符	*daoshi*	道士
Chongsheng guan	崇聖觀	*daotan*	道壇
Chongxu guan	沖虛觀	*daotang*	道堂
chou	丑	*Daoxue keyi*	道學科儀
Chu	楚	*Daoxue zhuan*	道學傳
chu	廚	*Daozang jiyao*	道藏輯要
Chuci	楚辭	*Daozang xubian*	道藏續編
Chūinryū	中院流	Daqi	大器
chukuang	觸壙	*Datang liudian*	大唐六典
Chunfu	純甫	*daxing fanqi fu*	大行梵氣符
Chunqiu fanlu	春秋繁露	*Daxue yanyi lunduan*	大學演義論斷
Chunqiu yi	春秋億	*Daxue yi*	大學億
Chunyang shengzu	純陽聖祖	Dayu	大禹
Chunyu Yi	淳于意	*de*	得
Ci'en si	慈恩寺	Deming	德明
citang	祠堂	Deng Yougong	鄧有功
Ciyi jing	雌一經	Dengling shi	鄧陵氏
congci	叢祠	*dengshan*	登山

Dengxi	鄧析	Fang Dacong	方大琮
Dengzhen du fuming	登真度符命	Fang Fengwu	方逢午
Di	弟	Fang Huan	方渙
dianku	填庫	Fang Jue	方玨
Dianlue	典略	Fang Wen	方汶
diao	調	Fang Wenzhao	方文照
die	牒	Fang Xian	方咸
ding	鼎	Fang Xun	方詢
Dingguang fo	定光佛	*fang yankou*	放焰口
dixian	地仙	Fang Zhong	方仲
Diyi juetan	第一覺壇	Fang Zhuangyou	方壯猷
Diyi kaihua tan	第一開化壇	*fangji*	方技
Diyi tan	第一壇	*fangliang*	方良
Dizang	地藏	Fangshan pai	方山派
Donghua dijun	東華帝君	*fangxiang shi*	方相氏
Donghua pai	東華派	*Fangzhai cungao*	方齋存稿
Dongji jiulong fuming		Fanyu	番禺
	東極九龍符命	*Fanyu xian xuzhi*	番禺縣續志
Dongjing hui	洞經會	*Fayuan zhulin*	法苑珠林
Doumu	斗母	*Feizhi yin*	飛質印
Du Fu	杜甫	*fendeng*	分燈
Du Lüzu sanni yishi shuoshu guankui		Feng Yan	馮衍
	讀呂祖三尼醫	Fengdu	酆都
	世説述管窺	*fengpian*	風片
Du Yangdong	杜陽棟	*Fengsu tongyi*	風俗通義
Du Yongchang	杜永昌	*Fengxue jiaozi shu*	風雪教子書
Duan Chengshi	段成士	*Foshan yaoye zhi*	佛山藥業志
Duan Yucai	段玉裁	*Foshan zhongyi xiangzhi*	
Duren jing	度人經		佛山忠義鄉志
Duren shangjing dafa	度人上經大法	*foshou guo*	佛手果
Dushi lunduan	讀史論斷	*fu*	符
		Fu Xi	伏羲
egui	餓鬼	*fuming*	符命
Enhong	恩洪	*fushui*	符水
Ezhou	鄂州	Fuyou dijun	孚佑帝君
		Fuyou dijun jueshi jing	
fa	法		孚佑帝君覺世經
fa puti xin	發菩提心	*Fuyou shangdi tianxian jinhua zongzhi*	
faguo	發果		孚佑上帝天仙
fahui	法會		金華宗旨
falun	法輪	Fuzhou	福州
fan	梵		
Fan Ao	范鰲	Gai Gong	蓋公
Fan Ben	范貢	*gancao tang*	甘草湯
Fan Changsheng	范長生	*ganguo*	甘果
Fan Li	范蠡	*ganlu*	甘露
Fang Ciweng	方祠翁	Ganquan	甘泉

Gaogong daoshi　　高功道士
gaoqian　　高錢
Gaotang fu　　高唐賦
gaozi　　糕仔
Ge Hong　　葛洪
Ge Xuan　　葛玄
Gelao　　仡佬
gewu　　格物
geyi　　格義
gongde fashi　　功德法師
Gongde wenjian　　功德文檢
Gongmo　　貢末
Gongshan she　　公善社
Gongyang yishi　　供養儀事
Gongyu shuyuan　　攻玉書院
Gu hongmei ge　　古紅梅閣
Gu shuyinlou cangshu

　　古書隱樓藏書
Guan Yin　　關尹
guanding　　灌頂
Guang　　光
Guangchengzi　　廣成子
Guangdong nianjian

　　廣東年鑑
Guanghuazi Huijue

　　廣化子惠覺
Guangji zhenjun　　廣濟真君
Guangzhou　　廣州
Guansheng dijun　　關聖帝君
Guansheng dijun mingsheng jing zhujie

　　關聖帝君明聖
　　經注解
Guanyin　　觀音
Guanzizai　　觀自在
guhun　　孤魂
guibing　　鬼兵
guidao　　鬼道
guishi　　鬼師
guiwu　　鬼巫
guizhu　　鬼主
guizu　　鬼卒
Guochao qixian leizheng chubian

　　國朝耆獻類徵
　　初編
Guodian　　郭店
guoshi　　國師
Gushi shijiu shou　　古詩十九首

hai　　亥
Han Fei　　韓非
Han He　　漢河
Han Yu　　韓愈
Hanfeizi　　韓非子
Hanshi waizhuan　　韓詩外傳
Hanshu　　漢書
Hanyang　　漢陽
Hanzhong　　漢中
He Baiyun　　何白雲
He Qizhong　　何啓忠
Hefu tongzi　　合符童子
Henan Fangshi　　河南方氏
Heqiao　　何喬
Hong'en lingji zhenjun

　　洪恩靈濟真君
honggui　　紅龜
Hongjiao enshi　　宏教恩師
hongyuan　　紅員
Hou Hanshu　　後漢書
Houcun xiansheng daquan ji

　　後村先生大全集
Hua Zhushi　　華主事
huahu　　化胡
Huainanzi　　淮南子
Huajian shan　　花尖山
Huang Xuanxian　　黃玄憲
Huang Zhonghuang

　　黃中黃
Huang Zongxi　　黃宗羲
Huangdi　　黃帝
Huangdi sijing　　黃帝四經
Huangfu Mei　　皇甫枚
Huangfu Peng　　黃甫朋
Huangjing hui　　皇經會
Huang-Lao　　黃老
Huanglong guan　　黃龍觀
Huanglu dazhai yi　　黃籙大齋儀
Huanglu zhaiyi　　黃籙齋儀
huangquan　　黃泉
Huangsha　　黃沙
Huangshi gong　　黃石公
Huanzhu qiao　　環珠橋
Huayangguo zhi　　華陽國志
Hubei　　湖北
Hui Shi　　惠施
huiguang　　迴光

huihe	會合	*Jingming yuanliu*	淨明源流
Huijue	惠覺	Jingming zhongxiao dao	
Huijue dizi Jiang Yupu shouzhong			淨明忠孝道
shi	惠覺弟子將予	*Jingming zhongxiao lu*	
	蒲守中氏		淨明忠孝錄
Huilan	慧蘭	*jingshe*	精舍
Huixing shantang	惠行善堂	*jingshi*	靜室
Huiyuan	慧遠	*jingsi*	精思
hunqi	魂氣	*jingtu*	淨土
		Jinhua keyi	金華科儀
Ikeda On	池田温	Jinhua Taiyi	金華太乙
		Jinjing	禁經
Ji tiannü shier xinü fa		*jinshi*	進士
	祭天女十二溪	*Jinshu*	晉書
	女法	Jishan	積善
jia	甲	Jishan li	積善里
jia	家	*Jiu Tangshu*	舊唐書
Jia Yi	賈誼	*jiujin*	九金
jiaci	家祠	*Jiuku zhenfu*	救苦真符
jiamiao	家廟	*jue*	訣
jiang baxian	降八仙	Jueqi	決氣
Jiang Shuyu	蔣叔輿	Juetan	覺壇
Jiang Yupu	蔣予蒲	Jueyuan baotan	覺源寶壇
jiangbi	降筆	Jueyuan bentan	覺源本壇
jianjue	劍訣	Jueyuan jingshe	覺源精舍
jianshou	劍手	Jugong	巨公
jiao	醮	Jupo jingshe	菊坡精舍
jiaobing	醮餅	*juren*	舉人
jiashou	假手	*jushe*	居舍
jiazhi	加枝	Jutao yin	巨韜印
jibi	乩筆	*juzi*	巨子
Jidu dacheng jinshu	濟度大成金書		
Jidu jinshu	濟度金書	*kaipi fu*	開闢符
jie	劫	*kanwei*	龕位
jie	解	*kaozheng xue*	考證學
Jiebi	解敝	Ke Yanggui	柯陽桂
jiefa yin	結法印	*kechuan*	客船
jiejie	解結	Kobayashi Taichirō	小林太市郎
jieyin	結印	Kong-Mo	孔墨
Jijiao fa	祭醮法	Kongzi	孔子
jijiu	祭酒	Kou Qianzhi	寇謙之
Jilian keyi	祭煉科儀	*kuangzu*	狂阻
Jin Yunzhong	金允中	Kunlun shan	崑崙山
Jing	景		
jing	敬	La	臘
jing	精	Lan'gong	蘭公
jingbao	敬包	Lao	獠

Lao Dan	老聃	*Lingbao wufu xu*	靈寶五符序
Laojun yinsong jiejing	老君音誦戒經	Lingji gong	靈濟宮
Laozi yi	老子億	Lingji xinggong	靈濟興宮
leiju	雷局	Lingji zongmiao	靈濟宗廟
Li	李	*Lingjiao jidu jinshu*	靈教濟度金書
Li Bo	李白	Lingjue	領決
li chang	離腸	*lingwei*	靈位
li diji	理地紀	*liren*	里人
Li Hu	李虎	*litou*	里頭
Li Mingche	李明徹	Liu Du'an	劉度菴
Li Qingfu	李清馥	Liu Jia	陸賈
Li Qingqiu	李清秋	Liu Kezhuang	劉克莊
Li Shangyin	李商隱	Liu Shouyuan	柳守元
Li Si	李斯	Liu Tishu	劉體恕
Li Te	李特	Liu Xiang	劉向
Li Wenyuan	李文沅	Liu Yuzhen	劉玉真
Li Xiong	李雄	Liu Zongliang	劉宗良
Li Yi	李億	Liu Zongyuan	柳宗元
Li Ying	李郢	*Liu Zongyuan quanji*	
Li Zhaoji	李兆基		柳宗元集全
Li Zhi	李贄	Liu Zongzhou	劉宗周
Li Zhongsheng Tang		*liudao*	六道
	李眾勝堂	*Liujia feishen shu*	六甲飛神術
Li Zhuguo	李柱國	*liujia zhi yaozhi*	六家之要指
Li Zi'an	李子安	*liuyi*	六藝
Li Zongjian	李宗簡	*Lixu*	隸續
Liang Qian	梁潛	*lixue*	理學
Liang Ren'an	梁仁庵	Long Yu	弄玉
Liang Wudi	梁武帝	*Longghu shan bichuan shoujue*	
liangzhi	良知		龍虎山秘傳
lianhua	鍊化		手訣
lianhua fa	鍊化法	Longhan	龍漢
lianshi	鍊師	Longmen	龍門
Liezi	列子	Longnü si	龍女寺
Liguan zhutian fu	歷關諸天符	Longqiao	龍嶠
Liji	禮記	*lou*	樓
Lin Lingzhen	林靈真	*lü*	律
Lin Wenjun	林文俊	Lü Chunyang	呂純陽
Lin Ziyao	林自遙	Lü Dongbin	呂洞賓
Lingbao	靈寶	Lu Wenchao	盧文弨
Lingbao dalian neizhi xingchi jiyao		Lu Xiujing	陸修靜
	靈寶大鍊內旨	Lu Yinfang	陸吟舫
	行持機要	*luanji*	鸞乩
Lingbao duren dafa	靈寶度人大法	Luci gang	鸕鶿港
Lingbao lingjiao jidu jin shu		Lujiang	盧江
	靈寶領教濟度	*Lunheng*	論衡
	金書	*Lunyu*	論語
Lingbao liuding bifa	靈寶六丁秘法	Luo Chi	羅池

Luo Qinshun	羅欽盾	*mingwang*	明王
Luofu shan	羅浮山	*Mingzhen ke*	明真科
Luoshen fu	洛神賦	Minnan	閩南
Luotian jiao	羅天醮	*Minzhong lixue yuanyuan kao*	
Luqiao	綠翹		閩中理學淵源考
Lüshi chunqiu	呂氏春秋	Mo	貊
Lüzu	呂祖	*mo*	摩
Lüzu quanshu	呂祖全書	Mo	墨
Lüzu quanshu zongzheng		Mo Chou	莫愁
	呂祖全書宗正	*moluo*	魔羅
Lüzu shi xiantian xuwu taiyi jinhua		*Mouzi lihuolun*	牟子理惑論
zongzhi	呂祖師先天虛	*muquan*	墓券
	無太乙金華		
	宗旨	*Nah mouh louh*	喃無佬
Lüzu xunyu	呂祖訓語	Nanchang	南昌
Lüzu yaoqian	呂祖藥籤	Nanhai	南海
Lüzu zhenjing	呂祖真經	*Nanhai xianzhi*	南海縣志
		Nankang	南康
Magong	馬公	*Nanshi*	南史
malao	麻雞	Ni Heng	禰衡
mao	卯	*ni*	覽
Maojun	茅君	Ning Quanzhen	寧全真
Maoshan	茅山	*niwan*	泥丸
Mawangdui	馬王堆	*nü*	女
Mazu	媽祖	Nüqing	女青
Meng Jingyi	孟景翼	*Nüqing guilü*	女青鬼律
Meng Ke	孟軻		
Meng Sheng	孟勝	Ouyang Xiu	歐陽修
Meng Xi	孟喜		
Meng Zhizhou	孟智周	Pan Jingguan	潘靜觀
mengbu	夢卜	Pan Lang	潘郎
Mengshi	孟氏	Pan Yi'an	潘易菴
Mengzi	孟子	Pan Yue	潘岳
mianyang	麵羊	Panhu	槃瓠
mianzhu	麵豬	*Paodian liuzi shu*	拋點劉子書
miaoyu	廟宇	Pei Songzhi	裴松之
Miedu wulian shengshi miaojing		Peng Meng	彭蒙
	滅度五煉生尸	Piling	毘陵
	妙經	*pingfu*	憑附
migui	米龜	*po diyu yinzhou*	破地獄印咒
milao	米雞	*Po diyu zhenfu*	破地獄真符
Min Yide	閔一得	*Po'anji*	泊菴集
Minbei	閩北	Pou	裒
Mindu ji	閩都記	*poyufu*	破獄符
ming	名	Pozhuan yin	婆縛印
ming	命	*pudu*	普度
Mingru xue'an	明儒學案	*Pugao sanjie fu*	普告三界符
mingtang	明堂	Puquan she	普勸社

qi	氣	Ru	儒
Qi Ying	耆英	Rui Lin	瑞麟
qi'an jiao	祈安醮		
qia	掐	*san enzhu*	三恩主
qian	牽	San Lüshi	三閭氏
Qiande	乾德	*sanbao*	三寶
Qianfu lun	潛夫論	*Sanbao yin*	三寶印
Qianheng	乾亨	*Sandong zhunang*	三洞珠囊
Qianjin yifang	千金翼方	*sanfang han*	三方函
Qiankun yizhang tu	乾坤一掌圖	Sangong jiuqing	三公九卿
Qianlong	乾隆	*sanguan*	三官
Qianshan	乾善	*Sanguo zhi*	三國之
qianshi	籤詩	*Sanhuang zhai*	三皇齋
Qianwei	乾維	*sanjie*	三界
Qianxin	乾心	*Sanni yishi shuoshu*	三尼醫世説述
Qianyuan	乾元	Sanqing	三清
Qianzhen ke	千真科	Sanqing qibao gong	三清七寶宮
Qidiao shi	漆雕氏	Sanshan	三山
qin	琴	*Santian neijie jing*	三天內解經
Qin Guli	禽滑釐	Sanxingdui	三星堆
qing shifu	請師父	Sanyuan gong	三元宮
Qingbu	青布	Shan Tao	山濤
qingge	清歌	*shan'gen*	善根
Qingpu	青圃	Shangdi	上帝
qingshi	清室	Shangqing	上清
Qingsong guan	青松觀	*Shangqing lingbao dafa*	
Qingyuan	清遠		上清靈寶大法
Qingyuan xianzhi	清遠縣志	*Shangqing liujia qidao bifa*	
qitou	魁頭		上清六甲祈
Qiu Changchun	邱長春		禱秘法
Qiuzu yulu	邱祖語錄	*Shangshu*	尚書
Qu Yuan	屈原	*shangzhang*	上章
Quan Tangshi	全唐詩	Shangzhi tongzi	上智童子
Quanshu zhengzong	全書正宗	*Shanlue fu*	山略附
Quanzhen	全真	*shanshe*	善社
Quanzhou	泉州	*shanshu*	善書
Quduo	瞿多	*shantang*	善堂
		Shanyu rentong lu	善與人同錄
Randeng	然燈	*shanzhen haiwei*	山珍海味
Ren An	任安	Shao Zhilin	邵志琳
Renpu	人譜	*shen*[a]	神
Renwang huguo boruo boluomi jing		*shen*[b]	身
	仁王護國般若	Shen Dao	慎到
	波羅蜜經	Shen Quanqi	沈佺期
renwang[a]	忍王	Shen Yue	沈約
renwang[b]	仁王	*shen'gen*	神根
Rong	戎	*shence*	神筴
Ronghui sanjiao	融會三教	*Shenggong caotang dashi jiyao*	

	省躬草堂大事	*si jiguan*	四雞冠
	紀要	*siguo*	思過
Shenggong lu	省躬錄	*siguo*	四果
Shengtian lu	生天錄	Sima Qian	司馬遷
Shenhu yin	神虎印	Sima Xiangru	司馬相如
shenjin shengye	神津生液	*simiao*	寺廟
shenjin shenshi	身盡神逝	Siming zhenjun	司命真君
Shennong	神農	*Sizhen hetong fu*	四鎮合同符
Shennü fu	神女賦	Song Bing	宋餅
Shentian sanquan	昇天三券	*Soushen ji*	搜神記
Shenxian zhuan	神仙傳	Su Lang	蘇朗
Shenxiao zishu dafa	神霄紫書大法	Su Shi	蘇軾
shenzhou	神咒	Sulao guan	酥醪觀
shi	詩	Sumen	蘇門
Shi Qiu	史鰌	Sun Simiao	孫思邈
Shi zhuanhui lingpin	十轉回靈品	Sun Xing	孫性
Shicheng	石城	Sunshi	孫氏
shifang	十方	Sunü	素女
shifu	詩賦		
shihui zhai	十迴齋	Taihe dong	太和洞
Shiji	史記	*taiji*	太極
Shijing gong	石井公	*Taiji zhenren feixian baojian*	
Shilei guhun wen	十類孤魂文	*shangjing (xu)*	太極真人飛仙
Shiquan hui	十全會		寶劍上經序
shishe	詩社	Taiping dao	太平道
Shiyi	詩億	*Taiping dongji jing*	太平洞極經
shizuo	獅座	*Taiping jing*	太平經
shouguo	首過	*Taiping yulan*	太平御覽
shoujin	壽金	*Taishang chishe shengtian baolu*	
shoujue	手訣		太上敕赦生天
shouyin	手印		寶錄
Shu	蜀	*Taiyi dijun dongzhen xuanjing*	
shu	疏		太一帝君洞真
shu	術		玄經
Shujing	書經	*Taiyi jinhua zongzhi*	太乙金華宗旨
Shun	舜	Taiyi jiuku Tianzun	太乙救苦天尊
Shunqu	順渠	Taiyin	太陰
Shunqu xiansheng wenlu		Tan Changzhen	譚長真
	順渠先生溫錄	*Tangchao haofang nü*	唐朝豪放女
Shuowen jiezi	説文解字	*tangda*	糖塔
Shuoyuan	説苑	*tanzhi*	彈指
shushu	術數	*tao^a*	叨
Shuye	叔夜	*tao^b*	掐
Shuyi	書億	Tao Hongjing	陶弘景
shuyuan	書院	Tao Qian	陶潛
Shuzhu shan	漱珠山	Tao Shi'an	陶石菴
si	思	Tao Yan	陶炎
si	巳	*taozhi*	掐指

Tenglong yin	騰龍印	Wang Ji	王璣
ti	題	Wang Mang	王莽
Tian Pian	田餅	Wang Qizhen	王契真
Tian Shu	田叔	Wang Shouren	王守仁
Tian Wangsun	田王孫	Wang Wei	王維
Tian Yannian	天延年	Wang Xianzhi	王獻之
Tiandi	天帝	Wang Xuanhe	王懸河
tiandi jiao	天帝教	Wang Yangming	王陽明
Tiandi shizhe	天帝使者	Wang Yanxiang	王延相
Tianhuang yin	天皇印	Wang Yingshan	王應山
Tianhuang zhidao taiqing yuce		Wang Zhaojun	王昭君
	天皇至道太清	*Wangfu shi*	望夫石
	玉冊	*Wanggong shendao bei*	
tianjin	天金		王公神道碑
tianjun	天君	Wangwu shan	王屋山
tianku	天庫	Wangye jiao	王爺醮
Tianlao	天老	Wei	威
tianqian	天錢	Wei Mou	魏牟
tianshen	天神	Wei Ruyi	魏如意
Tianshi	天師	Wei Xiao	魏校
Tianshui	天水	Wei Zheng	魏徵
Tianxia	天下	Wei Zhuangqu	魏莊渠
Tianxian	天仙	*Weishan zuile*	為善最樂
Tianxian xinzhuan	天仙心傳	Wen Feiqing	溫飛卿
tianxiang	天相	Wen Tingyun	溫庭筠
Tianxin zhengfa	天心正法	Wen Weng	文翁
Tianzun	天尊	*Wenji*	文姬
tie	貼	*wenjian*	文檢
Tie'an ji	鐵菴集	*Wenxuan*	文選
Tong'an	同安	Wong Tai Sin	黃大仙
tongji	童乩	*wu enzhu*	五恩主
Tongren	通仁	Wu Yang	巫陽
Tongshan she	同善社	Wu You	吳祐
Tongwa yiyuan	東華醫院	*wu zhuoshi*	五濁世
tongzi ke	童子科	Wu[xing] dadi	吳[姓]大帝
Toulong bi yi	投龍壁儀	Wuchang	武昌
Toulong songjian	投龍送簡	Wucheng	武城
Tu Yu'an	屠宇菴	Wudi	五帝
tuchen	圖讖	*wugong*	午供
Tudi gong	土地公	Wuhu shan	五虎山
Tuo Xiao	它嚚	*wulao*	五老
tutan zhai	涂炭齋	*Wulian jing*	五鍊經
		Wulong	烏龍
Wanfa fanzong	萬法皈宗	*Wushang biyao*	無上秘要
Wanfa guizong	萬法歸宗	*Wushang huanglu dazhai licheng yi*	
Wang Chang	王昌		無上黃籙大齋
Wang Chong	王充		立成儀
Wang Dao	王道	Wushen	烏沈

Wusheng laomu	無生老母
Wushi	吳氏
Wushi shan	烏石山
wushou	五獸
wuxin	五辛
Wuxing pian	五行篇
wuxiu	五秀
Wuzhen pian chanyou	悟真篇闡幽
Xi Kang	稽康
Xi Shi	西施
Xiajie zhifu li	下界直符吏
Xiang	湘
xiangbing	香餅
Xiangfu shi	相夫氏
Xiangli shi	相里氏
xiangren	鄉人
xiangshi	香室
xianguan	仙館
Xiangying miao	祥應廟
Xiangying miaoji	祥應廟記
xiangyou qian	香油錢
xianshi	賢師
Xiantian dao	先天道
Xiantian xuwu taiyi jinhua zongzhi	先天虛無太乙金華宗旨
Xianxue	顯學
Xianyi guan	咸宜觀
Xianyou zhenjun	顯佑真君
Xiao	瀟
Xiao Shi	蕭士
Xiao Yan	蕭衍
xiaolian	小斂
Xiaoliang si	蕭梁寺
xiaolong zipai	小龍仔牌
Xiaoyou dong	小有洞
Xici	繫辭
Xie Daoyun	謝道韞
Xin Tangshu	新唐書
Xinshan tang	信善堂
Xinshu	新書
Xinyu	新語
Xiong Qufei	熊去非
Xiongnu	匈奴
Xiqiao shan	西樵山
Xiqiao yunquan xianguan shiji	西樵雲泉仙館詩集
Xiuyuan jingshe	修元精舍
Xiwangmu	西王母
Xu	徐
Xu Jingyang	許旌陽
Xu Shen'an	許深菴
Xu Xun	許遜
Xu Zhenjun	許真君
Xu Zhi'e	徐知鄂
Xu Zhizheng	徐知證
xuan bifan kai zangfu fashi fu	宣秘梵開臟腑法食符
xuan kai yanhou fu	宣開咽喉符
xuan poyu fu	宣破獄符
Xuandu daxian yushan jinggong yi	玄都大獻玉山淨供儀
xuanjiang	宣講
Xuanpu shan lingkui bilu	玄圃山靈匱秘籙
Xuantian shangdi	玄天上帝
Xuanyin	玄印
xuanyuan tan	玄元壇
Xue Hui	薛惠
Xue Yanggui	薛陽柜
Xuepen hui	血盆會
xun	巽
Xunyang	潯陽
Xunzi	荀子
Xuxian hanzao	徐仙翰藻
Xuxian zhenlu	徐仙真錄
Xuzu	許祖
yan	沿
Yan Song	嚴嵩
Yang Hou	楊厚
Yang Qing	陽慶
yangqi	養氣
yankou	焰口
Yanshi	顏氏
Yaochi jinmu	瑤池金母
Yaoxiu keyi jielü chao	要修科儀戒律鈔
Yaoyong wupin dan	要用物品單

Ye	鄴		難陀羅尼焰口
Ye Mingchen	葉名琛		軌儀經
Ye Zongmao	葉宗茂	Yulanpen hui	盂蘭盆會
yi	意	Yunquan xianguan	雲泉仙館
Yi	彝	*Yuqie jiyao yankou shishi yi*	
Yihe lou	亦鶴樓		瑜伽集要焰口
Yijing	易經		施食儀
Yili	儀禮	*Yuqing jing*	玉清經
yin	印	Yuqing tang	餘慶堂
yin	寅	Yuzhang	豫章
Yin Wen	尹文		
Ying Shao	應邵	*zai*	宰
Yingwu zhou	鸚鵡洲	Zai Quheng	載衢亨
Yingyuan gong	應元宮	*zaju*	雜居
yinjiao	銀角	*zangsuo*	藏所
yinyang	陰陽	*Zanling ji*	贊靈集
Yinzhiwen tushuo	陰騭文圖説	Zeng Chunshou	曾椿壽
yishe	義舍	*zhai*	齋
yiwen	移文	*zhaijie*	齋戒
Yixin she	一新社	*zhaishe*	齋舍
Yong'an xiang	永安鄉	*zhaishi*	齋室
you	酉	*zhaitang*	齋堂
You Qi	尤麒	Zhan Ruoshui	湛若水
you yan san guan	游宴三官	Zhanbei feng	折碑峰
youxin lang	有心郎	Zhang	張
Youyang zazu	酉陽雜俎	*zhang*	章
Yu Liang lou	臾亮樓	Zhang Daoling	張道陵
Yu shantang	與善堂	Zhang Gao	張高
Yu Xuanji	魚玄機	Zhang Jue	張角
Yuan Miaozong	元妙宗	Zhang Ling	張陵
yuan	員	Zhang Lu	張路
Yuan Zhen	元真	Zhang Shuang'an	張爽菴
Yuanhuo shan	遠火山	Zhang Shujing	張叔敬
yuanqi	元氣	Zhang Xu	張續
Yuanshi fuming	元始符命	*zhangjue*	掌訣
Yuanshi tianzun	元始天尊	*zhangshi gui*	障施鬼
Yuanxu	原序	Zhao	昭
Yue Chengong	樂臣公	Zhao Fenliang	招奮良
Yue wumu wang	岳武穆王	Zhao Lianshi	趙鍊師
Yuedong	粵東	Zhao Zunsi	招尊四
Yuefu	樂府	*Zhen'gao*	真誥
Yuegang yuan	越崗院	*zheng renshi*	正人事
Yueshi	樂氏	*zhengfa*	正法
Yuexiu shan	粵秀山	*Zhengjian gongde die*	正薦功德牒
Yuhuang benxing jing		Zhengyi	正一
	玉皇本行經	*Zhengyi fawen jingtu kejie pin*	
Yujia jiyao jiu anan tuoluoni yankou			正一法文經圖
guiyi jing	瑜伽集要救阿		科戒品

Zhengyi fawen taishang wailu yi
　正一法文太上
　外籙儀
Zhengyi jiaomu yi 正一醮墓儀
Zhengyi jiaozhai yi 正一醮宅儀
Zhengyi jie'e jiaoyi 正一解厄醮儀
Zhengyi licheng yi 正一立成儀
Zhengyi lun 正一論
Zhengyi weiyi jing 正一威儀經
zhenmu wen 真墓文
zhenyan 真言
Zhenzhong hongbao yuan bishu
　枕中鴻寶苑秘書
Zhenzhong sushu 枕中素書
zhi tianzheng 治天政
Zhibao tai 至寶台
zhicheng 至誠
zhifu 值符
zhihun 滯魂
zhijue 指訣
Zhiqi 志器
Zhiqiu 志秋
Zhiyi 智顗
Zhizhuo 志卓
Zhong Ziqi 鍾子期
zhongdang 種黨
Zhongli Quan 鍾離權
Zhongliang shi 仲良氏
zhongmin 種民
Zhongshan 中山
Zhongxiao jie 忠孝街
Zhongyong 中庸
zhongzi 種子
zhou 咒
Zhou Chong 周崇
Zhou Daotong 周道通
Zhou Dinglai 周鼎來
Zhou Qi 周棄
Zhou Ruli 周汝厲
Zhou Shixiu 周世修
Zhou Side 周思得

Zhou Sui 周燧
Zhou Yehe 周埜鶴
Zhou Yi 周毅
Zhou Yue 周説
Zhouli 周禮
Zhouyi yi 周易德
Zhouyi zhengyi 周易正義
Zhu Faman 朱法滿
Zhu Gui 朱珪
Zhu Hong 珠宏
Zhu Quan 朱權
Zhu Xi 朱熹
Zhu Yuanzhang 朱元璋
Zhu Yunyang 朱雲陽
zhuang 狀
Zhuang Xing'an 莊富菴
Zhuang Zhou 莊周
Zhuangzi 莊子
Zhuguo jiumin zongzhen biyao
　助國救民總真
　秘要
Zhuyuan 竹園
zhuzi 諸子
Zhuzi Fang 朱紫方
zi 子
Zi Gong 子貢
Zi Si 子思
Zi Zhang 子張
Zi'an 子安
zibo 自弑
Zichan 鄭自產
Zimo 茲莫
Ziran zhaiyi 自然齋儀
zisong 自訟
zize 自責
Zong 賨
zongheng 縱橫
zongzi 粽子
zu 祖
zumiao 祖廟

Names of Authors Cited

Akizuki Kan'ei	秋月觀英
Araki Kengo	荒木見悟
Asano Haruji	淺野春二
Asano Yūichi	淺野裕一
Chen Bing	陳兵
Chen Cheng-siang	陳正祥
Dong Qixiang	董其祥
Duan Yuming	段玉明
Fan Chunwu	範純武
Fukui Fumimasa	福井文雅
Fukui Kōjun	福井康順
Fukunaga Mitsuji	福永光司
Fuma Susumu	夫馬進
Furuie Shinpei	古家信平
Guan Xiang	關翔
Harada Masami	原田正已
Hu Fuchen	胡孚琛
Huang Junjie	黃俊傑
Huang Shiqing	黃拾青
Ikeda Tomohisa	池田知久
Jiang Boqian	蔣伯潛
Kamitsuka Yoshiko	神塚淑子
Kawai Kōzō	川合康三

Kobayashi Masayoshi	小林正美
Kobayashi Yoshihiro	小林義廣
Kokusho Kankōkai	國書刊行會
Kondō Hiroyuki	近藤浩之
Li Huichuan	李匯川
Li Ling	李零
Li Qing	李慶
Lin Guoping	林國平
Liu Xiangming	劉向明
Liu Zhiwan	劉枝萬
Liu Zhiwen	劉志文
Liu Zhongyu	劉仲宇
Lü Chuikuan	呂鐘寬
Luo Yixing	羅一星
Mabuchi Masaya	馬淵昌也
Maruyama Hiroshi	丸山宏
Matsumoto Kōichi	松本浩一
Misaki Ryōshū	三崎良周
Mitamura Keiko	三田村圭子
Miyakawa Hisayuki	宮川尚志
Mizokuchi Yūsō	溝口雄三
Mizuno Minoru	水野實
Mori Yuria	森由利亞
Nan Huaijin	南懷瑾
Ōfuchi Ninji	大淵忍爾

Pang Pu   龐朴
Peng Wenyu   彭文宇

Qiao Qingquan   喬清拳

Rueh Yih-fu   芮逸夫

Sahara Yasuo   佐原康夫
Sakade Yoshinobu 阪出祥神
Sakai Tadao   酒井忠夫
Sano Kōshi   佐野公治
Shiga Ichiko   志賀市子
Shimamori Tetsuo 島森哲男
Shiratori Yoshirō 白鳥芳郎
Song Enchang   宋思常

Takeuchi Fusashi 武内房司
Tsuchiya Masaaki 土屋昌明

Wang Jianchuan   王見川
Wang Ming   王明
Wang Qiugui   王秋桂
Wang Zhizhong   王志忠

Xiao Dengfu   蕭登福
Xu Dishan   許地山
Xu Xiaowang   徐曉望

Yamada Masaru   山田賢
Yamada Toshiaki 山田利明
Yang Cenglie   楊曾烈
Yoshikawa Tadao 古川忠夫
Yoshioka Yoshitoyo 古岡義豐
Yu Min   愚民

Zheng Zhenduo   鄭振鐸

Contributors

Co-editors

LIVIA KOHN is Professor of Religion and East Asian Studies at Boston University. She received her Ph.D. from Bonn University, Germany, after which she undertook post-doctoral studies at Kyoto University, Japan. A specialist of medieval Chinese religion and especially Daoism, she has written and edited many works, including *Taoist Meditation and Longevity Techniques* (1989), *Early Chinese Mysticism* (1992), *The Taoist Experience* (1993), *Laughing at the Tao* (1995), *God of the Dao: Lord Lao in History and Myth* (1998), and *Daoism Handbook* (2000).

HAROLD D. ROTH received his Ph.D. from the University of Toronto and served as visiting lecturer at the University of Alberta and at the School of Oriental and African Studies, London. He is currently Professor of Religious Studies and East Asian Studies at Brown University, specializing in Chinese religion and early Daoist thought. Major publications include *The Textual History of the Huai-nan Tzu* (1992) and *Original Tao: Inward Training and the Foundations of Taoist Mysticism* (1999).

Contributors

ASANO HARUJI is Associate Professor of Chinese Studies at Kokugakuin Junior College in Sapporo. He specializes in the understanding of contemporary ritual in Chinese society and has undertaken fieldwork with a focus on Daoist ritual in Taiwan since the 1980s. He has published various articles in prestigious journals, such as *Tōhōshūkyō* (1995) and *Girei bunka* (1996).

SUZANNE CAHILL is Adjunct Associate Professor in the History Department at University of California-San Diego. She is the author of *Transcendence and Divine Passion: The Queen Mother of the West in Medieval China* (Stanford University Press, 1993).

MARK CSIKSZENTMIHÀLYI is Associate Professor of Religion at the University of Wisconsin at Madison. He is the co-editor, with Philip B. Ivanhoe, of *Essays on Religious and Philosophical Aspects of the Laozi* (State University of New York Press, 1999)

EDWARD L. DAVIS is Associate Professor of Chinese History at the University of Hawai'i. He holds a B.A. from Harvard College and an M.A. and Ph.D. from the University of California at Berkeley. He is the author of *Society and the Supernatural in Song China* (University of Hawai'i Press, 2001) and co-editor of the *Encyclopedia of Contemporary Chinese Culture* (Routledge, forthcoming).

TERRY F. KLEEMAN is Associate Professor of Chinese and Religious Studies at the University of Colorado, Boulder. He is the author of *A God's Own Tale: The Book of Transformations of Wenchang* (State University of New York Press, 1994) and *Great Perfection: Religion and Ethnicity in a Chinese Millennial Kingdom* (University of Hawai'i Press, 1998).

MABUCHI MASAYA is Professor of Chinese Thought at Gakushūin University and focuses on the understanding of Ming-dynasty philosophy. He has published papers in both volumes edited by the Society for the Study of Daoist Culture (1994; 1998) as well as in the important journal *Chūgoku tetsugaku kenkyu* (1990).

MARUYAMA HIROSHI is Associate Professor of East Asian Religion at Tsukuba University. He is one of Japan's foremost scholars on questions of contemporary Daoist ritual and has undertaken extensive fieldwork in Taiwan. He is published widely in such prestigious journals such as *Tōhōshūkyō* (1986; 1991), *Shakai bunka shigaku* (1986), and *Acta Asiatica* (1995).

MITAMURA KEIKO is Lecturer of Chinese Studies at Meikai University in Chiba. She is especially interested in the study of medieval Daoism and has variously studied its texts and worldview. Her writings appear in the volumes edited by the Society for the Study of Daoist Culture (1994) as well as in *Tōhōshūkyō* (1998) and *Kōza dōkyō* (1999).

MORI YURIA is Associate Professor of Chinese History and Culture at Waseda University in Tokyo. His area of specialization is the history of the Quanzhen lineage in the Ming and Qing dynasties. His publications explore this almost unknown area of Daoist and Chinese history, appearing in the volumes edited by the Society for the Study of Daoist Culture (1994; 1998) as well as in *Tōyō no shisō to shūkyō* (1998) and *Kōza dōkyō* (1999).

PETER NICKERSON is Assistant Professor of Religion and Asian and African Languages and Literature at Duke University. His publications include "The Great Petition for Sepulchral Plaints" (in Stephen R. Bokenkamp, ed., *Early Daoist Scriptures* [University of California Press, 1997]) and "A Poetics and Politics of Possession: Taiwanese Spirit-Medium Cults and Autonomous Popular Cultural Space" (forthcoming in *Positions: East Asia Cultures Critique* 9.1 [2001]). He is currently completing a book manuscript, *Taoism, Bureaucracy, and Popular Religion in Early Medieval China.*

CHARLES D. ORZECH is Associate Professor and Head of the Department of Religious Studies at The University of North Carolina–Greensboro. He is the author of *Politics and Transcendent Wisdom: The Scripture for Humane Kings in the Creation of Chinese Buddhism* (Pennsylvania State University Press, 1998).

SHIGA ICHIKO is Lecturer of Chinese Anthropology at Tokyo Seitoku University. She focuses especially on the development of contemporary forms of Daoism in Hong Kong and southern China. She has published widely in such journals as *Kōza dōkyō* and recently brought out a book entitled *Kindai chūgoku no shamanizumu to dōkyō* (Tokyo, 1999).

TSUCHIYA MASAAKI is Associate Professor of East Asian Thought at Yokohama University. He is primarily interested in the early Daoist movements and in questions of self and self-understanding in traditional China. His publications cover various subjects in this general area and have appeared in the volumes edited by the Society for the Study of Daoist Culture (1994; 1998).

Index

academies, Confucian, 198; membership in, 199
Acala, 216
acāryas, 215
accommodation, and identity, 215
Aiyu shantang, 201
alchemy, and *pudu,* 228
altar: arrangement of, 291; of awakening, 175–176, 183; as body, 222; disciples of, 173; and healing, 172; in modern Daoism, 185–209; offerings on, 277, 279, 281; preparation of, 275; protection of, 261; in Qing, 167; setting up of, 259
Amah, 120, 122
Amitābha, 176–177
Amoghavajra, 215–217
amṛta. See sweet dew
ancestors: anxiety about, 72, 75; cult for, 160; offerings for, 290; temple for, 152–153; worship of, 75
Ancestral Hall, 158, 160, 163
anger, 14
animals, five, 276, 282; in offerings, 288; sacrificial, 278
announcement, 65, 261–263; ceremony of, 259–260; for dead, 66; in ritual, 257
Aofeng, 151, 155, 157, 161, 163
Aofeng shutang, 159
apocrypha, Buddhist, 213. See *chenwei*
appropriation, 215
Asano Haruji, 18
Asano Yūichi, 83

"At the Temple Washing Silk Gauze," 121
autobiography, 43
Avalokitesvara. *See* Guanyin

Ba people, 11, 25, 28–35; beliefs of, 26; Daoist attraction of, 27; kingdom of, 29
Ba youhun zhenfu, 263
Baidu pai, 154
Baihe guan, 190
Bailong jingshe, 167, 170–171, 173
Baiyun dong, 198
Baiyun guan, 179
Baiyun shan, 193
Baldrian-Hussein, Farzeen, 194
ballads, 112
bamboo, 122
Bamboo Grove, Seven Sages of, 111, 116, 118–119
Bamen kaidu Tianzun, 225
Bamen yanqin shenshu, 253
Ban Gu, 89–90, 98
banjiao, 31
banquet: as audience, 226; in *fang yankou,* 221–223; and offerings, 282; in *pudu,* 225–227; ritual, 10
Banshun Man, 35
Bao Jing, 191
Baodao tang, 196, 203
Baopuzi, 71, 244, 284, 286
Baosheng dadi, 160
Baosong baohe ji, 203, 205, 208
Baoyuan taiping jing, 94

barbarians: Chinese views of, 30–32;
  conversion of, 31
Beijing, 151, 176
Beimeng suoyan, 125
beiyin, 156
benevolence, 130
Berger and Luckmann, 4
Bian Que zhenzhong bijue, 99
bigu, 287
blood: magic of, 284–286; sacrifices,
  10, 18, 27, 280–284, 291
Bo Ya, 116, 123
boats, 104, 109, 111–116, 124
bodhi, and Dao, 216
bodhicitta, 222–224, 228
bodhisattvas, 162; in ritual, 223
body: as altar, 222, 226; as cosmos, 228;
  in Daoism, 12; at death, 67–68; defilements of, 45; and hand signs, 237;
  lightness of, 287; as microcosm, 52;
  and mind, 51–52; spirit, 271; as state,
  226, 228
Bokenkamp, Stephen, 220, 231
Boltz, Judith, 220, 227
boundaries, and identity, 2
bowls, as offerings, 277
Brahmā, 225, 231; in hand signs, 239–
  240; language, 220
buddhas: assembly of, 223–224; invocation of, 221, 223; of the past, 158;
  in ritual, 223–224
Buddhism: comparison with, 99; and
  Daoism, 58; and Daoist identity, 7;
  and Daoist ritual, 231–234; discipline
  of, 31; Esoteric, 213–234; and guilt,
  41–42; and literati, 157; and Ming
  Daoism, 137–138; in Ming dynasty,
  10, 131, 143, 235–255, 274; and
  modern cults, 205; and mortuary
  rites, 74–75; offerings in, 279; and
  popular religion, 163; ritual of, 15,
  16–17, 256; temples of, 104; understanding of, 35
Budong, 216
bureaucracy: imperial, 107; otherworldly, 10, 58–77. *See also* officials
butterfly dream, 114

Cahill, Suzanne, 14
Cai Wenji, 121
cakes, as offering, 276, 283
candies, as offering, 276–277, 283
candles, as offering, 275, 283, 291

Canhua gong, 198
Canton, spirit-writing in, 187, 189
Cao Cao, 27, 29
"Capturing Willows by the Riverside,"
  112–113
Catholics, and identity, 6
Cedzich, Angelika, 60–61
Celestial Elder. *See* Tianlao
Celestial Masters: beginnings of, 99–100;
  confessions in, 39–40; early history
  of, 96–97; and ethnic groups, 26, 28,
  33; and identity, 7–8; merit rituals of,
  256–273; new Daoism under, 58–77;
  ritual of, 274–294
Celestial Monarch. *See* Tiandi
Ceng Yiguan, 190, 192
Central China, 23
chamber of tranquility. *See* oratory
Chan Buddhism, 158, 162
Chang'an, 102, 104, 105, 118
Changchun daojiao yuanliu, 190–192
Changchun xianguan, 200
Changqu lidu nü tuoluoni zhoujing, 241
Changsheng lingfu, 263
Changsheng shu, 166
Changsheng shu xuming fang hekan, 166
Changzhou, 167
Chanhui wen, 56
chanting, 267
Chen Minggui, 190
Chen Mou, 166, 173
Chen Qiyou, 97
Chen Rongsheng, 259, 275
Chen Tao, 118
Chen Tiquan, 195
Chen Xianzhang, 140, 146
Chen Zhong, 98
Cheng Mou, 172
Chengdu, 25
chengfu, 218
Chenhou Yinzi dui, 99
Chen-Li Ji, 195
Chenmu, 169
chenwei, 24, 92
Chi Daomao, 46
Chi Tan, 46
chicken, blood of, 284
Chijingzi, 94
children, and spirit-writing, 196–197,
  206
Chiyou, 71, 75
Chongsheng guan, 104
Chongxu guan, 190–192, 204

Christianity: guilt in, 41; history of, 99; revelation in, 96–97

Chu, 25, 105; clans of, 112; king of, 107

Chuanxi lu, 132, 145

Chuci, 62, 114, 117, 123, 124

Chunqiu fanlu, 56

Chunqiu yi, 145

Chunyang [shengzu]. *See* Lüzu

Chunyang guan, 192

Chunyu Yi, 93–94

Ci'en si, 104

citang, 153

city god, 262, 265

Ciyi jing, 246

Clark, Hugh, 162–163

Clart, Phillip, 187

clothing, in Daoist identity, 104–111, 123–124

Cold Food Festival, 117–118

Colpe, Carston, 214

commitment: in Daoism, 8, 9–10; and identity, 4–5

commoner, clothes of, 110

Complete Perfection. *See* Quanzhen

confession, 39–57; acts of, 46; in modern Daoism, 20; terms for, 39

Confucianism: academies of, 198; and Buddhism, 213, 217; classification of, 97; and Daoism, 58; and Daoist rites, 65; and healing, 41; and Ming Daoism, 137–138, 145; in modern cults, 187; offerings in, 279, 281–282, 284; and popular religion, 162; and religious identity, 7; ritual of, 256

Confucius, 84–87, 91, 130; in Ming Daoism, 138; and souls, 69

consecration, 221–222, 225

conversion, 217

corpse, preparation of, 64–66

cosmogony, 132–134

cosmology, 17, 60

crucible, 228

Csikszentmihàlyi, Mark, 13–14

Cuanyu lieyu aotuo shenyu, 239

culture: encounters of, 218; and identity, 6

Dacheng, 29

Dadao jia lingjie, 30, 37

Dadong zhenjing, 34

Dai Zhen, 145

Daizong (Tang emperor), 216–217

Daluo tian, 120

Dan Ranhui, 166

Dangqu, 29

Dao: and bodhi, 216; grace of, 262; in Han dynasty, 89–90, 98; levels of, 137; in Ming, 130, 133; principle of, 132; root of, 134; and transcendence, 135; versus *fa*, 152

daochang, 275

Daode jing, and Buddhism, 214

Daodian lun, 246–247

Daofa huiyuan, 236, 249–250, 251, 252, 284, 286

Daoism: areas of, 8; and Buddhist practice, 235–255; Buddhist terms in, 231; early schools of, 88–89; identity in general, 7–11; key concepts of, 8; metaphors in, 226–227; origins of, 96–97; poetry of, 102–126; and popular religion, 149–164; schools of, 83; shift in studies of, 149; sociological development of, 81–101; term, 96; women in, 102–126

Daoists, 27; definition of, 139; literati, 7, 8–9; redhead and blackhead, 253, 292

daojia, 83, 139

daojiao, 139

Daojiao yishu, 30–31

Daomen kelue, 40, 284

daotan, 13, 16, 185–209; growth of, 206; list of, 188

Daoxue keyi, 292

Daoxue zhuan, 287

Daozang jiyao, 166, 172–174, 176, 178, 183

Daozang xubian, 166

Dark Warrior, 188

Datang liudian, 235

dates, 287; as offering, 284

Davis, Edward, 15

Daxue, 216–217

Daxue yanyi lunduan, 145

Daxue yi, 145

de. *See* virtue

dead: liberation of, 59; offerings for, 290; rituals for, 58–77, 255–273; tablets for, 156

death: avoidance of, 74; as punishment, 52

DeGroot, J.J.M., 219

demon soldiers. See *guizu*

demons: control of, 247–248; killing of, 243; offerings for, 276, 282; rites for, 27. *See also* exorcism

Deng Yougong, 237
Dengxi, 98
descent, of gods, 196
desires, 52, 288
destiny: control over, 256; ruler of, 188; of world, 264
devotion, 288
dhāraṇi, 228, 231, 239–240. *See also* mantras
dharma, 216–217, 223, 225, 231
Dharmadhātu, 223
Di people, 31
Dianlue, 39
differentiation, 3
Dingguang fo, 158, 163
Dipīmkara, 158
Dipper: in hand signs, 236, 239–240, 242–244, 249–250, 252; invocation of, 249; Mother of, 192
disasters: avoidance of, 193; and morality books, 187, 200–201
discipline, religious, 106
diseases, dispelling of, 267. *See also* healing
divination, 93, 156; and Daoism, 82; and Ming Daoism, 128; in temples, 155
Divine Empyrean, 237
Division of Lamps, 259
Diyi kaihua tan, 173, 183
Dizang, 224
documents: burning of, 260; contents of, 261; editing process of, 266; envelopes of, 261; notes on, 260; in rituals, 256–273; types of, 257
Donghua dijun, 205
Donghua pai, 271
Dongji jiulong fuming, 263
Dongjing hui, 34
Doumu, 192
dragon cards, as offerings, 278–279, 289
dragons: as hand sign, 239; as messengers, 289; as offerings, 289; talisman of, 271; talisman order of, 263
drugs. *See* medicines
drunkenness, and poetry, 113, 115–116, 118–119
Du Collection, 259–260, 261, 263, 264–265, 267, 269, 270
Du Fu, 108, 111
Du Lüzu sanni yishi shuoshu guankui, 180
Du Yangdong, 191
Du Yongchang, 258–259
Duan Chengshi, 63

duck, blood of, 284
Duren jing, 267
Duren shangjing dafa, 247–248, 268
Dushi lunduan, 145
"Dwelling in the Mountains," 110–111

"Early Autumn," 118
Earth: Department of, 271; Door of, 243, 245; god of, 261–262, 265; and hand signs, 252; officials of, 69; *qi* of, 51; realm of, 263; spirits, of, 52
eccentricity, in poetry, 115, 116, 118
egui. See hungry ghosts
Eight Immortals, 196
elite, local, 151–153
elixir, concoction of, 285
energy. See *qi*
enlightenment: essence of, 224; proof of, 175; seed of, 222–224
Envoy. *See* Tiandi shizhe jie
equivalence, 221; in translation theory, 215–217
Erikson, Erik, 1–2
Ernst, C.W., 230
eroticism, 104, 115, 116–117, 121–122, 123
Esposito, Monica, 165, 166, 172, 182
essence. See *jing*
ethnicity, 11; in China, 7; and identity, 6, 23–38; in modern Asia, 32–33; understanding of, 34–35
exorcism, 61, 62–64, 71–73, 241–242; and hand signs, 238, 246, 249; in modern Daoism, 193

fa, 152
family shrine, 160
Fan Ao, 173
Fan Ben, 29
Fan Changsheng, 29
Fan Li, 93
fang. See methods
Fang Ce, 155
Fang Ciweng, 161
Fang Dacong, 153–154, 161–162
Fang family, 149–164
Fang Fengwu, 161
Fang Hong, 153
Fang Huan, 161
Fang Ji, 155
Fang Jue, 153, 155
Fang Lue, 163
Fang village, 197

Fang Wen, 161
Fang Wenzhao, 161
Fang Xian, 161
Fang Xun, 161
fang yankou, 16, 213–234; description of, 221–225
Fang Zhao, 163
Fang Zhong, 161
Fang Zhuangyou, 161
fangliang (demon), 62
Fangshan, 155, 159
Fangshan pai, 154
fangshi, 17, 244; and hand signs, 237
fangxiang, 62–64, 69, 71, 74
Fangzhai cungao, 138
Fanyu, 202
Fanyu xian xuzhi, 202
Fayuan zhulin, 284
fendeng, 259
Feng Yan, 93
Fengdu, 226–227, 265
Fengsu tongyi, 63
Fengxue jiaozi shu, 253
Festival: Cold Food, 117; of Hungry Ghosts, 199; Mid-Autumn, 196–197
festivals, 158, 162, 185; annual, 199; and local temples, 158
fire: as passions, 224; phase of, 51; in ritual, 222–223
fisherman, 111
five directions, 278
Five Emperors, 290, 293
Five Marchmounts, 59–60
Five Pecks of Rice, 100
five phases, 51; hand signs for, 243
flow, going with, 114, 115, 124
flowers, 289; as offering, 275, 283, 291
"Following the Rhymes of My Western Neighbor," 117
food: distribution of, 230; as offering, 275; raw versus cooked, 280. *See also* blood, sacrifices
Former Heaven, 174, 176
Foshan, 194–195
Foshan yaoye zhi, 195
Foshan zhongyi xiangzhi, 194
freedom, and identity, 111, 116
Freud, Sigmund, 1
fruit, 290; of immortals, 287; as offering, 275–276, 283, 286–288, 291
Fu Xi, 93, 130
Fujian, 149–164, 187, 271
Fukui Kōjun, 41

funerary rites, 291–292
Fuxing, 203
Fuyou [dijun]. *See* Lüzu
Fuyou dijun jueshi jing, 196
Fuyou shangdi tianxian jinhua zongzhi, 165
Fuzhou, 151

Gai Gong, 95
games, and spirit-writing, 196–197
ganlu. See sweet dew
Ganquan wenji, 143
Gansu, 29
Gaogong daoshi, 257, 259
Gaotang fu, 107
Gaoxiong, 258, 261
gati, six, 221, 225, 230–231, 265
Ge Chaofu, 231
Ge Hong, 40, 71, 244; and mudras, 17
Ge Xuan, 65
Gelao people, 27, 35
genealogies, in Song, 154
generals, celestial, 261
Gennep, Arnold van, 70
geomancy, 157
gewu, 136
geyi, 214, 230
ginger, as offering, 277
"Given to a Neighbor Girl," 105
goats, as offerings, 276, 278, 280–282
goddess, Daoist, 107, 189
gods: and ghosts, 160; local, 153
"Going Along the Yangzi River," 114
gold, as offering, 278, 283, 289
Gongde wenxian, 258
Gongshan she, 186
Gongyang yishi, 253
Gongyu shuyuan, 198
good works, 186–187, 189
goodness, 131–132, 135; basic, 140, 142; counterfeit, 138; and healing, 202; practice of, 201; and righteousness, 131; root of, 37; sprouts of, 135; utmost, 136
government, and hand signs, 252
grain: abstention from, 287; and elixir, 285; ground, 287–290; as offering, 276, 283
Granet, Marcel, 64, 100
grave-securing writs, 58–77
Gray, Isabella, 192–193
Gray, John Henry, 192–193
Great Clarity, 241–243
Great Master, 85, 98

Great One. *See* Great Unity
Great Peace: confessions in, 39–57; ideal
    of, 28, 31; and identity, 7–8, 11, 12
Great Perfection, 29
Great Ultimate, 132, 137
Great Unity, 132, 134, 170, 176, 177,
    182, 245
griffon mask, 63, 74
grottoes, 121–122
growth, 267
Gu hongmei ge, 168
Gu shuyinlou cangshu, 166, 176–180, 182
Guan Yin, 98
Guandi, 187, 193
guanding, 221–222
Guangchengzi, 202, 208
Guangdong, Daoism in, 185–209
Guangdong nianjian, 190–191, 193
Guangdong tongzhi, 191
Guangji zhenjun, 175
Guansheng dijun mingsheng jing zhujie,
    187
Guanyin, 160, 223, 231
guhun. See souls, orphaned
guilt, 41, 43, 44–45, 54–55
Guizhou, 33
guizu, 27, 39, 55
Gujilue, 191
Guo Qingfan, 97
Guochao qixian leizheng chubian, 172
Guodian, 81
Gushi shijiu shou, 118

Habsbawm, Eric, 91
hair, in poetry, 115–116
Hall of Light, 246
Han dynasty: healing in, 39–57; manu-
    scripts of, 81; mortuary rites in,
    13, 58–77; in poetry, 109, 118;
    taxonomies in, 81–101
Han Fei, 130
Han River, 112, 114, 117
Han Yu, 145, 157, 159
hand signs, 17, 220, 235–255; descrip-
    tion of, 245; emergence of, 237; lists
    of, 239, 242, 243; in motion, 247–
    251; origins of, 244–247; pictures
    of, 240, 244, 248, 250; texts on, 236,
    237–238; words for, 235
"Handing Over My Feelings," 115
hands, right versus left, 252
Hanfeizi, 75, 86–88
Hangzhou, 23

Hanshi waizhuan, 98
Hanshu, 14, 53, 88, 89, 94, 97, 98, 99
Hanyang, 114
Hanzhong, 25–27, 29
Haoli, Elders of, 65, 67–68
Harada Masami, 26
Harper, Donald, 26
Hayes, Glen, 231
He Baiyun, 198
He Jinmei, 261
He Qizhong, 204–205, 208
healing: in early Daoism, 39–57; and
    hand signs, 238, 241, 249; and
    identity, 7, 12; and lineage forma-
    tion, 172; and modern cults, 189,
    194–196
Heaven: anthropomorphic, 50; ascent
    to, 264; compassion of, 52; and
    consciousness, 49–51; and modern
    cults, 189, 194–196; as cranium, 228;
    and disease, 44; Gate of, 243, 245;
    God of, 281; gods of, 45; and heal-
    ing, 12, 54–55; light of, 176; lord of,
    52; music of, 176; offerings to, 39;
    order from, 266–267; principle of,
    132, 140–142; punishments of, 47,
    55; and radiance, 51; rebirth in, 264;
    refuge in, 46; sublimation into, 272
Heavenly Sovereign, hand sign for,
    239–240
Heavenly Worthies, 225, 231, 241–243,
    268
Hefu tongzi, 268
hell: busting of, 218, 220, 224–225; de-
    struction of, 263, 269; money for,
    230; rescue from, 16. See also *fang
    yankou*
hells, nine, 268–269
Henan, 151
Henan Fangshi, 155
Henry, A. M., 191
Heqiao, 261
herbs, and poetry, 108
Herd Boy and Weaver Girl, 117–118
Hertz, Robert, 72
Hetu, 92
hexagrams, 156
Highest Clarity, 241–243
Highest Emperor, 286
Hinduism, 215
Hmong people, 35
Hocart, A.M., 219
homa, 222–223, 228

Hong Kong: Daoism in, 16, 185–209;
   jiao in, 220; spirit-writing in, 167
Hong'en lingji zhenjun, 151
Hong'en lingji zhenjun miaojing, 163
Hongjiao enshi, 174
Honolulu, 220
Hou Hanshu, 39, 53, 55, 95
Houcun xiansheng daquan ji, 161
Houcun xiansheng quanji, 154, 158
Hua Zhushi, 129–130
huahu. See barbarians
Huainanzi, 56, 90–91
Huajian shan, 200
Huang family, 259
Huang Xuanxian, 205
Huang Zhonghuan, 169
Huang Zongxi, 128, 140
Huangdi, 13, 59, 74–75, 91–93, 95, 99,
   100, 208
Huangdi sijing, 81
Huangfu Mei, 103, 125
Huangfu Mi, 69
Huangfu Peng, 238–239
Huangji hepi xianjing, 179
Huangjing hui, 34
Huang-Lao, 13, 24, 81, 91–92, 94, 95, 99
Huanglong guan, 190
Huanglu dazhai yi, 288–290, 292–293
Huanglu jiao, 158
Huanglu zhaiyi, 292–293
Huangshi gong, 288
Huanzhu, 193
Huayangguo zhi, 26, 27
Hubei, 112, 117
Hui Shi, 98
Huijue, 182
Huilan, 113
Huixing shantang, 202
Huiyuan, 214, 230
Huizong (Song emperor), 237–238
hungry ghosts, 221, 225–228, 229–230,
   231; offerings for, 276, 280–281, 282
Hymes, Robert, 152, 154

identity: and apocalypse, 187; and
   coherence, 138; in Daoism, 7–11;
   definition of, 2; and economic
   reality, 283; and freedom, 111, 116;
   limitations of, 105, 107; through
   lineage, 180; of Master Zhuang,
   171; Muslim, 215; perspectives
   of, 138–139; and popular religion,
   149–164; and prejudice, 214; as

process, 3, 8, 272; and religion, 1–11;
   through ritual, 256–257; theory of,
   1–6; and translation, 213–234; in
   Western thought, 1–2; word for, 1;
   with world, 223. *See also* self
immortals: commentary of, 180; descent
   of, 197; and food, 287; in poetry,
   110, 116, 122; prefaces by, 172; prescriptions of, 195–196, 199; and
   revelation, 166, 168; ritual transformation into, 222; in Song, 162; in
   Song-Ming, 151; types of, 74. *See also*
   séance; spirit-writing
incense: as offering, 275, 283, 291;
   chamber for, 45
initiation, 220, 229
ink, as offering, 278
inner alchemy, and hand signs, 237
inner nature, 132, 143. *See also* mind
inner organs, 51
inscriptions, 156
institutions: in Han, 95–96; and identity;
   and lineages, 84
integration, 3
intention, 51, 53
invocations, 222–224
Islam, 215

Jade Clarity, 226, 241–243, 252
Jade Emperor, 163, 281; birthday of, 199
jade yang, 228
Jakobson, Roman, 216, 231
James, William, 1
Japan, 24, 33; invasion, 204
Ji tiannü shier xinü fa, 292
Ji Yugong, 125
Jia Yi, 98
jiaci, 160
Jiang Boqian, 85
Jiang Shuyu, 266
Jiang Yupu, 15–16, 165, 173; altar of,
   174–175; followers of, 183
Jiangsu, 16, 24
Jiangxi, 152, 154, 162
Jianzhi lue, 192
jiao, 10, 18, 99, 158, 185; altar of, 283;
   definition of, 274–275; offerings in,
   286; for peace, 257–258
jiashou, 37
Jidu dacheng jinshu, 270, 285
Jidu jinshu, 268, 270
Jiebi, 98
Jijiao fa, 292

Jijie, 99
jijiu, 27, 28, 55
Jilian keyi, 253
Jin Yunzhong, 262, 286–287, 293
jing, 44
Jin'gai shan, 176–180, 181
Jin'gai xindeng, 180
Jingming (school), 16, 166, 169–172,
     180–182
Jingming yuanliu, 169–170
Jingming zhongxiao dao, 169
Jingming zhongxiao lu, 169, 179
jingshi. See oratory
Jinhua keyi, 182
Jinhua Taiyi, 170
Jinjing, 245
Jinshu, 35, 45
Jishan li, 157
Jishan xiantan, 204
Jiu Tangshu, 99
Jiuku zhenfu, 263
Johnson, Mark, 216–217
journey: as metaphor, 217–218; post-
     mortem, 66–69, 71–72. *See also*
     boats
judgment: and afterlife, 59–60; and
     metaphors, 217; powers of, 142;
     and sins, 53, 54
Jueqi, 30
Jueyuan bentan, 175
Jueyuan tan, 173, 183
Jung, C. G., 165
Jupo jingshe, 200

kalpas, 177, 187, 264
Kant, Immanuel, 1
kaozheng xue, 138
karma, 265, 288, 290; abrogation of,
     225; in China, 218; destruction
     of, 227, 230; road of, 226
Kawai Kozō, 43
Ke Yanggui, 192
Kierkegaard, Soren, 1
King Mu, 188
kingdom, Daoist, 29
kings, humane, 217
kitchen feasts, 157
Kleeman, Terry, 11, 181, 293
knife, as hand sign, 243
knots, untying of, 269–270
knowledge: and action, 140; pure, 135,
     140–141
Kobayashi Yoshihiro, 154

Kong-Mo, 91
Kongzi. *See* Confucius
Korea, 33
Kou Qianzhi, 40
kuangzu, 63
Kuhn, Dieter, 125
Kuhn, Thomas, 70, 73
Kumārajīva, 214
Kunlun shan, 121, 239

lads, 268–269. *See also* talisman lads
Lagerwey, John, 219, 257, 266
Lakoff, George, 216–218
landowners, in Han, 86
Lan'gong, 169
Lao Dan, 98
Lao people, 27, 31
Laojun yinsong jiejing, 40–41
Laos, 33
Laozi: emigration of, 31; revelation by,
     24; versus village cults, 149; worship
     of, 193
Laozi: in Han, 82; and literati Daoists,
     7, 8; meditation in, 100; in Ming,
     14–15, 127–146
Laozi yi, 127–146
"Late Spring Sketch," 108, 114
laws, and traditions, 85
lecture sessions, 187, 189
ledgers, of sins, 52–53
LeFevre, André, 216
Legalists, 83, 88
Leibniz, Wilhelm, 1
letters, 290
Li Bo, 108, 111, 116–117
Li Hu, 26
Li Ling, 93
Li Mingche, 192
Li Qingfu, 161
Li Qingqiu, 190
Li Shangyin, 119
Li Si, 98
Li Te, 29
Li Wenyuan, 182
Li Xiong, 29
Li Yi, 102, 119
Li Ying, 106
Li Zhaoji, 195
Li Zhi, 145
Li Zhongsheng Tang, 195
Li Zi'an, 113
Li Zongjian, 198
Liang Qian, 144

Liang Ren'an, 201
liangzhi, 135–136, 140, 142
Liaoning, 23
libationer. See *jijiu*
Liezi, 100, 145
light, 224
Liji, 63
Lin Lingzhen, 268
Lin Wenjun, 138
Lin Ziyao, 239
lineages: and aristocracy, 10; consciousness of, 160; creation of, 168, 178, 181; in Daoism, 9–10; duality in, 169–170; in early Daoism, 81–101; establishment of, 156; formation, 165–184; and identity, 180; legitimacy of, 166; legitimation through, 205; membership in, 89; in modern cults, 205; names of, 88–89, 170; nine, 90; orthodoxy, 175; and ritual, 257; rural, 157; scroll of, 179; in Song, 149–164; succession of, 179; and texts, 13; transmission in, 84
ling, 231, 246
Lingbao: brilliance of, 226; and Buddhism, 7; Daoists of, 292; and death, 67; and hand signs, 238; and mudras, 17; relief through, 227; revelations of, 65; ritual of, 69, 219–220, 263, 271, 274; scriptures of, 231
Lingbao dalie neizhi xinchi jiyao, 220
Lingbao duren dafa, 293
Lingbao lingjiao jidu jinshu, 220
Lingbao liuding bifa, 292
Lingbao wufu xu, 285, 293
Lingji gong, 15, 150–151, 155, 158–159, 163
Lingji xinggong, 161
Lingji zongmiao, 156
Lingjiao jidu jinshu, 286
Lingjue, 30
lingwei, 185
litanies, precious, 259, 267–268, 271
literati Daoists, 14–15, 191, 194
Liu Du'an, 170
Liu Jia, 99
Liu Kezhuang, 162
Liu Shouyuan, 174
Liu Tishu, 167
Liu Xiang, 74, 94
Liu Yuzhen, 169
Liu Zhiwan, 258
Liu Zhongyu, 239–240

Liu Zongyuan, 145, 156–157, 159
Liu Zongyuan quanji, 156, 161
Liu Zongzhou, 56, 144
Liujia feishen shu, 253
living, rites for, 275
Lixu, 35
lixue, 127
local elite, 187, 191, 194, 199, 200–201, 203–204, 206
Locke, Herbert, 1
lodges, 193
long life, talisman of, 263
long night, 265. *See also* hell
Long Yu, 122
Longghu shan bichuan shoujue, 252
Longhan, 264
Longmen lineage, 16, 171, 175–180, 182, 189, 204–205
Longnü si, 187
Longqiao hermitage, 176–177
Lord Lao, 30. *See also* Laozi
Lord of Ghosts, 27, 35
lotus blossom, 224
Lu, 85
Lü Chuikuan, 258
Lü Dongbin. *See* Lüzu
Lu Jiuyuan, 146
Lu Wenchao, 98
Lu Xiujing, 40, 284
Lu Yinfang, 205
luanji, 155
Luci gang, 114
Lujiang, 287
Lunheng, 49, 74, 99
Lunyu, 84–86, 128, 142
Luo Qinshun, 140
Luofo shan, 189–191, 193–194, 206
Luofu zhinan, 191
Luoshen fu, 123
Luoshu, 92
Luotian jiao, 158
Luqiao, 102
Lüshi chunqiu, 48, 49, 85, 97–98
Lüzu: legends of, 194; in modern Daoism, 185–209; names of, 173–174; and Qing lineages, 16, 165–184
Lüzu quanshu, 165, 167–169, 171
Lüzu quanshu zongzheng, 166
Lüzu shi xiantian xuwu taiyi jinhua zongzhi, 166, 182
Lüzu yaoqian, 199
Lüzu zhenjing, 197

Mabuchi Masaya, 14
Macao, 203, 207
magic, 26; of blood, 284–286; and
    Daoism, 149
Magong, 187
maid, murder of, 102, 105, 124
Man people, 23, 31; types of, 35
mandala: eight-sided, 231; Vajradhātu,
    216
mandates: in ritual, 257; twelve, 268–
    269; to underworld, 259–262, 271–
    272; of yin and yang, 270
mantras: in *fang yankou*, 10, 221–222,
    224; and hand signs, 239–240; in
    pudu, 219–220; in ritual, 228–229
Maojun, 169
Maoshan, 155
mapping, in religions, 217–218
markets, for religions, 219
Maruyama Hiroshi, 17–18, 34
material culture, and Daoism, 14,
    102–126
Mawangdui, 81, 99–100
Mazu, 145, 160
McRae, John, 34
meat: dried, 285; as offering, 277–278,
    280–284, 291
medicine: and cults, 205–206; and
    Daoism, 82; and Ming Daoism, 128;
    and modern cults, 189, 201–203
medicines: and modern cults, 194–196;
    peddlers of, 194–196; revelation of,
    195–196, 204
meditation, 45, 106, 199
melancholy, 105, 108–109, 110, 113,
    117, 121, 124
memorial, 259–260, 290
Mencius, 81, 117, 132, 135
Meng Jingyi, 64–65, 66, 74
Meng Ke, 98
Meng Sheng, 98
Meng Xi, 95
Meng Zhizhou, 64
mengbu, 155
merit, officers of, 265
metaphor: of guest in ritual, 222; and
    religion, 11, 14, 17, 214–218, 221,
    228–229; studies of, 231
methods, and lineages, 88–89, 91–92,
    98; in Han, 87
Miedu wulian shengshi miaojing shenjing,
    67, 69, 238

milk, as offering, 285–286; taboo of,
    292–293
Milky Way, 106, 117
millenarianism, 26
Min County, 149–164
Min Yide, 15–16, 166, 175–180, 183
Minbei, 151, 159
mind: examination of, 246; in Ming
    Daoism, 127–146; and phenomena,
    134, 140; and *qi*, 50–52; substance of,
    136, 140, 142–143; transcendence of,
    135–136, 140–141
Mindu ji, 154, 161
ming (school), 45, 55
Ming dynasty: hand signs in, 17, 235–
    255; *Laozi* in, 14, 127–146; offerings
    in, 285; order in, 158; pharmacies
    in, 195; ritual in, 257, 261, 268–272;
    Taiping jing in, 42
Mingru xue'an, 128, 129, 140–142
mingtang, 246
mingwang, 216–217
Mingzhen ke, 268
Minnan, 151
Minzhong lixue yuanyuan kao, 159
mirror, in translation, 216–218
Mitamura Keiko, 17
Mo Chou, 112
Mo people, 31
models, 89
Mohism, 95; hierarchy of, 98
Mohists, 83, 88, 98
Mol, Hans, 2–6
Moling, 176
monasteries, 152; in Guangdong, 191
money: incense,190; for lost souls, 259;
    as offering, 278, 288–289; for spirits,
    269
Monkey God, 193
moon, in ritual, 224
morality: Confucian, 117; and death, 61;
    and ethnicity, 31, 37; and healing,
    46, 52; and health, 41; and Heaven,
    44–45; and mind, 135; in Ming
    dynasty, 141–142; and ritual, 10;
    root of, 130
morality books, 16, 189; and eschatol-
    ogy, 187; in modern Daoism, 186–
    187; and pharmacies, 196; and
    sickness, 202–203
Mori Ogai, 125
Mori Yuria, 15–16

Mother Goddess, 189
mountain, entering of, 245
Mouzi lihuo lun, 42
Mozi, 41, 84–87, 91
mudra: in Daoism, 10, 17, 235–255; as
    Daoist term, 247; in *fang yankou*, 224;
    in *pudu*, 219–220; as seal, 239, 252
muquan, 59
music, 109
myths, and identity, 5–6

Nah mouh louh, 193–194, 207
Nanchang, 168
Nanhai, 195, 197–198
Nanhai County, 186
Nanhai xianzhi, 192, 198–199
Nanjing, 176
Nankang, 162
Nanshi, 74
nature, Daoist, 106
Needham, Joseph, 61
Neo-Confucianism: Daoist assimilations
    of, 32; and Daoist rites, 65; and Ming
    Daoism, 127–146; and rural order,
    158
neolithic, 23
New Testament, of Dao, 61
Ni Heng, 121
Nickerson, Peter, 12–13
Nida, Eugene, 216, 230
nightmares, banishing of, 246
Nine Ministers, 25
Nine Obscurities, 265
"Nineteen Songs from a Nomad Flute,"
    121
Ning Quanzhen, 266
Nirvāna, 228
niwan, 228
No exorcism, 62–64
nonbeing, 132, 134, 177
noon sacrifice, 276
Northern Emperor, 252
Nüqing, edicts of, 66
Nüqing guilü, 27

objectivation: in Daoism, 8–9; and
    identity, 3–4
offerings: consumption of, 284–285; in
    fang yankou, 224; and healing, 40;
    history of, 284–285; placement of,
    289; in ritual, 18, 271, 274–294
officials: celestial, 256, 266–267; of

Earth, 69; as gods, 288; imperial,
    218; and local elite, 154; metropoli-
    tan, 158; names of, 267; needing
    paper, 290; offerings for, 282; at
    Qing court, 172; receiving money,
    269; as spirit masters, 172; of under-
    world, 259, 261–262, 265
Ōfuchi Ninji, 41–42, 44, 258–260, 270,
    293
"On a Pavilion Hidden in the Mist," 110
Opium War, 200
oratory, 41–42, 45, 53
order, through ritual, 256
orders: of execution, 266; to other-
    world, 257
ordination, in Qing, 179; rituals of, 229
organizations, today, 185–186
organs, 12
Orthodox Unity. *See* Celestial Masters
Orzech, Charles, 16, 236
Ouyang Xiu, 145

painting, 157
Pan Jingguan, 171
Pan Lang, 120
Pan Yi'an, 169–170, 172–173
Pan Yue, 120
Pang, Duane, 219–220
Pangu shan, 162
Panhu, 33
paper, as offering, 278, 290
paradigms, in early Daoism, 58–77
paradise, 121–122
Pardon, Writ of, 259, 261, 263–267,
    270–271
"Passing Ezhou," 111–112
Patriarch Lü. *See* Lüzu
Payne, Richard, 221
peace, offering for, 275
Pearl River, 186, 189, 192–193, 194,
    202
Pei Songzhi, 39
Peng Meng, 98
penitence, 47, 53
People's Temple, 5
petitions: for dead, 61, 65, 66–67; and
    healing, 39–40; in ritual, 257, 290
pharmacies, 195–196
Pidian liuzi shu, 145
pigs, as offerings, 276, 278, 280–282
Piling, 167, 171–172, 178
pillow books, 94, 109

planchette, 155, 192–193, 196–197.
    See also séance; spirit-writing
plum trees, 122–123; blossoms of, 162
pluralism, and identity, 6
Po diyu zhenfu, 263
Po'anji, 144
"Poem Following the Rhyme Words of
    Three Sisters," 120
"Poem to the Refined Master," 107
poetry, 102–126; societies for, 198
Pool of Blood, 259
popular religion: beliefs of, 26; and
    Daoism, 58–77, 149–164; and Daoist
    offerings, 18, 274–294; and modern
    cults, 16, 189; and modern Daoism,
    193–194; offerings in, 279, 281, 282–
    283; ritual of, 256
population, expansion of, 204
possession, 156
precepts: and healing, 46; and lineage,
    179; nine, 272
Precious Litany, 18
preta. See hungry ghosts
Priest of High Merit. *See* Gaogong
    daoshi
priests: as bureaucrats, 272; in her-
    mitages, 191; and offerings, 275;
    redhead, 284; today, 33; urban,
    193–194. See also *jijiu;* officials
primordial beginning, 264; Heavenly
    Worthy of, 268; talisman of, 263
principle: and Dao, 136; of Dao, 132;
    and mind, 143
prison, in poetry, 111
proto-Daoism, 61
pudu, 16–17, 213–234, 259, 265; de-
    scription of, 225–228; similarities
    with *fangyan kou,* 219–220, 228–230
pūjā, 222
Puji tan, 195, 201
punishment: death as, 52; through
    Heaven, 47, 55; for wrong offerings,
    290
Puquan she, 186
Pure Land, 177, 221
pure songs, 109, 118
purgatory. *See* hell
purification: in alchemy, 285; and sins,
    45
purity: and offerings, 285–286; in ritual,
    280, 283
Purple-Robed Fangs, 153, 154, 159, 162
Putian, 154, 159, 162

qi: and consciousness, 50–51; in cosmos,
    12, 44; and healing, 54; in Ming,
    136, 140–141; nurturing of, 110;
    strength of, 285; yin, 246
Qi Ying, 199
qi'an jiao, 257
Qianfu lun, 74
Qianjin yifang, 245
Qiankun yizhang tu, 253
Qianzhen ke, 238
qin. See zithers
Qin, 81, 85; conquest, 24
Qin Guli, 98
Qing dynasty: Daoism in, 15–16, 154,
    190–194; Daoist lineages in, 165–
    184; hand signs in, 235, 252
Qingbu, 151
Qingpu, 150–151
Qingshui zushi, 160
Qingsong guan, 205
Qingyuan County, 200
Qiu Changchun, 167
Qiu Chuji, 169, 171, 205
Qiu Xigui, 97
Qiuzu yulu, 171
Qu Yuan, 105, 112, 117
Quan Tangshi, 102–126
Quanshu zhengzong, 165, 172–174, 175,
    182–183
Quanzhen (school): in Guangdong,
    192; lineages in, 16, 167, 170–172,
    175–181; and modern cults, 189–
    190, 204–207; and nationalism, 32;
    patriarchs of, 169–170, 189
Quanzhou, 187
Quduo, 241
Queen Mother of the West, 121–122

rainmaking, 48–49
Randeng, 158
rebirth, realms of, 221
Refined Master, 107, 108, 114
registers: in Daoism, 218; of death, 65;
    descent of, 266; in Heaven, 264
religions: definition of, 35; encounter
    of, 219; interaction of, 213–215, 236;
    types of, 214–215
Ren An, 95
Renpu, 56
renwang, 217
Renwang huguo boruo bolomiduo jing, 213
Renwang jing, 217
requiem. *See* rites, of merit

"Return from Fishing," 106
revelation: by immortal, 180; through
  Lüzu, 168, 174–175
"Rhapsody on the Parrot," 121
Rig Veda, 231
righteousness, 131
rites: distinctions in, 256; of merit, 18,
  185, 199, 256–273; in Ming Daoism,
  134; of passage, 70; preliminary, 283;
  travel, 71–72
ritual: Buddhist versus Daoist, 213–234;
  in Daoism, 10; documents in, 256–
  273; of flaming mouths, 213–234;
  and hand signs, 235–255; and healing, 39, 46; history of, 270–271;
  homa, 216, 222–223; and identity, 5,
  8–9; identity of, 219–220; mortuary,
  13, 58–77, 185; offerings in, 274–
  294; for protection, 246–247; standardization of, 257; structure of,
  70; study of, 256–257; today, 17–18;
  translation of, 213–214; of universal
  salvation, 213–234; Vedic, 221–222,
  231
Robertson, Maureen, 125
Rong people, 30
Ronghui sanjiao, 138
Roth, Harold, 99–100
Ru, 81, 83, 86, 88; masters of, 98
Ruan Zhao, 108–109, 111
Rui Lin, 193
Rulers of Darkness, 18
rushe, 157

sacralization, 3, 6
sacrifice: attitude of, 288; for dead, 61–
  62; travel, 71; for Wangye, 293
Sacrificial Hall, 153–154, 159
"Sad Thoughts," 109, 118
sages, 82
saints, 9
Śākyamuni, 130–131. *See also* buddhas
saliva, swallowing of, 246
salvation, talismans for, 264
San Lüshi, 112
Sandong zhunang, 30, 245, 247, 287
Sangren, Stephen, 231
Sanguo zhi, 39, 40
Sanhuang, texts of, 75
Sanhuang zhai, 292
Sanni yishi shuoshu, 180
Sanqing, 192
Sanshan, 154

Sanshui xiaolu, 125
Sanskrit: spells in, 239–240; terms
  in Chinese, 215–216
Santian neijie jing, 40
Sanxingdui, 24
Sanyuan gong, 192
sarcasm, 106
Sarvatathāgatatattvasaṃgraha, 221
Saso, Michael, 219, 253, 258
Schipper, Kristofer, 32, 207, 257–258
scholars: projects of, 34; views of, 9
schools: in Han, 83; in Warring States,
  87
scripts, ancient, 25
scriptures, at ordination, 179
seals, 269
séance: by children, 196–197; description of, 167, 176–177, 192–193, 204;
  and sickness, 202
seclusion, 108, 115, 191
"Secret of the Golden Flower," 165–184
seed people, 35
seed syllable, 222–224
Seidel, Anna, 26, 59, 60, 61, 69, 72, 75,
  94, 165
self: affirmation of, 43; blame of, 46–
  47, 48–49, 54; consciousness of, 152,
  161; cultivation of, 82, 136, 140, 180,
  186; definition of, 149–150, 256; expression of, 14, 122; identification
  of, 138–139; images of, 109–110,
  112; punishment of, 47; reflection
  on, 141; understanding of, 291
"Sending Someone My Innermost
  Feelings," 122
senses, six, 265
"Sent to Wen Feiqing," 119
"Sent to Zi'an," 113
separation, pain of, 113
Seven Treasures, 261
sexual rites, 7
sexuality: and music, 116–123; in poetry,
  107, 109, 119–120, 121–122; in ritual,
  220
Shaanxi, 29
shamanism, 27, 62–63, 74, 238, 244
shame, 47, 54, 120, 123
Shan Tao, 119
Shang dynasty, 23, 24
Shangdi, 169
Shangqing, 7, 66, 107; lineage, 169;
  and poetry, 122, 124; and revelation,
  93

Shangqing lingbao dafa, 247–248, 262–
    267, 292–293
Shangqing liujia qidao bifa, 292
Shangshu, 134
Shangzhi tongzi, 268
Shanlue fu, 180
shanshu. See morality books
Shanxing, 275
Shanyu rentong lu, 199–200
Shao Zhilin, 15–16, 165, 167–170, 178,
    181
Shaoyuan (king), 71
Shen Dao, 98
Shen Quanqi, 118
Shen Yue, 56
Shenggong cantang, 196, 202, 204
Shenggong caotang dashi jiyao, 202
Shenggong lu, 202
Shengtian lu, 264
Shenhu, 261
Shennong, 91–93
Shennü fu, 123
Shenxian zhuan, 40, 55
Shenxiao zishu dafa, 251
Shi Qiu, 98
Shi Zhaolin, 182
Shi zhuanhui lingpin, 268
Shicheng, 112
Shiga Ichiko, 13, 16, 167
shihui zhai, 268
Shiji, 13, 81, 88, 92–94, 95, 97, 99
Shijing, 124
Shilei guhun wen, 230
Shiliu pinjing, 182
Shimamori Tetsuo, 100
Shintō, 24
Shiquan hui, 187
Shisan jing zhushu, 97, 99
Shiyi, 145
shoujue. See hand signs
shouyin, 235
Shu, 25
shu. See methods
Shujing, 29
Shun, 30, 87, 116–117, 130
Shunde County, 204
Shunqu, 128
Shunqu xiansheng wenlu, 129–131, 135–
    137, 145–146
Shuowen jiezi, 74
Shuoyuan, 74
Shuye, 117–118
Shuyi, 145

Shuzhu shan, 192
Sichuan, 11, 24–25, 29, 31–32, 33
sickness, 39–57; and modern cults,
    201–203
silk, 111, 278, 289
Sima Qian, 81, 88–89, 90, 91–92, 95, 98
Sima Tan, 89, 98
Sima Xiangru, 25, 116–117, 119
simiao, 160
simplicity, 109, 115
sincerity, 50
sins, 39–57, 288; and death, 265–266
Sioux, 2
Siu, Helen, 162
Six Dynasties: Buddhism in, 214;
    hand signs in, 238; image in, 105;
    mortuary rites in, 74; ritual, 271;
    talismans in, 263
six schools, 88
snake, charming of, 245
social work, 186
societies: charitable, 193–194, 200, 206;
    local, 157
sociology: in Han, 95; of modern cults,
    203–204; and priesthood, 149–150;
    in Song-Ming, 149–164
soma, 222
Song Bing, 98
Song dynasty: Daoism since, 7, 37; fes-
    tivals in, 162; hand signs in, 237–238,
    241–244, 252; lineages in, 152; local
    elites in, 159; Lüzu in, 194; national-
    ism in, 11, 32; offerings in, 288; reve-
    lation in, 180; ritual in, 65, 257, 261,
    267, 270–272; *Taiping jing* in, 42
Song Yu, 107, 114, 117
souls: invocation of, 246; journey of, 65–
    66, 68–69; obstructed, 230; offerings
    for, 280; orphaned, 221, 225–228,
    265, 276, 282; salvation of, 275;
    sprites of, 246; sublimation of, 259;
    summoning of, 63; transfer of, 272;
    understanding of, 75; and under-
    world, 59–60
soup, as offering, 275, 283
Soushen ji, 288
Southern Song dynasty, 152
Southern Tang dynasty, 151–152, 161
spells: and hand signs, 239, 245–248;
    and healing, 39; phonetic, 240–241;
    in *pudu,* 219, 220, 225
spirit: departure of, 67–68; root of, 44
spirit mediums, 155–156

spirit money, 278
spirits, feeding of, 227, 230
spirit-writing: and access to gods, 181; in
    modern Daoism, 185–209; in Qing,
    165–184
Spring and Autumn period, 84, 86, 88,
    95
Staal, Frits, 221
stars: as hand sign, 239, 242–243,
    249–250; in poetry, 117
statutes, 179
Stewart, Tony K., 17, 215–217, 230
Strickmann, Michel, 58, 61, 93, 96–97,
    99, 229–230
Su Lang, 172
Su Shi, 145
Sūkhavatī, 177
Sulao guan, 190–191
Sumen, 168
summons, to underworld, 266
Sun Guangxian, 125
Sun Simiao, 245
Sun Xing, 53
Sunū, 92
sweet dew, 221–223, 228, 230
sword, and hand signs, 236, 238–239,
    241–243
symbols, 11
syncretism, 17, 213–214

tablets, funerary, 156, 185, 207
taboo, of meat, 280
Taihe dong, 200
Taiji zhenren feixian baojian shangjing
    xu, 37
Tainan, 258, 273
Taiping. See Great Peace
Taiping dongji jing, 42
Taiping guangji, 40
Taiping jing, 12, 13, 39–57, 94; history
    of, 42–43
Taiping yulan, 63
Taishang chishe shengtian baolu, 264
Taiwan: Daoism in, 17–18, 185–209, 253;
    ritual in, 219, 256–273, 274–294
Taiyi dijun dongzhen xuanjing, 245
Taiyi jinhua zongzhi, 15–16, 165–184;
    editions of, 165–166; in Jingming,
    167–172; in Quanzhen, 175–180;
    in Tianxian, 172–175
Taiyi jiuku Tianzun, 225
Taiyi lineage, 170, 182
Taiyin, 66

talisman lads, 261, 268–269
talisman orders, 260, 263–264, 267–269,
    271
talisman water, 40–41, 206; as offering,
    275–276
talismans: and blood, 284; and dead, 67;
    and hand signs, 238, 245–247; and
    healing, 39–40, 74; matching of,
    269; and mortuary rites, 65, 74; pres-
    entation of, 262; in pudu, 225–227;
    in ritual, 257, 260–262; for under-
    world, 226, 264
Tan Changzhen, 167
Tang (Shang ruler), 48–49, 50
Tang caixi zhuan, 125
Tang dynasty: Buddhism in, 213, 215,
    284; codes of, 103–104; Daoist life
    in, 102–126; hand signs in, 236, 240,
    246, 252; texts in, 35
Tangchao haofang nü, 103, 125
Tangshi jishi, 125
tantra, 222–223, 240
Tao Hongjing, 285
Tao Jing'an, 178
Tao Qian, 116–118
Tao Shi'an, 176–178
Tao Yan, 287
Tao Yuanming, 162
tapas, 222
tathagātas. See buddhas
taxonomies, 81–101; stages of, 84
tea, as offering, 275, 283, 291
teeth, clapping of, 246
temple cults: benefactors of, 157; and
    Daoism, 149–164
temples: gods in, 192; household, 161;
    and Quanzhen lineage, 190; today,
    33, 185–186
ten directions, 259, 263, 290
Tenfold Return, Rite of, 268
texts: categories of, 89; chanting of, 193;
    classification of, 81–101; compilation
    of, 178; Daoist, 13; editing process
    of, 168; imaginary transmission of,
    178; revealed, 90–94; revisions of,
    173; sets of, 83; of three traditions,
    199; transmission of, 86–87, 94–97,
    166, 176, 177–178; versions of, 173
Thailand, 32–33
theology, and identity, 2
things, investigation of, 136
Three Bureaus, 28
Three Caverns, 65–66, 68

Three Dukes, 25
Three Heavens, 263
Three Kingdoms, 116
Three Pure Ones, 192, 225, 261–262, 275, 283
Three Sisters, 120
three teachings, 131, 137–138
Three Treasures: offerings for, 286; seal of, 269
Three Worlds, 283, 290; talisman of, 264
throats, opening of, 224, 227
thunder: and hand signs, 236, 249–251, 252; rulers of, 269
thunder rites, 237
Tian Pian, 98
Tian Shu, 95
Tian Wangsun, 94
Tian Yannian, 53
Tiandi, 59–60, 66, 73–75, 201
Tiandi shizhe jie, 59–60, 73–75
Tianhuang zhidao taiqing yuce, 237–238, 252, 253
Tianlao, 65
Tianshi dao. *See* Celestial Masters
Tianshui, 29
Tiantai shan, 271
Tianxian lineage, 16, 172–174, 182
Tianxian xinzhuan, 182
Tianxin zhengfa, 33, 236, 241–243
Tie'an ji, 153–154, 161
tiger: as hand sign, 239–240; paper, 278, 284
ti/yong, 152
tofu, as offering, 277–278
Tomb, Sire of, 59, 67–68
tomb contracts, 13, 58–77; terms for, 73–74
Tong'an County, 162
tongji, 155
Tongshan she, 189, 205
Tongwa Hospital, 201
Toulong bi yi, 292
Toulong songjian, 292
traditions: and early Daoism, 84; oral, 238
trance, 196
transcendence: through Dao, 135; in Ming Daoism, 135, 140; in poetry, 110
translation: definition of, 230; and religion, 236; and syncretism, 214–218
transmission, across lineages, 181

treasury, 259, 261; loan from, 269–270
trees, fruits of, 286–287
tribes, 23
trigrams, 145, 170
Tsuchiya Masaaki, 12
Tu Yu'an, 168–169, 170, 172–173
Tudi gong, 261
Tuo Xiao, 98
Turner, Bryan S., 82
Turquoise Pond, 121
tutan zhai, 42

underworld, 65–66, 262; kings of, 267–269; road to, 259
unity, of action and knowledge, 141
Universal Salvation, rite of. See *pudu*
urbanization, of modern cults, 102–103
utopia, 29

vajra, 219–220, 226; in Daoism, 231; in *fang yankou*, 224
van Gulik, Robert, 103
Vedas, 221
vegetables: as offerings, 286–287; smelling, 276, 280, 285, 287, 292
vegetarianism, and ritual, 280
vidyārāja, 216–217
Vietnam, 33
virtue, 130, 132–133
"Visit on Refined Master Zhao," 108
visualization: in Buddhism, 221, 223; in *fang yankou*, 224; and hand signs, 249, 252; in *pudu*, 228; in ritual, 220, 267

Wailu yi, 36
Wanfa fanzong, 253
Wanfa guizong, 197
Wang Chang, 105–106
Wang Changyue, 178–179
Wang Chengzan, 160
Wang Chong, 49, 50
Wang Chunfu, 128–129
Wang Dao, 14–15, 127–146; Laozi adoption of, 130–135; life and work, 128–129; teachers of, 139–141
Wang Ji, 56
Wang Kunyang, 178–179
Wang Mang, 25
Wang Ming, 43
Wang Qiugui, 253
Wang Qizhen, 247, 262
Wang Shouren, 127

Wang Tingxiang, 140
Wang Wei, 108
Wang Xianzhi, 45–46
Wang Xuanhe, 245
Wang Yangming, 14, 127, 129–146
Wang Yingshan, 161
Wang Zhaojun, 112
Wangfu shi, 117
Wanggong shendao bei, 128
Wangwu shan, 121
Wangye jiao, 257
Warring States, 62, 70, 81–101;
    taxonomies in, 86–88
water, imagery of, 111
wealth, 288
Weaver Girl, 118
Weber, Max, 82–83, 97
Wei Mou, 98
Wei Ruyi, 200
Wei Xiao, 129
Wei Zheng, 202
Wei Zhuangqu, 146
Weishan zuile, 197, 207
Wen Feiqing, 119
Wen Tingyun, 119
Wen Weng, 25
Wenji, Lady, 120, 122
wenjian, 257
Wenlu. See *Shunqu xiansheng wenlu*
Wenxuan, 107
Wilhelm, Richard, 165
wine, as offering, 275, 283, 285, 291
women: in Daoism, 102–126; and Daoist
    identity, 14; in modern cults, 205
Wong Tai Sin, 195, 201–202
worship, in ritual, 267
Writ of Pardon, 18
writing utensils, as offerings, 278,
    288–291
Wu Peiyi, 43
Wu Yang, 62
Wu You, 53
Wu[xing] dadi, 160
Wuchang, 112, 114
Wucheng, 128
Wudi (Liang emperor), 115
wugong, 276
Wuhu shan, 154
Wulian jing, 67, 69, 238
Wushang biyao, 75, 292
Wushang huanglu dazhai licheng yi, 266
Wusheng laomu, 189
Wushi shan, 153

wuxin, 276
Wuxing pian, 81, 100
Wuyi shan, 160
Wuzhen pian chanyou, 171

Xi Kang, 118–119
Xi Shi, 120–121
Xiang River goddess, 117
Xiangying miao, 159, 163
Xiantian dao, 189, 205
Xiantian xuwu taiyi jinhua zongzhi,
    165–166
Xianyi guan, 102
Xianyou zhenjun, 175–177
Xiao River goddess, 117
Xiao Shi, 122
Xiao Yan, 115
Xiaolan, 162
Xiaoliang si, 115
Xiaopeng xianguan, 200
Xiaoyou dong, 120
Xici, 92, 137
Xie Daoyun, 120–121
Xiguan, 204
Xin Tangshu, 27
Xinghua, 153
Xinshan tang, 167, 197, 203, 206, 207
Xinshu, 98
Xinyu, 99
Xiong Qufei, 159
Xiongnu, 121
Xiqiao Baiyundong zhi, 198
Xiqiao shan, 195, 198, 201
Xiqiao yunquan xianguan shiji, 198, 203
Xiqiu shan, 195
Xiuyuan jingshe, 192–193, 204
Xiwang mu, 121–122
Xu Brothers, 15, 149–164
Xu Jingyang. *See* Xu Xun
Xu Shen'an, 170
Xu Xun, 169–170
Xu Zhi'e, 151
Xu Zhizheng, 151
Xuandi (Chen emperor), 42
Xuandu daxian yushan jinggong yi, 220,
    225–228, 231
Xuanpu shan lingkui bilu, 238–239, 240–
    241, 244, 247
Xuanyuan xianguan, 199
Xuanzong, 32, 239
Xue Hui, 137, 146
Xue Yanggui, 182
Xuepen hui, 158

Xunyang, 287
Xunzi, 48, 81, 86–88, 89, 135
Xuxian hanzao, 151, 153, 155–158, 160, 162
Xuxian zhenlu, 151, 153, 157, 163

Yamada Masaru, 187
Yamada Toshiaki, 41, 42, 293
Yan Song, 128
Yang, C. K., 97
Yang Hou, 95
Yang Qing, 94
Yang Xiong, 135
yangxing, 109
Yangzi River, 112, 114–115, 152, 156
Yao (ruler), 87, 130
Yao people, 11, 32–33
Yaochi, 120
Yaochi jinmu, 189
Yaoxiu keyi jielü chao, 64–68
Yaoyong wupin dan, 275
Yates, Robin, 92
Ye, 29
Ye Mingchen, 200
Ye Zongmao, 204
Yellow Monarch. *See* Huangdi
Yellow Register Rite, 258, 262, 265, 270
Yellow River, 92
Yellow Springs, 61, 74
Yellow Stones, Lord of, 288
Yi people, 27, 35
Yihe lou, 203
Yijing, 92–93, 95, 99, 136–137, 145, 156–157; and Buddhism, 214; and lineage names, 170
Yili, 64
Yin Wen, 98
Ying Shao, 63
Yingwu zhou, 114
Yingyuan gong, 192, 204
yin-yang, 94; cosmologists, 88; and Ming Daoism, 128, 137
Yinzhiwen tushuo, 195
yishe, 28
yiwen, 65
Yixin she, 186
Yogatantras, 228
Yong'an, 259
Yong'an xiang, 258
Yongle (Ming emperor), 15, 151
Yoshikawa Tadao, 42, 53
Yoshioka Yoshitoyo, 42, 230
You Qi, 138

Youyang zazu, 63
Yu, the Great, 112, 130
Yu Liang lou, 115
Yu shantang, 202
Yu Xuanji, 14, 102–126; biography, 102; works on, 103; writings of, 103–104
Yuan dynasty: academies in, 159; Jingming in, 169; nationalism in, 32; ritual in, 257, 261, 269–272; ritual manual of, 221
Yuan Miaozong, 238
Yuan Zhen, 117
Yuanhuo shan, 112
Yuanshi fuming, 263
Yuanshi tianzun, 268
Yue Chengong, 95, 99
Yue Jugong, 99
Yuedong, 172
Yuefu, 112
Yuegang yuan, 191
Yuexiu shan, 191–192
Yuhuang benxing jing, 34
Yujia jiyao, 241
Yujia jiyao jiu anan tuoluoni yankou guiyi jing, 253
Yulanpen hui, 158
Yunji qiqian, 37
Yunnan, 33–34
Yunquan xianguan, 186, 191, 199, 201, 203–204
Yuqie jiyao yankou shishi yi, 220
Yuqing jing, 32, 37
Yuqing tang, 158
Yushan tang, 203–204
Yuzhang, 168
Yuzhen, 169

Zai Quheng, 172
Zangwai daoshu, 182, 270, 285
Zanling ji, 151, 156
Zeng Chunshou, 258
Zeng Collection, 258–259, 270
zhai, 18, 41, 53, 263; definition of, 274–275
zhaijie, 45
zhaitang, 155
Zhan Ruoshui, 14, 24, 129, 140–141, 143–145
Zhanbei feng, 112
Zhang Daoling, 47, 58, 65; biography of, 40
Zhang Gao, 239

Zhang Jue, 39, 40
Zhang Lu, 26, 27, 30, 40; biography
    of, 39
Zhang Shuang'an, 168
Zhang Shujing, 59–60
Zhang Xiu, 39
Zhang Xu, 64
Zhao Fenliang, 196
Zhao Lianshi, 107–108
Zhao Zunsi, 202
Zhejiang, 176, 271
Zheng Zichan, 162
Zhen'gao, 107, 285
Zhengjian gongde die, 272
Zhengyi. See Celestial Masters
Zhengyi fawen jingtu kejie pin, 30
Zhengyi fawen taishang wailu yi, 31, 37
Zhengyi fawen Tianshi jiaojie kejing, 35
Zhengyi jiaomu yi, 284
Zhengyi jiazhai yi, 284
Zhengyi jie'e jiaoyi, 284
Zhengyi licheng yi, 286
Zhengyi lun, 65, 74
Zhengyi weiyi jing, 41
zhenmu wen, 59
Zhenyan, 219, 240; and mudras, 17
Zhenzhong hongbao yuan bishu, 94
Zhenzhong sushu, 99
Zhibao tai, 204–207
Zhiyi, 31
Zhong Ziqi, 116, 123
Zhonghuang, 169
Zhongli Quan, 172, 182
Zhong-Lü zhuandao ji, 183
Zhongshan, 23
Zhongxiao jie, 259
Zhongyong, 143
Zhou Chong, 161
Zhou Daotong, 136, 145
Zhou Dinglai, 162
Zhou dynasty, 23, 24, 25
Zhou family, 149–164
Zhou Qi, 93
Zhou Ruli, 161

Zhou Shixiu, 161
Zhou Side, 270, 285
Zhou Sui, 153, 162
Zhou Yehe, 167, 169, 173
Zhou Yi, 161
Zhou Yue, 153, 162
Zhouli, 62
Zhouyi yi, 145
Zhouyi zhengyi, 99
Zhu Faman, 64
Zhu Gui, 172
Zhu Hong, 56
Zhu Quan, 237
Zhu Xi, 127, 132–133, 136, 138–
    139, 140–142, 144, 146, 158;
    and academies, 159
Zhu Yuanzhang, 158
Zhu Yunyang, 171
Zhuang Xing'an, 170–172
Zhuang Zhou, 98
Zhuangzi: and Buddhism, 214; among
    Han schools, 85, 86–88, 92, 97–100,
    114; and literati Daoism, 7, 8; in
    Ming Daoism, 131, 144–145; versus
    village cults, 149
Zhuguo jiumin zongzhen biyao, 238,
    242–243, 244, 248–249, 252, 253
Zhuo Wenjun, 116
Zhuyuan, 202
Zhuzi Fang, 153
Zi Gong, 87
Zi Si, 81
Zimo, 27
Ziran zhaiyi, 263
Zisong, 56
zithers, and Daoist identity, 104, 116–
    123, 124
Zize, 56
zodiac positions, and hand signs,
    247–251
Zong, 35
Zongyang gong, 178
zumiao, 152–153
Zürcher, Erik, 220, 230, 231